Early Modern Literature in History

Series editors
Cedric C. Brown
Department of English
University of Reading
Reading, UK

Andrew Hadfield
School of English
University of Sussex
Brighton, UK

Within the period 1520-1740, this large, long-running series, with international representation discusses many kinds of writing, both within and outside the established canon. The volumes may employ different theoretical perspectives, but they share an historical awareness and an interest in seeing their texts in lively negotiation with their own and successive cultures.

More information about this series at
http://www.palgrave.com/gp/series/14199

Edel Lamb

Reading Children in Early Modern Culture

palgrave
macmillan

Edel Lamb
School of English
Queen's University Belfast
Belfast, UK

Early Modern Literature in History
ISBN 978-3-319-70358-9   ISBN 978-3-319-70359-6   (eBook)
https://doi.org/10.1007/978-3-319-70359-6

Library of Congress Control Number: 2017961113

Cover illustration: Image from William Hornbye's 'Hornbyes Hornbook' (1622). ART Collection / Alamy Stock Photo.

Printed on acid-free paper

This Palgrave Macmillan imprint is published by Springer Nature
The registered company is Springer International Publishing AG
The registered company address is: Gewerbestrasse 11, 6330 Cham, Switzerland

For David, Amelia and Ewan

ACKNOWLEDGEMENTS

The research for this book was initially undertaken during postdoctoral fellowships. I am indebted to the Australian Research Council's Discovery Project Scheme for a Postdoctoral Fellowship at the University of Sydney (Project ID: DP0988452) and to the Irish Research Council for a Postdoctoral Fellowship at University College Dublin. I am also grateful to University of Sydney and University College Dublin for additional funding to undertake archival research. Thanks to Queen's University Belfast for significant support, particularly additional travel funding and a period of research leave.

My approach has been shaped through many discussions with Mark Burnett, Kate Chedgzoy, Danielle Clarke, Margaret Harris and Liam Semler. I thank each of them sincerely for their mentorship of this project, and of me. I would not be at this stage without their enthusiasm, encouragement, feedback and support. Particular thanks are due to Mark and Kate for their continued support for my work, and to Ramona Wray and Adrian Streete for their constant encouragement and invaluable advice. Thanks too to Lucy Munro for many conversations about early modern childhood. Naomi McAreavey, Kate Flaherty and Angie Dunstan offered much needed encouragement and friendship at every stage—to them, many thanks.

The early ideas for this project emerged during a fellowship at the Huntington Library, and this book is indebted to work undertaken there. Thanks also to the Bodleian Library, the British Library, the Centre for Kentish Studies (especially Helen Orme), the Library of Trinity College Dublin, Newcastle University Library, Queen's University Library (especially Diarmuid Kennedy) and State Library Victoria for access to materials. Chapter 4 builds on the early findings of this work, published in *The Child in British Literature* (Palgrave Macmillan, 2012) and in *Young Shakespeare, Actes des Congrès de la Société Française Shakespeare* 34 (2016). Thank you to the editors, Adrienne Gavin and Laetitia Sansonetti, and the readers for their feedback. Many thanks to Ben Doyle, Cedric Brown and Andrew Hadfield for their belief the project, and to Camille Davies. I would also like to thank the reader for supportive and stimulating comments.

This book was completed at three institutions (Queen's University Belfast, University College Dublin and University of Sydney) and draft material was presented at many seminars and conferences (including the Shakespeare Association of America, the Société Française Shakespearean, Australian and New Zealand Shakespeare Association, and Australian and New Zealand Association for Medieval and Early Modern Studies, and at Canterbury Christ Church University, Newcastle University, Nottingham Trent University and the University of Western Australia). I am extremely grateful for the support and feedback generously offered by colleagues and friends in each of these places, and I would like to particularly thank the following: Christina Alt, Geraldine Barnes, Daniel Bender, Gina Bloom, Yan Brailowsky, Fran Brearton, Bernadette Brennan, Hannah Burrows, Vic Burrows, Andrew Carpenter, Will Christie, David Coleman, Rob Conkie, Ruth Connolly, Eileen Corrigan, Luca Crispi, Nicholas Daly, Derek Dunne, Ewan Fernie, Alan Fletcher, Susanne Greenhalgh, Matthew Grenby, Huw Griffiths, Jane Grogan, Kate Harvey, Moyra Haslett, Jennifer Higginbotham, Anne Holloway, Annamarie Jagose, Mark Johnston, Claire Jowitt, Stephen Kelly, Ed Larrissy, Steffi Lehner, Karin Lesnik-Oberstein, Rory Loughnane, Philippa Maddern, Shehzana Mamujee, Gail McConnell, Clare McManus, Gordon McMullan, Kathryn McPherson, Kathryn Moncrief, Fiona Morrison, Alex Murray, Emily O'Brien, Stephen O'Neill, Ricki O'Rawe, Andrew Pepper, Mike Pincombe, Ursula Potter, Andrew Power, Fiona Ritchie, Daniel Roberts, Margaret Rogerson, Fred Schurink, Rosalinde Schut, Edel Semple, Bev Sherry, Paul Simpson, Gavin Smith, Dan Soule, Caroline Sumpter, Stephanie Tarbin, Lyn Tribble, William West, Bob White and Michael Witmore. Thanks also to many enthusiastic postgraduate students at Queen's for lively conversations about Shakespeare and childhood.

Family and friends have been hugely supportive, patient and encouraging over many years. I would especially like to thank Clare Boyle,

Marie-Claire Henry, David and Ashlene Lamb, Chris Lamb, Mary Lamb, Clare and Colin McCoy, Noel and Tara McGarry, Stephen McGarry and Sarah Cosentino, Peter O'Hare and Rochelle O'Hara, Dave and Caroline Spencer, Damien and Louise Trainor. Special thanks to Naomi McAreavey and Martin Canavan for a Dublin 'home'. Thanks to Noel and Alice McGarry, especially for many hours of childcare! A special thanks to Eilís Devaney, for a place to stay, for many conversations about books—whether Renaissance or those shared in our childhoods—and for encouraging me on many occasions to keep going but also reminding me that it was time to finish!

My parents, Martin and Ursula Lamb, have made this book possible in more ways than I can acknowledge. For 'snipping' the pages, for a home between many moves, for many hours of childcare, and for belief and encouragement at every stage, thank you. Amelia and Ewan McGarry have been welcome interruptions to my thinking about early modern childhood and have wonderfully transformed my experiences of childhood reading. To David McGarry, who went there and back again; who put many things on hold, and held everything together; who restored confidence and energy when mine wavered: thank you above all.

Contents

1 Introduction: Reading Child Readers   1

2 'A Good Child Is One that Loves His Book': Literacy, Religious Instruction and the Child as Reader   29

3 Books for 'Childish Age': Youthful Reading Cultures in Early Modern England   71

4 Reading Boyhood: The Books and Reading Practices of Early Modern Schoolboys   107

5 'This Girle Hath Spirit': Rewriting Girlhood Reading   151
         ↳ Read

6 'I Remember When I Began to Read': Remembering Childhood Reading   191

Bibliography   231

Index   251

CHAPTER 1

Introduction: Reading Child Readers

Children are Bookes; and Bookes men's children are
In them is stampt the Father's character.[1]

Reading Children in Early Modern Culture is a study of children, their books and their reading experiences in late sixteenth- and seventeenth-century Britain. It is about the significance of reading to early modern childhood and of childhood to early modern reading. Children occupied an important role in early modern textual cultures. The proliferation of advice and how-to manuals in the period often specified children and the young as important recipients of advice on how to speak, behave, worship and acquire new skills.[2] Children were, William Martyn's early seventeenth-century equation of children and books suggests, central to the imaginative conceptualization of print culture. Images of print were also at the heart of understanding childhood, with John Earle describing the child as 'a man in small letter' in 1628.[3] Childhood and youth were often characterized through associations with particular books and reading practices. Margaret Cavendish, for instance, depicts the 'difference between Youth and Age' in terms of reading 'the Horn-book' and reading an 'Old Chronicle' in her *Sociable Letters* (1664).[4] Children were also readers, creative 'users', consumers and producers of the literature of the period.[5] Investigating children as readers, this study interrogates the ways in which early modern textual cultures constructed distinct concepts of childhood

© The Author(s) 2018
E. Lamb, *Reading Children in Early Modern Culture*,
Early Modern Literature in History,
https://doi.org/10.1007/978-3-319-70359-6_1

1

and impacted on the experience of being a child.[6] It explores the ways in which early modern childhoods were produced by literacy and reading experiences through an analysis of literary representations of children as readers and of historical evidence of the reading experiences of those defined as 'children' in early modern society. It argues that while reading was undoubtedly a formative experience for early modern literate children, it was more significantly constitutive of childhood identities and experiences. *Reading Children* focuses on how early modern children read: how they were imagined as readers; how they were instructed and advised to read; how, where and when they read and used their books; and how they negotiated childhood through reading. It begins, in this introduction, by asking how we might read these early modern child readers: how were children defined in the period; where is the evidence of their reading practices and experiences located; and how might we in the twenty-first century interpret this evidence of the elusive figure of the early modern child reader, imagined and historical?

Imagining the Child as Reader

One early modern book that was directed in part at children as readers and that addresses their early encounters with literary cultures gestures towards the manifold connections between children and texts in the period. William Hornby's *Hornbyes Hornbook* (1622) subjects the reading practices of early modern children to comic scrutiny through its satirical account of formative youthful encounters with the hornbook. The hornbook, a page of text mounted on wood containing the alphabet, sample syllables and the Lord's prayer, was commonly used by sixteenth- and seventeenth-century boys and girls from diverse social backgrounds in learning how to read.[7] It is the book that characterizes the young in Cavendish's formulation. It was often the first and, according to Hornby's text, the most important book of early modern childhood. *Hornbyes Hornbook* provides an overview of the benefits of the hornbook for all alongside a tale of the author's own schoolboy experiences at St Peterborough Free School to offer humorous insight into 'How schollers do begin, and how they grow'.[8] Hornby aligns the processes of learning to read with the early stages of life, although he admits that this literacy is not always achieved in childhood. Describing the hornbook as 'first Arts Nurse', he figures the book as an alternative to the physical nourishment provided by nurses or mothers, contributing to the prevalent image of texts as substitute parents in the period.[9] Hornby thus depicts reading as a crucial formative experience, here facilitating movement of the early modern male child out of the feminized spaces of infancy though reading and learning.[10] He implies that use of the hornbook is essential before progressing to other educational texts, identified as the primer, psalter, Bible, Latin ABC, '*Pueriles*', Cato, Cicero, Ovid, Corderius' *Dialogues*, Terence and Horace (B3v–B4r), and ultimately to the sciences, arts and law or all 'the worlds knowledge' (Br). In this representation, the hornbook instigates a transformation from the illiterate infant to the professional adult male through reading. *Hornbyes Hornbook* implies that it is by learning to read and through repeated reading experiences that children become adult in early modern culture.

Becoming adult through reading is a common image in the period, and Hornby's depiction of reading as part of a scholarly process that produces civic subjects is in line with the aims of many educational programmes. His recommended reading list, which demonstrates the central role of religious material to early literacy instruction, is also exemplary of the reading advocated at grammar schools. Although Hornby also commends his book to maidens, he focuses primarily on the literate schoolboy reading under supervision. The boy, he suggests can learn his '*A.B.C.*', syllables and vowels from the hornbook, but it is only with the 'Masters rule' that he learns 'how he may put together' (B2v). The woodcut on the book's title page reinforces this favoured method of youthful reading in its depiction of the boy leaning against the schoolmaster's knee and pointing out his letters under the gaze of his teacher.[11] This intimate relationship is offered as an alternative to the common violent pedagogy of the period, that Hornby's text refutes, even though the rod placed on the nearby table serves as a reminder of the threat of corporal punishment in schooling in the period.[12] Through repeated recommendation of how children should read in the visual image and comic rhyme contained in this book, Hornby suggests some common practices of childhood reading. However, he also acknowledges that child readers might appropriate the hornbook for their own ends. The child at petty school, for instance, does not read the hornbook but sees it as an object of 'sport' (B2r), using it as a 'weapon' (B2r) when he falls out with his school-fellow, as 'agreeing with their childish yeares' (B2r). Other children read the book but 'learne in waste'. They are reprimanded in the warning that this mode of reading produces the 'Thrid-bare *Poet*, or the Ballad-maker' and the drunken '*Pot-Poet*' (B6v–B7r). The recommendations of parents, educators, employers, religious authorities, printers and authors on what books children should read and on how and where they should read them were widely circulated in educational texts, advice books and conduct manuals and in the prefaces of the books aimed directly at a young readership. Yet Hornby's comic depiction of books misread and misused reminds us that early modern children were also agents in their own reading, and engaged with textual cultures in independent and often unexpected ways.

Hornbyes Hornbook offers an insight into some of the books, reading spaces and ways of reading associated with early modern childhood, and gestures towards differences in these according to gender and social status. It also represents itself as a book for the young. Dedicated to youthful patrons, Robert Carr, 'scarce' in his teens (A4r), the 12-year-old Thomas Grantham and the 'young' Rochester Carre (A6r), it claims to be 'respondent unto youthfull yeares,/Fit for your young dayes and minoritie,/ Untill you come to senioritie' (A3v). Recognizing the young as patrons, readers and potential market, it is one example of the diverse texts that directly address early modern children and youths as a particular category of reader in the period. Hornby compares his 'tale' of his own schooldays with romances and histories such as that 'of valiant *Guy*' and 'the Mirror of Knight-hood' (B7r–v), which, as this book explores, were widely perceived to be among the books desired by children, although their elders often warned against them. However, he simultaneously identifies an adult readership for his *Hornbook*, calling on the various professions, judges, justices, lawyers, constables, poets and school masters to remember 'the seede and graine/Of skill' (B4v) to which 'they were first beholden' (B7r). Hornby exploits the imagery of childhood and early reading experiences, producing a text that simultaneously functions as wry nostalgia for older readers and participates in contemporary debates on education. *Hornbyes Hornbook*, therefore, like many early modern English books functions as a book for children and a book for adults; as recreational reading, didacticism and politicized commentary.

Reading Children in Early Modern Culture focuses on the figure of the child reader to investigate the multiple connections between children and their books exemplified by *Hornbyes Hornbook*. Hornby's book is one of many early modern texts that identify the child as one potential reader, recommend modes of reading as a child and depict children's reading experiences. This study suggests that in this period of expanding print culture and increasing literacy levels, authors and printers identified readers in aged terms, and it explores the extent to which fresh understandings of children as readers emerged in this age-inflected marketplace. John Locke made a transformative contribution to concepts of childhood, children's education and to the production of texts specifically for the child reader when he famously bemoaned the lack of an 'easy pleasant book, suited to his capacity' that might 'tempt' the child to read at the end of the seventeenth century.[13] However, earlier authors, pedagogues and publishers had begun to recognize the importance of attending to the distinct needs of the child as reader much earlier. A range of sixteenth- and seventeenth-century texts imagined the child reader, addressing this reader directly on title pages, in prefaces and dedications and via direct address within the main text, and by manipulating the material book to present content in ways perceived to facilitate the cognitive engagement of this reader. Covering the period from the first mid-sixteenth-century printings of the frequently produced *ABC for Children*, an adaptation of the established *ABC* text that identified children as the primary audience, to Locke's comments on books for children, *Reading Children in Early Modern Culture* examines diverse English-language texts that were adapted for, printed for and marketed to children and the young. It evaluates these texts alongside the reading practices recommended by authors and publishers and the advice offered by other moralists, guardians and teachers, to investigate how this textual culture imagined the distinct abilities of the child. By evaluating this construction of an imagined child reader, this book suggests that textual cultures produce concepts of childhood and proposes that this sheds new light how childhood was understood in the period.

Extensive catalogues of children's books in the early modern period have brought to light many texts that identify children as readers in the period.[14] They include instructional manuals, didactic, moral and religious texts, parental advice books, riddles, fables, pictorial encyclopaedias, histories, romances, satires, comic tales, poems, broadsheets, drolleries and collections of compliments and conjurer's tricks. Yet, although these catalogues and anthologies usefully bring examples of early modern children's books and reading to light, they do not fully consider what they might disclose about childhood identity. *Reading Children* considers these aspects of literary and literate cultures in the period. It evaluates the paratextual material of early modern books for children, following scholarship that pays renewed attention to what Jennifer Richards and Fred Schurink call the '"textuality" of reading'.[15] It argues that, by representing the young as a distinct category of potential readers, these texts indicate a wider cultural recognition of discrete identities associated with the early stages of the life cycle. These books often recognize youthful readers alongside their older counterparts, demonstrating nuanced cultures of reading in the period by attending to what Teresa Michals calls a 'mixed-age' audience.[16] They negotiate the aged states of imagined readers with varying material, textual and cognitive needs in response to changing imperatives of education, religious literacy and the demands of an expanding market for books. The connections between childhood and the history of printing have been well examined. Neil Postman famously argued that childhood was invented in the Renaissance as a result of the printing press and the related imperative to become literate.[17] The distinct innovation of the eighteenth-century market of books for children and its connection to modern concepts of childhood has been clearly demonstrated, and scholars of earlier literatures have equally contextualized this argument with evidence that texts were produced for children throughout history.[18] *Reading Children* argues for important connections between the expanding cultures of literacy and print the sixteenth and seventeenth centuries, but rather than proclaiming the invention of a new concept of childhood or staking a claim for the 'origins' of children's literature, it unpacks the ways in which the construction of the idea of the child in print culture relates to and informs wider understanding of children in textual cultures.[19] It proposes that the recognition of children as unique types of readers was not restricted to print culture with many—including parents and teachers—producing manuscript texts to meet the distinct educational needs of their children. It examines how varied genres in print and manuscript acknowledge children as one potential—or the intended—reader and how this defines the child. It explores the extent to which authors, publishers, parents and teachers assume or recommend a set of reading practices specific to early modern children and youths and asks what this reveals about concepts of childhood in the period.

Childhood is commonly represented in early modern culture as a vulnerable stage during which physical features and cognitive faculties might be shaped through external influences, and this is a prevalent idea in the intersecting discourses of childhood and reading. Reading was perceived to have a formative influence during the early stages of the life cycle. Some early modern commentators even suggested that it could shape the child before birth. In the early seventeenth century, Jacques Guillemeau warns expectant mothers against 'lamentable and fearefull tales', claiming they might imprint upon the unborn child.[20] For Dorothy Leigh, reading is essential to the physical and moral development of the child during the early years of life, as she advises her children to read the Bible but also warns that if they 'read it without meditating theron, it doth the soule no more good then meate and drink doth the body, being seene and felt and never fed upon'.[21] *Hornbyes Hornbook* suggests that it is through reading that young boys begin the process of becoming future poets, scholars and judges. The practical benefits of reading are also highlighted in numerous commentaries on the purposes of reading for early modern girls. In 1572 Jane Tuttoft urges that her daughter learn to 'write and read and cast accounts and to wash and brew and to bake and dress meat and drink and so I trust she will prove herself a great good housewife'.[22] In her fictional representation of an uncle choosing books for his 7-year-old niece in 1656, Margaret Cavendish suggests that he 'chose her such books to read in as might make her wise … to lay a ground and foundation of virtue, and to teach her to moderate her passions, and to rule her affections'.[23] The mid-seventeenth-century bookseller, William London, shares the view that reading is crucial to shaping the child as an adult, claiming that the 'reading of History' 'wean[s] from a childish effeminacy, and train[s] our minds to manlike actions, snatching us from the vanity of youth and corrupt society'.[24] From the early sixteenth century, moralists emphasized the importance of reading for children to occupy the mind so that they did not have the 'leyser to muse or delyte in other fantasies'.[25] Robert Boyle recalls that he read 'the strange Adventures Amadis de Gaule; & other Fabulous & wandring Storys' as a 10-year-old convalescent in 1637 to engage his 'restlesse Fancy'.[26] Boyle's recollection of his reading imagines childhood as a period of fancy and overwrought imagination, which during this period of physical illness is contained through reading. Humanist practices of reading in the period meant that readers frequently read for a particular purpose, for instance the acquisition of scholarly or spiritual knowledge or practical skills, the cultivation of the mind, morals or manners.[27] The varied ends and contexts for early modern children's reading shed light on multiple concepts of childhood in the period, depicting it as a stage of physical and mental development, a time of fancy and the period during which practical skills are acquired and gendered identities are forged. Attending to this humanist understanding of reading and influenced by seminal work on this topic, this book explores how the processes of reading to acquire literacy and reading for salvation in Protestant culture (in Chap. 2), reading for pleasure in the context of an expanding book market (in Chap. 3) and reading for the acquisition of scholarly knowledge and practical skills in educational contexts (in Chaps. 4 and 5) impact on childhood identity.

Childhood, as many scholars have shown, is multiple and contingent; informed and produced in relation to local contexts.[28] *Reading Children* argues that early modern textual cultures produced manifold constructs of childhood. Children are perceived in various ways depending on the context—the aims, spaces and modes—of reading. This is reflected in early modern texts that refer to a range of categories of readers associated with childhood: the child, the youth, the boy and the maid or girl. The following chapters explore how different types of child readers are imagined in early modern literary cultures in relation to the contexts of religion, print markets, leisure reading, education and the schoolroom, and genre: the 'good child' in Chap. 2, the 'childish' or 'youth' reader in Chap. 3, the 'boy' in Chap. 4, the 'girl' in Chap. 5, and the memory of childhood reading in Chap. 6. The first two chapters evaluate how the child is figured in texts produced for his or her salvation and pleasure. Chapter 2 proposes that an original concept of the child as reader emerges in a post-Reformation context through the increasing attention to teaching literacy as an element of religious subjectivity. Focusing on religious books directed to teaching the young how to read and recommending reading to those in the early stages of literacy acquisition, it argues that a series of religious texts for children build on and complicate this idea of the child reader to produce the category of the 'good child' reader. Chapter 3 considers how an alternative child reader was imagined in books claiming to offer pleasure and delight. Analysing how the paratextual elements of books in the late sixteenth and seventeenth centuries urged the young to read in distinct ways, the chapter argues that a certain mode of reading was defined as childish or youthful. These chapters propose that these modes of reading might be practised by the young, and situates them in relation to what we know about children's access to and ownership of texts in the period, but it proposes that reading particular texts or reading in certain ways might also position the early modern reader, no matter what his or her age, as childish. The early modern child reader is a discursive entity, and these diverse representations of what it might mean to read as a child produce complex concepts of childhood and childhood reading in the period.

The production of diverse concepts of childhood through the imagining of child readers in print and manuscript culture is just one dimension of the fascinating interactions between children and textual cultures in early modern Britain. The books that attend to children as readers shed new light primarily on adult attitudes towards or understandings of the role of reading in childhood. This is, of course, an important element in understanding early modern childhoods; yet the experiences of young readers in this period—the texts they read and the reading practices they employed—are also crucial to evaluating the child as reader in the period. As Jennifer Heller and Carol Chillington Rutter point out in their analyses of early modern advice books, the texts that address a child reader might simultaneously be material objects produced with specific children in mind, passed to those children and attending to the experiences of childhood.[29] The experience of reading these texts, as well as other material, form a crucial part of early modern children's identities. *Reading Children* simultaneously attends to historical child readers, investigating the reading experiences of the young to evaluate the ways in which their engagements with texts impacted on their childhoods. It seeks, therefore, as many recent studies of reading have done, to bring together the representations of readers and of reading experiences and the historical readers of those books, combining a consideration of the textuality and the materiality of reading.[30] By combining an analysis of the representation of the child as reader and children's reading experiences, it is possible to consider not only how childhood was understood but also how it was experienced in early modern culture. This study contends that while prescriptive advice on children's reading emphasized the production of well-informed adulthoods through literacy, the reading experiences of the young also offered a unique opportunity for readers to negotiate their identities as children. As Roger Chartier proposes, 'the discursive and material forms of texts read' and the 'codes and conventions' of a reading impact on the reading experience; but they cannot wholly determine the responses of specific readers to specific texts.[31] Early modern children's reading often involved an active and creative reading of a text, informed by the reader's age, gender and social status, as well as their location within a reading community.[32] Early modern children responded to the texts produced for them in unexpected ways, demonstrating autonomy as early modern readers.

This autonomy is evident in the fact that children did not only read the texts recommended to them. While boys and girls from a range of social backgrounds read material claiming to be for children, they also read numerous texts not recommended to or explicitly intended for them, ranging from Ovid to medieval romances to the works of George Chapman, Edmund Spenser, Ben Jonson and William Shakespeare. They encountered diverse texts in a range of contexts and forms, and they read them silently and aloud, alone and communally, with their elders and their peers, in diverse spaces including the bed, the closet, the parlour, the schoolroom and the field. For many early modern children their first encounter with texts was mediated through the oral storytelling and instruction of those who cared for them in infancy and early modern childhood. While some children learned to read as young as age 2, for others it was later. Some children read the manuscript texts prepared by parents, often mothers, for their early instruction, or the manuscripts and printed texts made available in early modern schools. Many were given their books by fathers, mothers, godparents and grandparents, and read these in ways approved by their guardians in the home. John Rastrick, for example, describes his encounters with the Bible at a very early age when 'Father would shew me the Minister's Texts, and tell me some of the Historys of the Bible when I used to sit on his Knee', a shared experience which continued once Rastrick learned to read and he would read his psalter on his father's knee.[33] Other children shared their early encounters with texts with their siblings. Elizabeth Isham recalls how she and her sister would share responses to their reading and how she and her siblings would read extracts from the Bible aloud every morning and night.[34] This practice of the communal reading aloud of godly books may have been a common experience for early modern children, but the young also read other genres aloud and collectively.[35] Two early seventeenth-century child poets allude to winter evenings spent reading.[36] Roger North recalls how, in the 1650s, his sister would recite romances to 'diver[t] her Sisters and all the female Society at work together'.[37] The practice of shared familial reading by the fireside is also hinted at in *The Cobbler of Canterbury* (1590), which claims that 'When the farmer is set in his chair turning (in a winter's evening) the crab in the fire, here he may hear, how his son can read, and when he hath done, laugh while his belly aches', a representation of a reading experience that both acts to shape how readers use the text and potentially discloses contemporary practice.[38] Intergenerational communities of readers are also depicted in Shakespeare's *Titus Andronicus* as Titus invites Lavinia and young Lucius into the closet to read 'sad stories' together.[39] Children's reading experiences were often communal and intergenerational, guided within the home or school.

Yet children were not restricted to reading what guardians or teachers gave them. A manuscript riddle book compiled by the Holme children in the 1640s and passed on to their youngest sibling indicates the ways in which children may have accessed textual material and appropriated it for their own ends. The production of this book by children and read by children gestures towards the shared cultures of childhood made possible through early textual engagement and children's participation as aural consumers, readers and writers.[40] Other children borrowed material from neighbours, bought it from peddlers and some encountered books 'lying' in the house.[41] Children often read alone, beyond the guidance of older generations. Some children read while at work.[42] Isham describes reading in her closet; while Lucy Hutchinson claims she would 'steal into some hole or other to read'.[43] While this was an approved act of spiritual meditation in Isham's case, this was a disruptive act for Hutchinson, who hid away to read following her mother's disapproval of her commitment to reading books, an act which was sanctioned by her father as part of her schooling. Elizabeth Cary's daughter claims a similar experience, when her father supported her reading as a child by giving her a copy of Calvin's *Institutes* but her mother prevented her from reading, leading to Cary reading illicitly at night, buying candles from the servants to facilitate this.[44] Elizabeth Isham also read against parental wishes. Although she was allowed to read books from her father's household library he refused to lend her the 'play books' she desired, leading to her reading of copies provided by her nurse instead.[45] This book will argue that such autonomous and disruptive reading practices facilitate the assertion of childhood identities by children, and this is explored in Chaps. 4 and 5. These chapters advance the argument that the contexts of reading impact on the ways in which the child is imagined and trained as a reader by focusing on the books used to educate early modern boys, in Chap. 4, and girls, in Chap. 5. Building on Heidi Brayman Hackel's seminal scholarship on the gendering of early modern reading practices to consider the extent to which readers and reading practices are gendered and aged, these chapters examine the intersections of gender, age and education in defining childhood to argue that the books for training children at school and home contribute to the period's concepts of boyhood and girlhood.[46] Yet these chapters will also focus on the ways in which literate boys and girls drew on their educational experiences to deploy their reading material—through the annotations on their books and their translations of what they read—to negotiate their own experiences of what it might mean to be a child, or more specifically a boy or girl, in the period.

Defining the Child (Reader)

The historical child or youth, particularly the boy-as-reader and girl-as-reader, is often discerned in the material evidence at moments of resistance. It is in the reading experiences that depart from recommended practice or the moments in which the young engage with their books (the content of the text or the space provided by the page) that readers are often defined as children: that is, in the moments when the young do not read, as they are advised to, in order to become civil, educated, professional or adult, but instead use their reading to explore alternative subjectivities, the state of being a boy, a girl or a child. Early modern child readers might, therefore, be evaluated in Michel de Certeau's terms, as consumers who appropriate their texts for their own ends.[47] However, this disruptive element that characterizes the reading experiences of many of the early modern children considered in this book might also be accounted for by the nature of the extant evidence. Extant descriptions of reading experiences often draw attention to readings that diverge from expectation, that somehow provoke comment, or in the case of children, even rebuke or punishment. This is particularly the case in the depictions of reading in early modern diaries and memoirs, as writers reflect on their exceptional reading practices as children.[48] However, it is also a result of how childhood is defined in the period. The history of childhood, as Ludmilla Jordanova has argued, is a methodologically difficult subject because 'definitions of the child are locally not biologically forged, and accordingly historians have no stable subjects for study'.[49] Definitions of childhood in early modern culture are varied. The child is, in one sense, defined by chronological age, yet even across tracts outlining the traditional ages of man there is disparity in the years accorded to this stage of the life cycle. Henry Cuffe suggests an element of fluidity in definitions of childhood when he defines childhood as stretching from birth to 24 and incorporating the states of 'infancy', 'boyhood', 'budding and blossoming age' and 'youth' in his *The Differences of the Ages of Man's Life* (1607).[50] John Ferne's *The Blazon of Gentry* (1586) and the anonymous *The Office of Christian Parents* (1616) both define childhood or 'peurillitye or childish yeeres' as stretching from 7 to 14. However, the latter qualifies this with a differentiation between males and females stating that for maids childhood ends at 12, as it is at the ages of 14 and 12 that boys and maides, respectively, 'beginne the flower of youth, preparing it selfe to the state of manhood or marriage'.[51] Even within definitions of childhood according to years, other factors come in to play, including gender and social contexts such as marriage.[52] Early modern childhood, therefore, is in part an aged category but is not fixed nor is it solely determined by biology or chronological age. Instead childhood is often defined in relation to social contexts. In addition to the school and marriage, the child or the state of childhood was variously defined in relation to the parents and elders in the context of family; the status of apprentice or servant to a master in contexts of service; denoted the individual who could not yet fully recite the catechism in religious institutions and the subject who could not yet take full responsibility or stand over an oath in legal and political terms. As Keith Thomas has persuasively argued, childhood was often determined in relation to authority.[53] It signified a subservient status, or a lack of economic, legal, sexual or even cognitive awareness or independence. Age, gender and class, the contexts of learning, family, religion, economics and marriage determined early modern childhoods in a variety of ways and the identity of the child was produced in relation to these factors. This book seeks to explore how cultures of reading also contributed to the state of being a child. It considers literacy and reading experiences alongside age, gender and social status in the construction of early modern childhoods. It evaluates on the one hand how expanding textual, and particularly print, cultures identified a particular category of reader as a child or in a state of childhood, and asserted a programme for reading specific to this entity and to the related and often overlapping categories of boy, maid and youth. On the other hand, it assesses the ways in which individuals' reading experiences produced their identities as children (the good child, the youth, the boy and the girl). It does not seek to uncover evidence of what texts early modern readers encountered at a certain age, but how, through their marginalia, memories or the contexts of their reading experiences, they were defined or asserted themselves as children.

It is in the moments in which children use their reading to assert their subjectivity against established authority that they are most commonly defined as children. Early modern texts suggest that reading is a way in which children gain the ability to challenge social, aged and gendered hierarchies. A preface 'To the Youthful Gentry' in *The Mysteries of Love and Eloquence* (1658) points out that 'a wench of fourteen, with a few Dramatic *Drayton* and *Sidney* Quillets' can 'put to the *non plus* a Gallant of thirty' and 'such a Lass [can] defeat a Gentleman of some years standing at Inns of Court'.[54] A servant in early seventeenth-century drama *The Wit of a Woman* warns 'olde men may teach to spell, but young folks will put together', hinting at the autonomous uses by children of their literacy.[55] This is perhaps most evident in the writing of children such as Elizabeth Cary (1585–1639), Rachel Fane (1613–1680), Abraham Cowley (1618–1667) and Elizabeth Delaval (*c.* 1648–1717) considered in Chaps. 5 and 6. Young readers respond to their reading by producing their own texts, copying diverse material from spiritual maxims to riddles, annotating their books, commenting on their encounters with literary cultures and drawing on their reading in the translations, poetry, prose and drama that they write. These texts in turn occasionally became the reading material of their peers, resulting in literary cultures produced by children for children; reading communities that shape childhood reading. Yet, as Kate Chedgzoy reminds us, early modern childhood, like childhood in any period, is not unmediated.[56] It is, Ludmilla Jordanova warns, impossible to recover separate histories of children. They do not occupy separate 'worlds' nor have an 'autonomous, authentic voice' in which 'a separate history could be rooted'.[57] The experiences of children are, as Jordanova states, 'inevitably bound in with the world of adults, through which they learn their languages, mental habits and patterns of behaviour'.[58] They are bound more specifically, in relation to this study, with the world of adults who teach them to read and who monitor and produce much of their reading material and experiences. The child readers who produce their own texts responded to texts produced by, recommended by or even forbidden by adult authors, printers, educators and guardians. Yet early modern children demonstrated remarkable variety and agency in their reading experiences, building on their reading to become producers of literature for and about childhood and evincing a cognitive capacity that challenges early modern understanding of childhood as a time of limited mental faculties. As Michael Witmore points out, children were perceived to be cognitively inferior in early modern culture, with writers such as Thomas Wright proposing that children 'lacke the use of reason, and are guided by an internal imagination'.[59] This attitude towards childhood as a time of the imagination and of lacking art and understanding is reflected in literary cultures through the associations of particular literary forms with childhood. Writing that is perceived to be inferior, for instance, is often dismissed as childish. Thomas Campion calls rhyme 'childish titillation', Gabriel Harvey transcribes two brief rhymes as 'Children's Songs' and Margaret Cavendish alludes to her early writings as 'my Baby-books', using the term to account for what she deems to be the inferior quality of her early writing.[60] Yet, as *Reading Children* shows, the ways in which early modern children read and respond creatively to their texts facilitates the expression of their childhoods in original ways. Although many of the representations of children as readers discussed in this monograph depict reading as a child as a mode of reading with lesser understanding and diminished responsibility, this concept of childish reading is also appropriated by the young through their creative engagement with their books to negotiate and reimagine their childhoods. Reading did not just instil identity for early modern children; reading was a means of shaping what it meant to be a child. This monograph thus challenges the definition of childhood as a vulnerable state, determined by a lack of autonomy or understanding. In *The Poetics and Politics of Youth in Milton's England*, Blaine Greteman persuasively demonstrates the extent to which the language of early modern children complicates the threshold between childhood and adulthood.[61] *Reading Children* contends that children's agency and creativity as readers also challenges this threshold, and reveals childhood as distinct state of being rather than simply a transitional stage on the way to becoming adult. A fresh understanding of what it means to be a child can, therefore, be discerned through close attention to the reciprocal relationships between children and reading cultures in early modern Britain.

Locating children in early modern reading cultures, however, is not straightforward. Children are represented as readers in a range of sources: in educational, didactic and religious texts, portraiture, woodcuts, poetry, prose and drama. *Reading Children* considers all of these sources to discern what Kate Flint terms 'rhetoric of reading practices' of children.[62] However, as Flint highlights, such sources 'build up a picture of widespread assumptions about what, when, and how' children should read, but does not necessarily disclose anything about their reading practices.[63] While Matthew Grenby suggests that the representations of children's reading might provide genuinely useful evidence of reading practices and Helen Smith usefully proposes that, although they 'cannot allow us unmediated access to the early modern reader but can help us to locate that reader in her environment', the reading experiences of early modern children are challenging to recover.[64] This in part due to the fact that they are difficult to define; it is also a consequence of the scarcity of evidence. As historians of reading have highlighted, reading often leaves no traces.[65] This is a particular problem in the early modern period given that reading was often the first element of literacy acquired. Many readers would not have been able to write in order to annotate their texts or leave other written accounts of their reading experiences. These readers constitute a gap in the historical record as they often leave no traces. Moreover, it is possible that even if young readers annotated their texts these may not have survived given the fragile nature of many of the texts directed towards them and the intense use to which they may have been put by young readers.[66] A sixteenth-century tract for Dutch children on how to preserve their books concludes that the best method of preservation is not to give them to children at all![67] Yet extant evidence indicates that children did handle, annotate and mark their books in diverse ways. William Sherman has highlighted some of the ways in which children 'use' books: writing their signatures, practising their writing and colouring in the bibles and other books that came into their hands.[68] Annotations and marginalia are a crucial source for an evaluation of the early modern reading experience, and a range of books considered in this study provide further evidence of children using books in this way. Yet, as Sherman points out, markings on a text, particularly the use of the leaves in a book to practise basic writing, do not necessarily indicate ownership or readership of a text. Nonetheless, as Juliet Fleming and Jason Scott-Warren have shown, such 'graffiti' are meaningful and worthy of interpretation.[69] As Sherman highlights, these readers' marks may provide specific examples of use rather than general rules, but they do reveal encounters of individuals with their books.[70]

More problematic, however, is the fact that doodles and signs of limited writing ability—such as practising handwriting—do not necessarily mean that the annotator is a child. Readers of all ages may have had limited writing abilities or may have drawn on books in ways that appear child-like. Most authors of textual annotation cannot be easily identified as children: markings on a text rarely designate age or draw attention to the writer or reader's context. In some instances, the provenance of a text (for example, books that formed part of early modern school libraries) indicate the annotator's identity, and in some cases young boy readers signal their status as members of a school. These marginalia, such as those evaluated in Chap. 4, shed some light on a youth's engagement with a text. More significantly they illuminate the encounters of individuals defined by their context as children—in this case the school—with their books. The scarcity of markings by the young on early modern texts means that analysis of these examples cannot offer a paradigm for the textual cultures of early modern childhood across social, economic, geographical and gender lines, but such markings signal the potential ways that children engaged with and used their reading material, and gesture towards the diversity of childhoods and children's reading experiences in early modern Britain. Some well-educated children left more substantial evidence of their reading through their writing. The educational exercises undertaken by early modern school children, their gathering of exempla in notebooks and their translations of what they read, offer an important source of evidence not only of what the young read but how they engaged with and used this material.[71] The school exercises of early modern girls, specifically Elizabeth Cary and Rachel Fane, form the focus of Chap. 5. Although in both these cases, it is likely that these exercises were undertaken between the ages of 11 and 16, these individuals are defined as children because of the contexts in which they read and write, rather than their chronological ages.

Diaries, letters and memoirs are among the most rewarding sources when seeking evidence of how children engaged with their texts.[72] Such accounts not only provide contextual information on the young readers—such as age, relational status and space and reason for reading—but often refer to using terminology of childhood. Much of the evidence of children's reading experiences considered in this monograph is located in autobiographical texts or in literary representations of what, when, where and how children read. Yet, these representations need to be evaluated, like the paratextual addresses to intended child readers and fictional representations of children as readers, as discursive constructs influenced by range of factors. The children memorialized in portraiture, such as the 2-year-old 'Miss Campion' depicted with hornbook in hand (1661), or in biographies, such as the extraordinary childhoods of the 'famous' and 'eminent Divines' of Samuel Clarke's collection (1662), often depict exceptional reading abilities either to display the talents of advanced children or to serve as an example to others. As Ramona Wray has noted, autobiographical texts 'might seem a privileged place to look for reading habits', but even these are complicated by the fragmentary nature of the evidence provided combined with the tendency to 'fi[t] the mould' of the form.[73] This is complicated further in relation to children's reading, as the child's reading experience is filtered through the retrospective perspective of an adult writer remembering their childhood in ways that facilitate the literary construction of their adult self. Chapter 6 focuses on such retrospective recollections of childhood reading to explore the extent to which childhood reading is represented specifically in this genre. Although autobiographical texts may offer limited information on the material reading practices of children, this chapter proposes that these representations illuminate the ways in which childhood, like adult masculinity or femininity, is a discursive construct and explores how it is constructed through the intersections of memory, reading and writing.[74] This chapter demonstrates the extent to which the child as reader functions in early modern literary cultures as an image in textual articulations of a developing adult self. It suggests that autobiographical writing offers another distinct conceptualization of the child as reader. In this genre, childhood is reimagined.

REIMAGINING THE CHILD READER

Reading Children in Early Modern Culture, therefore, aims to explore multiple manifestations of child as reader in early modern literary cultures. It is unique in its consideration of how early modern childhood is produced through the combined representation and participation of children in reading cultures. It is indebted to recent studies of early modern reading that bring together representations of readers and historical readers.[75] In particular, it takes its cue from Heidi Brayman Hackel's exemplary methodology of reconstructing 'both the strategies recommended to readers and the practices in which they then engaged' and balancing these 'constructions and representations of readers … against their practices' in her historicization of early modern readers.[76] As Brayman Hackel urges, it is necessary to 'return to the archives with the questions that literary theory has raised but cannot fully answer'.[77] Brayman Hackel does this through her focus on women readers; others have achieved this through case studies of exceptional scholarly readers; and William Sherman looks more widely at what evidence of book use reveals about a range of early modern readers.[78] Matthew Grenby's impressive study of eighteenth-century child readers develops this methodology specifically for a consideration of children as readers. Pointing out that there is a structural clash between the fields of book history and children's literature studies, Grenby argues that 'children are not, and have never been, readers in the sense that book historians usually envisage'.[79] Instead, of offering 'a single new model of the child reader', he considers evidence of book use by children in ownership records and marginalia, alongside publication history and representations of children as readers in a range of textual and graphic sources.[80] As Grenby persuasively argues, 'intermingling of sources and methods' helps to expose 'the ideological work being performed … by particular representations of reading, and take us as close as it is possible to get to ... the eighteenth-century child reader'.[81] Yet, as Ludmilla Jordanova has pointed out, there is 'no direct access to the experience of children'.[82] *Reading Children in Early Modern Culture* investigates the early modern child reader by bringing together wide-ranging representations of the child reader and childhood reading in the texts produced for children, in texts about children as readers, in recollections of reading as well as the traces of book ownership and engagement left by annotations and children's writing in order to shed light the multiple dimensions of the child as reader in the late sixteenth and seventeenth centuries. By evaluating this evidence together, a detailed, albeit—in Jordanova's terms— 'fragmented' picture of early modern child readers begins to emerge.[83]

This book thus contributes to the increased critical interest in early modern childhoods. Scholarship on this topic has flourished since the beginning of the twenty-first century. Studies of Shakespearean childhoods and performance cultures, by scholars such as Kate Chedgzoy, Susanne Greenhalgh, Robert Shaughnessy, Lucy Munro, Carol Chillington Rutter and Michael Witmore, radically transformed the critical landscape by arguing for the importance of the child to early modern literature and culture, and demonstrating the importance of further exploration of cultures of childhood in order to chart a more comprehensive history and examine the multiple and contingent constructs of childhood in the period.[84] This has been taken forward in examinations of the gendering of the Shakespearean child in studies by Katie Knowles on boyhood and Deanne Williams and Jennifer Higginbotham on girlhood, as well as re-examinations of the institutions in which childhood was shaped in monographs by Lynne Enterline, Jeanne McCarthy, Julie Ackroyd and edited collections by Deanne Williams and Richard Preiss, Naomi Yavneh and Naomi Miller.[85] Attending to the construction of childhood in relation to gender, education, economics and the institutions of theatre and school, this work has advanced the crucial task of unpacking the multiple connections between attitudes towards and experiences of childhood, and has offered new and varied definitions of what it means to be a child in this period. It has been crucial in establishing the diversity and richness of cultures of childhood in the period, yet has simultaneously signalled the vast range of material not yet investigated. The representation of children as readers, their reading practices and reading experiences, offers an important context for an interrogation of the importance of the child to early modern literary cultures. Edited collections, such as *Childhood and*

Children's Books in Early Modern Europe, 1550–1800, and book chapters signal importance of this area, gesturing towards the importance of literature and reading to early modern children and the significance of the child to early modern literary culture.[86] Yet to date the reading of children in the sixteenth and seventeenth centuries has not been fully investigated.

As Joseph Campana has highlighted, two key approaches to early modern childhood have emerged in this scholarship. Many scholars have focused on the material realities and voices of children in what Campana has termed 'archive fever' to recover the experiences of children.[87] Others have prioritized childhood as a concept separate from the lived experiences of children. Developing the critical contention that childhood is a historically and socially contingent construct, this monograph explores the concepts of childhood constructed by early modern textual cultures. It brings together these two strands by positioning the reading experiences of children alongside representations of childhood in the books produced for them and in accounts of how they should participate in early modern textual cultures. *Reading Children in Early Modern Culture* takes forward Kate Chedgzoy's proposal that scholars need to consider in tandem the 'connected questions of how childhood is to be defined and how children are to be known perceived and enabled to articulate their own kinds of knowledge'.[88] This approach discloses much about the complex and multiple contexts that shaped ideas and experiences of childhood in the period. It enables a fresh consideration of early modern childhood, but also of cultures of reading and of literary and book history from a new perspective; what Kate Chedgzoy calls a 'child-centred' perspective.[89] Through an analysis of the prevalence of this category of reader in the period, this monograph establishes the significance of childhoods to literary cultures pre-1700.

Reading Children in Early Modern Culture thus interrogates the concept of the child reader, asking how this is produced within the cultures of early modern textual production and reading, and what role this played in shaping wider understandings of childhood and children's experiences. It suggests that reading not only constructed childhood, but also the different purposes, spaces and ways of reading, in other words the distinct nature of the reading experience, created varied concepts of the child as reader. It ultimately argues that reading—what you read, how you read, how you imagine and present these reading experiences to others—was a crucial part of the identity of many early modern children, as well as adults reflecting back on their passage through the various stages of the early modern life cycle. However, not all early modern children could read. This monograph considers multiple forms of 'literacy' and 'reading'. It is interested in range of textual encounters, including the oral transmission of texts to children, children who could read encountering the written word in print and manuscript, children who could both read and write leaving evidence of their reading, and the distinct ways that early modern boys and girls who acquired advanced literacy in multiple languages engaged with their books. Yet, given low literacy levels in the period, this does not take into account the high proportion of children who could not read and for whom reading was not a crucial part of their experience or identity.[90] Cultures of reading are one way in which childhood was shaped, and many children and versions of childhood fall beyond the scope of this study. Nonetheless, as the examples considered in this book indicate, for those children who could read, reading was significant to their social development, to the negotiation of their childhoods and to their future adulthoods. This book thus reframes Frances Dolan's key question about early modern women and literacy, to ask what difference does children's literacy make.[91] If reading is a mode of negotiating the state of being a child, did the ability to read allow a number of early modern children the opportunity to experience a childhood? Childhood is not a universal experience. It was—and despite increasing emphasis on the rights of the child continues in some cultures to be—seen as a privilege.[92] Literacy and reading may have been one way in which the young of late sixteenth- and seventeenth-century Britain could access and experience a version of childhood.

NOTES

1. William Martyn, *Youth's Instruction* (London, 1612), n.p.
2. Jennifer Heller, *The Mother's Legacy in Early Modern England* (Aldershot: Ashgate, 2013), 1–10; Judith John, 'I Have Been Dying to Tell You: Early Advice Books for Children', *The Lion and the Unicorn* 29.1 (2005): 52–64; Louis B. Wright, 'Handbook Learning of the Renaissance Middle Class', *Studies in Philology* 28.1 (1931): 55–86.
3. Cited in Anna French, *Children of Wrath: Possession, Prophecy and the Young in Early Modern England* (London: Routledge, 2016), 35.
4. James Fitzmaurice, ed., *Margaret Cavendish: Sociable Letters* (London: Garland, 1997), 186.
5. On early modern children as readers, see Andrea Immel and Michael Witmore, ed., *Childhood and Children's Books in Early Modern Europe, 1550–1800* (London: Routledge, 2006); Seth Lerer, *Children's Literature: A Reader's History from Aesop to Harry Potter* (Chicago: University of

Chicago Press, 2008), 81–103; Nicholas Orme, *Medieval Children* (New Haven: Yale University Press, 2001), 298–304. On early modern children as authors, see L. C. Black, 'Some Renaissance Children's Verse', *Review of English Studies* 24.93 (1973): 1–16; Cedric Brown, 'Recusant Community and Jesuit Mission in Parliament Days: Bodleian MS Eng. Poet. B 5', *Yearbook of English Studies* 33 (2003): 290–315; Kate Chedgzoy, 'A Renaissance for Children?', Newcastle Upon Tyne ePrints, http://eprint. ncl.ac.uk/pub_details2.aspx?pub_id=196398, deposited 20 Nov. 2013; Kate Chedgzoy, '"Make me a Poet, and I'll quickly be a Man": Masculinity, Pedagogy and Poetry in the English Renaissance', *Renaissance Studies* 27.5 (2013): 592–611; Kate Chedgzoy, 'Playing with Cupid: Gender, Sexuality and Adolescence', in *Alternative Shakespeares 3*, ed. Diana E. Henderson (London: Routledge, 2008), 138–157; Lucy Munro, 'Infant Poets and Child Players: The Literary Performance of Childhood in Caroline England', in *The Child in British Literature*, ed. Adrienne Gavin (Basingstoke: Palgrave Macmillan, 2012), 54–68. See also consideration of girls as readers and producers of literature in the seventeenth century in Deanne Williams, *Shakespeare and the Performance of Girlhood* (Basingstoke: Palgrave Macmillan, 2014).

6. This study is thus influenced by critical approaches to childhood which, since Philippe Ariès' landmark study, *Centuries of Childhood* (New York: Vintage, 1962), have read childhood as a historically and culturally specific concept. For a summary of approaches to childhood post-Ariès, see Margaret King, 'Concepts of Childhood: What We Know and Where We Might Go', *Renaissance Quarterly* 60 (2007): 371–407; Karin Lesnik-Oberstein, 'Childhood and Textuality', in *Children in Culture: Approaches to Childhood*, ed. Karin Lesnik-Oberstein (Basingstoke: Palgrave Macmillan, 1998), 1–28.

7. See Andrew Tuer, *The History of the Horn-Book* (London: The Leadenhall Press, 1861), 2 vols.

8. William Hornby, *Hornbyes Hornbook* (London, 1622), A3v. Further references will be given in the text.

9. See Douglas Brooks, ed., *Printing and Parenting in Early Modern England* (Aldershot: Ashgate, 2006).

10. On childhood as feminine, see Naomi Miller and Naomi Yavneh, 'Introduction: Early Modern Children as Subjects: Gender Matters', in *Gender and Early Modern Constructions of Childhood*, ed. Naomi Miller and Naomi Yavneh (Aldershot: Ashgate, 2011), 1–16.

11. See cover image of this monograph.

12. On the intimate and violent elements of early modern pedagogy, see Alan Stewart, *Close Readers: Humanism and Sodomy in Early Modern England* (Princeton: Princeton University Press, 1997).

13. John Locke, *Some Thoughts Concerning Education* (London, 1693), 186. On the influence of Locke, see Lerer, 104–128.

14. See Jane Bingham and Grace Scholt, *Fifteen Centuries of Children's Literature* (London: Greenwood Press, 1980); Ruth Bottigheimer, *Bibliography of British Books for Children and Adolescents, 1470–1770* (New York: Stony Brook University Libraries, 2008); Patricia Demers, ed., *From Instruction to Delight: An Anthology of Children's Literature to 1850* (Oxford: Oxford University Press, 2008); F. J. Harvey Darton, *Children's Books in England: Five Centuries of Social Life* (Cambridge: Cambridge University Press, 1982); William Sloane, *Children's Books in England and America in the Seventeenth Century* (New York: Columbia University Press, 1955); Mary Thwaite, *From Primer to Pleasure in Reading: An Introduction to the History of Children's Books in England* (London: The Library Association, 1972); Warren Wooden, *Children's Literature of the English Renaissance* (Lexington: University Press of Kentucky, 1986).

15. Jennifer Richards and Fred Schurink, 'Introduction: The Textuality and Materiality of Reading in Early Modern England', *Huntington Library Quarterly* 73.3 (2010): 345. See also Evelyn Tribble, *Margins and Marginality: The Printed Page in Early Modern England* (London: University Press of Virginia, 1993).

16. Teresa Michals, *Books for Children, Books for Adults: Age and the Novel from Defoe to James* (Cambridge: Cambridge University Press, 2014), 2.

17. Neil Postman, *The Disappearance of Childhood* (New York: Vintage, 1984), 20–51. See also Patricia Crain, *Reading Children: Literacy, Property and the Dilemmas of Childhood in Nineteenth-Century America* (Philadelphia: University of Pennsylvania Press, 2016) on the intersections between literacy, print and concepts of childhood; Karin Lesnik-Oberstein, *Children's Literature: Criticism and the Fictional Child* (Oxford: Clarendon Press, 1994), 48, on the perceived need for books that corresponded to the ontology of the child. Seth Lerer '"Thy Life to Mend, This Book Attend": Reading and Healing in the Arc of Children's Literature', *New Literary History* 37.3 (2006), 634, who claims that 'if the child is kin to letter or to page [in Puritan culture], then the sustained study of the letters and the pages of the world becomes the key to understanding childhood'; Anja Müller, *Framing Childhood in Eighteenth-Century English Periodicals and Prints, 1689–1789* (Aldershot: Ashgate, 2009) on the production of concepts of childhood by eighteenth-century print media.

18. For an overview of approaches to the history of children's literature see Matthew Grenby, *The Child Reader*, 'The Origins of Children's Literature', in *The Cambridge Companion to Children's Literature*, ed. Matthew Grenby and Andrea Immel (Cambridge: Cambridge University Press, 2009), 3–18.

19. In this respect, my approach is influenced by changing definitions of 'children's literature'. See Edel Lamb, 'The Literature of Early Modern Childhoods', *Literature Compass* 7.6 (2010): 412–423.

20. Jacque Guillemeau, *Childe-Birth, or, The Happy Deliverie of Women* (London, 1612), 26.

21. Dorothy Leigh, *The Mother's Blessing* (1616), in *Women's Writing in Stuart England: The Mothers' Legacies of Dorothy Leigh, Elizabeth Joscelin, and Elizabeth Richardson*, ed. Sylvia Brown (Stroud: Sutton Publishing, 1999), 23.

22. Cited in Anthony Fletcher, *Growing Up in England: The Experience of Childhood, 1600–1914* (Yale: Yale University Press, 2008), 259.

23. Margaret Cavendish, *The Contract*, cited in Barbara Ravelhofer, '"Virgin Wax" and "Hairy Men-Monsters": Unstable Movement Codes in the Stuart Masque', in *The Politics of the Stuart Court Masque*, ed. David Bevington and Peter Holbrook (Cambridge: Cambridge University Press, 1998), 259.

24. William London, *A Catalogue of the Most Vendible Books in England* (Newcastle, 1658), G1r.

25. Cited in Wendy Wall, *Staging Domesticity: Household Work and English Identity in Early Modern Drama* (Cambridge: Cambridge University Press, 2002), 13. See also Geoffrey Whitney, *A Choice of Emblemes* (London, 1586), 172, who urges young people to 'Watche, write, and reade, and spende no idle hower.'

26. Lori Humphrey Newcomb, 'Gendering Prose Romance in Renaissance England', in *A Companion to Romance: From Classical to Contemporary*, ed. Corinne Saunders (Oxford: Blackwell, 2004), 133.

27. See Anthony Grafton, 'The Humanist as Reader', in *A History of Reading in the West*, ed. Guglielmo Cavallo and Roger Chartier (Cambridge: Polity Press, 1999), 179–212.

28. See Anna Davin, 'What Is a Child?', in *Childhood in Question: Children, Parents and the State*, ed. Stephen Hussey and Anthony Fletcher (Manchester: Manchester University Press, 1999), 16–36; Ludmilla Jordanova, 'New Worlds for Children in the Eighteenth Century: Problems of Historical Interpretation', *History of the Human Sciences* 3.1 (1990): 69–83.

29. Jennifer Heller, *The Mother's Legacy in Early Modern England* (Aldershot: Ashgate, 2011), 5; Carol Chillington Rutter, *Shakespeare and Child's Play: Performing Lost Boys on Stage and Screen* (London: Routledge, 2007), 156.

30. On this approach, see Heidi Brayman Hackel, *Reading Material in Early Modern England* (Cambridge: Cambridge University Press, 2005), 1–16; Stephen Colclough, *Consuming Texts: Readers and Reading Communities, 1695–1870* (Basingstoke: Palgrave, 2007), 5–7; Richards and Schurink, 350.

31. See Roger Chartier, *The Order of Books: Readers, Authors and Libraries in Europe between the Fourteenth and Eighteenth Centuries*, trans. Lydia Cochrane (Cambridge: Polity Press, 1994), 2, 5.
32. On communities of readers, see Chartier, 1–23; Colclough, 7–14.
33. Andrew Cambers, *Godly Reading: Print, Manuscript and Puritanism in England, 1580–1720* (Cambridge: Cambridge University Press, 2011), 95–96.
34. See Chap. 6.
35. See Fletcher, 99; Cambers, 68.
36. Black, 1.
37. Cited in Kate Loveman, *Samuel Pepys and His Books: Reading, Newsgathering, and Sociability, 1660–1703* (Oxford: Oxford University Press, 2015), 153.
38. Cited in Catherine Belsey, *Why Shakespeare?* (Basingstoke: Palgrave Macmillan, 2007), 12.
39. William Shakespeare, *Titus Andronicus*, in *The Norton Shakespeare*, ed. Stephen Greenblatt et al. (New York: W. W. Norton & Co., 2008), 3.2.80–84.
40. See Edel Lamb, 'The Riddles of Early Modern Children's Worlds', in *Material Worlds of Childhood in North-Western Europe c. 1350–1800*, ed. Philippa Maddern and Stephanie Tarbin (London: Routledge, 2017).
41. See Margaret Spufford, *Small Books and Pleasant Histories: Popular Fiction and Its Readership in Seventeenth-Century England* (Cambridge, 1981), 74; Abraham Cowley, *The Works of Mr. Abraham Cowley* (London, 1668), 144.
42. The 13-year-old Thomas Tryon learned to read with the help of his 'Fellow-Shepherds' in the fields in the 1640s (Spufford, 28–29). In the 1660s, Samuel Pepys sees a 'little boy' reading the Bible to a fellow shepherd (Hugh Cunningham, *The Invention of Childhood* [London: Random House, 2006]), 80. John Rastrick recalls how he took a book with him to read while he tended cows in the field in summer 1665 (Cambers, 112).
43. Elizabeth Isham, *My Booke of Rememberance*, ed. Elizabeth Clarke et al., *Constructing Elizabeth Isham*, University of Warwick, http://web.warwick.ac.uk/english/perdita/Isham/index_bor.htm, accessed 7 Dec. 2011, 10r; N. H. Keeble, ed. *Memoirs of the Life of Colonel Hutchinson* (London: Phoenix Press, 2000), 14.
44. Heather Wolfe, ed., *Lady Falkland: Life and Letters* (London: Continuum, 2004), 108.
45. Isham, 26r.
46. See Brayman Hackel, 7.
47. See Michel de Certeau, *The Practice of Everyday Life*, trans. Steven Randall (Berkeley: University of California Press, 1988).

48. See Kate Flint, *The Woman Reader, 1837–1914* (Oxford: Clarendon Press, 1993), 15, who notes that much of the extant evidence concerning individual readers comes from those who are reflective about their own practices, which 'perhaps calls into question their claim to typicality'.

49. Jordanova, 79.

50. Henry Cuffe, *The Differences of Ages of Man's Life* (London, 1607), 117–118.

51. John Ferne, *The Blazon of Gentry* (London, 1586), 169; *The Office of Christian Parents* (London, 1616), L1r.

52. See Davin, 16–36. See also Paul Griffiths, *Youth and Authority: Formative Experiences in England 1560–1640* (Oxford: Clarendon Press, 1996), 20, on early modern definitions of the stages of the life cycle.

53. Keith Thomas, 'Age and Authority in Early Modern England', *Proceedings of the British Academy* 62 (1976): 205–248.

54. *The Mysteries of Love and Eloquence* (London, 1658), A5r.

55. *The Wit of a Woman* (London, 1604), C3v.

56. Chedgzoy, 'Renaissance', 21.

57. Jordanova, 78.

58. Jordanova, 79.

59. See Michael Witmore, *Pretty Creatures: Children and Fiction in the English Renaissance* (Ithaca: Cornell University Press, 2007), 39. On early modern perceptions of children's cognitive abilities, see also Evelyn Tribble and Nicholas Keene, *Cognitive Ecologies and the History of Remembering: Religion, Education and Memory in Early Modern England* (Basingstoke: Palgrave Macmillan, 2001), 132–151.

60. See Joseph Campana, 'Boy Toys and Liquid Joys: Pleasure and Power in the Bower of Bliss', *Modern Philology* 106.3 (2009): 470–471; Eleanor Relle, 'Some New Marginalia and Poems of Gabriel Harvey', *Review of English Studies* 23.92 (1972): 404; Fitzmaurice, 188.

61. Blaine Greteman, *The Poetics and Politics of Youth in Milton's England* (Cambridge: Cambridge University Press, 2013).

62. Flint, 73. See also Sasha Roberts, *Reading Shakespeare's Poems in Early Modern England* (Basingstoke: Palgrave Macmillan, 2003), 13.

63. Flint, 73.

64. Matthew Grenby, *The Child Reader, 1700–1840* (Cambridge: Cambridge University Press, 2011), 22–23; Helen Smith, '"More swete unto the eare/than holsome for ye mynde": Embodying Early Modern Women's Reading', *Huntington Library Quarterly* 73.3 (2010): 414.

65. Brayman Hackel, 2; Margaret Ferguson, *Dido's Daughters: Literacy, Gender and Empire in Early Modern England and France* (Chicago: University of Chicago Press, 2003), 74.

66. William Sherman, *Used Books: Marking Readers in Renaissance England* (Philadelphia: University of Pennsylvania Press, 2007), 5, points out that a more heavily used book is more vulnerable to decay.

67. M. H. Porck and H. J. Porck, 'Eight Guidelines on Book Preservation from 1527: How One Should Preserve All Books to Last Eternally', *Journal of Paper Conservation* 13.2 (2012): 17–25.

68. Sherman, 84. See H. Jackson, *Marginalia: Readers' Writing in Books* (New Haven: Yale University Press, 2001), 21, on the ways in which young children tend to use books for drawing or writing practice.

69. Juliet Fleming, *Graffiti and the Writing Arts of Early Modern England* (London: Reaktion Books, 2001); Jason Scott-Warren, 'Reading Graffiti in the Early Modern Book', *Huntington Library Quarterly* 73.3 (2010): 363–381.

70. Sherman, xvi.

71. As evidenced in Lynn Enterline, *Shakespeare's Schoolroom: Rhetoric, Discipline, Emotion* (Philadelphia: University of Pennsylvania Press, 2012).

72. Cambers, 41, points out that 'diaries and autobiographies provide evidence of reading practices that is unparalleled by other textual sources'.

73. Ramona Wray, 'Recovering the Reading of Renaissance Englishwomen: Deployments of Autobiography', *Critical Survey* 12.2 (2000), 33. See also Grenby, *The Child Reader*, 14.

74. On the need to move beyond essential views of the child and to apply theory to childhood, see Lesnik-Oberstein, 'Childhood', 1–25; Erica Burman and Jackie Stacey, 'The Child and Childhood in Feminist Theory', *Feminist Theory* 11 (2010): 227–237.

75. See Colclough, 1–26, for useful analysis of developments in the history of reading.

76. Brayman Hackel, 8–9.

77. Brayman Hackel, 7.

78. For example, Lisa Jardine and Anthony Grafton, '"Studied for Action": How Gabriel Harvey Read His Livy', *Past & Present* 129 (1990): 30–78; William Sherman, *John Dee: The Politics of Reading and Writing in the English Renaissance* (Amherst: University of Massachusetts Press, 1995).

79. Grenby, *The Child Reader*, 10. See also Crain, 18, who points out that book history has failed to take account of discourses of childhood.

80. Grenby, *The Child Reader*, 10.

81. Grenby, *The Child Reader*, 35.

82. Jordanova, 78.

83. Jordanova, 76.

84. Kate Chedgzoy, Susanne Greenhalgh, Robert Shaughnessy, ed., *Shakespeare and Childhood* (Cambridge: Cambridge University Press, 2007); Lucy Munro, *Children of the Queen's Revels: A Jacobean Theatre Repertory*

(Cambridge: Cambridge University Press, 2005); Chillington Rutter; Witmore. See also Mary Bly, *Queer Virgins and Virgin Queans on the Early Modern Stage* (Oxford: Oxford University Press, 2000); Edel Lamb, *Performing Childhood in the Early Modern Theatre: The Children's Playing Companies, 1599–1613* (Basingstoke: Palgrave Macmillan, 2009); Morris Partee, *Childhood in Shakespeare's Plays* (New York: Peter Lang, 2006).

85. Julie Ackroyd, *Child Actors on the London Stage, circa 1600* (Brighton: Sussex Academic Press, 2017); Enterline; Jennifer Higginbotham, *The Girlhood of Shakespeare's Sisters: Gender, Transgression, Adolescence* (Edinburgh: Edinburgh University Press, 2013); Katie Knowles, *Shakespeare's Boys: A Cultural History* (Basingstoke: Palgrave Macmillan, 2014); Jeanne McCarthy, *The Children's Troupes and the Transformation of English Theatre 1509–1608* (London: Routledge, 2016); Deanne Williams, *Shakespeare and the Performance of Girlhood* (Basingstoke: Palgrave Macmillan, 2014); Deanne Williams and Richard Preiss, ed., *Childhood, Education and the Stage in Early Modern England* (Cambridge: Cambridge University Press, 2017); Yavneh and Miller, ed., *Gender and Early Modern Constructions of Childhood*. See also articles by Joseph Campana on early modern childhood, including 'The Child's Two Bodies: Shakespeare, Sovereignty, and the End of Succession', *English Literary History* 81.3 (2014): 811–839.

86. See Immel and Witmore; Lerer, *Children's Literature*; Adrienne Gavin, *The Child in British Literature* (Basingstoke: Palgrave Macmillan, 2012); Mary Hilton, Morag Styles and Victor Watson, ed., *Opening the Nursery Door: Reading, Writing and Childhood 1600–1900* (London: Routledge, 1997); Celia Keenan and Mary Shine Thompson, ed., *Studies in Children's Literature, 1500–2000* (Dublin: Four Courts, 2004),

87. Joseph Campana, 'Shakespeare's Children', *Literature Compass* 8.1 (2011): 5.

88. Chedgzoy, 'Introduction', in *Shakespeare and Childhood*, 17.

89. Chedgzoy, 'Make', 595.

90. On early modern literacy levels, see Chap. 2, 33.

91. Frances Dolan, 'Reading, Writing, and Other Crimes', in *Feminist Readings of Early Modern Culture*, ed. Valerie Traub, M. Lindsay Kaplan and Dympna Callaghan (Cambridge: Cambridge University Press, 1996), 144.

92. See Crain, 60.

CHAPTER 2

'A Good Child Is One that Loves His Book': Literacy, Religious Instruction and the Child as Reader

This your first ABC, and best Primer is
Whence, having thoroughly learnt the Christcrosse row,
You may with comfort to Our Father goe,
Who will you to that highest lesson bring
Which Seraphins instruct his saincts to sing.[1]

In his 'Verses on a Bible Presented to Lady K[atherine] C[ork]' (*c.* 1624), Thomas Pestell describes the Bible as a path to literacy and salvation for the young Katherine Boyle. This forty-line poem was likely inscribed upon a Bible presented to the 10-year-old-girl who had recently arrived in the household of her intended husband, heir of Lord Beaumont.[2] In the concluding lines, Pestell, the household chaplain, establishes this Bible as the 'first' and 'best' reading book for the young girl. Defining it as her ABC and Primer he compares it to the basic reading books used to instruct the young in literacy which contained, for the most part, religious material, and he recommends that Boyle makes this book her primary source for lessons in literacy and religion. The language of learning pervades the poem. In addition to the final images of learning the 'Christcrosse row'—the alphabet prefixed by the figure of the cross in early hornbooks—and the 'highest lesson' of God, the poem opens with an image of the world as 'gods large book wherein we learne/Him'.[3] While, the poem claims, the world offers lessons that are difficult to discern, 'His word' becomes the focus of learning. This enlightenment offered by the Bible's

© The Author(s) 2018
E. Lamb, *Reading Children in Early Modern Culture*,
Early Modern Literature in History,
https://doi.org/10.1007/978-3-319-70359-6_2

'rays' is, according to Pestell, particularly directed to children. Claiming that it may 'dazle & confound the wise', he depicts the word as 'a gentle light to children's eyes'. In subsequent lines the Bible is compared to a garden that delights 'little ones' and in which they can gather 'fruicts for taste, & flow'rs for sight'. This account of the multi-sensory experience of reading is not uncommon in a culture in which collections of religious material, such as *The Garden of Godly Delights*, or catechisms such as Robert Abbot's *Milk for Babes*, compared the reading experience to gathering spiritual and material nourishment.[4] Yet Pestell's depiction is notable for its emphasis on the particular suitability of children to participate in this practice. He portrays a gentle educative process through reading via this gentle light and garden imagery. Directing Boyle's reading further by urging her to 'Behold that blessed babe within this booke', he sets up the Christ child as a point of identification. His claims that 'tender Virgins love to looke' on 'babes' suggests a common experience of youth but also this young maid's planned future as wife and mother. In addition, Pestell highlights the book's status as material object by advising the young girl on when to read it—'Read it when first you rise &, gone to bedd'—and where to store it—'Under your pillow, let it bear your head'. Pestell evokes the book as the girl's companion, revered object and moral guide. These dedicatory verses render the Bible personal reading material and precious object for this young girl. They imaginatively transform the Bible into a children's book: an ABC, a book in which 'little ones' can take 'delight' and gather 'the fruit of knowledge', and a book in which the young reader can learn through beholding another child.

Pestell's personalization of this Bible as the material property and spiritual guide for one particular child is representative of the processes through which becoming literate in early modern culture overlapped with the shaping of religious subjectivity. It discloses the ways in which these experiences were both frequently associated with the early textual encounters of children. Although the Bible was not adapted specifically for children in English until the late seventeenth century, it was widely recommended as a crucial text for Protestant children, male and female, from across the social spectrum in early modern Britain.[5] In her 1616 advice book, Dorothy Leigh urged that all children be taught to read the Bible and suggests that one of the main aims of learning to read this book is for children 'to learne how to serve God, their King & Country by reading' (31), gesturing towards the political import of early literacy.[6] In his 1660 children's book, *A Little Book for Little Children*, Thomas White advocates the Bible as essential reading material 'when thou canst read'.[7] Thomas

Lye's *The Child's Delight* (1671), an instructional reading book, claims that its main aim is 'speedily to inable children, accurately to read the Bible'.[8] Lady Grace Mildmay recalls her sixteenth-century childhood experiences of her mother giving her a Bible to read, while the non-conformist minister Oliver Heywood similarly recollects his mother 'continually putting us upon reading the scriptures' in the early 1630s.[9] Fathers provided bibles to Elizabeth Isham, who describes the bibles bought for 'us his children' in the early seventeenth century as her 'chiefest treasure', and to Issac Archer who remembers his unwillingness to read the Bible which his father forced upon him in his childhood in the 1640s.[10] In 1629 Lady Brilliana Harley requests her husband to send a Bible for their 5-year-old-son, Ned, who has begun to delight in reading.[11] The accounts for Francis Lynn's school expenses at Westminster Grammar School in May 1689 indicate his father's purchase of three essential items: 'A Bible, Practice of Piety and a comb'.[12] The Bible seems to be have been an essential purchase for early modern parents as part of their duty in bringing up their children. It was also, in many cases, the impetus for and the mode of determining literacy in childhood in post-Reformation England. As William Sherman points out 'the Bible was closely connected to the drive towards literacy' to the extent that 'literacy did not just mean reading; it meant reading the Bible'.[13] Religious texts were central to methods of literacy acquisition in the period. The child's first book teaching the basic skills of reading—the hornbook or ABC book—combined alphabetical instruction with the Lord's Prayer. More substantial ABC books merged alphabetical basics with catechetical instruction. In grammar schools, proficiency was often measured by the child's ability to read the Bible.[14] For early modern children, learning to read was a religious experience.

This chapter examines the extent to which becoming literate in early modern religious culture shaped ideas about childhood. As Alec Ryrie argues, post-Reformation culture was a 'bookish' one and the complex relationship between Protestants and the written word meant that although the illiterate could be zealous Protestants, they were excluded from what was to many a central part of that experience: direct access to the word of God.[15] This chapter analyses the books printed to facilitate the acquisition of basic literacy and religious knowledge—from the first authorized version of *The ABC with Catechism* of 1551 to the religious reading books of the 1690s—to argue that the child is identified in this textual culture as distinct type of reader. Building on existing work on childhood within Protestant and particularly Puritan culture, I suggest that an original understanding of the child as reader emerges within post-Reformation attitudes towards literacy.[16] Through an analysis of early ABC books, I propose that textual cultures produced a concept of the child reader characterized both by literacy level and age, and demonstrate how authors and printers, including John Bunyan in *A Book for Boys and Girls* (1686), continued to develop the concept of this reader in the seventeenth century through the innovative design of religious ABCs targeted at the young. I then consider the religious books recommended to and written for children who had acquired basic literacy. Through a case study of Thomas White's *A Little Book for Little Children* (1660), James Janeway's *A Token for Children* (1671) and Robert Russel's *A Little Book for Children and Youth* (*c.* 1693–1696), I evaluate the books and reading practices recommended to aid children in developing their religious subjectivities. These authors align the reading of 'good books' with being 'good' children, demonstrated aptly by Russel's clear formulation 'A good child is one that loves his Book'.[17] They offer detailed accounts of what it means to be a 'good' child through narratives of exemplary children and through direct addresses and instructions to the reader. These books have often been cited in children's literature scholarship as among the earliest examples of the form. Patricia Demers, for instance, includes Puritans as among the first to write specifically for children and Gillian Avery suggests that the limited number of child-slanted books in the seventeenth century were almost exclusively religious.[18] While acknowledging that religious printed texts constitute the majority of what might be termed books for children in the sixteenth and seventeenth centuries, in the ways that they claim to be primarily for children and deploy a range of strategies to facilitate reading and learning by the child, this chapter moves forward from such debates to investigate the ways in which these books frame literacy and reading as markers of what it means to be a 'good' child. It will argue that religious books for children determine what it means to be a good child in terms of reading practices and reading experiences. Ultimately it aims to evaluate the extent to which this literary and religious recognition of childhood produces a shared concept of the child as reader.

LEARNING TO READ

To learn to Read, good Child, give heed,
For 'tis a precious Thing:
What may compare with Learning rare!
From hence doth Virtue spring.[19]

Benjamin Keach's mid-seventeenth-century ABC and catechism for children, *Instructions for Children*, highlights the importance placed by many on learning to read. Keach deploys the language of being a 'good' child in this first precept to his child reader, suggesting that learning to read leads to moral virtues as well as, the economic implications of precious and rare imply, practical success.[20] Despite extensive scholarship on literacy in the early modern period, it has not been determined how far-reaching such calls to reading may have been. Literacy levels continue to be contested since David Cressy's seminal study of the topic, yet scholars largely agree that the ability to read was widespread and that literacy rates increased throughout the sixteenth and seventeenth centuries, although this varied according to gender and class.[21] A variety of social, cultural and technological shifts underlie increasing literacy, not least the wider accessibility of texts following the introduction of the printing press, developments in education and religious reformation.[22] Learning to read was important no matter what your age. This is reflected in the large range of texts produced to assist in the acquisition of literacy, including the anonymous and oft-printed *An ABC for Chyldren* (1561) to S. W.'s *Most Easie Instructions for Reading Specially Penned for those of Yeares* (1610).[23] Although children were not the only ones in need of instruction, they became key beneficiaries of efforts to extend literacy. Thomas Newbery's *A Booke in Englysh Metre, of the Great Marchaunt Man Called Dives Pragmaticus* (1563) was intended to be 'very preaty for children to rede: whereby they the better and more readyer, rede and wryte wares and Implementes', and aimed to provide a basic knowledge of the merchant's business alongside literacy to children likely to enter this profession.[24] From this trade-specific text to J. G.'s *A Play-Book for Children To Allure Them to Read* (1694), which aimed to teach basic literacy using alphabetized sequences of sentences often using examples from daily life, children were encouraged to read for a variety of purposes and using a range of methods.[25] Pedagogues recognized the diverse benefits of training children in reading.[26] In his 1582 treatise on bringing up and educating children, Richard Mulcaster insists 'I make *reading*, my first and fairest principle of all other.'[27] Reading, he suggests, should be taught first as this 'most frutefull principle, in training of the minde', as it will eventually provide access to religion, law and knowledge as well as 'hel[p] to do all thinges well' and benefit the health and physical development of the young, as 'loud reading scoureth all the veines ... encreaseth heat ... suffereth not superfluous humours to grow grosse and thicke'.[28] Charles

Hoole, a mid-seventeenth-century Yorkshire teacher, also recommends early instruction in reading. Ideally, he suggests, a child should be taught to read before entering school: he 'hath a great propensity to peep into a book' between the ages of 3 and 4.[29] Hoole's focus is on training school-boys, for whom reading was an essential requirement if they wished either to enter an apprenticeship or grammar school, but he also indicates the wider benefits of learning to read early, including gaining 'habit and delight in reading' and to 'sweeten their (otherwise sowr) natures, that they may live comfortably towards themselves, and amiably converse with other persons'.[30] For humanist educators such as Mulcaster and Hoole, reading helped shape children's health and sociability as well as preparing them academically and professionally.

Despite the identification of this range of benefits, religion recurs as a primary context in accounts of teaching reading. With the post-Reformation emphasis on the importance of the written word as a significant element of individual relationships with God, reading was perceived to be a crucial means of accessing religious knowledge and practice, primarily through the reading of the Bible.[31] The Bible was a significant object in becoming literate, as reading its text was a common means of measuring reading proficiency. John Brinsley's dialogue between two schoolmasters, *Ludus Literarius*, suggests that the measure of literacy for entry into grammar school was that children should 'be able to read English: as namely, that they could reade the New Testament perfectly'.[32] Hoole claims to have heard of teachers who have taught 'little children not much above four years old to read distinctly in the Bible in six weekes', but notes that he allows two or three years for 'learning to read English perfectly' before moving on to Latin.[33] Oliver Sansom claims that when he was 'put to school to a woman' in the early 1640s when he was 6 he made such progress that 'in about four months time, I could read a chapter in the Bible pretty readily'.[34] In these accounts the Bible is evoked as the central focus of the learning experience: it is the rationale for learning and the mode of testing that ability.

Teaching children to read also permitted dissemination of knowledge of the Bible to previously illiterate households as, according to Bishop Whitgift in the sixteenth century, those 'being not able to read themselves, by means of their children reading to them at home, receive instruction and edifying'.[35] The practice of having children read the Bible aloud for the benefits of their less able peers and elders continued. Lady Alice Lucy frequently had one of her children read biblical passages to the others before supper in the 1640s.[36] In 1667 Samuel Pepys records the 'pleasant and innocent sight' of a 'little boy' reading the Bible to his master, a shepherd.[37] Training children to read benefited their illiterate elders, but was more significant for their own religious instruction. Religious moralists stressed the particular benefits of teaching children to read. Almost one hundred years after Mulcaster cites 'access to religion' as one of the ends of learning how to read, Richard Baxter urged 'By all means let children be taught to read, if you are never so poor whatever shift you make, or else you deprive them of a singular help to their instruction and salvation.'[38] By the late seventeenth century to not teach basic literacy in childhood is to 'deprive' children in both educational and religious terms. More specifically, reading is one aid towards salvation.

The dissemination of religious beliefs was thus a significant impetus for teaching children to read and informed the teaching processes. This is further evidenced by the fact that the first literacy books encountered by many children on what John Locke termed 'the ordinary road' of the hornbook, primer, psalter, and New Testament contained religious material.[39] Similar ABC texts—either in manuscript, hornbook or print—and methods were used whether the child learned to read at home under the instruction of parents, siblings or tutors, at places of work, or the formal schoolroom.[40] The hornbook and basic ABC books, which often claimed to teach English and Latin in the six weeks noted by Hoole, combined the alphabet, capitalized and non-capitalized in black letter, roman and italic typefaces with lists of the vowels and basic letter combinations with common prayers and the commandments.[41] Children who used them may have learned from them as both auditors and readers. While various late sixteenth- and early seventeenth-century schoolmasters suggested innovative ways of using these texts in order to learn the alphabet and basic reading skills in English, key methods are repeated across their suggestions.[42] In *The Education of Children* (1588), William Kempe proposed a cumulative learning process, first knowing 'letters by their figures', then sounding 'them aright by their proper names' and finally 'join[ing] them together, the vowels with the vowels in diphthongs and the consonants with vowels in other syllables'.[43] In 1659, Charles Hoole further advocated this method, stating that 'The usual way to begin with a child, when he is first brought to Schoole is to teach him to know his letters in the Horn-book, where he is made to run over all the letters in the Alphabet or Christ-cross-row both forwards & backwards, until he can tel any one of them which is pointed at.' Having 'got some knowledge of their letters, & a smattering of some syllables and words in the horn-book', the child should then progress to the ABC or primer and 'name the letters, and spell the words, till by often use they can pronounce (at least) the shortest words at first sight'.[44] Pronunciation was an important element of the reading process and numerous tracts recommended that the child recite the alphabet, vowels, consonants, letter combinations and syllables included in the hornbooks and ABCs repeatedly so that through continued association between the sounds and the visual text they would acquire the ability to read any word.[45] Sounding out early sample material was perceived to be the first step towards religious knowledge. In an account of the early reading experiences of the young Marta Hatfield in the mid-seventeenth century, James Fisher claims 'Even while she spelled words and syllables, she spelled out Christ.'[46]

The child put this learning into practice by turning to the sample material included in the latter part of the hornbook or ABC, and this material was primarily religious in content, including the Lord's Prayer, the Articles of the Faith, the Ten Commandments and 'precepts of good lyvynge' including 'feare God' and 'love God'.[47] These short texts were frequently provided in English and Latin, fulfilling the book's aim of teaching reading in both languages. Becoming literate in English and Latin, as Patricia Demers points out, was a process of instilling the fundamentals of the faith.[48] This continued as children progressed from these basic ABCs to the *The ABC with Catechism* and *The Primer*, books in English that also contained prayers and the commandments with the addition of catechisms, graces, liturgical offices, psalms and litanies.[49] Some texts explicitly articulated the dual emphasis on literacy and faith.[50] One seventeenth-century grammar school text demonstrates the extent to which acquiring other forms of literacy continued to overlap with religious instruction. Elisha Coles' *Nolens Volens, Or, You Shall Make Latin Whether You Will or No* (1677) is a textbook on grammar but contains *The Youth's Visible Bible*, an alphabetical arrangement of key words with accompanying woodcuts and scriptural examples in English and Latin.[51] Having mastered the rudiments of Latin grammar this collection of biblical words and extracts serves as a basis for schoolboy practice. Advancing skills of literacy formed part of an extended process of indoctrination.

Early modern ABC books, therefore, often functioned as ABCs in a dual sense. As well as teaching the fundamentals of the alphabet and language, the basic prayers held within them were also what Richard Bernard called 'the ABC of our religion' in 1613.[52] The benefits of this alphabet-ized format for fixing religious prayers and precepts in memory were rec-ognized by many, with E. C., for instance, producing a religious manual for children which arranged basic scriptural lessons around the letters of the alphabet in *An A.B.C. or Holy Alphabet ... to Enter Young Beginners in the Schoole of Christ* (1626). Recognizing that this may seem 'too vulgar, or meane a project', the author upholds his method as fitting to deliver 'some rudiments that may yield instruction to poore ignorant people ... and set forward young beginners, not capable for their weaknesses of the benefit of any artificiall method, in that their holy course'.[53] Alphabetization is recognized beyond the basic ABC book as a fitting mode of instilling knowledge.

The ABC format was officially sanctioned as a useful mode of training children in religious beliefs with the publication of *The ABC with Catechism* in 1551.[54] Catechisms and primers had been used as a method of religious instruction in English, orally and via reading, from the early sixteenth cen-tury.[55] Yet the standardization of this early reading material in the mid-sixteenth century signals the extent to which literacy, religious knowledge and concepts of childhood coalesce. Following the model of earlier ABC books, this new format opened with similar instructional material in the form of the alphabet in multiple print types and various letter and syllable combinations. Yet it was more extensive, including basic numerical instruc-tion, the short form of catechism, and concluding with a series of prayers.[56] Recommended on the statutes of many schools and by a range of educa-tors, it seems likely that *The ABC with Catechism* was one of the first books encountered by many early modern children, whether read aloud to them by parents or masters or handed to them as readers, for a period spanning over 150 years.[57] It was perceived to be for the youngest of learners, who would move on to *The Primer with Catechism*, which contained additional material such as a almanac, prayers, psalms and sentences from scripture, and then progress to Nowell's longer and more complicated catechism.[58] In this sense then, *The ABC with Catechism* was a book for those begin-ning their learning, whether in religion or reading, to equip them with the basic skills necessary to progress towards knowledge and understanding as well as to admission to the Church through confirmation. Learning to read thus frequently meant the same thing as learning religion. Increased literacy in early modern culture often signalled a progression to spiritual knowledge.

THE ABC BOOK AND THE 'CHILD' AS READER

Childhood was widely recognized in early modern England as a formative stage of life in which basic precepts could be instilled. The child was not only perceived to be open to learning; images of childhood as a formative stage highlighted the necessity of beginning the processes of moral and educational learning in the early years. Bartholomew Batt, for example, compares the need to instruct children and fashion their behaviours to the swaddling of infants who 'so soone as they be borne, be carefully tended, roled and swaddled, that they grow not crooked and deformed'.[59] The production of ABC books for catechetical instruction forged an association between the earliest years and basic learning, putting forward an ideal model of religious instruction beginning as soon as the child could learn to read. Yet in practice religious novices or those in the early stages of literacy acquisition were not necessarily children in terms of age. Authors and printers identified a wide range of novice listeners and readers for this basic instructional book. While the earliest edition of *The ABC with Catechism* specifies children as the primary users, stating on the title page that it is 'an instruction to be learned of euerye chylde before he be brought to be confyrmed' (an injunction repeated on extant editions up to the 1630s), from the 1660s the title page extends this to 'every person before he be brought to be confirmed by the Bishop'.[60] A range of basic instructional religious texts deploy an image of the young reader as someone who was both young in years and in understanding. Title pages and prefatory material commonly categorized these readers as a combined group of the young and ignorant. Thomas Cobhead, for instance, writes religious instruction for '*the Exercise of Youth, and Simple Sort of People*' (1579), Robert Cawdry aims at '*instructing the youth, and ignorant persons in the principles and groundes of Christian religion*' (1580) and Thomas Doolittle's catechetical exercise in *The Young Man's Instructer, and The Old Man's Remembrancer* (1673) claims to be 'fitted to the capacity of children and the more ignorant sort of people'.[61] The claim of being for both young and old, for those lacking in knowledge and those seeking to refresh their knowledge, might form part of a marketing strategy, leading, as Ian Green points out, to works being described as being suited to a much wider readership or as having a larger number of uses than might originally have been imagined.[62] Yet this identification of young readers alongside others in need of advice highlights a perceptual connection between those young in age and those lacking in religious knowledge.

Throughout the sixteenth and seventeenth centuries, children were frequently classed with uneducated or illiterate adults, and this acquires a particular resonance in religious contexts in which this pre-educative state equates to ignorance of the faith.[63] In *An A.B.C. or Holy Alphabet*, E. C. claims his book is for the young and the ignorant in its dedicatory epistle and concludes by highlighting that 'children' should be 'taught' and 'instruction' given to those that 'remain children in understanding'.[64] Childhood is further equated with a lack of knowledge in the common image of the parental-instructor and the child-learner. In catechisms, such as John Craig's *The Mother and Child* (1611), Dorothy Burch's *A Catechism of the Several Heads of the Christian Religion* (1646) and Robert Abbot's *Milk for Babes* (1646), the child is deployed as an image of the recipient of catechetical instruction. These 'mother-directed' catechisms designate the instructor as mother and the catechumen as child, reflecting common practice but also positioning the child as an image of the recipient of religious instruction.[65] Maternal spiritual advice books further develop this concept of a child as figure who needs textual guidance and advice, particularly on spiritual matters. While many are written by mothers addressing their own children, including Elizabeth Joscelin's manuscript legacy to her unborn child (1622) and Dorothy Leigh's printed address to her sons (1622), such books were circulated, published, imitated by male authors and made available to a range of readers.[66] As Jennifer Heller argues, although they do not always address 'historical children' they do 'address the vulnerable child reader'.[67] Leigh's text, for example, claims to be 'for all parents to leave as a Legacy to their Children, but especially for those, who by reason for their young yeeres stand most in need of instruction'.[68] Therefore, even though readership varies, these books represent text as surrogate parent who 'mothers' an imagined young and impressionable reader.[69] They function as both material items, often handed down from mother to child reader and signalling an exchange of literacy and spiritual guidance through the generations, and as textual constructions of an imagined reader who is positioned as child.[70] The recurrent metaphor of the child as religious novice or ignorant in matters of the faith forges a concept of the child reader as reading to learn: to become literate and to become a religious subject.

Therefore, although the acquisition of religious knowledge and the processes of learning to read are not limited to the stage of the life cycle known as childhood, these activities are widely associated with it in the early modern period, and writers and publishers exploited this. Edmond

Graile's *Little Timothe His Lesson* (1611), for instance, is not a lesson for the young but instead a scriptural summary 'comprised in Meeter, for the helpe of memory, and instruction of the ignorant in the Writings of God' that exemplifies the early instruction of the biblical Timothy who, in his early childhood, 'could talke and Scriptures tell'.[71] The child as reader is held up here as a model for religious instruction. This association between childhood and early literacy learning was so widely recognized that it was also invoked to ridicule older would-be readers. Learning the ABC is comically represented as a childish act by Nicholas Breton who writes in 1600 that 'To learn the babies A,B,C/Is fit for children, not for mee'.[72] In 1618, he ironically portrays those who do not succeed in their learning as prolonging infancy through to their old age, writing 'there are some that in their Child-hood are so long in their horne booke, that doe what they can, they will smell of the Baby till they cannot see to read.'[73] Thomas Dekker's mock-advice book, *The Gul's Horne-booke* (1609), similarly styles itself as an instructional manual through the use of the term 'hornbook' and comically suggests that the young men using it are childish.[74] This concept of the child reader formed within models of literacy acquisition and religious instruction was thus appropriated beyond these contexts as a source of humour and derision.

These ironic uses of the imagery of ABCs and hornbooks imply that successful learning is crucial to progressing beyond infancy and early childhood. In a poem 'To the little Children' attached to his 1587 tract on petty schools, Francis Clement suggests that the acquisition of literacy is a necessary part of growing up. He insists to his imagined 'little child' reader to 'Come make your choyce, let toies alone,/and trifles: Learne A, B'.[75] The turn to reading, books and learning is represented as a choice that entails leaving 'toies' and 'trifles' and moving away from the spaces of play to education, here in the learning of trades.[76] The title-page woodcut on the 1563 edition of *The Whole Book of Psalms* depicts a similar transition from toys to books. Its image of a father directing his family in the singing of the psalms shows a small boy on the mother's left-hand side, not yet breeched and holding a hobby-horse.[77] A larger, more mature boy is shown in contrast, sitting on the mother's right, reading from a book, presumably his book of psalms.[78] Like Clement's verse, this illustration posits an ideological model of movement from toys to books as the child gets older. In the context of the psalm book, it is specifically a shift from infant play to spiritual reading. The transition from play and childhood to learning and ageing is reflected in the accounts of early modern adults remembering their experiences of learning how to read. Commenting on his childhood learning, Thomas Tryon claims that, having been sent to school at the age of 5 in the 1630s he was 'addicted to play, after the Example of my young School-fellows' and, as a result, 'scarcely learnt to distinguish my Letters'.[79] Adam Martindale, born in 1623, remembers that prior to being given an ABC by his godmother at the age of 6 he was 'all for childish play, and never thought of learning'. On receiving this small book, however, he embarked on a process of learning to read this book, then the primer, the Bible and 'any other English book'.[80] Learning to read is discursively constructed as one step away from childish play and ignorance to religious subjectivity. The child becoming literate in this metaphorical representation signifies an individual embarking on this process. To be a child reader represents the first step towards spiritual understanding.

Through such representations of the ideal processes of becoming literate, the image of child as reader encapsulates the early stages of literacy acquisition and a commitment to learning matters of the faith. Yet instructors and authors also recognized the needs of the material child. Many seventeenth-century mothers produced their own texts to fit the abilities of their children, including Elizabeth Walker, who produced 'a plain familiar Catechism, suited to their Capacity, whilst very young'.[81] In printed editions, brevity was a central factor in making a book suitable for children. When Nowell adapted his official catechism for the youngest learners he produced a shortened version.[82] Robert Abbot's substantial and widely published catechetical text for mothers instructing their children, *Milk for Babes* (1646), similarly offers brief catechetical instruction 'for Children' in two brief versions preceding the main text.[83] Almost fifty years later, John Mason's fourteen-page *A Little Catechism, with Little Verses, and Little Sayings, for Little Children* (1692) takes this practice further. As well as punning extensively on the suitability of 'little' books for 'little' children, this octavo text carries this through to its physical size.[84] The extant title page of a catechism from the 1630s claims to be 'So Short for Little Children, That they may understand, and Learne it by two or three yeares of their Age'.[85] An earlier sixteenth-century version, on which this may be based, claims on its title page to be 'A Short Catechisme for little children learned by one at three yeares of age'. Following the format of *The ABC with Catechism*, it provides alphabetical information, a catechism, followed by prayers and the commandments. The catechism is brief but is further adapted to the format of father and child, and the book interestingly also includes scriptural extracts in the form of 'Fatherly advice for little yong children'.[86] This book shapes the form and content of religious instruction to the experiences of the 'little' child. The reprint of Benjamin Keach's seventeenth-century primer indicates the continuation of these strategies through to the early eighteenth century. *Instructions for Children; The Child and Youth's Delight* (*c.* 1710) provides three age-graded catechisms presented as dialogues between a father and his 3-year-old, his 10-year-old and his more 'mature' son.

Keach's primer, first printed in the 1660s, exemplifies the development of the ABC genre. Like many books of basic religious instruction for children, by the seventeenth century, it incorporates instruction in the alphabet and faith with other general instruction. Preceding the catechetical material, such texts often present the alphabet to aid literacy acquisition but Keach's book also includes guidance on how to tell the time, convert currency, basic arithmetic, punctuation, how to draw up a receipt or bond and a brief dictionary. While religious instruction remains central, this book constitutes an introduction to basic skills perceived to be necessary for the young. In combining this diverse material, it facilitates learning specifically by the child, aiming to instil literacy through an introduction to the alphabet and print types, to pass on religious knowledge through catechisms suited to their capacity, and to introduce other skills that may aid them as they proceed in life. Furthermore, its claim that it will bring 'delight' builds on the creative techniques used by early modern authors and teachers to facilitate the learning and reading experience of the young child by 'alluring' them.[87] Charles Hoole, for instance, offers 'A way to teach little Children to read English with delight and profit' in *The Petty-Schoole*, and recommends games involving letters on dice, on pieces of paper in boxes or accompanied by pictures to help children learn to recognize the letters before proceeding to the contents of *The ABC with Catechism* and *The Primer with Catechism*.[88] Pictures are used in a range of early modern ABC books, such as Festus Corin's *The Childe's First Tutor*, printed in 1664, which, 'knowing that Children are much delighted with pictures', includes woodcuts alongside statements introducing children to the alphabet in order 'to induce them to be the more apt in attaining of their learning'.[89] These alphabetical statements and images, focusing for the most part on animals, from apes to dogs to unicorns, are provided to entice the child before the book offers moral and religious guidance in the form of maxims and catechetical instruction and prayers contained in the later sections of the book. One of these lessons is: 'A good Childe will learn his Book: a bad will not learn his Lesson'.[90] The child reader is offered a model within the text for his or her own reading practices.

One of the most well-known deployments of innovative techniques to teach both the ABC and spiritual matters is John Bunyan's *A Book for Boys and Girls: or, Country Rhimes for Children* (1686). Often cited as an example of early children's literature, it constitutes a significant development of early instructional literature.[91] Claiming to teach 'what the Letters be,/And how they may improve their A. B. C.' in a brief section entitled *'An help to Chil-dren to learn to read Eng-lish'*, it explicitly positions itself as a replacement for the traditional ABC and catechism by concluding 'I shall forbear to add more, being perswaded this is enough for little Children to Prepare themselves for Psalter, or Bible'.[92] In contrast to the catechetical material, prayers or scriptural extracts provided in other ABCs, Bunyan writes a series of verses on religious and spiritual matters. While some reflect directly on prayers and religious practices, others look to children's worlds as the focus of meditations on God. It contains emblems that draw on familiar objects—such as the egg, bee, fish, spider, fig-tree—and others that specifically present subjects and objects relevant to childhood experience. 'Girls and Boys' are used as images in the verses (62); a number of poems are from the perspective of children ('The Awakened Child's Lamentation', 'Of the Child with the Bird at the Bush') or are about children (including 'Upon the Boy on his Hobby-Horse', 'Of the Boy and Butter Fly', 'Upon the whipping of a Top', 'The Boy and Watchmaker', 'Upon the Boy and his Paper of Plumbs', 'Upon the Disobedient Child' and 'Upon the Boy dull at his Book') and their toys, their rewards and their experiences. Other authors recognize the benefits of facilitating children's learning through the depiction of familiar experiences and objects. Another late seventeenth-century ABC, J. G.'s *A Play-Book for Children To Allure Them to Read* (1694), includes illustrations and familiar subject matter to offer an alternative to the 'large leaves, close Stuft, with things not understood by Children, and many times in a black Print, as if the design had been to frighten from, rather than to allure to, Learning'.[93] In addition to hinting at apples as a reward for successful learning in its sample reading material beginning 'Ap-ples are for Children that know the Let-ters', *A Play-Book* alludes to a number of experiences that were likely common to early modern children, including combing for headlice, boys beating drums, inkhorns, 'Mar-vils' or marbles, described as 'pret-ty play-things for Chil-dren', and the whipping top, and includes two alphabetized sequences that focus on animals.[94]

J. G. emphasizes the need to use particular methods in the production of a text in order to facilitate use by children in this 'tender Age' to 'decoy Children into reading', wondering that so many writers 'forget the variable nature of young ones'.[95] Both *A Book for Boys and Girls* and *A Play-Book for Children* set out to make basic learning easier and more enjoyable for a young readership, aiming to facilitate use by a material child reader. In doing so, they hint at some common experiences and material worlds recognizable to a group of readers which they identify as children. While J. G.'s book is secular rather than religious in its focus and is likely influenced by new ideas about the role of play in educating children, presented famously in John Locke's *Some Thoughts Concerning Education* (1693), Bunyan's earlier book emphasizes the child as a distinct reader, anticipating Locke's insistence that books should be 'suited to a child's capacity and notions' and to 'the Age and Inclination of the person'.[96]

Yet Bunyan's *A Book for Boys and Girls* simultaneously complicates the idea of child readership. The children deployed in the verses are emblematic.[97] The boy in 'The Boy and the Watch-maker' is, the comparison informs us, 'an Emblem' of 'a Convert' (55). The child is representative of a type, signalling a lack of understanding. The metaphorical language of childhood is carried through to the book's prefatory material. Although the title page proclaims it as a book for 'Boys and Girls' or 'for Children', the address to the reader comments on this. It clarifies that it is for:

> Boys and Girls of all Sorts and Degrees,
> From those of Age, to Children on the Knees.
> Thus comprehensive am I in my Notions;
> They tempt me to it by their childish Motions.
> We now have Boys with Beards, and Girls that be
> Big as Old Women, wanting Gravity. (A1v)

For Bunyan, his imagined child readers are both those that are young but also 'children' of any age. These 'Old Women' and bearded children he defines as such in terms of their behaviour or 'childish Motions'. He proceeds to comment on those 'Bearded men' who 'act like Beardless Boys' and women who 'please themselves with childish toys' (A1v). The notion of acting childishly and of being addicted to 'childish toys' continues throughout this opening address as these terms are repeated, particularly when Bunyan states his aim to 'entice' them to 'mount their Thoughts from what are childish Toys,/To Heav'n' (A2r). Like other books for children in the period, Bunyan positions toys in opposition to literacy and spiritual thoughts. To leave childishness behind entails the setting aside toys for the reading book.

The format of the ABC book, combined with basic religious instruction in the sixteenth and seventeenth centuries, thus put forward a complex understanding of childhood and of the child reader. In one sense, these books aiming to instil literacy and a basic knowledge of spiritual matters imply that the position of the child is one of ignorance and a lack of knowledge. In promoting literacy, and particularly religious literacy, they hint that progression beyond childhood comes through learning. They do this by appealing to a range of readers who were 'babes' or 'children' in terms of knowledge. Yet, at the same time, the strategies used in many of these books adapt this basic instructional material and direct it to readers in particular stages of the life cycle. Through processes of simplification and characterization, and the inclusion of subjects common to childhood experience, these books gesture towards a significant cultural recognition of the youthful child as a distinct type of reader. Producing printed material suited specifically for children's needs forges a culture of childhood and suggests a communal experience of childhood characterized by distinct cognitive abilities, rather than simply urging a transition to a knowledgeable adulthood. This is evident in the religious books written for 'little' children in second half of the seventeenth century. Three books written for Puritan children—Thomas White's *A Little Book for Little Children*, first published in the 1660s, James Janeway's *A Token for Children*, which was printed in two volumes in the 1670s, and Robert Russel's two-volume *A Little Book for Children and Youth*, printed in the 1690s—are fascinating case studies for thinking about books for and attitudes towards the child reader who had acquired the basic literacy urged by the religious ABCs.

'LITTLE' BOOKS FOR 'LITTLE CHILDREN'

If learning to read was the first step to entering the faith and potential salvation, what should the young child who had mastered their ABC read next? As ABC books and the accounts of children's early reading experiences indicate, the religious novice was expected to progress from the ABC and basic catechetical instruction to the primer and ultimately to the Bible. Yet a range of books were recommended to and encountered by children reading for their faith. Recalling her childhood reading in the mid-sixteenth century, Lady Grace Mildmay claims that her mother allowed her to read 'Musculus's *Common Places, The Imitation of Christ,* Mr. Foxe's *Book of Martyrs*' in addition to the Bible. Suggesting that through this limited reading, '[I] found myself the better established in the whole course of my life', Mildmay views her childhood reading, and her mother's influence on this, as establishing lifelong reading practices that enabled her to live well as a religious subject.[98] Reading in childhood is depicted in this context as a formative step towards adulthood. This reading list comprises books that were widely recommended to all ages in order to assist in leading a virtuous life. The books she mentions are not specifically adapted for children and the reading of such books is certainly not unique to childhood. Instead Mildmay's reading as a child is the reading of a godly adult. This is a pervasive element of religious culture in post-Reformation England, with an immersion in godly books frequently depicted as the duty and the good practice of the religious subject. Yet the particular benefits for children are highlighted throughout the sixteenth and seventeenth centuries. Robert Prudom recalls reading and being converted to a better life upon reading Foxe's *Book of Martyrs* or *Acts and Monuments* aged 14.[99] Susanna Perwich apparently read one of a range of religious books 'every night in her bed, immediately before sleep, and then fed upon them on her first waking, by which means she increased much in knowledge'.[100] John Rastrick, claims that his childhood reading made him 'inquisitive' about religion and 'delighted' and 'much affected' him in his autobiographical recollection of his early reading of 'Minister's Texts, and Historys of the Bible' on his father's knee, his collection of psalms and Bible extracts as a 10-year-old *c.* 1660, and his reading of 'the Bible and other good books', as well as books that 'We had in our Family', including 'Dyke's Deceitfulness of Man's Heart and Dent's Plain man's path way to H'.[101] According to Lucy Hutchinson, her husband Colonel John Hutchinson, had Lewis Bayly's *The Practise of Pietie* read to him by his maid before he could read. These early prayerbook encounters enabled him to begin 'to apprehend … something of eternity and of sinne'.[102] Such prayerbooks were often recommended and given to the young. Elizabeth Isham read and owned a range of prayerbooks from a young age, including a prayerbook given to her by her mother, her grandmother's copies of Thomas Sorocold's *Supplications of Saints,* Henry Bull's *Christian Prayers and Meditations* and Bayly's *Practise*.[103] In the mid-seventeenth century, Anne Clifford donated a copy of Bayly's *Practise* to 'Boyes in the Howses', along with Michael Sparke's *The Crums of Comort* and Nicholas Themylthorpe's *A Posie of Godly Prayers.*[104] Prayerbooks were thus read to and placed in the hands of boys and girls in a range of households. These prayerbooks and spiritual guides were given to them to instil practices of daily reading that would be continued through life. In one respect, therefore, having gained literacy and a basic knowledge of faith children became akin to their adult counterparts as religious readers. They read the same books, regularly in the same ways—committing prayers to memory and reading scripture and religious meditation daily.[105] John Rogers recalls that, as child in the 1620s he read daily, memorizing his morning and evening prayers, and out of a book, reading these prayers and the Bible 'over and over and over again'.[106] Children such as Rogers had acquired the reading practices that were expected to be continued into the adulthood of godly readers. In this context of religious reading, these children who had advanced beyond the ABC and instructional texts moved into a culture of religious reading that no longer differentiated readers according to age categories.

Yet, in the seventeenth century religious books began to recognize the child as a distinct literate participant in this reading culture. As mentioned at the opening of this chapter, bibles were not specifically adapted for children until the end of the seventeenth century but extracts from the Bible were included in the ABC texts discussed here, in aids and introductions to Bible reading, and in anthologies for youth such as Nathaniel Crouch's *Youth's Divine Pastime for Children* (1691), which contained 'forty remarkable scripture stories turned into English verse'.[107] Children were encouraged to read 'good Books, especially those for children' together in the seventeenth-century household of Philip Henry, gesturing towards the existence of a range of 'good' or religious books produced specifically for the young.[108] Religious guides offered spiritual and moral instruction to the young in the form of dialogues and poems.[109] Thomas Willis' *The Key to Knowledge* (1682), which directly addresses the child and youth in its preface, combines prayers for children and divine poems by George Herbert, John Donne, Francis Quarles, Richard Crashaw and the child-author Abraham Cowley with a catechism for the young.[110] H. P. also combines diverse material, including two narratives of exemplary children by Henry Jessey and verses about and addressing the young by Abraham Chear, as religious guidance for children in *A Looking Glass for Children* (1673). Chear's verses include poems sent to his young relatives during his imprisonment in the 1660s and advise young girls and boys on matters of faith, reading the Bible and good behaviour and thus offer another instance of poetry being used to guide children.[111] Along with Keach's verses, Willis' inclusion of divine poems and Bunyan's rhymes might be said to constitute what Green describes as a 'new genre' of 'religious verse for children and young people'.[112] Willis' selection of 'certain verses, from some of our Divine Poems' hints at a rationale for the deployment of this literary form as he claims to offer 'Profit and Delight' in a mode that is 'more fit to be Imprinted on the Memories of Young People than Prophane Songs'.[113] If songs being widely circulated in ballad form were attracting the attention of the young, these religious writers offer an alternative form of verse to attract their imaginative engagement.[114]

Prayerbooks also included prayers specifically for children. 'The child's praier' in Edward Hutchins' *David's Sling against Great Goliath* (1589) deploys imagery of infancy and breastfeeding to figure the child as recipient of God's word.[115] Thomas Sorocold's *Supplications of Saints* (1612) contains a number of prayers for children in varying situations, while a prayer for children appears in the eighth edition of Michael Sparke's *The Crums of Comfort With Godly Prayers* (1628).[116] The additional prayer in Sparke's collection follows two prayers for servants, while Sorocold's prayers (one for children during their 'parents life time', one for 'Orphans' and one for all children) are located in a section containing prayers for people of 'several estates', including wives, widows and servants. The positioning of these children's prayers indicates the ways in which being a child is recognized here as a distinct social role. The content of the prayers also attends to the social status of childhood, highlighting the importance of obedience to parents and betters, and 'our Parents and Governors, whom thou hast set over us'.[117] Moreover, the prayers identify aspects of being young that need particular attention. Through these prayers children vocalize what it means to be a child, stating that 'I who am a childe in age, understanding and discretion' and emphasizing their 'tender years'.[118] They pray particularly for restraint given the 'untamednesse of my youth' and the suppression of 'proud nature' to 'subdue our carnall lusts, to over-rule our unruly willes, to bring into order our irregular affections'.[119] These prayers for children draw on and propagate commonly held beliefs that the young were unruly, lacking in reason and tended towards evil.[120] This idea recurred throughout religious literature of the period. Bayly's *The Practise of Pietie*, for instance, meditates in detail on the miseries of the infant and youth, claiming the latter is 'an untamed beast … whose actions are rash and rude … and Ape-like delighting in nothing but toies and bables'.[121] Like the association of the young and those who are 'childish' in behaviour in ABC books, Bayly reduces the young to indulging in toys. The remedy that he proposes for this state is reading and prayer. In religious literature for children and about childhood, reading is repeatedly depicted as offering a transition from childish toys to faith and salvation.

The importance of reading *good* books in childhood is emphasized in a number of books claiming to be for children in the latter half of the seventeenth century. Robert Russel's *A Little Book for Children and Youth*, published in two parts the 1690s, is explicit in its statement that being a good child depends upon reading. The first part offers a short catechism and a prayer in addition to 'Instructions for young Children' on how to be a 'good child' through a series of depictions of good and bad children; while the second offers nine directions or lessons with woodcuts on how to 'escape Hell and go to Heaven' (4) that present the horrors of hell in a typically Puritan fashion. Yet, as Hannah Newton points out, Russel tailors his descriptions to suit his young audience.[122] He describes hell as 'a dreadful place, worse Ten Thousand times than thy Parents beating thee' (I, A7r). It educates children in religious beliefs but mediates this in terms that they will understand. Russel's motivation for writing, he claims, is his 'sad Experience' of the number of 'lewd, wicked Children' in towns and on streets (I, A4r). After a brief preface advising parents and governors on the importance of instilling good religious practices in children, he proceeds to address children directly, reaching out repeatedly to 'My dear Child' (I, A4r; I, A4v; I, A5r) and insisting on the benefits of reading 'this little book' (I, A4r) as well as others. Depicting one element of wicked behaviour as children who play at school and who do not focus on their reading lessons, he offers the contrasting image of the good child as one who learns (I, A4v), minds (I, A6r) and reads books. In the second book he states 'A good child is one that loves his Book' (II, 8), with accompanying woodcuts of the good child at prayer with a book in his hand (II, 7) and another entitled 'Good Children at School a learning their Books' (II, 9). To learn to read and to continue to read not only prepares children for adulthood or future salvation, it also shapes their identities as children, making them 'good' children rather than remaining in what Russel seems to suggest is their natural state as 'wicked' or 'bad' children. Despite the fact that Russel's books likely post-date John Locke's articulation of the child as a *tabula rasa*, he propagates earlier seventeenth-century Puritan perceptions of the child as depraved and in need of learning and instruction, not play.[123] He imagines the child holding this book in his or her hand (I, A4v) and ponders that 'this Boy, or this Girl, that is reading this Book, begins to be resolved to become [one of] God's Children' (I, B2r). This recurs in the second volume when he asks his reader:

> Now, my dear Child, how doest thou do? How is it with thee since the time I made thee that little book? Now methinks there stands a little Boy, with tears in his Eyes, that is ready to tell me, saying *I am heartily sorry that I have been such a wicked Child […] I will for the time to come, learn and study my Book and my Catichism,* […] And methinks there stands a pretty Girl that looks very wishfully, as if she had a mind to be a Child of God: Now methinks she begins to say, *Well, I am resolved never more to be stubborn and rebellious […] I will endeavour to spend my time in reading my Book, and in studying the Word of God.* (II, 4)

Russel directly engages with his imagined readers, seeking a response about the effect of his first book. He pre-empts this response. By evoking an affective image of the reader's response to his text—the boy crying, the girl wishful and both resolved to read and dedicate their time to God—he establishes an ideal reader: the young child, male or female, who is moved to spiritual learning by the experience of reading his book. Moreover, Russel himself is affected by these imagined child readers. He proceeds by offering an ecstatic account of his response to these children. Asking 'My good Girl, my dear Boy, art thou thus resolved?', he exclaims, 'O there is my sweet Child indeed! My brave Child! O it is my lovely Child! Now God loves thee' (II, 5). No reader response is required as Russel is overcome by the images of the affected children saved from 'Hell-fire' by reading his book.

Russel's engagement with his imagined child readers continues as he offers companionship and further guidance. He states 'I am hear making thee another little Book' in order to 'encourage thee to continue to be a good Child' (II, 5). Through his book, he positions himself as substitute parent, teacher and spiritual guide. The second book does not include a note to parents and governors. Instead Russel builds on his imagined pre-existing relationship with the child reader and emphasizes his continued engagement. One transformative reading experience, it seems, is not enough. Russel suggests that being a good child requires ongoing reading and exposure to the 'Patern of a good Child, one that is a Child of God' (II, 5). Russel puts forward a concept of 'good' childhood as shaped and informed by repeated engagement with books. He does not only recommend his own books. In the first book, he urges the 'dear Child' to 'pray thy good Mother to buy thee a little Book call'd *A Token for Children*' (I, A4v) as a way of seeing further examples of good children who 'learn their Book, and their Catechism ... serve God; and obey their Parents' and who are now 'among glorious Saints and Angels' (I, A4v–A5r). Russel suggests the salvation of children from a life of wickedness and an eternity of 'Hellfire' (I, A7r) through immersion in a textual culture of exemplary children. He thus participates in a wider culture of the provision of spiritual guidance through examples of 'good' religious subjects, famously offered by seminal early modern books such as Foxe's *Book of Martyrs*. More particularly, Russel builds on earlier, popular efforts to adapt this religious textual culture for children, including Henry Jessey's two pious children in *A Looking Glass for Children* and the children who die young in White's *A Little Book for Little Children* and Janeway's *A Token for Children*.[124] The book that he urges children to read, Janeway's *Token*, is also, to some extent, his model.

Russel's depiction of 'good' children thus draws on earlier books that offer extreme examples of what it means to be a good child through their depictions of child death. In 1660, Thomas White appended *A Little Book for Little Children* containing 'several examples both ancient and modern of children eminent in holiness' (title page) to his *Manual for Parents*, first published in 1660. Just over a decade later, two volumes of James Janeway's *A Token for Children* were first entered on the Stationers' Register. This martyrology in two parts describes the deaths of thirteen exemplary children, male and female, from a range of social backgrounds— from the beggar child to the shopkeeper's son to the child of an eminent bishop.[125] These stories included retellings of already publicized child deaths as well as original stories, some of which, Janeway claims, 'are taken *verbatim* in writing from their dying lips'.[126] Janeway's books were widely reprinted in England and America, attesting to their wide and continued readership, while White's book was subsequently printed as a stand-alone text, appearing in its twelfth edition by 1702.[127] The extensive publication history of these books signals the cultural fascination with these exemplary children and gestures towards a wide and enduring readership, possibly of children, for the books. It is likely that Russel was taking advantage of this market for books for children depicting exemplary 'good' children, and his two volumes have much in common with the earlier books, including the direct address to children, the instruction through example of how to be a child of God, and the depiction of children's tendency to wickedness and their potential futures in hell fire. The books carefully reference each other; like Russel recommending that children read Janeway, Janeway urges children to read White (I, A11v). These books intertextually create an imagined reading list for the child and establish a group of children's books with common themes and aims.

Yet while Russel offers instruction on how to live well, Janeway's and White's books focus on dying well.[128] Their guidance on how to live as a good child is mediated through accounts of the deaths of these exceptional boys and girls. As Ralph Houlbrooke points out, these books are informed by the conviction that children are not too young to be damned and that a good death is a fitting end to a godly life.[129] Indeed, Janeway explicitly reminds parents and teachers of this in his opening address, stating 'whatever you think of them, Christ doth not slight them; they are not too little to dye, they are not too little to go to Hell, they are not too little to serve their great Master, too little to go to Heaven' (I, A4 r). He implies a conflict in attitudes towards children, suggesting with 'whatever you think' that those in close relationships with children do not always recognize their spiritual culpability. As well as being a book for children, his first volume stands as a useful reminder to parents and teachers that they can be responsible for the 'Conversion and Salvation' (I, A4r) of their children by teaching them. He tasks them with speaking to children 'about their miserable condition by Nature' and with putting 'your Children upon Learning their Catechism and the Scriptures, and getting [them] to pray and *weep* by themselves after *Christ*' (I, A1v). Like Russel, Janeway recommends an affective engagement with religious books.[130] In particular, he advises parents on the ways in which they should encourage their children to read his book, proposing:

> Let them Read this Book over an hundred times, and observe how they are *affected*, and ask them what they think of those Children, and whether they would not be such? … Incourage your Children to read this Book, and lead them to improve it. (I, A4v–A5r)

Janeway recommends a shared reading experience. Observed by parents the child should read the book repeatedly. The parents should then engage with the child, leading them, exploring their responses and the emotional effects of their reading experience. It is through reading his book repeatedly, the examination of responses and discussion of the exemplary behaviour contained within the stories that the child, Janeway implies, will find the way to 'Christ and Heaven, and Salvation' (I, A4r).

Janeway expounds the benefit of good reading by occupying the position of surrogate parent in his preface 'containing directions to children' (I, A6r). Through a series of informal questions, he asks his reader if he or she notes how his exemplary children demonstrate duty to parent, their readiness to learn scripture and catechisms, how they lived 'holy' lives and how they died 'joyfully' (I, A6v). He thus establishes his stories as models against which the reader should measure their own behaviour. He repeatedly, affectionately questions his readers, calling them 'dear lambs' (I, A6r) and 'dear Children' (I, A6v). Yet this gentle engagement is balanced with accounts of the realities of death and hell, as he instils fear into his readers through graphic accounts of hell fire (I, A8r). Directing the readers' responses in moments such as 'But tell me, my dear Children, and tell me truly, Do you do as these Children did?' (I, A6v), 'How dost thou spend thy time?' (I, A7r), 'do you keep in to read your book, and to learn what your good parents command you?' (I, A7r), he aims to instruct through an interactive reading experience. He asks a series of eleven numbered questions as a way of talking to his readers (I, A7r). Some of these deal directly with the reading of his book as he interrogates how the child reads, questioning whether the child reads out of necessity before forgetting the experience or if the child is 'affected [...] in the Reading of this Book?' (I, A8r). The reader, he implies, should be 'affected' to shed a tear and to fall on their knees 'begging that God would make you like these blessed Children' (I, A8r–v). He envisions, in a manner similar to Russel's, 'that pretty Lamb begin to weep' (I, A8v). This is Janeway's ideal and idealized reader: 'a sweet Child', 'my brave Child indeed' who becomes 'resolved for Christ and for Heaven' (I, A9r).

White's book similarly emphasizes the importance of reading to his readers. He too presents a series of children who all die young as models of good behaviour. He suggests that by reading 'these stories of Holy Children', his 'dear Children', or his readers, should 'long to be like them' (83). White imagines that the experience of reading his book instils empathy, longing and imitation in his child readers. The behaviour they should imitate is again characterized by good reading practices. One of the children he presents reads a little of a book on the Passion of Christ every day, and ultimately takes so much delight in his book that his parents have to hide it from him (75–76). White presents reading as akin to one of the commandments in his account of one child who responded to his father's questions of 'who bid you learn your book? And there is no command-ment saith thou shalt learn thy book?' with 'It is said, *Thou shalt honour thy Father and thy Mother*, you bade me learn my book' (55). He suggests that the same young boy, who dies around the age of 8, demonstrates his knowledge 'in the things of God' through 'his reading books, and mark-ing them with a line in the Margent' (56). The child asks that no bell is rung at his death and instead 'good books' should be given to do others good (60). Reading good books and recommending good books to oth-ers is a crucial part of what constitutes the pious practices of these children.

In addition to presenting models of reading practices, White's book opens with a series of chapters offering guidance to his child readers. One chapter, 'What Books Children are to read', recommends 'the *Bible*, and the *Plain Man's Pathway to Heaven*, a very plain holy book for you; get the *Practise of Piety*; Mr. Baxter's *Call to the Unconverted*; Allen's *Alarum to the Unconverted*; read the Histories of the Martyrs that dyed for Christ' (17–18). His reading list is in line with other accounts of what children should read for their spiritual education, including the Bible, Bayly's prayerbook and Foxe's text, and alongside religious books offering guid-ance to the ignorant. Two of White's exemplary boys read these books. One takes much delight in Bayly's *Practise*, while another has marked 'many precious things' in Baxter's *Call to the Unconverted* (59). White also recommends 'treatises of Death, and Hell and Judgement, and of the Love and Passion of Christ' (18). Like Russel and Janeway, he urges his child readers to encounter through their reading the terror of Hell and the alternative of Heaven and Christ's love. Janeway's children read the books recommended by White and others: the scriptures and the Bible, cate-chisms and primers, Foxe's *Book of Martyrs* and the books of Richard Baxter.[131] One child, Sarah Howley, additionally reads books that 'make Religion her business', including *The Best Friend in the Worst of Times*, Swinnock's *Christian Man's Calling*, and makes *The Spiritual Bee* her 'great companion' (I, 4). One boy reads Drayton's poems about Noah's flood by himself and uses it to gain further knowledge and understanding of the scripture (II, 7). Many of the children read what Janeway repeatedly describes as other 'good books'.

It is also important how the children read. Godly reading required active engagement and reflection. Leigh, for example, advises her children that to 'reade with profit' they must 'not onely reade, but gather some fruite out of it, and ever when you begin to read any part of scripture, lift up your harts, soules and minds unto God'.[132] Almost all of Janeway's narratives promote the engaged reading of good books as central to the 'exemplary Lives, and Joyful Deaths' (I, title page) of children.[133] These diligent children turn away from play and commit themselves to learning, prayer and reading. They learn to read quickly, love school, take notice of what they read, 'run' to their books 'without bidding' (II, 4) and rejoice and delight in their books. John Harvy, for instance, turns away from an opportunity to play and entreats a schoolmistress to teach him to read 'before most Children are able to know their letters' (II, 66), reaffirming the division between play and reading continually put forward in early modern religious books for children. The desire of these children to read surpasses all other basic necessities. Harvy ignores medical advice when deteriorating eyesight prevents him from reading between the ages of 6 and 7. When alone he continues to 'stand by the windows, and read the Bible and good Books; yea he was so greedy of reading the Scripture, and took so much delight in it, that he would scarce allow himself sometimes time to dress himself for reading' (II, 73). He continues to do this until he loses his sight as a result. Reading may have a detrimental effect on his physical being, but Janeway's sick children, as Seth Lerer points out, find spiritual health through reading.[134] This surpasses any physical requirements. On one occasion in Janeway's narratives reading is depicted as a 'more sweet' alternative to food (I, 33) and on another a boy frequently leaves his dinner to 'go to his Book' (II, 4). Janeway thus builds upon the image of reading as spiritual nourishment and as a basic bodily requirement conveyed in catechetical texts that align religious learning as milk for babes.

Janeway and White both recommend repetitive reading by children. White suggests that they might 'mark in the margent, or by underlining the places you find most relish in, and that take most special notice of, and that most concern thee, that you may easily and more fully find them again' (18). This interactive process of reading aids children in revisiting crucial textual moments. Reading good books repeatedly, responding affectively and meditating upon the examples offered is depicted as a method of living and dying as a 'good' child. One girl in Janeway's book makes her book 'her delight' before her death, aged 4 or 5, and 'what she read she loved to make her own' (I, 29). Another observes what 'did most warm her heart' in her reading of 'good Books' (I, 33). Another is very 'attentive when she read(s) the Scriptures' and is 'much affected with them' (I, 41), and a boy labours to understand and remember his reading (II, 5). These reading practices are idealized further when Janeway depicts children who are moved to weeping by their encounters with prayer and books. One girl is 'so strangely affected in reading of the Scriptures, that she would burst out into tears, and would hardly be pacified, so greatly was she taken with Christs sufferings' (I, 29). This is the reading experience Janeway asks of his child readers: that they be moved to empathy and religious understanding. It is a practice recommended more widely to children in the period. Elizabeth Walker encouraged her daughters to read the 'Lives of Holy, Exemplary Persons, especially of those who were so while Young that she might doe several things at once; both perfect their Reading, and inform their Judgements, and inflame their Affections to an imitation of their early Piety', while Martha Hatfield, another exemplary child presented as a model for others in Fisher's *The Wise Virgin* (1653), 'would read by her mother out of such good books … with much affection'.[135] Reading as a good child entails this affected response to exemplary tales. Some of Janeway's children continue to value their books and reading experiences on their death bed. Sarah Howley gives her Bible as a 'Legacy to one of her brothers', urging him to 'use it well for her sake' (I, 13). Susanna Bicks gives her mother 'Mr. DeWit's Catechise Lectures' and entreats her to keep it 'as long as she lived from her sake', and gives her little Sister her 'other Book as my remembrance' (II, 57). John Harvy spends the two weeks preceding his death in 'religious duties and preparing for his death', but also continues to gather observations from his 'great book', Baxter's *Saints' Everlasting Rest*. His final request, in spite of his loss of eyesight and great pain, is to his mother that he may have Baxter's book to 'read a little more of Eternity before I go' (II, 84). These children exemplify the importance of reading 'good' books carefully and repeatedly in order to be good children and to die 'joyful deaths'.

For these authors, therefore, a good death in childhood necessitated religious understanding and, in all cases except one, the reading and understanding of good books. Of course, these children are exemplary and are not necessarily representative of early modern children, good or bad. Janeway's converted children are set against a series of depictions of wicked children, who turn to play, refuse to learn and do not read. His models eschew the company of such 'common children' (II, 16). Yet despite Janeway's insistent claims that these are true accounts, neither the depictions of the 'good' or 'bad' children are necessarily accurate.[136] Both are offered as extremes in order to instruct Janeway's child readers in how to read and act as 'good' children. Nonetheless, they share and recommend a wider concept of what it means to be a good and religious child.

Reading to Become Children

The books by White, Janeway and Russel might be described as children's books, or, as many scholars have termed them, early examples of children's literature, in the ways in which they frame themselves as being for children through their titles, prefatory material, direct addresses to imagined child readers and their depiction of young subjects with whom the reader is urged to identify. They differ from the notional concept of the child as reader signifying those who were lacking in understanding as well as years. They identify children at a particular stage in the life cycle as material entities with their own cultures, and draw on this material culture of childhood to propose models of exemplary childhood piety. As Courteney Weikle-Mills proposes, it may be that this extensive literature dedicated specifically to children 'could result from the need to differentiate "children in years" from other kinds of metaphorical children'.[137] These narratives of good children view the child as a distinct category of reader, requiring these textual aids to facilitate the reading process, and so build on the techniques deployed to encourage children's reading and religious learning in ABCs and catechetical texts. Yet these books also recommend particular reading practices, suggesting that it is not only what books the child reads but how he or she reads them that determines whether or not the child performs the role of ideal child reader and enters the imagined community of 'good' children.

Of course, as Carolyn Steedman points out, 'The essence of being a good child is taking on the perspective of those who are more powerful than you.'[138] These representations of good child readers are shaped and held up as exemplary models by adults. Nonetheless, they shed light on nuanced perceptions of childhood in religious textual culture. Religious books produce one understanding of the child reader as seeking literacy and religious knowledge, which by implication defines children as the young and as those lacking knowledge. They highlight the importance of becoming literate as a crucial route to knowledge and understanding, and to embark on a path towards salvation. This raises important questions about definitions of childhood, and indeed of adulthood, in early modern religious contexts. If literacy is perceived to be an important aspect of defining good children and religious subjectivity, does this mean the substantial illiterate portion of early modern England could not become either good children or adults in spiritual terms? The oral engagement with

catechisms, the examples of reading the Bible aloud, sermons which provided similar examples of good behaviour and the example of an illiterate
beggar boy in Janeway's text, who achieves understanding through oral
instruction and discourse, shows that this emphasis on reading is just one
element of what defines the good child or knowledgeable individual.[139]
Moreover, these exemplary 'good' child readers read with understanding
and engage affectively with their texts to achieve higher levels of religious
knowledge, demonstrating cognitive capacities that challenge the alternative definitions of childhood within religious culture. Nonetheless, in
these books aiming to instruct in literacy, religious knowledge and 'good'
behaviour, there is, unsurprisingly an emphasis on the importance of
learning to read. What and how you read is depicted as a formative experience into an enlightened adulthood but more significantly as a good child.
Reading practices are presented in these books as constitutive of childhood experience and subjectivity. This is perhaps most clear in the depictions of children's deaths. These boys and girls who die young are eternally
children; fixed through these accounts of their reading practices as good
children and as children of God.

This understanding of childhood reading applies to a range of children,
male and female, from a multiple social backgrounds. Janeway describes
exemplary boys and girls who range from the children of bishops and
shopkeepers to the street beggar. From the country boys and girls of
Bunyan's book to the children on the town streets of Russel's text to
Janeway's English and Dutch children, these books draw on children that
are geographically diverse. In his adaptation of the narratives of the two
Dutch children, Susannah and Jacob Bicks, however, Janeway claims that
he is presenting this narrative 'for the benefit of English children' (II, 25),
suggesting a more targeted understanding of children and their reading
practices. Yet Janeway's book was substantially reprinted in the colonies
throughout the seventeenth and eighteenth centuries and continued to be
hugely popular. The Boston cleric Cotton Mather produced his own collection of accounts of child deaths in the Massachusetts Bay Colony, and
this book, *A Token for the Children of New England,* was appended to the
first colonial printing of Janeway's work in 1700.[140] Janeway's narratives
for English children thus offer a concept of good child readers that was
ultimately extended beyond national, geographical and historical
boundaries. This concept of the 'good' child, defined by literacy and reading practices, becomes common to a range of historical children's reading
experiences.

NOTES

1. Thomas Pestell, 'Verses on a Bible Presented to the Lady K[atherine] C[ork]', in *Verse in English from Tudor and Stuart Ireland*, ed. Andrew Carpenter (Cork: Cork University Press, 2003), 154–155.
2. On Boyle's childhood, see Ruth Connolly, '"A Wise and Godly Sybilla": Viscountess Ranelagh and the Politics of International Protestantism', in *Women, Gender and Radical Religion in Early Modern Europe*, ed. Sylvia Brown (Leiden: Brill University Press, 2006), 286–288.
3. On the Christ-cross row, see Patricia Crain, *The Story of A: The Alphabetization of America from The New England Primer to The Scarlet Letter* (Stanford: Stanford University Press, 2002), 20.
4. On the 'godly garden' tradition, see Susan Felch, 'Introduction', in *Elizabeth Tyrwhit's Morning and Evening Prayers*, ed. Susan Felch (Aldershot: Ashgate, 2008), 34–36. On catechisms as providing nourishment, see Paula McQuade, 'Introduction', in *Catechisms for Mothers, Schoolmistresses and Children, 1575–1750*, ed. Paula McQuade (Aldershot: Ashgate, 2008), xiv–xv.
5. See Ruth Bottigheimer, *The Bible for Children: From the Age of Gutenberg to the Present* (New Haven: Yale University Press, 1996), 43–45.
6. Dorothy Leigh, *The Mother's Blessing* (1616), in *Women's Writing in Stuart England: The Mothers' Legacies of Dorothy Leigh, Elizabeth Joscelin, and Elizabeth* Richardson, ed. Sylvia Brown (Stroud: Sutton Publishing, 1999), 31.
7. Thomas White, *A Little Book for Little Children* (London, 1702), 17–18. All references are from this twelfth edition and are given in the main text. This edition is the same as the first, except that it contains an additional section titled 'Youth's Alphabet'. See Thomas White, *A Manual for Parents ... To Which is Added, A Little Book for Little Children* (London, 1660) and Judith St. John, *The Osborne Collection of Early Children's Books, 1566–1910: A Catalogue* (Toronto: Toronto Public Library, 1958), 774.
8. Thomas Lye, *The Child's Delight* (London, 1671), A4r.
9. Linda Pollock, ed., *With Faith and Physic: The Life of a Tudor Gentlewoman, Lady Grace Mildmay 1552–1620* (London: Collins and Brown, 1993), 28. Anthony Fletcher, *Growing Up in England: The Experience of Childhood, 1600–1914* (New Haven: Yale University Press, 2008), 99. For other examples of recollections of reading the Bible as a child, see Alec Ryrie, *Being Protestant in Reformation Britain* (Oxford: Oxford University Press, 2013), 272.
10. Elizabeth Isham, *My Booke of Rememberance*, ed. Elizabeth Clarke et al., *Constructing Elizabeth Isham*, University of Warwick, http://web.warwick.ac.uk/english/perdita/Isham/index_bor.htm, accessed 7 Dec.

2011. Matthew Storey, ed., *Two East Anglian Diaries 1641–1729: Issac Archer and William Coe* (Woodbridge: Boydell Press, 1994), 47–48.

11. Thomas Taylor Lewis, ed., *The Letters of the Lady Brilliana Harley* (London: Camden Society, 1854), 5.

12. John Sargeaunt, *Annals of Westminster School* (London: Methuen, 1898), 285–286. 'Practice of Piety' refers to Lewis Bayly's frequently reprinted prayerbook, discussed later in this chapter.

13. William Sherman, *Used Books: Marking Readers in Renaissance England* (Philadelphia: University of Pennsylvania Press, 2007), 72.

14. See Juliet O'Connor, 'The ABC of Horn-Books', *La Trobe Journal* 77 (2006): 42–43.

15. Ryrie, 170. On Protestantism and literary cultures, see also Andrew Cambers, *Godly Reading: Print, Manuscript and Puritanism in England, 1580–1720* (Cambridge: Cambridge University Press, 2011); Brian Cummings, *The Literary Culture of the Reformation: Grammar and Grace* (Oxford: Oxford University Press, 2002), 1–53; Ian Green, *Print and Protestantism in Early Modern England* (Oxford: Oxford University Press, 2000); Kate Narveson, *Bible Readers and Lay Writers in Early Modern England: Gender and Self-Definition in an Emergent Writing Culture* (Aldershot: Ashgate, 2012).

16. Others have argued for radical invention of childhood in this context. See C. John Sommerville, *The Discovery of Childhood in Puritan England* (Athens: University of Georgia Press, 1992); Carmen Luke, *Pedagogy, Printing and Protestantism: The Discourse on Childhood* (New York: State University of New York Press, 1989); Neil Postman, *The Disappearance of Childhood* (New York: Vintage, 1984), 37–38. Studies of childhood in relation to early modern religion have focused for the most part on Protestant cultures. This study continues this focus, given that the majority of books for children in the period were produced within the context of authorized religious practice. On Catholicism and childhood, see Lucy Underwood, *Childhood, Youth and Religious Dissent in Post-Reformation England* (Basingstoke: Palgrave Macmillan, 2014); Alison Shell, '*Furor Juvenilis*: Post-Reformation English Catholicism and Exemplary Youthful Behaviour', in *Catholics and the 'Protestant' Nation: Religious Politics and Identity in Early Modern England*, ed. Ethan Shagan (Manchester: Manchester University Press, 2005), 185–206.

17. Robert Russel, *A Little Book for Children and Youth* (London, *c.* 1693–1696), 8. Further references are given in the text.

18. Patricia Demers, ed., *From Instruction to Delight: An Anthology of Children's Literature to 1850* (Oxford: Oxford University Press, 2004), 46; Gillian Avery, 'The Puritans and Their Heirs', in *Children and Their Books*, ed. Gillian Avery and Julia Briggs (Oxford: Clarendon Press, 1989), 97.

See also Seth Lerer, *Children's Literature: A Reader's History, from Aesop to Harry Potter* (Chicago: University of Chicago Press, 2008), 81–103.

19. Benjamin Keach, *Instructions for Children: Or, The Child's and Youth's Delight* (London, [1710]), 6. This is most likely a reconstructed edition of Keach's original text, *The Child's Instructor*, printed in 1664 but destroyed due to this Baptist minister's disagreements with the Church's views on infant baptism. Keach claims to have rewritten it from memory *c.* 1672. On the relationships between the versions of Keach's primer see David Copeland, *Benjamin Keach and the Development of Baptist Traditions in Seventeenth-Century England* (Lewiston: Edwin Mellen Press, 2001), 23–30, 164–165.

20. On the perceived values of literacy in early modern England, see David Cressy, *Literacy and the Social Order: Reading and Writing in Tudor and Stuart England* (Cambridge: Cambridge University Press, 1980), 1–15.

21. Cressy's assessment of literacy levels based on signature rates in the 1640s concluded levels of illiteracy of 70% among men and 90% among women (72–73, 191–201). Scholars have contested these conclusions by challenging Cressy's definitions of literacy and his methodologies, largely on the grounds that writing is not the only indicator of literacy. For challenges to his conclusions, see Jennifer Andersen and Elizabeth Sauer, 'Current Trends in the History of Reading', in *Books and Readers in Early Modern England: Material Studies*, ed. Jennifer Andersen and Elizabeth Sauer (Philadelphia: University of Pennsylvania Press, 2002), 1–21; Heidi Brayman Hackel, *Reading Material in Early Modern England* (Cambridge: Cambridge University Press, 2005), 57–60; Margaret Ferguson, *Dido's Daughters: Literacy, Gender and Empire in Early Modern England and France* (Chicago: University of Chicago Press, 2003); Juliet Fleming, *Graffiti and the Writing Arts of Early Modern England* (London: Reaktion Books, 2001), 9; Adam Fox, *Oral and Literate Culture in England, 1500–1700* (Oxford: Clarendon Press, 2000); Jonathan Goldberg, *Writing Matter: From the Hands of the English Renaissance* (Stanford: Stanford University Press, 1991), 242–243; Keith Thomas, 'The Meaning of Literacy in Early Modern England', in *The Written Word: Literacy in Transition*, ed. Gerd Baumann (Oxford: Clarendon, 1986), 97–131; Eve Sanders, *Gender and Literacy on Stage in Early Modern England* (Cambridge: Cambridge University Press, 1998); Edith Snook, *Women, Reading and the Cultural Politics of Early Modern England* (Aldershot: Ashgate, 2005), 8–10; Margaret Spufford, *Small Books and Pleasant Histories: Popular Fiction and its Readership in Seventeenth-Century England* (London: Methuen, 1981), xviii, 19–44; Tessa Watt, *Cheap Print and Popular Piety 1550–1640* (Cambridge: Cambridge University Press, 1991), 7.

22. See Goldberg, 47–49; David Vincent, *The Rise of Mass Literacy: Reading and Writing in Europe* (Cambridge: Polity Press, 2000). Robert Houston, *Literacy in Early Modern Europe: Culture and Education 1500–1800* (London: Longman, 2002) and Lawrence Stone, 'The Education Revolution in England, 1560–1640', *Past and Present* 28.1 (1964): 41–80, note the associations between education and religion in increasing literacy levels. H. S. Bennett, *English Books and their Readers: 1475 to 1557* (Cambridge: Cambridge University Press, 1970), 29; Cressy, 1–5; and Luke consider the combined associations between Reformation and advances in printing with reading abilities. Ian Green, *The Christian's ABC: Catechisms and Catechizing in England c. 1530–1740* (Oxford: Clarendon Press, 1996) notes that, although there is no evidence of an official plan to further elementary instruction, this instruction was provided as a result of a combination of sustained increase in educational provision and religious and political pressures (68–69).

23. *An A.B.C. for Chyldren* (London, 1561); S. W., *Most Easie Instructions for Reading Specially Penned for the Good of Those Who Are Come to Yeares* (London, *c*. 1610).

24. Thomas Newbery, *A Booke in Englysh Metre* (London, 1563), title page.

25. J. G., *A Play-Book for Children To Allure them to Read* (London, 1694).

26. Helen Jewell, *Education in Early Modern England* (London: Macmillan, 1998), 93–94.

27. Richard Mulcaster, *Positions Wherein Those Primitive Circumstances Be Examined, Which Are Necessarie for the Training Up of Children* (London, 1581), 30.

28. Mulcaster, 29–30, 60.

29. Charles Hoole, *The Petty-Schoole* (London, 1659), 2. Early modern pedagogues differed on the age at which they believed children should learn to read and enter school, recommending a variety of ages between 3 and 7. See Cressy, 27. Some children may have learned even earlier. A portrait of Miss Campion, a member of the Essex family, depicts her holding a horn-book at the age of 2 years and 2 months in 1661. See Andrew Tuer, *The History of the Horn-Book* (London: The Leadenhall Press, 1861), II, 65.

30. Hoole, *The Petty-Schoole*, 27.

31. See Cambers, 6; Kenneth Charlton, 'Women and Education', in *A Companion to Early Modern Women's Writing*, ed. Anita Pacheco (Oxford: Blackwell, 2002), 10; Narveson, 5; Ryrie, 257–261.

32. John Brinsley, *Ludus Literarius* (London, 1627), 13.

33. Hoole, *The Petty-Schoole*, 12, 23.

34. Cited in Spufford, 24.

35. Cited in Fox, 38.

36. Fletcher, 99.
37. Cited in Thomas, 106.
38. Richard Baxter, *A Christian Directory* (London, 1673), 548.
39. John Locke, *Some Thoughts Concerning Education* (London, 1693), 186. Matthew Grenby, *The Child Reader, 1700–1840* (Cambridge: Cambridge University Press, 2011), 40, points out that this curriculum had been standard throughout the seventeenth century.
40. For example, Adam Martindale learned to read at home aged 6 *c.* 1629 using an ABC given to him by his godmother 'by the help of my brethren and sisters that could read, and a young man that came to court my sister'. See William Sloane, *Children's Books in England and America in the Seventeenth Century* (New York: Columbia University Press, 1955), 7–8. Thomas Tryon was first taught to read at school at the age of 5 in the 1630s, but having failed there eventually he 'bought ... a Primer' at the age of 13 and used it when at work as a shepherd to learn to read under the guidance of his 'Fellow-Shepherds' (Spufford, 13–14).
41. On the content of the hornbook, see Tuer. For a description of the basic ABC text, see Green, *Christian's ABC*, 174–175.
42. See Rosemary O'Day, *Education and Society, 1500–1800* (London: Longman, 1982), 53–54.
43. William Kempe, *The Education of Children in Learning* (London, 1588), F2r–v. See also Edmund Coote, *The English Schoolmaister* (London, 1596), 2. For a detailed history of the processes of teaching reading, see Ian Michael, *The Teaching of English: From the Sixteenth Century to 1870* (Cambridge: Cambridge University Press, 1987), 14–134.
44. Hoole, *The Petty-Schoole*, 4, 20.
45. On learning to read as oral process, see Cressy, 20–21; Michael, 52–58.
46. James Fisher, *The Wise Virgin* (London, 1653), n.p.
47. See *An A.B.C for Children* (London, 1561); *An ABC for Children* (London, 1570). On the content of ABCs, see Bennett, 167; Green, *Christian's ABC*, 174–5; Michael, 111.
48. Demers, *From Instruction to Delight*, 2.
49. On the progression to these texts, see Bennett, 167; Craig Thompson, *Schools in Tudor England* (Washington: Folger Library, 1958), 8–10.
50. See, for example, *The Protestant Tutor, Instructing Children to Spell and Read English and Grounding Them in the True Protestant Religion and Discovering the Errors and Deceits of the Papists* (London, 1679).
51. Elisha Coles, *Nolens Volens: Or, You Shall Make Latin Whether You Will or No, Together with The Youth's Visible Bible* (London, 1677). On religious education at grammar school level, see Ian Green, *Humanism and Protestantism in Early Modern English Education* (Aldershot: Ashgate, 2009), 267–306.

52. Cited in Green, *Christian's ABC*, 280.

53. E. C., *An A.B.C. or Holy Alphabet* (London, 1626), A4r–A5v.

54. See Green, *Christian's ABC*, 174.

55. See Richard Halpern, *The Poetics of Primitive Accumulation* (Ithaca: Cornell University Press, 1991), 22; O'Day, 44; David Vincent, *Literacy and Popular Culture* (Cambridge: Cambridge University Press, 1989), 13.

56. See Green, *Christian's ABC*, 67. On catechisms for the young, see also B. Ritter Dailey, 'Youth and the New Jerusalem: The English Catechetical Tradition and Henry Jessey's Catechism for Babes (1652)', *Harvard Library Bulletin* 30 (1982): 25–34; Patricia Demers, *Heaven Upon Earth: The Forms of Moral and Religious Children's Literature to 1850* (Knoxville: University of Tennessee Press, 1993), 61–62; Ian Green, '"For Children in Yeeres and Children in Understanding": The Emergence of the English Catechism under Elizabeth and the Early Stuarts', *Journal of Ecclesiastical History* 37.3 (1986): 397–425; Gerald Strauss, *Luther's House of Learning: Indoctrination of the Young in the German Reformation* (Baltimore: Johns Hopkins University Press, 1978); Philippa Tudor, 'Religious Instruction for Children and Adolescents in the Early English Reformation', *Journal of Ecclesiastical History* 35.3 (1984): 397–425.

57. See Bennett, 167–169; T. W. Baldwin, *William Shakspere's Petty School* (Chicago: University of Illinois Press, 1943), 67; Green, *Christian's ABC*, 67; McQuade, 'Introduction', 176; O'Day, 56.

58. On Nowell's catechism, see Green, *Christian's ABC*, 188–192.

59. Bartholomew Batt, *The Christian Man's Closet* (London, 1581), 10. See also Anna French, *Children of Wrath: Possession, Prophecy and the Young in Early Modern England* (London: Routledge, 2016), 34–45; Paul Griffiths, *Youth and Authority: Formative Experiences in England, 1560–1640* (Oxford: Clarendon Press, 1996), 49–52; Edel Lamb, *Performing Childhood in the Early Modern Theatre* (Basingstoke: Palgrave Macmillan, 2009), 96–98.

60. See, for example, *An A.B.C. wyth a Cathechisme, That is to Saye, An Instruction to be Learned of Everye Chylde Before he be Brought to be Confyrmed* (London, 1551), STC 20.2. Extant later editions specifying child readers include 1601 (STC 20.7), 1605 (STC 20.8), 1633 (STC 21), 1636 (STC 21.2), 1637 (STC 21.3). The title page of 1668 has been altered to indicate instruction of 'every person'. See *The ABC With the Catechism, That is to Say, An Instruction to be Learned of Every Person Before he be Brought to be Confirmed by the Bishop* (London, 1668, ESTCR232988) and later editions of 1682 (Wing A38), 1687 (Wing A38A), 1698 (Wing A38B).

61. Thomas Cobhead, *A Briefe Instruction, Collected for the Exercise of Youth, and Simple Sort of People* (London, 1579), title page; Robert Cawdry, *A Shorte and Fruitefull Treatise of the Profite and Necessitie of Catechising* (London, 1580), title page; Thomas Doolittle, *The Young Man's Instructer and The Old Man's Remembrancer* (London, 1673), title page.

62. Green, *Christian's ABC*, 7.

63. Ruth Bottigheimer, 'The Child-Reader of Children's Bibles, 1656–1753', in *Infant Tongues: The Voice of the Child in Literature*, ed. Elizabeth Goodenough, Mark Heberle and Naomi Sokoloff (Detroit: Wayne State University Press, 1994), 45, suggests that this is the case until Locke differentiates between states of innocence and ignorance in the 1690s.

64. E. C., 90–91.

65. See Paula McQuade, '"A Knowing People": Early Modern Motherhood, Female Authorship, and Working-Class Community in Dorothy Burch's *A Catechism of the Several Heads of the Christian Religion* (1646)', *Prose Studies: History, Theory, Criticism* 32.3 (2010): 167–186; Kevin Hayes, *A Colonial Woman's Bookshelf* (Knoxville: University of Tennessee Press, 1996), 29.

66. See Brown, ed., *Women's Writing*, 3; Jennifer Heller, *The Mother's Legacy in Early Modern England* (Aldershot: Ashgate, 2011), 5, 43–49. They were also given to early modern children. Anne Clifford donates Leigh's book, among others, to 'Boyes in the Howses' in 1665. See Edith Snook, 'Reading Women', in *The Cambridge Companion to Early Modern Women's Writing*, ed. Laura Lunger Knoppers (Cambridge: Cambridge University Press, 2009), 47.

67. Heller, 5.

68. Leigh, 15.

69. Heller, 5. See also Ramona Wray, *Women Writers of the Seventeenth Century* (Tavistock: Northcote House, 2004), 39; Kristen Poole, '"The Fittest Closet for All Goodness": Authorial Strategies of Jacobean Mothers' Manuals', *Studies in English Literature, 1500–1900* 35.1 (1995): 69–88.

70. Heller, 182.

71. Edmond Graile, *Little Timothe His Lesson* (London, 1611), title page, n.p. Timothy is also held up as exemplary to children in White, 13.

72. Nicholas Breton, *Melancholike Humours* (London, 1600), Dv.

73. Nicholas Breton, *The Court and Country* (London, 1618), Cr.

74. Thomas Dekker, *The Guls Horne-booke* (London, 1609).

75. Francis Clement, *The Petie Schoole* (London, 1587), 9.

76. On the extent which toy and play stand for childhood in early modern culture, see Teresa Michals, 'Experiments before Breakfast: Toys, Education and Middle-Class Childhood', in *The Nineteenth-Century*

Child and Consumer Culture, ed. Dennis Denishoff (Aldershot: Ashgate, 2008), 29–42.

77. See also Anne Bradstreet's association of hobby-horse and child in 'Of The Foure Ages of Man', *The Works of Anne Bradstreet*, ed. Jeannine Hensley (Cambridge: Belknap Press, 1967), 51.

78. Reproduced in David Lindley, *Shakespeare and Music* (London: Arden, 2006), 67.

79. Cited in Spufford, 28–29.

80. Cited in Sloane, 7–8.

81. Anthony Walker, *The Vertuous Wife* (London, 1694), 69. See also Paula McQuade, *Catechisms and Women's Writing in Seventeenth-Century England* (Cambridge: Cambridge University Press, 2017), 56–88.

82. See Green *Christian's ABC*, 189–190.

83. Robert Abbot, *Milk for Babes* (London, 1646). See McQuade, 'Introduction', xxxi.

84. John Mason, *A Little Catechism with Little Verses and Little Sayings for Little Children* (London, 1692).

85. *A Catechism So Short for Little Children* (London, 1639).

86. *A Short Catechisme for Little Children* (London, 1589), B2r–v.

87. See title page of J. G.'s *Playbook* for use of the term 'allure'.

88. Hoole, *The Petty-Schoole*, title page.

89. Festus Corin, *The Childe's Tutor* (London, 1664), A2v. See also Charles Hoole, *Orbis Sensualium Pictus* (London, 1659), A4r–v, who claims 'Children (even from their Infancy almost) are delighted with Pictures, and willingly please their eyes with these sights.'

90. Corin, A4v.

91. For example, in Matthew Grenby and Andrea Immel, ed., *The Cambridge Companion to Children's Literature* (Cambridge: Cambridge University Press, 2009).

92. John Bunyan, *A Book for Boys and Girls* (London, 1686), A3r, A2v, A4r. Further references are given in the text.

93. J. G., title page.

94. J. G., 37, 39, 41. Animals are seen as of interest to children in the early modern period as bestiaries are frequently directed to children. For example, Edward Topsell, *The Historie of Four-Footed Beastes* (London, 1607), in addition to editions of *Aesop's Fables* for schoolboys and the alphabet of animals in Corin's and J. G.'s ABCs.

95. J. G., n.p.

96. Locke, 187, 243. Locke argued that children should be tenderly used, should be recognized as having distinct requirements and importantly 'must play and have play-things'. He develops this argument around play by suggesting that 'learning might be made a play and recreation to chil-

dren' (Locke, 176). See Margaret Ezell, 'John Locke's Imagery of Childhood', *Eighteenth-Century Studies* 17.2 (1983–1984): 139–155; Lerer, *Children's Literature*, 104–128.

97. See Mary Thwaite, *From Primer to Pleasure in Reading* (London: Library Association, 1972), 28–29. Green, *Print*, 398, suggests that it has more in common with the chapbook genre than an emblem book.

98. Pollock, 28.

99. Robert Prudom, *Truth Unavail'd by Scripture-Light* (London, 1699), 150–170. Isham, *Diary*, year 1621, and *Booke*, 17v. Elizabeth Isham also read it in her 13th year (Isham, *Booke*, 8r) and Elizabeth Walker's young daughters read Foxe under their mother's instruction (Walker, 71).

100. John Batchiler, *The Virgin's Pattern* (London, 1661), 20.

101. Cambers, 95–96, 55–56.

102. N. H. Keeble, ed., *Memoirs of the Life of Colonel Hutchinson* (London: Phoenix Press, 2000), 38–39.

103. Isham, *Booke*, 8r, 16v.

104. Snook, 47.

105. On common religious reading practices, see Cambers, 246–248 and Ryrie, 259–298.

106. Adrian Johns, *The Nature of the Book* (Chicago: University of Chicago Press, 1998), 410.

107. For example, *The Child's Bible* (London, 1677); R. B., *Youth's Divine Pastime*, 3rd edition (London, 1691). On Crouch's adaptations for children, see Demers, *Heaven*, 99–102; Green, *Print*, 400. On early editions of biblical stories for children, see Bottigheimer, *The Bible*, 43–35, and 'The Child-Reader'; Andrea Immel, 'James Pettit Andrews's "Books" (1790): The First Critical Survey of English Children's Literature', *Children's Literature* 28 (2000): 147–163; Andrea Immel, 'Some Picture Bibles and their Illustration', *Newsletter of the Children's Books History Society* 59 (1997): 20–22; Alexandra Walsham, *The Uses of Script and Print, 1300–1700* (Cambridge: Cambridge University, Press, 2004), 141.

108. Matthew Henry, *An Account of the Life and Death of Mr. Philip Henry* (London, 1699), 61.

109. For example, Benjamin Keach, *War with the Devil, Or, The Young Man's Conflict with the Powers of Darkness in a Dialogue … Chiefly Intended for the Instruction of the Younger Sort* (London, 1676); Thomas Sherman, *Youth's Tragedy, A Poem: Drawn Up By Way of a Dialogue … For The Caution and Direction of the Younger Sort* (London, 1671); Thomas Sherman, *Youth's Comedy, Or, The Soul's Tryals and Triumph, A Dramatick Poem* (London, 1680).

110. Thomas Willis, *The Key of Knowledge* (London, 1682).

111. See H. P., *A Looking Glass for Children* (London, 1673); Sloane, 170.

112. Green, *Print*, 398–401. Courtney Weikle-Mills, *Imaginary Citizens: Child Readers and the Limits of American Independence, 1640–1868* (Baltimore: Johns Hopkins University Press, 2012), 16, describes Bunyan's *Book for Boys and Girls* as one of the first poetry books for children.

113. Willis, 137–139.

114. See Watt's important study of the relationship between cheap print and piety. See also Spufford, 194–218.

115. The prayer includes 'make me a babe of thy familie, that I may suck the paps of thy word'. See E. H., *David's Sling against Great Goliath* (London, 1589), 109–111.

116. Thomas Sorocold, *Supplications of Saints* (London, 1612). Michael Sparke, *The Crums of Comfort, 8th Edition* (London, 1628). This prayer for children is retained in later editions of Sparke's collection of prayers. On Sparke's work, see Green, *Print*, 20–21, 259–260

117. Sorocold, 315; Sparke, C6v.

118. Sorocold, 317.

119. Sorocold, 314; Sparke, C6r.

120. The belief that children were prone to sin and lacking in reason was partially due to religious assumptions of the depravity of children (see Avery; see also H. P., *A Looking Glass*, in which the author claims to have compiled this book following his 'daily observation of Youths' great need of all endeavour to prompt them to that which is good, they being naturally addicted to be drawn away through their own inclinations, and the powerful prevalency of Satan to sin and disobedience' [Preface 'To the Reader', n.p.]). It also came from the understanding of the humours, specifically the predominance of moisture in young bodies that led to the drowning of reason and a lack of control over bodily processes. See Hannah Newton, *The Sick Child in Early Modern England, 1580–1720* (Oxford: Oxford University Press, 2012), 41. Gail Kern Paster, *Humoring the Body: Emotions and the Shakespearean Stage* (Chicago: University of Chicago Press, 2004), 13–14.

121. Lewis Bayly, *The Practise of Pietie* (London, 1613), E5r.

122. Newton, 211

123. On dating of Russel's texts, see Avery, 104; Kate Cregan and Denise Cuthbert, *Global Childhoods: Issues and Debates* (London: Sage, 2014), 27–28.

124. For other examples of early modern accounts of children on their death beds, see Ralph Houlbrooke, 'Death in Childhood: The Practice of the "Good Death" in James Janeway's *A Token for Children*', in *Childhood in Question*, ed. Stephen Hussey and Anthony Fletcher (Manchester: Manchester University Press, 1999), 37–56.

125. See Houlbrooke, 38–39 on sex and social backgrounds of subjects.
126. James Janeway, *A Token for Children: Being an Exact Account of the Conversion, Holy and Exemplary Lives, and Joyful Deaths of Several Young Children* (London, 1676), A5v. See also James Janeway, *A Token for Children. The Second Part. Being A Farther Account of the Conversion, Holy and Exemplary Lives, and Joyful Deaths of Several Other Young Children, Not Published in the First Part* (London, 1673). Further references to the two parts of Janeway's collection are given in the text.
127. See Houlbrooke on early editions of Janeway.
128. On literature teaching children how to die piously, see Heller, 162; Alec Ryrie, 'Facing Childhood Death in English Protestant Spirituality', in *Death, Emotion and Childhood in Premodern Europe,* ed. Katie Barclay, Kimberley Reynolds and Ciara Rawnsley (Basingstoke: Palgrave Macmillan, 2017), 109–128; Sloane, 54. On wider literature on 'godly dying', see Green, *Print*, 360–367.
129. Houlbrooke, 51.
130. On affective reading, see Katharine Craik and Tanya Pollard, 'Introduction', in *Shakespearean Sensations: Experiencing Literature in Early Modern England*, ed. Katharine Craik and Tanya Pollard (Cambridge: Cambridge University Press, 2013), 1–28; Narveson, 79–99.
131. See reading of the Bible and scriptures in Janeway I, 4, 21, 24, 33, 41, 44 and II, 3, 10, 19, 39, 72, 82; of catechisms and primers I, 24, 31 and II, 3, 51; of Foxe's *Book of Martyrs* II, 4; of Richard Baxter II, 82.
132. Leigh, 42.
133. Janeway's final account in part I is of a beggar boy who cannot read. This boy seeks learning and knowledge through listening to sermons, discourse and asking for instruction.
134. Seth Lerer, '"Thy Life to Mend, This Book Attend": Reading and Healing in the Arc of Children's Literature', *New Literary History* 37.3 (2006): 636.
135. Walker, 71. Fisher, n.p. The young Judith Isham seems to have had such a response to her reading of 'a new booke of Gerard's Meditations', when having 'sat up in the night to read it stayed up late to read it' she woke her sister Elizabeth the next morning to tell her 'what great joy she had being filled with devine love' (Isham, *Booke*, 28r). On the 'affective power of the early modern text', see Helen Smith, '"More Swete Vnto the Eare / than Holsome for Ye Mynde": Embodying Early Modern Women's Reading', *Huntington Library Quarterly* 73.3 (2010): 413–432.
136. Shell usefully highlights the flawed tendency to assume that fictional representations of naughty children are 'more true to life than exemplary ones' (188).
137. Weikle-Mills, 16

138. Carolyn Steedman, *Past Tenses: Essays on Writing, Autobiography and History* (London: Rivers Oram Press, 1992), 34.

139. See also Michael Mascuch, 'The Godly Child's "Power and Evidence" in the Word: Orality and Literacy in the Ministry of Sarah Wight', in *Childhood and Children's Books in Early Modern Europe, 1550–1800*, ed. Andrea Immel and Michael Witmore (London: Routledge, 2006), 103–126, for an important consideration of illiterate participants, especially children, in 'godly' cultures.

140. See F. J. Harvey Darton, *Children's Books in England* (Cambridge: Cambridge University Press, 1982), 56, 62; Hayes, 40; Sloane, 166–167, 224.

CHAPTER 3

Books for 'Childish Age': Youthful Reading Cultures in Early Modern England

the Scriptures thought I, what are they? A dead letter, a little ink and paper, of three or four shillings price [...] give me a Ballad, a Newsbook, *George* on horseback, or *Bevis of Southampton*, give me some book that teaches curious arts, that tells of old fables.[1]

The narrator of John Bunyan's *A Few Sighs from Hell* (1658) is not a 'good' child reader! In line with other religious writing for and about children, Bunyan, author of what have subsequently been claimed as two of the earliest examples of children's literature, implies that a path to salvation is determined through early reading practices.[2] Instead of reading 'the Scriptures', which as Chap. 2 demonstrated was expected of the 'good' child, Bunyan's damned rich man admits to reading various forms of small books and cheap print, including news books, ballads, chapbooks of the English heroes, Saint George and Bevis of Southampton, books of magic and fables. These diverse textual forms are discursively linked in this account of childhood reading through their opposition to recommended religious reading and through their appeal to the young reader. This representation of youthful tastes serves a specific function as moral exemplar. Writers on education, children's behaviour and religious and moral matters frequently highlighted the dangers for the young of reading the cheap print and chivalric tales cited by Bunyan, particularly post-Reformation when such tales were dismissed as sinful, enchanting and popish for readers of all ages.[3] These tales were often specifically associated with

© The Author(s) 2018
E. Lamb, *Reading Children in Early Modern Culture*,
Early Modern Literature in History,
https://doi.org/10.1007/978-3-319-70359-6_3

childhood reading practices. For some early modern readers such indulgence signified a foolish waste of time in childhood from which individuals might be saved upon discovering religious texts. Many spiritual narratives, for example, deployed an account of altered reading practices to mark the end of an ignorant childhood and the beginning of an age of spiritual awareness, including those of Vasavour Powell and Richard Baxter who recall delighting in 'Hystorical or Poetical Books, Romances' and 'romances, fables and old tales' above scripture before being converted by reading Richard Sibbes' biblical exegesis, *The Bruised Reed* (1631).[4] Elizabeth Delaval admits in her memoirs that in her 'childish age' she read 'ill chosen boock's, such as romances are', before realizing that this was a distraction from scripture and mending, what she calls, her 'childish' and 'ill chosen' ways of reading.[5] In accounts of spiritual conversion this image of childhood reading of tales, romances and 'curious books' is a narrative trope, yet it also works to align the young and the 'childish' with this element of textual culture in early modern England. Childhood, or 'childish' ways, are characterized in a range of sixteenth- and seventeenth-century depictions of reading by an indulgence in material termed by moralists as 'wanton and naughty ... or trifling' and as 'undecent bookes' capable of 'corrupt[ing] and ensnar[ing]' the young, from 'bookes, ballades, Songes, sonettes, and Ditties of dalliance' to 'Tale-books, Romances, Play-books, and false or hurtful History'.[6]

This chapter investigates the widespread associations between reading these forms and 'childish' age in early modern England in order to unpack an alternative understanding of the child as reader. A number of early modern printed texts identify what Teresa Michals calls a mixed-age audience in their paratextual material.[7] Prefaces of *Aesop's Fables*, educational books, commentaries on Virgil and title pages of prose works invite the young, variously defined as a 'child', a 'youth' and the 'young' reader, to read the text in one way and the old to read it in another.[8] They commonly represent the child in terms of limited cognitive capabilities and distinctive desires in relation to their reading material. Assessing what these age-graded reading practices disclose about childhood and about cultures of reading, this chapter examines how the young are associated with reading for pleasure in printed texts. Exploring the discursive connections between the young and reading as a form of entertainment and leisure, it contends that the childish or youthful reader is characterized by certain modes of reading. Michals points out in her recent study of the adult reader that, prior to the mid-eighteenth century, readers were primarily categorized in terms of social status and gender, rather than age. Yet, as Michals highlights, age in the sense of a stage in the life cycle, rather than a fixed numerical state, has always been an element in identifying readers in print culture. This chapter builds on her important reminder to see 'literary history within the social history of age' by examining the identification of readers and the recommendation of reading practices according to age categories in early modern England.[9] It explores the intersections of status, gender and age in determining a particular mode of reading: reading for pleasure.

This concept of the child as reader, this chapter suggests, is also shaped by developing print markets in the late sixteenth and seventeenth centuries, in which the young are imagined as potential consumers. Francis Kirkman, a mid-seventeenth-century author and bookseller, not only identifies the young as a potential readers of his books, he also represents children, male and female, as avid readers of the genres he produces, and develops strategies of marketing his books to the young by exploiting cultural associations between recreational reading and childhood. A number of anthologies also adapted existing genres of verse, riddles, commonplaces and instruction in basic skills and magic tricks to claim that new editions were particularly suited to the young, specifically through their emphasis on mirth and play. Through an analysis of these texts, this chapter argues for an emerging sense of youthful reading cultures in the period. By considering how early modern print cultures identified aspects of reading as suited to a young market, it asks what this tells us about concepts of childhood in the period and what it reveals about the young as buyers of books. Reflecting on practices of buying, sharing and accessing books among early modern young people, this chapter proposes that whether this perception of the childish reader constitutes a marketing strategy or a literary trope, it indicates the significance of age-graded reading practices in the period. While Michals acknowledges that the young reader is prioritized amidst the mixed-age audiences identified by early modern books, this chapter goes further to suggest that the young reader is highlighted in order to recommend a particular mode of reading.[10] Developing this monograph's interrogation of what it means to read as a child in early modern England, it explores an alternative understanding of the child as reader to the 'good' child of Chap. 2. As Paul Griffiths has highlighted, 'the meaning and representation of youth to some extent depends on the nature of the source before us'.[11] Books identifying the young as reading for recreation view childhood and youth in different ways from the strict moral treatises warning against the dangers of reading non-religious material during these formative stages of the life cycle, signalling the multiple understandings of the child as reader that circulated in early modern culture.

'CHILDREN READ FOR THEIR PLEASANTNESS': READING AS A CHILD

In his tract on child-rearing, *A Childe's Patrimony* (1640), Hezekiah Woodward complains about the tendency to 'fit our books' to different stages within childhood. He proposes that the child is as 'fit for *Aesop, Cicero,* or *Ovid,* as for the Childish book', but acknowledges that educational customs mean that in practice 'we fit ... this part of *Ovid* for this *form,* that part for another; *Virgil* to the fourth; and *Horace* to the fifth'. Referring to the tendency to recommend different books for the various levels in early modern grammar schools, he questions the need for this approach and suggests that it increases labour but makes 'the benefit the lesse'.[12] Woodward expands his rationale by explaining that once scholars have acquired basic knowledge of letters and syllables in English, or of declension and verb in Latin, then he may read any book. Based on accounts of teaching children how to read English and Latin in the period, it is likely that this is the case.[13] Children who had acquired basic reading skills would have been able to read these more advanced texts. Nonetheless children are presumed, and advised, to read books differently from those at later stages of the life cycle in a range of contexts in early modern culture. This was due, at least in part, to early modern understanding of the cognitive abilities of children. Children may have been able to master literacy, but they were perceived to less capable as readers than adults because they were deemed to have a mental capacity and reasoning abilities limited by 'the 'number of [their] yeares', meaning that some books were considered to be 'fitter for men' than the young.[14] As Chap. 2 demonstrated, early reading and religious books were produced to fit these perceived needs. But this practice extended beyond these genres. Some authors even produced multiple books on the same topic for different categories of reader. Richard Hodges, for example, wrote an arithmetic book for children, *The Childes Counting Book* (1624), and later produced a second book on the subject, *A Manual for Millions* (1631). As 'M. I. Philimathematic' highlights in his dedicatory verse to the latter, 'Thy first was wrote for Children, this for Men', before comically asking will the 'third' be to 'women' (A3r), gesturing towards the ways in which different types of readers with distinct material needs and cognitive capacities were recognized within print culture. This is also evident in the ways in which 'men' and 'children' were seen to approach the same books in different ways. In 1591 Sir John Harrington admits that children are capable of reading Virgil's *Aeneid* but he reflects on how their reading experiences are different from those of their elders. In 'A Brief Apology for Poetry' he questions:

> Do we not make our children read it commonly before they can understand it, as a testimonie that we do generally approve it? And yet we see old men study it, as a proofe that they do specially admire it: so as one writes very pretily, that children do wade in *Virgill*, and yet strong men do swim in it.[15]

Harrington, almost fifty years earlier than Woodward, recognizes the abilities of children to read complex texts, but also suggests that by necessity their reading involves a different type of engagement with those texts. Towards the end of the seventeenth century an anonymous adapter of Aesop's fables reflects further on the ways in which different types of readers within a mixed-age audience might read classical texts. The preface of *Aesop Improved* (1673) notes that:

> Men and children, may read the same books, but for different ends and purposes. Men may read those books for their Profundity which Children read for their Pleasantness. Or men may read the same books for their Solidity wisdome, and Judgement, which is in them, which children are taught merely for their fancy, stile and language.[16]

Like Harrington and Woodward, the anonymous translator hints that translations of ancient poetry and fables serve a useful purpose in educating children, developing their reading capabilities and to teach language and style. However, the translator goes further in the conceptualization of the child reader, marked in each of these accounts by both gender and age and as a particular category of reader distinct from the adult, or, more specifically, the man. Pointing to the varied reading methods of the child, which include reading for 'their Pleasantness' and being 'taught' the book, this preface implies that the content of this book not only offers literacy instruction but also moral instruction via the acquisition of improved manners or 'pleasantness'. This stands in contrast to 'profundity' sought by the 'men' who read the same book. Building on the recognition that children will learn more successfully if that learning is made enticing, 'pleasantness' also implies that the content of this book is somehow appealing or pleasant to children. In its representation of the relationship between children and textual cultures in seventeenth-century England, this preface foregrounds diverse aspects of children's reading experiences: guided and independent reading, instruction and delight.

The balance between didacticism and pleasure has been, as Jacqueline Rose famously pointed out, one of the most famous debates in the history of children's literature.[17] It is, moreover, one of the major reasons that early modern books for children have been overlooked in scholarship. Texts predating the supposed birth of children's literature in the eighteenth century have frequently been dismissed as basically instructional, and therefore not 'proper' children's books, in many histories of the genre which map a transition from education to pleasure, and which, as Daniel Kline highlights, artificially separate these two elements.[18] Such histories, often sharing F. J. Harvey Darton's definition of children's books as 'printed works produced ostensibly to give children spontaneous pleasure and not primarily to teach them', have justified the omission of many of the texts directed at children before the publication of John Newbery's *A Little Pretty-Pocket Book* in 1744.[19] *Aesop Improved* is just one example of the articulation of the dual elements seen to motivate reading in the books produced for children in the seventeenth century. Writers' attempts to appeal to and instruct their potential readers can be discerned in books for children, male and female, from this period. It is foregrounded constantly in debates on schooling in the late sixteenth and early seventeenth centuries as many pedagogues and educational theorists advocate a ludic culture of learning, which depends upon the idea that children will learn more effectively through delight. From Erasmus' recommendation that those teaching early literacy encourage the young by baking cookies and carving toys in the shapes of letters so that the alphabet can be memorized in 'a few days of fun and play' to John Brinsley's proposition in 1612 that masters should 'breede in the little ones a love of their masters, with delight in their books', delight in reading is central to many early modern educational programmes.[20] In his 1659 translation of Comenius' *Orbis Sensualium Pictus*, Charles Hoole insists that he intends '*To entice witty Children*' (A4r) by teaching them '*by sport and merry pastime*' (A4v).[21] In another account of what subjects and books should be taught at each stage of schooling, Hoole comments directly on the use of *Aesop's Fables* in terms of delight and learning. Writing that this 'book of great antiquity and of more solid learning than most men think' should be used in teaching the third form of grammar school, he proposes that his students should 'procure *Aesops Fables* then in English and Latine, and the rather because they will take delight in reading the Tales, and the moral in a Language which they already understand, and will be helped thereby to construe the Latine of themselves'.[22] 'Delight in reading' is promoted by these early modern pedagogues as effective educational strategy, in teaching basic literacy, morality and languages because it fits the distinct capacities—the understanding—of the young.

Play and pleasure are prominent themes in early modern books that identify children as potential readers. Even Woodward, alongside his complaints about suiting books to children's needs, suggests that children will learn to read more easily if masters 'draw them on with all pleasingness' (34) and admits that there must be 'great choice of the matter, such ever, is best *sutable*, which will be ever that, which is most *sensuall*' (161). Going one step further than simply recognizing the child reader as seeking the 'pleasantness' or 'pleasingness' in reading material, Woodward suggests an emotional and bodily reading experience through enticing the senses. For Woodward this is in keeping with his rumination on the inherent features of childhood. 'Childhood and youth', he writes, 'are ages of fancy' (98). Woodward is not alone in associating these early stages of the life cycle with 'sensuall' experience and fancy. As Michael Witmore has shown, children were commonly associated with fancy and imagination, 'guided' as Thomas Wright writes in 1604, 'by an internall imagination'.[23] This association between childhood and fancy or pleasing the senses is, Witmore has argued, central to the role of children in early modern literary cultures. It is also, I would suggest, crucial to the understanding of the child as reader. This is not to return to the traditional 'grand narrative' of children's literature as the emergence of books to delight children, nor to posit an argument that children's literature exists in the sixteenth and seventeenth centuries because of the presence of books to 'please' children; rather, the precarious balance between instruction and delight, between reading for learning and for 'pleasantness', characterizes the 'child' as a distinct type of reader in early books directed at all ages.[24]

The blend of instruction and pleasure in reading is not unique to children's books. It has also been crucial to the history of literature more generally as authors and critics have argued for the utility of the literary in offering instruction and delight. Yet, as Robert Matz points out, Horace's original expression of the 'profit and pleasure' dictum emerged from a culture in which moral profit was associated with the Roman elders and pleasure was associated with the young.[25] The most famous articulation of this maxim in early modern England in Philip Sidney's *An Apology for Poetry* (1595) is similarly concerned with the connections between age and poetry that pervade this author's work. In his *Apology* Sidney associates authorship with a period of youthful idleness, describing himself as 'in these my not old years and idlest times having slipped into the title of a poet'.[26] He presents his romance fiction, *The Countess of Pembroke's Arcadia*, in its preface as 'this idle work of mine', written at the request of his sister and suitable for reading at her 'idle times', and further describes it as 'toyfull books' and 'ink wasting toys' in letters to his siblings.[27] As Katherine Duncan-Jones persuasively argues, Sidney's representation of his writing as recreation above profitable pleasure is more than a conventional expression of modesty.[28] The depiction of books as offering pleasurable reading forms part of a wider depiction of romance as a feminized genre in early modern culture, suited to the female reader.[29] However, the depiction of *Arcadia* as a toy also constructs Sidney's work as youthful or early attempts at writing. Sidney's terminology of toys exemplifies overlaps in the associations of the genre with a gendered and aged status. On one level it presents his romance fiction, as Duncan-Jones points out, as a 'fantastic or trifling speech or piece of writing'.[30] The description of his fiction as a toy works to render it less dangerous. As Joseph Campana has argued, poetry and fiction are described by a number of early modern writers in ways that lessen the potential feminizing threat. As 'vaine toyes' literary works are less effective in transforming men into boys.[31] Yet the term's multiple implications in the period as meaning both amorous sport or dalliance, enhancing romance fiction's reputation as the eroticized reading material of women, as well as the material objects of children's play, in fact potentially reduces adult readers to children as they encounter these childish objects: books.[32]

Effeminate and youthful pursuits overlap in Sidney's representation of his romance. As Daniel Kline proposes in relation to readership in the medieval period, the 'question of age is as significant as that of gender, class, ethnicity, or religion'.[33] As is often the case in early modern culture, the young are aligned with the feminine as both are implicated, as authors and consumers, in the production of 'idle' or recreational works of literature.[34] The preface to an earlier romance explicitly establishes these associations between age, gender and the genre. Age categories are fore-grounded in the preface of the first English translation by Margaret Tyler of *The Mirrour of Princely Deedes and Knighthood* (*c.* 1578), also known as *The Knight of the Sun*. Repeatedly referring to her own advanced and 'staied' years in an effort to justify her subject matter as an older female translator, Tyler explains that in undertaking the task of translation she turned to 'mine olde reading'.[35] Tyler's preface presents romance as suitable for younger readers: her younger self and the 'young Gentlemen' that the original author wanted to inspire with courage. Age is thus emphasized alongside gender, which she acknowledges in her 'woman's worke' of 'manlinesse of the matter' and by appealing to female readers.[36] Age and gender are significant to authorship and readership in this seminal text in the history of romance fiction in England.[37] Tyler participates in early modern efforts to reinvent romance fiction by drawing on the conventional profit and delight maxim, stressing the profit provided by the historical matter and the delight for the young reader. *The Mirrour of Knighthood*, like many tales of chivalry and romance written, translated and reprinted throughout Europe in the sixteenth and seventeenth centuries, is commonly cited in derogatory terms as the reading material of children and youths. Vives provides an extensive list of romances and tales in various nations that have 'no other purpose, but to corrupt the manners of young folkes', including the English tales of King Arthur, Bevis of Southampton and Guy of Warwick—texts that are described by Edward Dering in 1572 as 'childish follye'.[38] *The Mirrour of Knighthood* in particular becomes a cliché for the idle reading practices of schoolboys, young students and youths more generally in the English cultural imagination. Francis Meres names it in 1598 as one of a number of books 'hurtfull to youth', in a list that also includes the English chivalric tales condemned by Vives and a number of romances.[39] In 1629, Francis Lenton draws on it in his caricature of the idle and love-stricken youth distracted from his studies by '*Don Quix Zot*, or else *The Knight o' the Sun*' and by '*Ben Johnsons* booke of Playes'.[40] In William Hawkins' *Apollo Shroving* (*c.* 1626), John Gingle is a boy satirically characterized by his knowledge of this book. When receiving his lessons on how to court a lady he draws on his reading of *The Mirrour of Knighthood*, recalling: 'This Claridiana was courted by the Knight of the Sunne. My Mother has read that booke to me.'[41] The only benefit of this book, it seems, is an instruction in courtship. These representations of romances and stories of chivalry as the desired reading material of boys and young men interested in matters of courtship and love above academic pursuits further implies that reading romances is both a childish and effeminizing act.[42] As scholars of early modern women's reading—particularly Heidi Brayman Hackel in her seminal study of female readers—have pointed out, such representations reveal more about cultural perceptions of the genre than historical reading practices.[43] They also reveal much about cultural attitudes towards the young. They convey the fears of educators and moralists that if children are not supervised in their reading, or are supervised by the wrong people as in the case of John Gingle and his mother, they will at worst be corrupted by erotic and effeminate matters and at best seek only pleasure and play in their reading material. As Katharine Craik highlights, if the young read combining pleasure with profit, in line with Horatian dictum, they might be 'nourished by way of wisdom, reason and understanding', but if they read solely for delight 'the consequences are disastrous'.[44] The fear is about how children will engage with their reading material—what lessons they will learn—rather than simply about the content of a particular text.

The anxieties surrounding children's reading material expressed from Vives through to the Puritan moralists of the later seventeenth century draw on wider cultural concerns that children naturally tend towards idle recreation and pleasure without profit.[45] A common representation of the earliest stages of the life cycle in the period was as an age of 'pleasure and delight' that 'lack[ed] the use of reason' to seek the benefits.[46] Anne Bradstreet, for example, characterizes 'Childishness' as 'all folly' with a 'silliness' that did only 'take delight,/In that which riper age did scorn and slight,/In Rattles, Bables, and such toyish stuff'.[47] This association of children with 'toyish stuff' and material not worthy of the consideration of 'riper age' also informed the representation of literary genres with some inferior rhymes, for instance, deemed only 'fit for children to heare and follow with their rattles and hobby horses' in Hawkins' *Apollo Shroving* (*c.* 1626).[48] Children are also characterized by an irrational commitment to play and toys in religious depictions, when exemplary children dedicated to prayer and reading are juxtaposed with the more standard child at play. Samuel Clark notes that William Gouge 'was more than ordinarily studious and industrious' as a schoolboy 'for when other boyes upon play-dayes took liverty for their sports and pastimes, he would be at his book, wherein he took more delight than others could finde in their Recreations'.[49] James Janeway uses a similar motif to describe the children in his *A Token for Children* (first published in 1671), stating of one child 'admirably affected with the things of God' that 'When other Children were playing, he would many a time and oft be praying.'[50] Educators and moralists saw this propensity to play as a feature of the young that should be brought under control by more profitable pursuits. However, this understanding of childhood and reading simultaneously opportunities for profit-seeking authors and publishers to market their texts by appealing to this pleasure-seeking youthful reader.

IMAGINING A YOUTHFUL MARKET: IDENTIFYING THE CHILD AS READER

There is no doubt that many authors recognized the opportunity to appeal to this notional young reader preoccupied with delight, including one seventeenth-century author and bookseller, Francis Kirkman. Kirkman's books cannily recognized the child reader as potential market, and represented children as such in both his paratextual material and narratives. In a nostalgic account of his childhood reading in his semi-autobiographical fiction, *The Unlucky Citizen* (1673), he represents his own desire to read certain types of books when he recalls:

> one of my School-fellows lent me *Docter Faustus* [...] The next Book I met with was *Fryar Bacon* [...] I came to Knight Errantry, and reading *Montelion Knight of the Oracle*, and *Ornatus* and *Artesia*, and the Famous *Parismus* [...] I proceeded on to *Palmerin of England*, and *Amadis de Gaul*; and borrowing one Book of one person, when I had read it my self, I lent it to another, who lent me one of their Books; and thus *robbing* Peter *to pay* Paul, borrowing and lending from one to another, I in time had read most of these Histories.[51]

Although this description of a transition from chapbook tales to romances is similar to Bunyan's account in terms of the type of material read as a child, it presents a different attitude towards such books as the reading material of the young. Kirkman offers a positive account of his immersion in tales as a schoolboy in the late 1630s or early 1640s, even evincing some pleasure at the extent to which he believed 'all I read to be true' (11). On finding sixpence he spends it all on a copy of *Fortunatus*, hoping that 'Lady *Fortune* would one time or other bestow such a Purse upon me as she did on *Fortunatus*' (10). He continues to demonstrate how his reading as a schoolboy shaped his expectations of life, claiming that 'being so wholly affected to them, and reading how that *Amadis* and other Knights not knowing their Parents, did in time prove to be Sons of Kings and great Personages; I had such a fond and idle Opinion, that I might in time prove to be some great Person, or at leastwise be Squire to some Knight' (11–12). Kirkman characterizes childhood reading by this immersion in the imaginative world, yet his attitude is mediated by the fact that, in contrast to Bunyan, it is not positioned within a spiritual narrative of conversion from an unruly childhood to a reformed adulthood.

It is, however, shaped by a different set of narrative conventions. Although Kirkman claims that *The Unlucky Citizen* contains 'all the remarkable passages of my life' (n.p.) and in many instances the information provided is autobiographical, his narrative repeatedly draws on contemporary fiction.[52] In his description of schoolboy reading, Kirkman appropriates the fictional narrative of a book that he later claims to have read: Cervantes' *Don Quixote*. Kirkman's list of texts mirrors the well-known knight, also an avid reader of the adventures of Don Bellianis, Amadis de Gaule and Palmerin of England. His immersion in these tales reflects Don Quixote's reading practices as books take 'possession of his imagination' until he 'conceived the strangest notion … to become a knight errant, and to travel about the world with his armour and his arms and his horse in search of adventures, and to practise all those activities that he knew from his books'.[53] Rather than draw on the *Don Quixote* narrative to critique the effects of romance fiction, Kirkman celebrates it. There is only one difference between himself and the fictional knight: while the 50-year-old character pursues his desire to imitate his books, the young Kirkman stops short of becoming another Don Quixote because, he claims, of fear and 'want of years' (13). In Kirkman's narrative of childhood, age permits a merging of his experiences as a schoolboy and the stories that he reads but simultaneously prevents him from taking this too far. In contrast to the moralists' warning against the reading of romance in youth, as children, particularly young girls, were perceived to be lacking in the knowledge that 'they are but fictions' and as a result 'they truly move being read', Kirkman defends romance reading among the young by comically demonstrating the limits of the formative effect of reading on the child.[54] The imagination of the child might be carried away by the stories he or she reads, but Kirkman suggests that the practical restrictions of being young mean that this is confined only to the mind.

Nonetheless, Kirkman's account shows that his childhood reading shaped him in other ways as he projects a narrative of development from the child to adult. As a translator, author and seller of romances, histories and books of 'Knight-errantry', Kirkman highlights the impact that the books had on him as a child in order to account for his subsequent career.[55] He creates a story of professional development from childhood reading experiences to his early forays into the professions of writing and printing. This moment in his autobiography also functions as a significant commercial strategy. He represents childhood reading through the eyes of the adult but also through the eyes of an entrepreneur in the world of print. Kirkman demonstrated his talents in this arena as a bookseller, reissuing over twenty-five pre-interregnum plays, and as an author, writing fictional works in a range of genres and translating a number of chivalric romances to, as Lori Newcomb suggests, meet new demands for leisure reading.[56] These talents are further revealed by the extent to which Kirkman uses this description of childhood reading to promote his works, including his schoolboy translation of *Amadis de Gaule*, which he published in 1652.[57] He also translated, wrote sequels to and published multiple versions of *The Honour of Chivalry* or *The Famous and Delectable History of Don Bellianis of Greece* between 1664 and 1673 and a version of *The History of Prince Erastus Son to the Emperour Dioclesian and Those Famous Philosophers Called the Seven Wise Masters of Rome* in 1674, recommending them to children and the 'Younger Sort'.[58] In the 1664 preface to the second part of *Don Bellianis of Greece*, he admits that 'in my minority I was a great lover of Books of Knighthood' and again compares himself to Don Quixote because of this youthful passion (*Honour of Chivalry*, A3v). In the preface to his collected volume of the three parts of *Don Bellianis* in 1673, he notes the popularity of chivalric tales and recommends the text that he publishes one year later, *The Seven Wise Masters*. He also deploys this advertising strategy in other works. For instance, he notes in his criminal biography of the notorious Mary Carleton that she 'took much pleasure in reading, especially Love Books, and those that treated of Knight Errantry' in her youth, 'believing all she read to be true', includes some French romances, such as *Cassandra* and *Cleopatra*, and chivalric tales published by Kirkman, including *Don Bellianis* and *Amadis de Gaule*.[59]

The representation of children's avid taste for chivalric tales in *The Unlucky Citizen* might be part of these canny marketing strategies. Kirkman's invocation of youthful reading practices is particularly interesting in this context. He goes further than simply depicting the keen interest of schoolboys in the tales that he published from the 1650s to the 1670s; he presents them as a market for these texts. He recalls buying his first book with a sixpence that he found and relates how he lent these books to his schoolfellows in exchange for others. Furthermore, he claims that he read these books during 'time I had from School, as *Thursdays* in the Afternoon, and *Saturdays*' (*Unlucky Citizen*, 11). He suggests that children are a potential market for certain types of reading material and that they will read in a certain way: for leisure in the unsupervised and unregulated spaces of free time outside the structure of the school. Whether this is an accurate representation of the young Kirkman's reading practices or a fictionalized account, it discursively links specific genres and modes of reading with children and identifies them as a market.

Kirkman's production of multiple editions of histories and romances hints that this is the market at which he was aiming. In the 1673 preface to *Don Bellianis*, he recommends a series of 'Historyes' and 'Romances' (n.p.), urging his reader to read these books in an order similar to that outlined in *The Unlucky Citizen*: beginning with *The Seven Wise Masters* and then moving on to *Fortunatus*, *Don Bellianis* and others, including *Parismus*, *Montelion Knight of the Oracle* and *Amadis de Gaule*. He particularly recommends *The Seven Wise Masters* to the 'Young Reader', noting that in this 'very pleasant Collection of variety of that Witty history' there are 'Pictures fitted to every particular History' for the 'Pleasure of the Young Reader' (n.p.). He proceeds by stating that 'This Book is of so great esteem in *Ireland* that next to the *Horn-Book*, and Knowledge of Letters, Children are in general put to Read in it' (n.p.). This claim, which Kirkman repeats in the preface to his 1674 edition of *The Seven Wise Masters of Rome*, is also found in other editions of this story.[60] This may be highly unlikely, as Margaret Spufford points out, nonetheless Kirkman's emphasis on the link between these tales and the young reader is notable.[61] Age is the primary factor through which Kirkman addresses his readers. In the preface to *Don Bellianis*, Kirkman recommends romances and histories to 'thou of what Age, or Sex soever', and he claims that both 'young and old' (n.p.) take much pleasure in reading *The Seven Wise Masters*. The title page of *The Unlucky Citizen* claims that it is 'Calculated for the Meridian of this City but may serve by way of Advice to all the Cominalty of England, but more particularly to Parents and Children, Masters and Servants, Husbands and Wives'. By reaching out to all ages, Kirkman appeals to wide readership rather than, to use Adam Smyth's term, a 'discrete class of readers'.[62] His invocation of children and the young as readers on the title pages and prefaces of his books positions the young as one group within a range of consumers. Yet the preface to Kirkman's *Don Bellianis* does attend carefully to its young readers. It insists on the benefits to any reader in 'these sorts of Historyes', but insists that 'if thou art Young, begin now' as it will enable the younger reader to 'presently' read with 'the more Profit and Delight' (n.p.). The profit that Kirkman promises is the development of reading skills, and he supports this claim by aligning this genre with the use of the hornbook as early reading material in Ireland. The delight comes in the reading of a story that Kirkman repeatedly describes as 'pleasant', 'delightful' and as providing 'Pleasure' to the young reader (n.p.). This aspect of reading is emphasized by Kirkman across his multiple editions of the text. He claims in the 1664 edition that he wrote it as 'harmless recreation' and hopes that 'it recreats or contents you in the reading, as much as it did me in the writing' (*Honour of Chivalry*, A4v). Kirkman's prefaces construct his versions of *Don Bellianis* as recreational reading with a specific appeal to the younger reader seeking delight. Through careful use of his prefatory material, Kirkman imagines multiple readers, old and young, seeking distinct combinations of profit and delight from their reading experiences.

Francis Kirkman thus defends his acts of translating, writing and selling romances, histories and chivalric tales by alluding to their potential benefits in educational contexts but he appeals primarily to those seeking 'harmless recreation' (*Honour of Chivalry*, A3r). He imagines his readers via his own reading practices as a boy, as depicted in *The Unlucky Citizen*. In his 1673 preface to *Don Bellianis* he describes readers of *Parismus* who are 'so highly pleased' by what they read 'that they have run through all the Books of this Nature and Quality' (n.p.), echoing his account of his experiences as a schoolboy when he was 'terrified[d]' and 'delighted' by stories to the extent that he was 'desirous of reading more of that nature' (*Unlucky Citizen*, 10–11). His recollection of his and his peers' buying, lending and reading of these books in their time 'from school' locates these potential young readers as indulging their imaginations in an unsupervised space, allocating an autonomy to the child reader in selecting their reading material and reading, not for profit or education, but for their imaginative pleasure.

The potential of books to offer pleasure, delight and a pastime to readers is, as I have suggested, not unique to Kirkman, although he is notable for his sustained investment in this literary trope. It is invoked in a range of late sixteenth- and seventeenth-century English texts when addressing a younger audience. Robert Greene, like Tyler and Kirkman, appeals to a varied readership for his romances *Alcida Greenes Metamorphosis* (first published in 1588) and *Menaphon* (first published in 1589).[63] The latter is described on its title page as a 'worke, worthy [of] the yongest eares for pleasure' and the former, although 'full of grave Principles to content Age', offers 'pleasant parlees, witty answeres' to 'satisfie' youth.[64] Greene and Kirkman, writing romances almost a century apart, defend the genre and appease parents and moralists by identifying the type of instruction or principles their books might impart. Yet they simultaneously identify the distinct tastes of younger readers and reach out to this aged category of reader. These writers exploit the gap between the prescriptive ideals of what children should read and what they perceive to signify the distinctive cultures of the young in early modern England. The identification of the discrete aspects of a potential youthful market develops, in one sense, as a result of rapidly expanding print cultures. With the increasing reproduction of texts and diversification of forms of cheap print by the late seventeenth century, a range of genres, including books of riddles, compliments and tricks, manuals on courtship, songbooks and ballads, were being adapted or reprinted with a statement of being for the young.[65] By 1694, J. G. proclaims in the preface to *A Play-Book for Children* that he is 'not ignorant of the Swarms of Books for Children' in justifying his publication of another book for the young.[66] As David Scott Kastan points out, 'Where, previously, desiring readers had to find books, books, it could be said, now found (and even made) readers'.[67] By the seventeenth century many of these books directed primarily or solely at a youthful readership claimed to offer, like Greene and Kirkman's earlier romances, 'pleasant', 'witty' and 'merry' content for the 'delight and recreation' of a group of age-inflected readers—the childish and young. Seventeenth-century editions of *The Book of Merry Riddles*, one of the most widely published early modern riddle books, demonstrate increasing attention to the child as reader of witty and pleasant material. Although the earliest extant edition dates to 1600, it was well known and read before this date, and was reprinted widely throughout the seventeenth century, incorporating variations to the content, layout and appeals to readership, and identifying children and youths as potential readers.[68] The 1617 edition, which contains 76 riddles, 16 'proper questions' and 133 'witty proverbs', claims to be 'No lesse usefull then behoovefull, for *any young man or childe, to knowe* whether he be quicke-witted or no'.[69] It constructs riddling as a masculine pursuit involving the acquisition and demonstration of wit in this printed circulation of riddles. The edition might be read as a test of the child's or young man's wit—to let him 'knowe whether he be quicke-witted or no'. In a culture in which young boys were trained to store up choice examples from their reading material for later use, these riddles and proverbs might be learned and practised at the appropriate occasion as a demonstration of wit, enabling the assertion of a masculine identity according to verbal talents and knowledge.[70] This is emphasized by a verse in a woodcut on the facing page that urges the reader to read the riddles rightly in order to be a 'wittie spark'. This edition presents reading, learning and transmitting riddles as a male pursuit particularly suited those in youth: children, young men or 'wittie sparks', another term for young men affecting smartness and often used to refer to the witty page boys of early modern drama.[71] Nathaniel Crouch's *Winter Evening Entertainments* (first advertised in 1685), another collection of riddles and jests accompanied by morals and wood-cuts, similarly emphasizes the role of riddling in facilitating the transition out of childhood for young boys by claiming 'Here's Milk for Children, Wisdom for Young Men,/To teach them that they turn not Babes again'.[72] These printed riddle books for children suggest that engagement with these books will enable the transition to a masculine adulthood.

In contrast, other anthologies of riddles for the young highlight the immersion in pleasure and youth provided by their content without dem-onstrating any potential 'profit' or education, and instead of encouraging their readers to 'turn not Babes again' encourage indulgence in the literary pastimes of the young. *Youth's Treasury, or, A Storehouse of Wit and Mirth* (1688), an anthology of the 'Choicest and Newest Songs', love letters, 'Pleasant Tales, Witty Jests and Merry Riddles', is indicative of the range of genres that were adapted and brought together under the aegis of being a collection for young readers.[73] It combines abbreviated versions of songs from contemporary broadside ballads, playhouse songs, comic tales (including one on the follies of old age), jests, riddles and some model compliments or 'protestations of love'. This text evolves from earlier seventeenth-century miscellanies or drolleries, registering a culture of mirth and leisure against Puritan models of reading for profit.[74] The divi-sion of profit and delight cannot be read solely as an indication of the traits of different age groups in the period as, in this context, it also forms part of a politicized comment on religious and social attitudes to leisure. Yet it simultaneously positions this culture of mirth as attractive for the young. Each section emphasizes that the material presented is 'new' in this 'trea-sury' for youth. This material is marketable in being presented anew for this category of reader.

The text is also striking in the ways that it imagines a communal identity among this age group erasing distinctions of gender and social status. The title page woodcut depicts a carnivalesque gathering of young men and women dancing with joined hands and no clothing under the supervision of a pedagogue figure, differentiated by the fact that he holds the symbolic objects of the teacher, a birch rod and book. This humorously imagines an alternative group of pleasure-indulging readers forging their own subversive culture and replacing the typical books of the pedagogue with this treasury. Another earlier example, *Sports and Pastimes* (1676), explicitly posits books of mirth for the young against contemporary Puritan texts recommended to children in an effort to morally educate them. Its instruction in the arts of tricks and magic is proclaimed as a 'touch of Hocus Pocus, or Leger-demain. Fitted for the delight and recreation of Youth'.[75] The title page draws a direct contrast with the terrifying tales of death, hell and damnation recommended to the child and printed specifically for them by Puritan writers, with the couplet '*There's no Hobgoblins here for to affright ye,/ But innocence and mirth that will delight ye*'.[76] Like *Youth's Treasury*, *Sports and Pastimes* draws on a range of popular texts and reprints these genres in a form that it claims to be suited for the young. It adapts miscellanies such as John Cotgrave's *Wits Interpreter, or the English Parnassus* (first published 1655) and the anonymous *Hocus Pocus Junior* (first published 1634), which combined tricks using eggs, balls, strings, cups and coins and a discussion of the art of witchcraft, science and 'other curiosities' with witty sayings, short poems, anecdotes and letters or statements for imitation. *Sports and Pastimes* acknowledges its debt to this tradition in the 'The Epistle to the Reader', which notes that tricks have been omitted that 'were in Print before' and directs the reader to '*English Parnassus, Hocus Pocus Junior*, &c.' (A3r). Like *Youth's Treasury*, it insists on the newness of its content while repackaging this popular format for the young. As promised on the title page, it offers only innocence and mirth, omitting the more serious discussion of the art of magic contained in other books of tricks. It includes tricks that the young might carry out to impress others, such as appearing to turn water into wine, making two coins into one, making invisible ink, getting revenge on maids, and making 'one laugh until the tears stand in his eyes'.[77] Some are directed at youths in a wide sense—for example, games that involve drinking companions—but many make use of materials that would have been available to children at a younger age, such as coins, ink and food. One requires using bells 'such as Children have at their Corrals' (16).

Sports and Pastimes is a 'book of curious arts' for children and youths, perhaps of the type that Bunyan had in mind in his recollection of childhood reading. The address to the reader proclaims that: 'The design of this was for the recreation of Youth, especially School-boys, whose wits are generally sharpned on such Whetstones' (A3r). Like many others directed to the young in the seventeenth century, it emphasizes recreation, delight and indulgence in wit as the defining features of youth, or in this case boyhood. It instructs the individual reader on how to carry out these tricks among their peers, as each is described through a detailed account of what actions the boys must make and an accompanying 'script' for the reader to recite performing the act. For example, the trick using bells directs the reader to:

> bid them view them, and put one in one hand, and one in the other hand, then put the second into the left hand, and say, Now you think they are both in one hand; which if they have seen your palm before, will imagine you have it still in your right hand, and shaking the right hand, the bell will jingle; then say, Which hand will you have them both in? They will be apt to say, the left, as thinking they are in the right, then opening both hands you leave them in wonder. (16–17)

This book requires an engaged and active form of reading. It provides delight to the individual young reader by offering instruction in this trick but in implying that this must be enacted to peers it forges a community among the reader and his audience. This is different from the reading group of schoolboys sharing books in Kirkman's account, yet it indicates another way in which reading might create a shared space for the young to indulge in recreation and delight. Whether or not books such as *Sports and Pastimes* were bought by children or read by them at all, these texts imagine a culture of children and the young by representing them as consumers of a particular type of text and as engaging with these texts in certain ways.[78] As Mary Ellen Lamb argues of the erotic gentlewoman reader, the child as a pleasure-seeking reader may not have been an early modern invention but it rises 'to special prominence in the book trade' as these diverse genres work to appeal to and imagine use by child readers.[79] Early modern books claiming to offer reading as a form of leisure identify a young reader, who, according to the title pages, prefaces and narratives, will engage with the book in particular ways: reading for wit, mirth, sport and pleasure.

BUYING BOOKS: THE PURCHASE—AND PESTER—POWER
OF EARLY MODERN CHILDREN

These books directed to a youthful readership indicate some of the ways in which those working in an expanding book trade might appeal to their potential market in terms of age. However, it is difficult to determine if there was a corresponding market of children who read or bought these books. It was clearly a worthwhile strategy to print or sell books that in some way targeted the younger portions of society. It was deployed by key figures from the earliest emergence of the book trade in England. William Caxton's first list of titles of print included four works in English aimed at children.[80] Maintaining a stock of books for grammar schoolboys was one means of ensuring a guaranteed trade, evidenced by the decision of Caxton's successor, Wynken de Worde, to print Robert Whittinton's Latin grammar through to the rivalry among stationers to hold the patent for grammar books in the early seventeenth century.[81] Regional booksellers, such as Stephen Wissenden in Canterbury in 1597 and Nicholas Jonson in the same location in 1640, kept a stock of the 'basic texts for children', including psalters, primers, hornbooks and ABCs.[82] The trade in books from England to Ireland was also, according to Mary Pollard, substantially in hornbooks, grammar books and other small books for children, with consignments to Cork in the 1570s including twelve copies of *The Seven Wise Masters of Rome*, the history noted by Francis Kirkman over one hundred years later as being held in so great esteem in Ireland that children learned to read using it.[83] Advice books ostensibly directed at children and youths also flourished throughout the seventeenth century with a range of tracts offering moral guidance through the voices of parents and other interested parties.[84] The widespread popularity of such texts addressing an imagined audience of children is indicated by the fact that ballads, such as *A Table of Good Nurture* (1625) and *An Hundred Godly Lessons that a Mother on her Death-Bed gave to her Children* (c. 1686–1688), imitated the genre and disseminated it in this cheap format.[85] This was an apt form to reach a young audience. In addition to the lower purchase cost, ballads hung on nursery walls and, as they would have also been learned and recited or sung, they may have even reached an audience of illiterate youths.[86] Nathaniel Crouch, operating under the pseudonyms Robert or Richard Burton, also adapted a number of genres for the young in his prolific reprinting and remarketing of texts in the latter half of the seventeenth century, including versions of Samuel Crossman's *The Young Man's*

Monitor (first published in 1664) as *The Young Man's Calling* (first published in 1685), *Remarks upon the Lives of Several Excellent Young Persons of Both Sexes* (1678), *The Apprentice's Companion* (1681) and *Youth's Divine Pastime* (1691).[87] Like Kirkman, Crouch was aware of the commercial effectiveness of appealing to the young, writing in *Youth's Divine Pastime*: 'He certainly doth hit the White/Who mingles Profit with Delight'.[88] Referring to Thomas White, author of *A Little Book for Little Children* (1660), he deploys the tradition of adapting religious texts for children as a potentially profitable strategy.[89] The anonymous translator of *Aesop Improved* also alludes to the extensive use of books by child readers, but also signals the limits of this readership. Referring to the substantial translation by John Ogilby, the preface claims:

> Doubtless the famous Oglesby had never provided so elaborate a Translation for but one hundred and twenty Fables, or whereabouts, or found encouragement to print but such a number in two volumes, with excellent Sculptures at a very great charge, and price, if notwithstanding the seeming prostitution of that book to the use of children, it had not had a very great esteem, amongst the wiser sort of mankind.[90]

Hinting at the lesser status of a readership of children, this dismissive account links questions of readership to economics via the language of 'charge' and 'price'. Children, according to this writer, do not constitute a sufficient market for books like *Aesop's Fables*. Nonetheless, they form a significant portion of its users, as he reprovingly suggests that an identification of children as readers and circulation of books to this readership, a strategy which he also uses, is akin to prostitution.

These books directed to a young readership indicate some of the ways in which those working in an expanding book trade might appeal to the market in terms of age but also highlight its limits. It is difficult to determine if there was a corresponding market of children who read or bought these books. Although printers and booksellers recognized the economic profit that might be made in reproducing a range of books purporting to be for the young, this does not necessarily mean that the young constituted a significant portion of the market for books.[91] A notebook collection of 144 riddles compiled by three children of the Holme family, including the teenage Randle Holme, at their home in Chester in the 1640s indicates that children may have accessed the genre of riddles in a number of ways.[92] It is possible that the children copied these riddles from printed riddle books for children. Over one third of the riddles in this manuscript are similar to those contained in the 1631 version of *The Book of Merry Riddles,* and riddles 17 to 21 not only have similar wording to riddles in another well-known riddle book, *The Riddles of Heraclitus and Democritus* (1598), but also follow the same sequence, suggesting direct copying from this book.[93] However, given the wide circulation of these riddles in oral as well as textual form, it is likely, as Adam Fox suggests, that many of these 'poorly worded and incomplete [...] juvenile scribblings [...]' were written from memory.[94] Nonetheless this manuscript collection of readers does shed light on children's reading and book ownership as it was shared and read by the Holme siblings. Early sections of the manuscript completed by one young scribe, for instance, are later read, corrected and completed by another of the children.[95] Moreover, it seems that this text was compiled by the young Holme children to be shared among themselves: a communal riddle book for use by the children of the household. Alice, the youngest Holme child, born in 1636, annotates the manuscript by signing her name in the final blank sheet in an inexperienced hand indicative of someone first learning how to write.[96] Although this might indicate book 'use' rather than readership, it is possible that Alice read the riddles contained in it, potentially learning, copying, reciting and making these riddles her own in ways not evidenced by the extant text. Her signature raises the possibility that the collection and reading of riddles and the associated demonstration of wit is the leisure activity of a group of children including, but not limited to, those responsible for the composition of the manuscript.

This shared riddle book signals the ways in which children may have creatively produced and read their own books, and indicates their consumption as readers of the material identified in printed culture as appealing to them. Yet it suggests a restricted market for such texts if children produced their own versions. The cost of books is, of course, a factor in ownership, and the Holme children are not alone in producing their own versions. Children were trained at school to compile quotations from their reading in a commonplace book for their future reading and use.[97] The young Elizabeth Isham 'finding a louse paper of the Epistles of Saint John ... folded it up and made mee a little booke of it', and keeping it in her pocket read 'it often to my selfe'.[98] Grammar schools may have provided a more ready market as some boys, or their parents, bought books for their education, such as John Lycoris, who bought his copy of Edward Cocker's *Arts Glory. Or The Pen-Man's Treasurie* (1657) in 1658 and Francis Lynn who was bought a Bible, *The Practise of Pietie* and 'Dr William's Catechism' by his father for his schooling in 1689.[99] However, in many instances boys accessed the copies owned by the school, which included handwritten editions compiled by the masters to avoid the cost of buying books.[100] Like Bunyan's narrator and Kirkman, many children read histories, romances and chivalric tales as recreation in their younger years, and remember this in their adult writing, but they offer limited details as to how they accessed these books.[101] When Richard Baxter recalls reading 'romances, fables and old tales' in his childhood in 1620s Shropshire, he does not reveal how he gets these books. However, elsewhere in his autobiography he recalls borrowing books from a neighbour as well as a pedlar who comes to the door, both possible sources of romances for the young reader.[102] The annotations of a number of boys on a 1503 edition of *Bevis of Southampton*, uncovered by Nicholas Orme, provide further evidence of the reading and ownership of such books during childhood.[103] John Betts, Thomas Betts and John Gowd mark this copy of *Bevis* with drawings, underlining, short sentences in Latin and statements of ownership in the early seventeenth century, indicating the sharing of reading material among young boys. Each crosses out or writes over the claim of the previous reader, marking the book as his own even if only temporarily. It is possible that the boys traded the book in the method suggested by Kirkman's *The Unlucky Citizen*, however, it is more likely that the boys came into contact with the book as part of their studies. In this case, a common schoolmaster may have loaned the book to the boys.

Early modern children commonly encountered their reading material via the decisions and purchases of adults. Some children accessed books as a result of charitable donations. Anne Clifford and Rachel Fane donated books to charity schools during their lifetimes, and the 1639 will of Francis Pynner states that the remainder of his money should be put to 'godly and charitable uses', including 'for the buyeing and providing of horne bookes and primers to be given to poore children of the said parish of St Maries, in Bury aforesaid'.[104] Some read their parents' books: Lady Jane Lumley, for example, had access to her father's library during her youth in the mid-sixteenth century and Abraham Cowley recalls in 1668 that he 'happened to fall upon' a copy of '*Spencers* Works' in his mother's parlour when he was younger than 12.[105] Others were given books as gifts, often by parents or godparents. In 1565, the schoolmaster John Brechtgirdle left his copies of schoolbooks to his godsons.[106] In the early seventeenth century, Lady Frances Egerton passed on her Bible and devotional works to her daughters and book for 'Young Gentlemen Readers' to her son'.[107] The author William Lower gave a copy of his romance translations to his young daughter, Elizabeth, in 1659.[108] Adam Martindale recalls that when he was 6, in 1629, his godmother gave him his first ABC.[109] Elizabeth Hassen's note on the front leaf of her copy of John Kettlewell's *The Practical Believer* (1688), that this book was 'given me by Mʳˢ Aspley who is my/Godmother/1697', may be another example of this practice.[110] In the 1650s, Ralph Verney promises to send his goddaughter, Anne Denton, 'halfe a dozen of the French bookes to begin your Library', recommending in particular that she read 'romances, plays, poetry, stories of illustrious (not learned) women'.[111] It is possible that Hannah Barrow received her copy of Richard Hodges' *The Grounds of Learning* (1650) as a Christmas gift.[112] In the early seventeenth century, Elizabeth Isham's mother gave her young daughter a number of prayer books, her father bought her a Bible, her grandparents left her copies of their prayerbooks and her nurse sent her an unnamed work by George Withers as well as 'play books'.[113] Isham also seems to regularly request access to her father's books, and is allowed to read many from his personal library, although she does note that he refuses to lend her 'playbooks'.[114] Her brother also lends her books, including 'Sir phillips sidnes Booke', which on reading in her twenties, Isham claims 'I hard much comended by some and others againe discomended the reading of such Bookes of love. but I found no such hurt.'[115] Her brother also facilitates his own daughters' access to reading material including romances, and his 15-year-old daughter Jane notes in a letter to him that 'I have not read any story book since you was here, only Sir Philip Sidney'.[116] Children's access to books may have been regularly mediated by the decisions of their elders, but this did not necessarily mean that their access conformed to prescriptive moral advice on what they should read.

Elizabeth Isham's extensive record of her reading and access to books throughout her life sheds light on this young reader's extensive and varied access to books, primarily mediated by family members. Yet Isham also bought her own books on one occasion. She recalls in her *Booke of Rememberance* that at the age of 11 or 12 she sold the eggs from her hen, 'gathered mony' and 'bought me 2 bookes'.[117] Whether or not the isolated instances of book buying remembered by Isham and by Francis Kirkman in *The Unlucky Citizen* are representative of wider practices of independent buying by early modern children, they indicate one way in which children may have had agency in the marketplace. Young people

who worked, such as youthful apprentices, may have also had some pur-
chasing power and provided a market for the wide range of books identifying the young as readers. However, generally the status of being a child
was identified as one of dependence, which would have included financial
dependence. Children lacking the means to buy may have asserted their
desires as consumers in other ways, for example, requesting certain books.
In Robert Russel's *A Little Book for Children and Youth* (*c.* 1693–1696),
he advises his child readers to get their mother to buy them a copy of
James Janeway's *A Token for Children* (1671).[118] William Wycherley's *The
Plain Dealer* (1677) offers a dramatic representation of this early modern
pester power of sorts when Jerry Blackacre, 'under age and his mother's
government', visits the bookstalls at Westminster Hall with his mother.
Jerry conveys his literary tastes, requesting '*St George for Christendom; or,
the Seven Champions of England*' or a 'play'. Yet given that he is a youth
under his mother's charge and lacking autonomy in this marketplace, he is
instead limited to the book that his mother wants him to read as preparation for the law: Sir Richard Hutton's *The Young Clerk's Guide*, first
printed in 1649.[119] Those defined by early modern culture as being children or youths had by definition limited agency as consumers, but they
may have held some influence over the parents and guardians who bought
them books.

'To Play the Childe Againe'

If children were limited as purchasers and were more likely to be given
books that would benefit their educational or religious upbringing by
those who bought their books for them, why did authors and publishers
market books of romance, delight and pastimes as suited to this age-
inflected community of readers? Francis Kirkman's framing of his
romances and histories hints at the potential benefits. He suggests in
the 1673 preface to his edition of *Don Bellianis* that it 'is convenient'
for all of 'what Age or Sex soever' to read 'these sorts of Historyes' and
urges:

> if thou art Young, begin now, or else when thou comest to be Old, and hast
> any leisure; and if one of these Books chances into thy hand, thou wilt be so
> pleased with it, that read them thou must, and be in danger to be laughed
> at by those of the Younger sort, who having already read them, and being
> past that Knowledge, Laugh at thy Ignorance. (n.p.)

With what Lori Humphrey Newcomb calls 'an ironic generational awareness' in which 'one must read the right books to keep up with one's generation', Kirkman primarily appeals to readers currently in the earlier stages of the life cycle and threatens shame to those who do not read these books in their younger years.[120] However, he proceeds by highlighting the advantages of reading these books in old age. He claims that those 'grave Citizens' who:

> in their latter dayes, having met with a Part of this History, or that of the Famous *Parismus*, have fallen so much in love with them, that they have become conceitedly Young and Amorous, and so highly pleased that they have run through all the Books of this Nature and Quality. (n.p.)

Kirkman claims to achieve two things by printing these romances. He makes available texts that are essential for the young to relate to their peers and he offers older readers an opportunity to return to youth. The reading experience offered by his books permits all, even those in the final stages of life, a means of becoming 'conceitedly Young and Amorous'. Kirkman's address 'To the reader' does not necessarily depend on an existing market but creates two potential groups of readers in order to justify its publication: young readers wanting to participate in the reading community of their age group and older readers to whom it offers an alternative pleasure—a release from adulthood and temporary return to youth.

Seventeenth-century books promising recreation and leisure to the young, therefore, do not rely on a youthful market or reveal much about what children actually read. Instead, by associating certain texts with children and youths, they suggest that to indulge in idle toys and recreational reading practices was to some extent a childish act. They draw on wider cultural perceptions of children as desiring play and pleasure to advertise a return to this pre-adult state through the reading experience. Religious and moral writings deemed this a dangerous and morally corrupt act. As George Halifax warns in his seventeenth-century advice book, 'to be eager in the pursuit of pleasure whilst you are *Young*, is dangerous; to catch at it in riper *Yeares*, is grasping a shadow that will not be held, besides that by being less natural it growth to be indecent'.[121] For ageing individuals in early modern society, a return to a state of childishness was an unattractive inevitability as old age was commonly depicted as 'second childishness', a stage of life when the mind again gave precedence to 'childish childhood'.[122] Yet the books discussed in this chapter construct a temporary return to a stage of life during which indulgence in folly, mirth and recreation was permissible, and even desirable. They provide a space for the momentary release from the restrictions of adulthood. Like William Hornby's call to professionals to remember 'the seede and graine/Of skill' to which 'they were first beholden' when offering 'A Tale' of his own childhood, which he claims exceeds the stories of 'valiant Guy' and the 'Mirror of Knight-hood' in *Hornbyes Hornbook* (1622), many early modern books ostensibly for children recognize the extent to which comic, pleasant and fantastical texts might offer older readers a wistful return to childhood, issues that continue to inform debates about the function and readership of children's literature today.[123] Texts like the riddle books, *Youth's Treasury* and *Sports and Pastimes* on the one hand constitute material objects, the toys of childhood, that might be shared and read together by the young. They also offer—via reading—a return to the imaginative state of play and fancy associated with childhood and youth in this period. In reading as a child, any early modern reader can, as Lady Arabella Stuart suggests when she plays children's games, 'playe the childe againe'.[124] Childhood is a performative state, and reading is one way in which this identity is constructed in early modern culture.

The framing of early modern books as suited to particular readers reveals more about perceived modes of reading, or the potential reading experience that the same text might offer to multiple categories of reader, than it does about the intended or actual readers of these books in early modern England. They produce a rhetoric of reading childishly. In bringing together associations between children, play and folly, these texts shed light on one understanding of childhood in the period as a distinct cognitive state and reveal what these books might offer to readers at all stages of the life cycle. They establish a set of reading practices that are inflected by age: practices that are deemed childish or youthful but that may be appropriated by any age group. This has significant implications for approaches to early modern children's literature. It is more productive to think in terms of what constituted childish or youthful reading practices than to attempt to recover a body of children's books in early modern England as 'children's literature'. For, as Roger Chartier argues in relation to popular culture, 'it is clear that the appropriation of texts, codes or values in a given society may be a more distinctive factor than the always illusory correspondence between a series of cultural artifacts and a specific sociocultural level'.[125] Whereas books for children in early modern England always overlap with those written for, marketed to or read by other types of readers, there are modes of reading and means of engaging with or appropriating texts that are constructed as childish or youthful. Books claiming to provide recreation and mirth and accounts of how they should be read and were read might only shed light on one side of this multi-faceted topic, but they do reveal a significant aspect of what it meant to read as a child in early modern England. In the marketplace of early printed texts, it is an opportunity for the reader—no matter what their age—to return to the pleasures, delight and folly that are, to a certain extent, expected of the young but deemed unacceptable in older age.

NOTES

1. John Bunyan, *A Few Sighs from Hell* (London, 1658), 157.
2. On Bunyan's *The Pilgrim's Progress* (1678) and *A Book for Boys and Girls* (1686) as children's literature, see Shannon Murray, '*A Book for Boys and Girls: Or, Country Rhimes for Children*: Bunyan and Literature for Children', in *The Cambridge Companion to John Bunyan*, ed. Anne Dunan-Page (Cambridge: Cambridge University Press, 2010), 120–136.
3. See Joshua Phillips, *English Fictions of Communal Identity, 1485–1603* (Aldershot: Ashgate, 2010), 122; Tessa Watt, *Cheap Print and Popular Piety, 1550–1640* (Cambridge: Cambridge University Press, 1991), 39–40.
4. Edward Bagshaw, *The Life and Death of Mr. Vavasour Powell* (London, 1671), 2; N. H. Keeble, ed., *The Autobiography of Richard Baxter* (New York: Rowman and Littlefield, 1974), 4–6. See Chap. 6 for discussion of this trope of childhood reading.
5. Douglas Greene, ed. *The Meditations of Lady Elizabeth Delaval* (Gateshead: Northumberland Press, 1978), 45.
6. Juan Luis Vives, *The Instruction of a Christian Woman* (London, 1592), C6r; Richard Baxter, *A Breviate of the Life of Margaret* (London, 1681), A2r–v. Thomas Salter, *The Mirrhor of Modestie* (London, 1579), B2v.
7. Teresa Michals, *Books for Children, Books for Adults: Age and the Novel from Defoe to James* (Cambridge: Cambridge University Press, 2014), 2.
8. Paul Griffiths highlights that youth is perceived as distinct from child-hood as a phase in the life cycle in many early modern contexts (*Youth and Authority: Formative Experiences in England 1560–1640* [Oxford: Oxford University Press, 1996], 18.) However, this chapter proposes that the terminology of being a child or youth intersect in the concept of read-ing childishly in younger years.
9. Michals, 3.

10. Michals, 20–21.
11. Griffiths, 18.
12. Hezekiah Woodward, *A Childe's Patrimony* (London, 1640), 161. Further references are given in the text.
13. See Chap. 2.
14. Francis Hawkins, *Youth's Behaviour* (London, 1651), title woodcut; Thomas Sprat, 'An Account of the Life and Writings of Mr. Abraham Cowley', in *The Works of Mr. Abraham Cowley* (London, 1668), A2r.
15. Cited in David Scott Wilson-Okamura, *Virgil in the Renaissance* (Cambridge: Cambridge University Press, 2010), 215.
16. *Aesop Improved* (London, 1673), n.p.
17. Jacqueline Rose, *The Case of Peter Pan* (Philadelphia: University of Pennsylvania Press, 1993), 54–55.
18. William Sloane, *Children's Books in England and America in the Seventeenth Century* (New York: Columbia University Press, 1955), 120; Daniel Kline, ed., *Medieval Literature for Children* (London: Routledge, 2003), 4.
19. F. J. Harvey Darton, *Children's Books in England* (Cambridge: Cambridge University Press, 1982), 1. For example, Peter Hunt, *An Introduction to Children's Literature* (Oxford: Oxford University Press, 1994); Mary Thwaite, *From Primer to Pleasure in Reading* (London: The Library Association, 1972). This has been challenged by more recent studies, for example, Matthew Grenby and Andrea Immel, ed., *The Cambridge Companion to Children's Literature* (Cambridge: Cambridge University Press, 2009).
20. Desiderius Erasmus, 'A Declamation on the Subject of Early Liberal Education for Children', in *The Collected Works of Erasmus*, ed. J. K. Sowards (Toronto: Toronto University Press, 1985), 339; John Brinsley, *Ludus Literarius* (London, 1627), A4r.
21. Charles Hoole, *Orbis Sensualium Pictus* (London, 1659), A4v.
22. Charles Hoole, *A New Discovery of the Old Art of Teaching Schoole* (London, 1660), 63.
23. Thomas Wright, *The Passions of the Mind* (London, 1601), 12. See Michael Witmore, *Pretty Creatures: Children and Fiction in the English Renaissance* (Ithaca: Cornell University Press, 2007), especially 39, 211.
24. David Rudd, 'Theorising and Theories: How Does Children's Literature Exist?', in *Understanding Children's Literature*, ed. Peter Hunt (London: Routledge, 2000), 15–29.
25. Robert Matz, *Defending Literature in Early Modern England* (Cambridge: Cambridge University Press, 2000), 2.
26. Philip Sidney, *An Apology for Poetry*, ed. Geoffrey Shepherd and R. W. Masten (Manchester: Manchester University Press, 2002), 81.

27. Philip Sidney, *The Countess of Pembroke's Arcadia*, ed. Katherine Duncan-Jones (Oxford: Oxford University Press, 1994), 3.

28. See Katherine Duncan-Jones, 'Philip Sidney's Toys', *Proceedings of the British Academy* 66 (1980): 161–178.

29. Heidi Brayman Hackel, *Reading Material in Early Modern England* (Cambridge: Cambridge University Press, 2005), 137–95; Helen Hackett, *Women and Romance Fiction in the English Renaissance* (Cambridge: Cambridge University Press, 2000), 101–129; Caroline Lucas, *Writing for Women: The Example of Woman as Reader in Elizabethan Romance* (Milton Keynes: Open University Press, 1989), 118–132.

30. Duncan-Jones, 161.

31. Joseph Campana, 'Boy Toys and Liquid Joys: Pleasure and Power in the Bower of Bliss', *Modern Philology* 106.3 (2009): 465–496.

32. Duncan-Jones, 161. *OED*, defs 1 and 6.

33. Kline, 9.

34. On gendering of childhood, see Naomi Miller and Naomi Yavneh, 'Early Modern Children as Subjects: Gender Matters', in *Gender and Early Modern Constructions of Childhood*, ed. Naomi Miller and Naomi Yavneh (Aldershot: Ashgate, 2011), 1–16.

35. Margaret Tyler, *The Mirrour of Princely Deedes and Knighthood* (c. 1578), in *The Early Modern Englishwoman: A Facsimile Library of Essential Works*, ed. Kathryn Coed, Part I, vol. 8 (Aldershot: Ashgate, 1996), A2r.

36. Tyler, A3r.

37. See Tina Krontiris, 'Breaking Barriers of Genre and Gender: Margaret Tyler's Translation of *The Mirrour of Knighthood*', *English Literary Renaissance* 18 (1988): 19–39.

38. Vives, D1r; Edward Dering, *A Briefe and Necessary Instruction* (London, 1572), A2v.

39. Francis Meres, *Palladis Tamia* (London, 1598), 268v.

40. Francis Lenton, *The Young Man's Whirligig* (London, 1629), 4.

41. William Hawkins, *Apollo Shroving* (London, 1626), 56.

42. On the long-standing association of romance with childish intellect, see Phillipa Hardman, 'Popular Romances and Young Readers', in *A Companion to Medieval Popular Romance*, ed. Raluca Radulescu and Cory James Rushton (Cambridge: Brewer, 2009), 150–164.

43. Brayman Hackel, 4; Juliet Fleming, 'The French Garden: An Introduction to Women's French', *English Literary History* 56.1 (1989): 19–51; Hackett, 6–9.

44. Katharine Craik, *Reading Sensations in Early Modern England* (Basingstoke: Palgrave Macmillan, 2007), 2. See also Mary Ellen Lamb, 'Apologizing for Pleasure in Sidney's "Apology for Poetry": The Nurse of Abuse Meets the Tudor Grammar School', *Criticism* 36.4 (1994): 499–520.

45. See Gillian Avery, 'The Puritans and their Heirs', in *Children and Their Books*, ed. Gillian Avery and Julia Briggs (Oxford: Clarendon Press, 1989), 95–118.
46. Edward Calver, *Passion and Discretion, in Youth and Age* (London, 1641), 13; Wright, 12.
47. Anne Bradstreet, 'Of The Foure Ages of Man', in *The Works of Anne Bradstreet*, ed. Jeannine Hensley (Cambridge: Belknap Press, 1967), 53.
48. Hawkins, 36.
49. Samuel Clarke, *A Collection of the Lives of Ten Eminent Divines* (London, 1662), 95–6.
50. James Janeway, *A Token for Children* (London, 1676), 19, 24.
51. Francis Kirkman, *The Unlucky Citizen* (London, 1673), 10–11. Further references are given in the text.
52. See Jody Greene, 'Francis Kirkman's Counterfeit Authority: Autobiography, Subjectivity, Print', *PMLA* 121.1 (2006): 18–19.
53. Miguel de Cervantes, *The Ingenious Hidalgo Don Quixote de la Mancha*, trans. John Rutherford (London, 2003), 26–27.
54. Jacques Du Bosc, *The Compleat Woman* (London, 1639), 12–15.
55. See Kirkman, *Unlucky Citizen*, 11, and the preface to Francis Kirkman, *The Honour of Chivalry* (London, 1664), A3v. Further references are given in the text.
56. Lori Humphrey Newcomb, 'Kirkman, Francis (b. 1632, d. in or after 1680', in *Oxford Dictionary of National Biography*, ed. David Cannadine (Oxford: Oxford University Press, 2004), http://www.oxforddnb.com/view/article/15672, accessed 9 Dec. 2011. See also R. C. Bald, 'Francis Kirkman, Bookseller and Author', *Modern Philology* 41.1 (1943): 17–32.
57. See Kirkman, *Unlucky Citizen*, 13–14. Francis Kirkman, *The Famous and Renowned History of Amadis de Gaule* (London, 1652).
58. Francis Kirkman, *The Famous and Delectable History of Don Bellianis of Greece* (London, 1673), n.p. Further references are given in the text. On the publication dates of Kirkman's three parts of *Don Bellianis*, see Bald, 31.
59. Francis Kirkman, *The Counterfeit Lady Unveiled* (London, 1673), 9–10.
60. Francis Kirkman, *The History of Prince Erastus* (London, 1674), A2v. On editions of *The Seven Wise Masters of Rome*, see Jane Bingham and Grayce Scholt, *Fifteen Centuries of Children's Literature* (London: Greenwood Press, 1980), 101.
61. Margaret Spufford, *Small Books and Pleasant Histories: Popular Fiction and Its Readership in Seventeenth-Century England* (London: Methuen, 1981), 74.
62. See Adam Smyth, *'Profit and Delight': Printed Miscellanies in England, 1640–1682* (Detroit: Wayne State University Press, 2004), 36–37.

63. See Paul Salzman, *English Prose Fiction, 1558–1700: A Critical History* (Oxford: Oxford University Press, 1985), 59–69.

64. Robert Greene, *Menaphon* (London, 1589), title page; Robert Greene, *Alcida Greene's Metamorphosis* (London, 1617), title page.

65. On the expanding book trade, see H. S. Bennett, *English Books and Readers 1603–1640* (Cambridge: Cambridge University Press, 1970); Alexandra Halasz, *The Marketplace of Print* (Cambridge: Cambridge University Press, 1997); David Scott Kastan, 'Print, Literary Culture and the Book Trade', in *The Cambridge History of Early Modern English Literature*, ed. David Lowenstein and Janel Mueller (Cambridge: Cambridge University Press, 2002), 81–116.

66. J. G., *A Play-book for Children* (London, 1694), n.p.

67. Kastan, 82.

68. Adam Fox, *Oral and Literate Culture in England, 1500–1700* (Oxford: Clarendon Press, 2000), 208; Malcolm Jones, '"Such pretty things would soon be gone": The Neglected Genres of Popular Verse 1480–1650', in *A New Companion to English Renaissance Literature and Culture*, vol. 2, ed. Michael Hattaway (Oxford: Blackwell Press, 2010), 376–377. Extant editions include 1600, 1617, 1629, 1631, 1660, 1672, 1673, 1685. See William Hazlitt, *Handbook to the Popular, Poetical, and Dramatic Literature of Great Britain* (London: John Russell Smith, 1867), 509. On the associations between childhood and riddles in the period, see Edel Lamb, 'The Riddles of Early Modern Children's Worlds', in *Material Worlds of Childhood in North-Western Europe c. 1350–1800*, ed. Philippa Maddern and Stephanie Tarbin (London: Routledge, 2017).

69. *The Booke O[f] Merrie Riddles* (London, 1617), title page. This is based on the 1600 edition, and is reprinted in 1629 and 1660.

70. See Chap. 4.

71. *OED*, def. 2.

72. Cited in F. J. Harvey Darton, 'Children's Books', in *The Cambridge History of English Literature*, ed. Adolphus William Ward (Cambridge: Cambridge University Press, 1930), 370.

73. *Youth's Treasury* (London, 1688), title page.

74. See Courtney Smith, 'The Seventeenth-Century Drolleries', *Harvard Library Bulletin* 6 (1952): 40–51; Smyth, 1–31.

75. J. M., *Sports and Pastimes* (London, 1676), title page. Further references are given in the text.

76. On terrifying tales for children, see Avery.

77. J. M., 7.

78. See Mark Burnett, *Masters and Servants in English Renaissance Drama and Culture* (Basingstoke: Palgrave Macmillan, 1997), 9, which suggests that books for servants were instrumental in creating a servant culture.

79. Mary Ellen Lamb, 'Inventing the Early Modern Woman Reader Through the World of Goods: Lyly's Gentlewoman Reader and Katherine Stubbes', in *Reading Women: Literacy, Authorship and Culture in the Atlantic World, 1500–1800*, ed. Heidi Brayman Hackel and Catherine Kelly (Philadelphia: University of Pennsylvania Press, 2008), 18.

80. See Nicholas Orme, *Medieval Children* (New Haven: Yale University Press, 2001), 296.

81. See Bennett, 167–169; Kastan, 86–87; Nicholas Orme, 'Children and Literature in Medieval England', *Medium Aevum* 68.2 (1999): 239. David J. Shaw, 'The Book Trade Comes of Age: The Sixteenth Century', in *A Companion to the History of the Book*, ed. Simon Eliot and Jonathan Rose (Oxford: Blackwell, 2007), 221.

82. See Peter Clark, 'The Ownership of Books in England, 1560–1640', in *Schooling and Society: Studies in the History of Education*, ed. Lawrence Stone (Baltimore: Johns Hopkins University Press, 1976), 107.

83. Mary Pollard, *Dublin's Trade in Books, 1550–1800* (Oxford: Clarendon Press, 1989), 34.

84. On the range and popularity of advice books, Judith St John, 'I Have Been Dying to Tell You: Early Advice Books for Children', *The Lion and the Unicorn* 29.1 (2005): 52–64; Louis B. Wright, 'Handbook Learning of the Renaissance Middle Class', *Studies in Philology* 28.1 (1931): 55–86.

85. *A Table of Good Nurture* (London, 1625); *An Hundred Godly Lessons that a Mother on her Death-Bed gave to her Children* (London, *c.* 1686–1688).

86. See Ben Jonson, *Bartholomew Fair*, in *The Cambridge Edition of the Works of Ben Jonson*, ed. David Bevington, Martin Butler and Ian Donaldson (Cambridge: Cambridge University Press, 2012), in which Cokes recalls 'the ballads over the nursery-chimney at home o' my own pasting up' (3.5.44–5).

87. See Avery, 99–101; Robert Mayer, 'Nathaniel Crouch, Bookseller and Historian: Popular Historiography and Cultural Power in Late Seventeenth-Century England', *Eighteenth-Century Studies* 27.3 (1994): 391–419; Jason McElligott, 'Crouch, Nathaniel [Robert Burton] (c. 1640–1725?)', in *Oxford Dictionary of National Biography*, http://www.oxforddnb.com/view/article/52645, accessed 16 Mar. 2011.

88. R. B., *Youth's Divine Pastime* (London, 1691), title page.

89. Avery, 99.

90. *Aesop Improved*, n.p. On early editions of Aesop, see Seth Lerer, *Children's Literature: A Reader's History, from Aesop to Harry Potter* (Chicago: University of Chicago Press, 2008), 110–111.

91. See Orme, *Medieval*, 296.

92. See British Library Harley Manuscript 1960. Randle Holme (b. 1627) enters the final 31 riddles. It is likely that the other scribes are his younger siblings: either Katherine (b. 1629), William (b. 1631), or Elizabeth (b. 1632/3). For more information on the manuscript and its scribes, see Fox, 209; Lamb, 'The Riddles'; Frederick Tupper, 'The Holme Riddles (MS. Harl. 1960)', *Modern Language Association* 18.2 (1903): 211–272.

93. See BL Harley MS 1960, 3r–v and riddles 27–29 and 50–51 in *The Riddles of Heraclitus and Democritus* (London, 1598), B2r-v; C3r-v. Just under one fifth are similar to those contained in the 1617 edition of *The Booke of Merrie Riddles*. On sources of the Holme riddles, see Fox, 209–210; Tupper, 215–217.

94. Fox, 209.

95. For example, the first scribe left the answer for riddle 106 blank and this was later completed by the third scribe, Randle Holme (BL Harley MS 1960, 11v).

96. See Lamb, 'The Riddles', on the identity of this annotator.

97. Kenneth Charlton, *Education in Renaissance England* (London: Routledge, 2013), 110.

98. Elizabeth Isham, *My Booke of Rememberance*, ed. Elizabeth Clarke et al., *Constructing Elizabeth Isham*, University of Warwick, http://web.warwick.ac.uk/english/perdita/Isham/index_bor.htm, accessed 7 Dec. 2011, 14r.

99. See Eve Sanders, *Gender and Literacy on Stage in Early Modern England* (Cambridge: Cambridge University Press, 1998), 167; John Sargeaunt, *Annals of Westminster School* (London: Methuen, 1898), 285–286. The signatures of John and Anne Licoris in 1658 and 1664 on the Newberry Library copy of Edward Cocker's *Arts Glory. Or the Pen-Man's Treasurie* (1657) might signal another example of the borrowing of books by siblings and the circulation of books within the domestic space (see Sanders, 167).

100. See Rosemary O'Day, *Education and Society, 1500–1800* (London: Longman, 1982), 52–76; Fred Schurink, 'An Elizabethan Grammar School Exercise Book', *Bodleian Library Record* 18 (2003): 174–196.

101. For example, Robert Ashley remembers reading *Bevis of Southampton*, *Guy of Warwick*, *The History of Valentine and Orson* and *The Life of King Arthur of Britain* as a 15-year-old. Robert Boyle read *Amadis de Gaule* during a period of convalescence aged 10. Richard Norwood recollects that he took 'great delight in reading in vain and corrupt books as *Palmerin de Olivia, The Seven Champions*' during his youth. See Matthew Grenby, 'Chapbooks, Children and Children's Literature', *The Library* 8 (2007): 281; Ronald Crane, 'The Reading of an Elizabethan Youth', *Modern Philology* 11 (1913–1914): 269–71; Lori Humphrey Newcomb,

'Gendering Prose Romance in Renaissance England', in *A Companion to Romance*, ed. Corinne Saunders (Oxford: Oxford University Press, 2004), 133; Wesley Frank Craven and Walter B. Hayward, ed., *The Journal of Richard Norwood* (New York: Scholar Press, 1945), 17.

102. Alec Ryrie, *Being Protestant in Reformation Britain* (Oxford: Oxford University Press, 2013), 282.

103. Orme, *Medieval*, 298–304. See Chap. 4 for further discussion.

104. See Edith Snook, 'Reading Women', in *The Cambridge Companion to Early Modern Women's Writing*, ed. Laura Lunger Knoppers (Cambridge: Cambridge University Press, 2009), 47; Caroline Bowden, 'The Notebooks of Rachel Fane: Education for Authorship?', in *Early Modern Women's Manuscript Writing: Selected Papers from the Trinty/Trent Colloquium*, ed. Victoria Burke and Jonathan Gibson (Aldershot: Ashgate, 2004), 173; Samuel Tymms, ed., *Wills and Inventories from the Registers of the Commissary of Bury, St Edmund's* (London: Camden Society, 1850), 176.

105. Marta Straznicky, *Privacy, Playreading, and Women's Closet Drama, 1550–1700* (Cambridge: Cambridge University Press, 2004), 19–47; Abraham Cowley, 'Of Myself', *The Works of Mr. Abraham Cowley* (London, 1668), 144.

106. See T. W. Baldwin, *William Shakespere's Small Latine and Lesse Greeke* (Chicago: University of Chicago Press, 1944), 490–491.

107. Brayman Hackel, 147.

108. See David Kathman, 'Lower, Sir William (*c.*1610–1662)', in *Oxford Dictionary of National Biography*, http://www.oxforddnb.com/view/article/17094, accessed 18 May 2017.

109. Sloane, 7.

110. See Newcastle University Library copy of John Kettlewell, *The Practical Believer* (London, 1688) (K238.1 KET).

111. Cited in Anthony Fletcher, *Growing Up in England: The Experience of Childhood, 1600–1914* (New Haven: Yale University Press, 2010), 245.

112. See Chap. 4, 133, and Maddy Smith, 'Value in Unexpected Places: The Sole Surviving Copy of *The Grounds of Learning*, a Seventeenth-Century Schoolbook', *Untold Loves Blog*, 7 Feb. 2017, http://blogs.bl.uk/untoldlives/2017/02/value-in-unexpected-places-the-sole-surviving-copy-of-the-grounds-of-learning-a-seventeenth-century-.html

113. Isham, 5r, 8r, 14r, 16v. See further discussion of Isham in Chap. 6.

114. Isham, 26r.

115. Isham, 26r.

116. Isaac Stephens, *Under the Shadow of the Patriarch: Elizabeth Isham and her World in Seventeenth-Century Northamptonshire*, Unpublished PhD dissertation (University of California Riverside, 2008), 177.

117. Isham,17v.
118. Robert Russel, *A Little Book for Children and Youth* (London, *c.* 1693–1696), vol. I, A4v.
119. William Wycherley, *The Plain Dealer*, in *The Country Wife and Other Plays*, ed. Peter Dixon (Oxford: Oxford University Press, 1996), 3.1.305–307, 3.1.315.
120. Lori Humphrey Newcomb, *Reading Popular Romance in Early Modern England* (New York: Columbia University Press, 2002), 151.
121. George Savile, *The Lady's New Year's Gift* (London, 1688), 155.
122. William Shakespeare, *As You Like It*, in *The Norton Shakespeare*, ed. Stephen Greenblatt et al. (New York: W. W. Norton & Co., 2008), 2.7.164; Bradstreet, 52.
123. William Hornby, *Hornbyes Hornbook* (London, 1622), B4, B7r–v. See U.C. Knoepflmacher, 'Children's Texts and the Grown-Up Reader', in *Cambridge Companion to Children's Literature*, 159–173.
124. Cited in Katherine Larson, '"Certein childeplayes remembred by the fare ladies": Girls and their Games', in *Gender and Early Modern Constructions of Childhood*, 67.
125. Roger Chartier, *Forms and Meanings: Texts, Performances, and Audiences from Codex to Computer* (Philadelphia: University of Pennsylvania State Press, 1995), 89.

CHAPTER 4

Reading Boyhood: The Books and Reading Practices of Early Modern Schoolboys

We send them to learn their grammar and their Terence, and they learn their playbooks![1]

'There is more direct evidence on the reading of schoolboys', Margaret Spufford suggests, 'than any other social group' in the early modern period. However, even this, she admits, 'remains pitifully little'.[2] The wide range of ABC books, primers and catechisms produced for the young learning to read at home and in the petty schools, and translations and textbooks written for the boys advancing their education at the all-male grammar schools, alongside the records of such schools, including curricula, statutes and lists of books owned, provide us with a substantial insight into the wide range of books that were recommended and accessible to this particular category of early modern child.[3] Scholarship on the early modern grammar school has facilitated consideration of the schoolboy as reader.[4] The exciting archival discoveries of scholars such as Nicholas Orme and Fred Schurink have shed further light on the books read by early schoolboys, in English and Latin, and on how they engaged with these books.[5] As Chap. 3 proposed, grammar schoolboys were recognized as a significant market for a range of books, from Thomas Newbery's representation of the scholar as the buyer of educational texts such as 'Primers, and abces and bookes of small charge' in 1563 to the late seventeenth-century anthologies of riddles, songs and verse that were adapted for and

© The Author(s) 2018
E. Lamb, *Reading Children in Early Modern Culture*,
Early Modern Literature in History,
https://doi.org/10.1007/978-3-319-70359-6_4

marketed to the youthful scholar.[6] Furthermore, as the epigraph to this chapter highlights, the books encountered at schools often exceeded the expectations of parents, educators or publishers. Articulating the fear that schoolmasters 'make all their scholars play boys', Gossip Censure suggests in Ben Jonson's *The Staple of News* (first published 1631) that boys were exposed to a range of reading experiences at school that took them beyond recommended curricula.[7] This chapter focuses on the books and reading experiences of early modern schoolboys to investigate the ways in which the gendered and aged identity of the *boy* was produced through diverse reading experiences. It argues that training in reading and the witty deployment of reading material enabled early modern schoolboys to assert their boyhood, a term that was used from the 1570s to refer to the state of being a boy.[8]

Cultures of reading are crucial to the early modern concept of the schoolboy. In woodcuts on late sixteenth- and early seventeenth-century schoolbooks, the boy at school is commonly depicted with book in hand, or at least on hand.[9] In the theatre, books functioned as staging properties to define a young male character as a schoolboy. In *How A Man May Chuse a Good Wife from a Bad* (1602) the 'ii or iii Boyes' are marked as schoolboys by 'their Bookes in their hands' when they come on stage to deliver their lesson before their master.[10] As Amanda Piesse has argued, young Lucius' bundle of books in Shakespeare's *Titus Andronicus* (1594), which includes Ovid's *Metamorphosis* given to him by his mother, and his 'status as receptor of standard schoolboy stories' align him with the figure of the schoolboy and disclose the wider deployment of education as a theme of the play.[11] In Shakespeare's *The Merry Wives of Windsor* (1602), John Marston's *What You Will* (1607) and Edward Sharpham's *Cupid's Whirligig* (1607) schoolboys are characterized through their ability, or their inability, to recite the lessons from the standard Latin grammar book of the sixteenth and seventeenth centuries: William Lily's *A Short Introduction of Grammer*.[12] Accounts of reading also characterize boys as young scholars in early modern plays. As this chapter demonstrates, William Hawkins' *Apollo Shroving*, written for performance by Hawkins' scholars at his grammar school in Suffolk *c.* 1626, depicts a variety of schoolboy characters, each defined by their relationships with their books. The schoolbook and knowledge of these books signified schoolboy status in early modern culture. Like the 'good' child discussed in Chap. 2, the ideal schoolboy is portrayed as committed to his book. Yet accounts of the early modern schoolroom in books for children and in drama, frequently depict the schoolboy as an unruly figure, frequently tempted by 'pleasure' or 'play to 'neglect his booke'.[13] This chapter reads depictions of boys and their schoolbooks in the books produced for the schoolroom and in fictional representations of the schoolroom on the early modern stage alongside marginalia of early modern schoolboy readers to analyse the constitutive role of reading in schoolboy identity.[14]

Critical work on the lessons of the schoolroom has focused on the men produced via the educational cultures of reading. The ways in which the humanist grammar school instilled masculine traits through the methods used to teach a range of subjects, particularly Latin literacy, have been examined in detail. Influenced by Walter Ong's seminal analysis of Latin instruction as a rite of passage through which boys became men, critics such as Richard Halpern have explored the extent to which 'formal schooling was intended to rescue elite male children from the contaminating effects of both a popular milieu and a feminine one'.[15] This analysis has been further refined by feminist critics who have complicated divisions between schoolroom and domestic culture and usefully extended analyses of educational reading to consider the extent to which boys and girls acquired gendered behaviours as they learned to read and write.[16] Despite variations in these readings, most scholars agree that literacy instruction of the early modern schoolroom had a significant role in producing gendered subjects, and that one of the aims of the humanist grammar schoolroom was to produce the adult masculine identities of its subjects. However, while much attention has been lavished on the men and women produced via educational cultures of reading, less has been paid to what these cultures reveal about the boys and girls participating in them. Education in grammar schools did produce versions of adult masculinity through instructing boys in the memorization, pronunciation and imitation of *exempla*; through recitation of reading with the appropriate gesture, vocals and audacity; and through training boys to draw on their learning to invent logical arguments.[17] Yet this model of masculine identity suggests that it is a state that must be acquired through learning and the appropriate performance of this learning, or as Michael Roper and John Tosh suggest, as a state that is 'never fully possessed, but must perpetually be achieved, asserted, and renegotiated'.[18] Such an understanding of masculine identity produced over time through the lessons of the schoolroom sits precariously alongside early modern social practices such as the rituals at the end of infancy that included the breeching of the boy and the movement from the domestic space to the space of work or the all-male institution of the grammar school, which worked to signal an immediate transition out of a feminized childhood towards masculine identity.[19] The diverse early modern cultural signifiers of gendered identity during these early stages of life raise significant questions about how the young boy positioned within this process of learning might be defined. What is the gendered status of the schoolboy who cannot yet, or chooses not to, adequately perform the traits that define ideal masculinity? This chapter argues that the witty schoolboy can manipulate his literacy to assert alternative senses of gendered and aged selfhood that do not sit easily within an oversimplified transition from a feminized infancy to adult masculinity. It suggests that although the early modern schoolroom aims to teach boys how to be men, through their school reading experiences boys also learn how to be boys: a category that is gendered but also aged and related to reading experience.

Judith Gardiner has persuasively argued that age categories should perform a more prominent role in gender theory. Age, she proposes, enables us to conceptualize gender developmentally and 'allows for the possibility of more adequate models'.[20] Attending to age categories complicates early modern manhood. In the period, manhood was associated with youthful prime or middle age, generally identified as the stage between 25 and 50 years old.[21] It is described in Henry Cuffe's *The Differences of the Ages of Man's Life* (1607), for instance, as 'flourishing man age' and 'the strongest age' in which 'a man is come to the highest degree of perfection'.[22] Other stages of the life cycle, whether infancy, childhood or boyhood, young age, youth or *adolescentia* that precede 'manhood' or old age and 'decrepit' old age that follow it, are determined by varying degrees in relation to this ideal stage.[23] The schoolboy's association with the aged categories of boyhood or young age exposes the ways in which early modern masculinity exists as a variety of categories on a developmental scale. Historically, schoolboys entered grammar school between the ages of 7 and 11, but this figure of the schoolboy is also associated more generally with youthful stages of the life cycle in early modern culture.[24] In Jacques' well-known characterization of boyhood in Shakespeare's *As You Like It* (1623), gender, age and learning coalesce in the image of the 'whining schoolboy with his satchel/And shining morning face, creeping like snail/Unwillingly to school'.[25] Moth, the witty page of Shakespeare's *Love's Labour's Lost* (1598) who, as Katie Knowles persuasively argues, characterizes 'the precocious sixteenth-century schoolboy', depicts the connections between age and schoolboy lessons as a seminal part of becoming a man.[26]

When he responds to Armado's question, 'What wilt thou prove?', with 'A man, if I live; and this, "by", "in", and "without", upon the instant', he offers to prove his master's love through a linguistic exercise and occupies the role of schoolteacher instructing his 'negligent student' and schoolboy performing his learning.[27] The grammar lesson delivered here reinforces the idea that manhood is something that must be proven or achieved. Yet it goes further in its comic juxtaposition of the slow process of becoming a man through ageing ('if I live') with the mastery of language and of love. Moth posits apparently conflicting modes of 'proving' a man: age, courtship and the display of learning. Manhood in this construction is not only a gendered state but also depends on temporality or age and on the display of learning—in this case, a command of prepositions and the proof of an argument. In these well-known Shakespearean examples, schooling is portrayed as crucial to the formation of masculine identity but learning is not the only factor in achieving manhood. Age and the deployment of learning are also vital.

Reassessing pedagogical practices through an analysis of the concepts of boyhood and manhood put forward by books produced to train boys in languages, verbal skill and logic, this chapter raises questions about the type of masculinity produced by the all-male institution of the grammar school.[28] Critics have extensively highlighted the gaps between the ideals and achievements of early modern pedagogy, and Lynn Enterline has recently complicated models of learning as producing manhood.[29] In *Shakespeare's Schoolroom*, she compellingly argues that the reading material and ways of reading taught to early modern schoolboys did not simply confer gentlemanly identity but led to the instillation of a range of gendered and class traits via empathy with classical figures, who were often female and non-authoritarian, and through the ways that the deployment of learning 'often took turns the boys' teachers did not seem to expect'.[30] Like Enterline, I focus on moments of dissonance between the ideals of the humanist schoolroom and the experiences of boys in the schoolroom, as depicted by these schoolboys themselves in traces of their reading and in fictional representations of boys at school, to interrogate the ways in which learning and reading produced gendered identity.[31] However, while Enterline argues that the educational processes which required students to mimic a host of passions that were not their own engrained what she terms 'habits of alterity' at the heart of schoolboy 'identity', I suggest that the ways of reading taught in the schoolroom enabled boys to forge a state of boyhood.[32]

As Katie Knowles' important study, *Shakespeare's Boys*, demonstrates, boyhood is an important cultural category that cannot be pinned down or singularly defined, but is determined by the ways in which historical and cultural contexts attach meaning to the figure of the boy.[33] This chapter begins by looking at the extent to which the books produced for school-boys posit an ideal model of instilling manhood through reading and learning, before examining how training in ways of reading and the community of the schoolroom produced what Halpern calls 'autonomous subjects' who assert their distinct identities as boys, a state inflected by their gender and status but also by their learning and their age.[34] It argues that the spaces of schoolboy reading, that is, the physical space and cultural practices of the schoolroom which encouraged communal reading and performances of dialogues and plays, as well as the margins of the texts that were often shared among schoolboys, are sites in which boys might offer alternative versions of age-specific masculine identity. It reads the dramatic representation of schoolboys as readers, focusing specifically on William Hawkins' *Apollo Shroving*, a play written by a schoolmaster but performed by the boys who had been trained to read in the ways outlined in this chapter. This chapter suggests that theatrical performance is one way in which boys can explore the potential impact of their schoolroom reading on their identities and suggests that the performance itself constitutes a reading experience. Finally, this chapter considers the traces left by boys of their encounters with schoolbooks in the form of marginalia to examine the ways in which some historical schoolboys created cultures of boyhood through communal interactions with their books. This chapter, therefore, reads the schoolroom as an arena in which a community of young readers interrogate what it might mean to be a boy.

BOOKS FOR SCHOOLBOYS

Early modern grammar schools provided a ready market for books, and printers and schoolmasters recognized this.[35] The statutes for schools in the sixteenth and seventeenth centuries and the educational reading lists recommended by pedagogues such as Charles Hoole and John Brinsley indicate the need for copies of diverse books ranging from the Bible to *Aesop's Fables*, from Erasmus' dialogues and Cicero's epistles to the poetry of George Herbert.[36] Dictionaries, books of grammar and classical texts were intended to aid in the instruction of Latin the grammar school, yet following the beliefs of humanist educators that religion, moral virtue, wisdom and eloquence should also be taught and might be best taught through the study of classical languages and literature, they were also recommended to teach this range of knowledge and behaviour.[37] Given the cost of books, these would not necessarily been produced for every schoolboy, but the need to have copies for school libraries and for use in the schoolroom by teachers and pupils in their lessons evidently led to high demand for seminal texts.[38] In the 1570s English printers began producing an extensive number of what one referred to as the 'most usuall schoole bookes in Latin' and some sought patents to control this particular area of the market.[39] In addition to producing multiple copies of the authorized Latin grammar book, William Lily's *Short Introduction of Grammer*, and John Withal's commonly used *Short Dictionary for Children* in English and Latin, new editions of Aesop, Cato, Cicero, Corderius, Erasmus, Horace, Ovid, Terence, Virgil and Vives were printed and distributed throughout England and beyond.[40] The majority of all books shipped to Irish merchants, for example, between 1570 and 1601 were hornbooks, grammars and 'small books for children'.[41]

While many editions of established texts were published for use in schools without specifically being adapted for the schoolboy, many were modified to suit the needs of this particular reader. On occasion this involved the compilation of handwritten texts by teachers for use by their students.[42] Other enterprising pedagogues took advantage of the opportunity to participate in an emerging industry of books for children, as they joined with printers to adapt school texts in ways that were influenced by their humanist backgrounds and that allowed them to put their own pedagogical theories into practice, with one seventeenth-century headmaster even setting up a press within the school.[43] Two seventeenth-century schoolmasters, John Brinsley, a schoolmaster at Ashby from 1600, and Charles Hoole, schoolmaster of Rotherham from the 1630s, are noteworthy for their commitment to preparing editions of a range of educational textbooks for use in schools alongside extensive tracts outlining their ideas for education, thus propagating their own pedagogical methods.[44] These included Brinsley's grammar book, *The Posing of Parts* (1612) and his translations of Cicero, Ovid and Virgil; Hoole's edition of William Lily's Latin grammar, his vocabulary book for 'little children' learning the Latin tongue and his translations of Comenius' *Orbis Sensualium Pictus* (1659) and Terence (1676); as well as both schoolmaster-authors' translations of, for example, Leonard Culmann's *Sentences for Children*, Cato, Corderius, Terence, Aesop and of Evaldus Gallus' *Pueriles Confabulatiunculae, or Children's*

Dialogues.[45] Aiming to facilitate use by the schoolboy reader, these books are particularly interesting for the ways in which they manipulate the content and material dimensions of the text to suit this reader. In doing so, they disclose the schoolmasters' understandings of what it means to be a schoolboy. As one sixteenth-century editor of Cato suggests, these authors 'playe the childe agayne' in order to create suitable books for young learners.[46] Hoole contends that the best teachers make 'condescension' to 'a Childe's capacity'.[47] By providing material that is specifically for boy readers, these schoolmasters imaginatively occupy this youthful space. Yet they also produce books that allow boys to inhabit this space of childhood. These books that explicitly aim to 'teache scholars how to be able to reade well, and write true orthographie', 'to furnishe them with varietie of the best morall matter, and with understanding, wisdom, and precepts of virtue, as they growe', 'to imprint Latin in their minds' and 'to grow in our owne English tongue … so to be fitted for divinity, law, or what other calling or faculty soever they shalbe after employed in' and to produce subjects worthy of both 'Church and Commonwealth' construct the scholars' identities as boys—a gender-specific category of childhood produced within this all-male schoolroom.[48]

The translations of Gallus' Dutch and Latin *Pueriles Confabulatiunculae*, printed in English by Brinsley as *Children's Dialogues, Little Conferences, or Talkings Together, or Little Speeches Together, or Dialogues Fit for Children* in 1617, and prepared by Hoole in a bilingual English and Latin edition in the early 1650s and published as *Children's Talke, English & Latine, Divided into Several Clauses: Wherein the Propriety of both Languages is kept, That Children by the Help of their Mother Tongue May More Easily Learn to Discourse in Good Latine Amongst Themselves* in 1659, exemplify many of the ways in which books were made suitable for schoolboys but also highlight the potential effects of training boys to read such material in particular ways.[49] Dialogues, such as those of Gallus and Corderius, were commonly used in English grammar schools for instruction in reading and speaking Latin, and were seen as particularly suited to younger children in the lower forms as, according to schoolmasters such as William Kempe, 'because Children learne first to talke familiarly with their fellowes or others, Dialogs are most easie for their capacitie'.[50] Gallus' dialogues in particular were recommended on various grammar school curricula from the late sixteenth century onwards, to the extent that an edition in Latin was one of the most widely published schoolbooks in England throughout the seventeenth century and was still being advertised as a typical schoolbook in Ireland in the early eighteenth century.[51] In spite of this no edition of this text printed in England survives from before 1666, except for Brinsley's and Hoole's editions, and another English-Latin version prepared by the linguist Joseph Webbe.[52]

Although Brinsley and Hoole's translations are both produced primarily for use by grammar school boys they differ significantly. Hoole prints the Latin translations alongside the English texts and includes dialogues set in a tavern and a dialogue in which one boy seeks permission to leave the schoolroom to answer his catechism. In contrast, Brinsley offers only the English text, censors dialogues that he believes are 'popish' or 'unmeete to season the children's mindes' (n.p.) and retains only those depicting schoolboys. Brinsley's text, therefore, not only acts as a learning resource for grammar school boys, it also adapts the content to ensure that it is suitable for and appealing to boy readers. It focuses on their experiences, offering interlinked dialogues that present methods of learning, punishment for lateness, rows and companionship among the schoolboys, and the tensions between home and school. These dialogues offer narratives of schoolboy experiences, albeit mediated by a schoolmaster-author. In addition, they foreground topical issues in early modern educational cultures. Stereotypes of the tyrannical headmaster ready to dole out punishment, and of the boy in need of punishment, recur in this text, and in school texts throughout the period.[53] Yet the relationship between boys and their schooling is also cast in a more positive light in the depiction of the ludic culture that is central to both Brinsley's and Hoole's educational philosophies.[54] These teachers prioritize play and pleasure as part of the boys' educational experiences. In this respect, Gallus' dialogues, which contain elements of schoolboy humour, camaraderie and present play alongside traditional schoolroom learning, are apt material for these translators. One of the dialogues retained by both Brinsley and Hoole represents play as beneficial to learning as pupils promise to 'ever obey your precepts [...] never offend [... to] bestowe the utter-most diligence in studying' (*Children's Dialogues*, 27) if their schoolmaster gives them leave to play. In another dialogue, two boys in the schoolroom apparently desire play over learning, but their claim that they would like to be 'runn[ing] in the fields', 'leap[ing] in the meadows', fishing, hunting or learning music (*Children's Dialogues*, 28–29) reveals their desires to engage in many of the physical exercises advocated by contemporary pedagogues.[55]

Like numerous books of dialogues produced for early modern schoolboys in the early stages of their grammar school education, such as Juan

Luis Vives' *Linguae Latinae Exercitatio* (1539) and translations of Mathurin Cordier's dialogues, these dialogues repeatedly highlight the processes of becoming masculine in the educational institution. One of the dialogues in Vives' collection, for instance, conveys the crucial function of the school in transforming the child into a man. It depicts a father instructing his young son that the only distinction between the boy and his animal is that while the dog 'cannot become a man. You can, if you will' by going 'where animals go, to come back men', that is, the school.[56] Various dialogues exploring the relationships between home and school reinforce the necessity of leaving the domestic space and the mother behind, and accepting the authority of the master and the schoolroom. For instance, one schoolboy, Bartholomew, defends his lateness to the master claiming that 'My mother commanded me to tarry a little' and blaming his mother, who was 'slacker in preparing' his meal (*Children's Dialogues*, 13). In a typical representation of the boy who recognizes the importance of school, Bartholomew claims that he left the house in spite of his mother, fearing the master's 'government' (*Children's Dialogues*, 13). In another dialogue set in the home, the schoolboy, Dionisius, dismisses his sister who has come to wake him by telling her to 'get thee gone & care for [thy] kitchen' (*Children's Dialogues*, 14). Suggesting that school is an experience that female family members cannot share or understand, he exclaims 'whilest thou prattlest here, the houre goeth away, stripes are prepared for me, which thou feeleth not' (*Children's Dialogues*, 14). Dionisius insists upon the separation between the space of the kitchen, which he establishes as a feminized domain, and the masculine space of the schoolroom to which he now belongs. This schoolbook reinforces, on one level, a reductive model of the domestic versus the schoolroom supported by the largely all-male structure of the grammar school system. It acknowledges learning, discipline and the movement to the schoolroom as early modern social practices that constructed boys' masculine identities as they aged.

While these examples assert a division between the feminized space of the home and the masculine space of the schoolroom, others complicate this model. In one dialogue a pupil who has been prevented from coming to school by his father, who has sent him to work in the fields, is reminded by the master that 'Your father hath command at home, I in the schoole' (*Children's Dialogues*, 17). The movement to the schoolroom represented in this text, therefore, is not only inflected by the gender dynamics of the grammar school but also by economic concerns and social status. The early modern grammar school, and these dialogues, aimed to produce scholarly adult men of a particular status and, according to this dialogue, this entails the rejection of family, labour and the domestic space.[57]

This book, like many others produced for young schoolboys in the seventeenth century, suggests that this status of being a 'man', as Brinsley terms it, is achieved through the ability to utilize logic to construct an argument, demonstrate knowledge and partake wittily in dialogue, and it offers a number of dialogues as examples for imitation.[58] In one of the dialogues two schoolboys, Henry and Gerarde, argue over a seat and in winning this debate Henry, the dialogue concludes, proves his manhood. Throughout the argument the boys mock each other through questions and riddles. When Henry, for example, tells Gerarde to 'sit where dogs sit', Gerarde responds 'And where do dogs sit?' whereupon Henry throws him from his lap to the ground, telling him 'Upon their buttocks' (*Children's Dialogues*, 7). This report of physical action is followed by further threats of violence as Gerarde claims he will hit his fellow pupil. Although Henry initially dares him to, stating that he will then 'find me a man', the two set aside violence when Henry points out their equality, saying: 'O thou mad fellow, may we fight here being consecrated to the same studies, indued with the same precepts of virtue? Get thee gone with such frivolous fables' (*Children's Dialogues*, 8). The movement from anger and violence to a logic and recognition of companionship maps a simplified transition from childhood to adulthood similar to the dialogues representing the separation from the home. Children were frequently associated with the emotional, and with imagination, in contrast to the traits of logic and rationality that Henry ultimately demonstrates.[59] It is perhaps significant that, in offering his response, Henry dismisses Gerarde's 'frivolous fables' or, as this phrase is glossed in the margins, 'pleasing and vaine tales, or babbling' (*Children's Dialogues*, 8) or translated in Hoole's edition as 'idle tales' (*Children's Talke*, 12). Richard Halpern has suggested that the classical curriculum of the grammar school was 'designed in part to alienate youth from more spontaneous forms of popular learning', signalled here by the insistence that the boys dissociate themselves from fables, vain tales and babbling.[60] Yet books of fables were often used in grammar schools by the youngest pupils as their first step to acquiring language, style and moral principles, thus pointing to, as Peter Mack notes, the intersections between popular and educational cultures rather than the exclusion of popular genres from the schoolroom.[61] Brinsley and Hoole even produced their own editions of fables, aimed at children ranging from 'little ones in their first years' who prefer 'play before learning' through to those at grammar school.[62] This dialogue insists upon a progressive model of learning, and hence a simplistic, and unrealistic, continuum of a developing masculine adult identity. In spurning Gerarde's responses as 'frivolous fables' that he must leave behind, Henry urges his fellow pupil to move beyond the pleasing tales of early childhood and of early schooling, as he suggests he has. In acknowledgement of this, Gerarde concludes: 'Now I judge thee [to be] a man, [both] generous and invincible' (*Children's Dialogues*, 8). For Hoole, this version of manhood is further inflected by class, as Gerarde confirms: 'Now I conclude thee to be a gentleman indeed and one that will not be easily beaten' (*Children's Talke*, 12). Rehearsing logic, and by extension rehearsing this dialogue, allows the boys in these dialogues and reading these dialogues to assert a particular version of masculine identity. Being a man or, more specifically, a gentleman is characterized here as an educated and elite gendered identity, signalled by the ability to deliver logical arguments and by its distance from feminized tales and gossip. What boys read is depicted as crucial to the production of adult gendered identities. Reading and learning from these dialogues potentially produces men worthy of the professions, church and the commonwealth, which Brinsley and Hoole suggest is a central function of education.

The Reading Practices of Schoolboys

Whether or not the use of these books in the early modern classroom produces such men is, of course, another question. The ideals of this humanist programme of education map a straightforward development from feminized childhood to adult masculinity characterized by logic, reason and wit. This representation of gender in relation to age has a clear ideological purpose as it offers a concept of manhood that is idealistic, achievable and stable. The versions of Gallus' early modern book for schoolboys posit similar models for becoming masculine through the depiction of the transitions from the spaces, relationships, languages and stories of childhood to those of adulthood. Yet if the dialogues imagine the development of the aggressive boy to the logical man through the rehearsal of one argument, in practice more sustained negotiation of gendered identity is required before the schoolboy users of these books become men. As Diane Purkiss has suggested, these dialogues work to form masculine identity through a repetitive engagement with these transitional moments, demanding repetition precisely because this concept of masculine identity is so unstable.[63] Repetition was central to the reading practices of the early modern schoolroom. While schoolmasters encouraged children to engage with their schoolbooks in different ways, depending on what subject was being taught as well as on the pedagogue's individual methods, repetitive engagement with books was common. Boys were invited to engage with the same texts over again but often in a distinct way on each reading, reading it for understanding, memorization, recitation and imitation.[64] The instructions provided by Brinsley and Hoole on how their schoolboys should read their books suggest that practical repetition further underpinned the cultural production of early modern masculine identity offered by their translations of the dialogues. Recommending that *Pueriles Confabulatinucale* be used in the second form of grammar school on Tuesday and Thursday afternoons, Hoole suggests that the boys should in the first instance read a whole dialogue themselves in both English and Latin to acquaint them with the 'matter of the book' and to 'enable them to read both the Languages more readily'.[65] In addition to its role as a useful way of teaching the 'speaking' of Latin, he thus also views it as a text to be read and to improve reading abilities. For Hoole, reading in English is a crucial part of the language lesson, as it is 'English examples' that 'best help to instruct their understandings in the meaning of what they read, and confirm their memories to keep it'.[66] On the second reading each afternoon, he proposes that the boys should construe the content, reading phrases aloud and then substituting alternatives to practise their command of grammar.[67] The boys should continue in these methods until they have 'gone this book so often over as to be well acquainted with its phrases'.[68] Brinsley also urges that schoolboys engage with his *Children's Dialogues* in multiple ways. In addition to this book being a tool for Latin-learning, he specifies that his edition should be used by children to, in his words, 'grow in our owne English tongue'.[69] The only text he provides in this edition is in English, although it is likely, as Ian Green suggests, that his students would have used this alongside a Latin version of the dialogues.[70] To further facilitate English-learning, Brinsley glosses some words and places what he calls 'over-harsh Grammaticall translations and phrases into the margent [...] lest the children should learne barbarism in our own tong' (*Children's Dialogues*, n.p.). While he seeks to teach Latin, he also strives for fluency of phrasing in the boys' use of English, possibly in response to increasing criticism of Latin language learning as impractical for the schoolboys who would go on to make their living as tradesmen.[71]

These books of dialogues are produced to be read by the boys individually and together, but they are primarily intended to be read or spoken aloud. Both Brinsley and Hoole emphasize that these dialogues are to assist 'young scholars to learne to speake and talke in Latin' (*Children's Dialogues*, n.p.). Given this emphasis on 'saying' the phrases and varying the grammatical constructions, it is likely these dialogues would have been read aloud, or even memorized and recited by groups of boys in the classroom 'without book'. This alternative act of reading, however, potentially functioned to similarly instil the traits of an ideal masculinity. Reading aloud was one way of developing the gendered and aged voice. As James Cleland suggested in 1607, the boy should learn to 'read with a sweet accent, not reading with a sharp shril voice as a woman, or with a rough and huske voice, as an old man doth, but with a pleasant harmonie'.[72] The boy is thus trained to forge an optimum masculine identity that expels the potentially feminine traits of the 'sharp shril' adolescent voice for boys at grammar school and also avoids the 'rough' voice of old age. The ideal reading voice is masculine but also youthful. Like 'manhood' in early modern tracts on age, it occupies a precarious position between the underdeveloped biological state of childhood and the inevitable decline of old age. Early modern masculinity, as Cuffe's accounts of aged identity suggest, was not just seen in terms of manhood, or of boyhood versus manhood; instead childhood, youth, manhood and old age were categories on a continuum of aged masculinity.

Reading aloud thus facilitates the cultivation of a particular version of masculinity between the vocal traits of childhood and old age. In this sense, reading aloud, particularly the recitation of these dialogues, functions in a similar manner to dramatic performance in the early modern grammar schools, which was frequently used as a means of training boys in the skills of the orator, and hence in the masculine traits of boldness and 'audacitye' in, to use Ursula Potter's term, the 'performance space' of the early modern classroom.[73] Yet, if these dialogues were performed as such by the schoolboys 'among themselves', as the title of Hoole's book implies, then these boys would also have had to take on and rehearse the voices of the dialogues' female characters.[74] Hence the boys potentially engaged with the parts of mothers and sisters, and the parts of teachers and masters, as much as with the schoolboy characters. Performing these dialogues aloud did not involve a straightforward identification of schoolboys with their fictional counterparts. However, it did involve a repeated engagement with the narratives of schoolboy experience, and the opportunity to train and control their voices, which, as Gina Bloom argues, was a crucial trait of the ideal masculine voice in early modern England.[75]

Brinsley and Hoole also suggested that their books should be read alone outside the schoolroom by those children with a basic knowledge in order to 'prepare their lectures afore-hand at home over-night'.[76] This was common practice, indicated by one schoolboy's account of his experiences at Westminster grammar school when he notes that 'Bewtwixt 9 and 11 those exercises were reade which had been enjoyned us over-night.'[77] Schoolboys were frequently urged to engage with their books in humanist-influenced schools in such independent ways. Hoole recommends that schoolboys be given access to a 'variety of books' and proposes that schools should be furnished with books for general use of scholars.[78] They were encouraged to read actively, not only in preparing their lessons but also in marking sample words and phrases on the printed text or by copying these examples into a commonplace book so that they had a list of words and phrases that they might later use in their own compositions.[79] Printed commonplace books were commonly used to aid this process of independent selections of examples that might be used by students in their own compositions, and while by the seventeenth century these were used widely, in the sixteenth century this genre was associated specifically with the schoolboy.[80] As a result, boys were trained to read independently and selectively, leading some scholars to argue that boys rarely read texts in their entirety but instead selected examples which they might re-use in their own writing and rehearsal of arguments.[81] The well-trained schoolboy reader would have memorized and been able to recite his reading matter; he would also be able to deploy it creatively. When the scholar Lampatho of Marston's *What You Will* complains that you could 'make a parrot now/As good a man as he in fourteen nights', he derides Simplicius, the play's fool, who has not been properly schooled and has simply acquired the ability to recite set pieces but not to 'vent a syllable/ Of his own creating'.[82] Ultimately, schoolboys were trained not only to read in particular ways but also to draw on their reading material in innovative ways.

In training boys as active and independent readers, therefore, pedagogues like Brinsley and Hoole produced boys who might deploy their reading material in ways that exceeded the schoolmasters' expectations. Their versions of Gallus' dialogues not only repeatedly re-imagine the act of leaving the spaces of early childhood, they also demand that children repeatedly engage with this moment through their recurring encounters with this book. Through the reading of the text in this variety of ways, the repeated recital of set pieces in English and Latin, and through training in witty dialogues and logical responses (which, these books imply, are means of achieving manhood), the schoolboy reader would, if the pedagogical methods were successful, be provided with the skills and materials necessary to become men. However, Brinsley's and Hoole's instructions on how their books should be used can only offer an ideal model of how they might be read and of what this reading might achieve. It is difficult to ascertain how widely these schoolmasters' versions of the dialogues and their teaching methods were used.[83] The publication of Brinsley's textbooks and treatises on pedagogical methods throughout the seventeenth century suggests that an audience existed for his methods and texts, and the dialogues of Gallus continued to be recommended in grammar schools throughout early modern Britain. Hoole's edition went through a number of editions suggesting some demand for his version of the book.[84] As with the reception of any text, however, it is possible, if not likely, that if this book was used in schools then seventeenth-century schoolboys, particularly boys trained to be active readers, may have engaged with it in ways that exceeded the schoolmaster-authors' intentions.

The content of the book raises the intriguing possibility of alternative appropriations of the instruction it provides. In addition to the boys represented in this text, such as Henry, who achieve a standard of learning and wit to gain equality or mastery over their companions, other boys in the dialogues draw on this education to respond to the schoolmasters. In one, a schoolboy responds quickly and logically to escape punishment from the master for taking a knife from another boy. In another, some boys avoid punishment by providing 'prettily cunning' (*Children's Dialogues*, 17) excuses for their lateness and in being able to answer correctly all the questions posed to them by the schoolmaster. An anecdote from the period implies that students did appropriate their learning in such ways. In one account, Richard Mulcaster, headmaster at St Paul's Grammar School between 1596 and 1608, is described as pausing before striking a boy to recount a 'merry conceyt'. Mulcaster apparently asks 'the banes of matrimony between this boy on his buttocks, of such a parish, on the one side, and Lady Burch, of this parish on the other side'. When another schoolboy interjects with 'all parties are not agreed', Mulcaster is apparently impressed by the 'witty answer' to the extent that both boys are spared punishment.[85] In this moment, as in the dialogues, boys exploit their learning to serve them in moments of youthful camaraderie that temporarily disrupt the schoolmaster's normal method of exerting his authority. The boys who encountered these English versions of Gallus' dialogues at school, therefore, gained an education in how to outwit their masters and parents, and might have appropriated this reading experience to assert a youthful defiance against the hierarchies of age, family and school.

However, as the Mulcaster anecdote suggests, this was to a certain extent acceptable and comic in the context of the schoolroom. In this space, boys are rewarded for their learning by the fantasy of triumph over, and on occasion an escape from, the ever-present threat of beating. It is a momentary release contained within this disciplined context of learning and, in this respect, these dialogues may have functioned in many ways like the licensed festivals of youthful misrule that took place across schools in the period.[86] This potential use of the dialogues is reinforced by Hoole's recommendation that they use it among themselves, recommending a shared community of schoolboy readers in his classroom who might draw creatively on the lessons learned from their experiences of reading his book. Moreover, by depicting well-versed schoolboys who have learned to construct an argument to provide 'prettily cunning' excuses for lateness or bad behaviour, and presenting boys who escape the violent punishment that pervades the dialogues by answering their master's questions correctly and wittily, these dialogues threaten to disrupt hierarchies of authority and age but this is contained within the context of the schoolroom. It is set up as the adept deployment of lessons learned. These boys use their learning carefully and creatively to challenge their masters and enjoy the shared experience of being a schoolboy. The learning intended to facilitate the progression of these young male characters to manhood in fact equips these characters with the material to produce their boyhoods. Yet these boyhoods are not formed solely through knowledge of school lessons but through the youthful characters' disruptive uses of them. As readers they assert themselves, as Michel de Certeau suggests, through a 'transformation of the social relationships' that determine their relation to their texts.[87] Using the reading practices and the reading material that they have been taught, they 'escape' the strictures of the schoolroom through their 'procedures of consumption'.[88] They draw out their knowledge to assert their identities as *boys*.

Reading as Boys

Early modern drama offers fascinating insights into the ways in which young scholars might extend the lessons of the schoolroom and use their reading material to explore their identities as boys. The representation of diverse masculine identities produced by the schoolroom in the theatre sheds light on the processes of subject formation via schooling as drama explores the intersections between school lessons, reading and age. Shakespeare's *Love's Labour's Lost* elucidates the intersections of age and learning in relation to the production of gendered subjects. Berowne, for instance, speaks out against the 'little academe' (1.1.13) as 'Flat treason 'gainst the kingly state of youth' (4.3.289). The pedant, Holofernes, is depicted as having passed the quick-witted stage of life in the imagery of old age deployed by Moth, when he claims that he has 'true wit' (5.1.53) which is 'Offered by a child to an old man, which is wit-old' (5.1.54). Although grammar school texts posit education as a crucial means of producing an ideal version of masculine identity, the theatre suggests that prolonged book-learning instead produces this stereotype of 'soft and slow' old men 'finding numbness' in what should be their 'nimble age'.[89] The scholar who stays too long at his books rather than putting his reading into practice is often characterized as falling short of ideal manhood. The titular scholar of John Fletcher's *The Elder Brother* (printed in 1637), Charles, is depicted as being too immersed in his book. Described humorously as 'read[ing] them over leafe by leafe three thousand times' and as 'eat[ing] and digest[ing] more Volumes', he must 'part with/This bookish contemplation' to prepare himself for action.[90] Charles' reading practices are further revealed to be flawed when he erroneously turns to his books again claiming 'I study now to be a man', a state that in this play can only be found through love and marriage.[91] In other plays, this unmanly addiction to books is presented more specifically via the imagery of age. The scholar of John Marston's *What You Will*, Lampatho, is associated with the latter stages of old age, described as 'a fusty cask,/Devoted to mouldy customs of hoar'd eld'.[92] His association with the characteristics of old age does not result from his chronological age but instead has been produced by his seven years of study, which 'wasted lamp-oil, bated my flesh,/Shrunk up my veins'.[93] He complains that his lessons or the 'company of old *frenetici*/Did eat my youth', extending the common metaphors of consuming knowledge to suggest that, instead of the appropriate consumption, or to use Erasmus' term, 'digestion' of learning, his lessons, like those of Charles, consume his manhood.[94]

Study and schooling are common experiences for many early modern boys and are portrayed as an appropriate pursuit during youth. Yet in these examples they are simultaneously depicted as potentially destructive to youth, unless they are mediated carefully. *Love's Labour's Lost*'s Moth, although not technically a schoolboy, is well versed in the lessons of the schoolroom. He demonstrates the knowledge of classical literature expected of the grammar school boy as he adopts the position of scholar and teacher in advising Armado on the examples he might use in his love letter. He displays his command of grammar and his ability to utilize logic in his exercise on the use of prepositions to express love. He further demonstrates his ability to appropriate lessons when he offers Holofernes the lesson from the hornbook, asking 'What is "a" "b" spelled backwards, with the horn on his head?' (5.1.42–43). Moth adapts the questions from this common text to pose the bawdy riddle that Holofernes does not understand as he naively answers 'Ba, *pueritia*, with a horn added' (5.1.44). While Moth continues to mock Holofernes, who can only offer nonsensical answers, the schoolmaster attempts to reduce this page to a lesser status. As well as calling him a child, or '*pueritia*', he attempts to dismiss the page to children's games, claiming 'Thou disputes like an infant. Go whip thy gig' (5.1.57).

Holofernes' repeated efforts to designate Moth a child or infant, and hence inferior, indicates the extent to which Moth has challenged the hierarchies of teacher–pupil and adult–child through this witty exchange. The autonomous manipulation of lessons beyond the schoolroom by this character, who is young and in a status of service, clearly challenge the authority of this 'old' schoolmaster. In doing so, they form part of the play's ridicule of the figure of the pedagogue and of what Patricia Parker calls the series of 'preposterous reversals'.[95] Moth's state as a boy is emphasized as he sets his knowledge against that of his master, 'the tender juvenal' against the 'tough senor', and against the schoolmaster, 'child' against the 'old wit'. As H. R. Woudhuysen points out, Moth is exclusively referred to throughout the play as the 'boy' or 'child', terms that associate him with Cupid in the play but which set him apart from all other characters, even those who temporarily adopt the positions of schoolboys or scholars.[96] Whether or not we read him as schoolboy, Moth is repeatedly constructed as a *boy* in terms of his youth, his social status and his deployment of learning. He is the 'well-educated infant' (1.2.85), 'a most acute juvenal'

(3.1.57) and 'pretty and apt' (1.2.17), that is '"pretty", because little [...] "apt" because quick' (1.2.20–21). It is this apt or quick wit that is his dominant characteristic and is representative of his boyhood. Like the boys who outwit their masters in Gallus' dialogues, Moth, the youthful *boy*, is characterized by his playful adaptation of the lessons of the horn-book and the grammar school to assert an aged and gendered status, distinct from manhood, but also distinct from the infant games with which Holofernes attempts to associate him and from the old age of the pedant. It is the witty and subversive deployment of learning from his position of service that characterizes Moth as the child, boy or juvenal.

Using reading and lessons disruptively is, therefore, common to the fictional boys of Gallus' dialogues and of this boy on the early modern stage. It is also a feature of the comic representation of schoolboys in William Hawkins' *Apollo Shroving*, a play written by a schoolmaster about schoolboys for performance by his schoolboys at their school in Hadleigh, Suffolk, *c.* 1626.[97] While, as Eve Sanders persuasively argues, many early modern plays shed light on educational processes and attitudes, the plays written by teachers for performance by the boys who participate in these processes are particularly revealing.[98] School drama depicts the practices of the schoolroom and simultaneously forms part of these practices, with many masters recommending it as a pedagogical tool in the period.[99] The printed edition of *Apollo Shroving* highlights its function in this respect as the note to the stationer contends that Hawkins described it as 'an essay of his owne faculty, and of the activity of his tenderlings' ('To my singular honest Stationer', n.p.). Yet school performances also offer a release from normal lessons and an opportunity for schoolboys to interrogate their learning in performances before their peers, educators and guardians.[100] School drama might form part of the ludic cultures of the classroom, and this is particularly pertinent in the case of *Apollo Shroving*, which is performed as part of annual Shrove Tuesday celebrations for parents and 'domestique friends' (n.p.). Forming part of these carnival celebrations, the play depicts a range of schoolboys, all of whom, except one, are far from ideal scholars. Each schoolboy is set up as a type even at the level of the list of Dramatis Personae, with boys depicting the 'diligent student', the 'perplexed scholar', the 'young fresh scholar', the 'hasty non-proficient', the 'truantly scholeboy', the 'lazy droane' and one who has turned away from learning to become a 'scholar of Captain *Complements*', a 'teacher of gestures and fashions' whose practices are set up in this play as a tempting but dangerous alternative to traditional schooling for many of the boys. This carnival performance is an opportunity for the boys to present their schooling to their parents in the audience, but also to mock it and their own behaviour as schoolboys. Performing in this play offers these Suffolk schoolboys an opportunity to comically explore their own relationships with their books.

Books and reading are at the centre of the play's depiction of all of the schoolboys. The diligent Philoponus is well versed in the authors commonly listed on grammar school curricula from the late sixteenth century. In keeping with his description of 'O'streaming overflowing Ovid' (13), his speeches are replete with literary allusion as he indulges in extensive citation of the authors he admires. In addition to Ovid, he proclaims 'melliflous *Tully*', 'Majestique *Virgil*. Grave *Quintillian*. Sententious *Socrates*. Vertuous *Seneca*. Plentifull *Plutarch*. Profound *Aristotle*. Divine *Plato*' as 'my solace, my guides, my instructers' (13). This boy's reading not only frames his speech, it is also his literal companion. It is likely that the common schoolbooks he mentions, readily available to a schoolroom performance would have been used as staging properties. In addition, Philoponus proclaims the companionship offered by his books, stating that he is not alone as 'My books and meditations are my companions that never fail me' (12). He proceeds to recount a 'private reading of Seneca', in which he and Amphibius, the perplexed scholar, participated. 'I remember', states Philoponus, 'how affectionately he [Amphibius] would take his booke into his bosome, and hugge it, and protest that this one sentence is able to make us honest men' (12). Philoponus' recollection reveals much about schoolboy interactions with their books. This elusive 'private reading' points towards the ways in which enthusiastic boys may have come together to read their school texts outside of the schoolroom. These books are materially and culturally valuable. Amphibius' reported fondness for the book figures it as both material companion and his route to 'honest' manhood. Philoponus, the diligent student, and his peer have learned to value their books and have internalized the schoolroom lesson that good reading practices lead to manhood.

Apollo Shroving, however, does not simply reiterate the ideal of the humanist schoolroom; it also reveals its potential failures. Opening with a prologue in Latin, this is quickly interrupted by a fictional female spectator, Lala, who cannot understand it and insists that the play is presented in 'honest English' and 'plaine dealing English poetry' (13) for the sake of the audience. This moment functions, as others have shown, to illuminate the gendered dimensions of early modern grammar school education, particularly the teaching of Latin.[101] The idea that the schoolroom might produce schoolboys who cannot communicate with others around them is taken further in the representation of Rowland Retro, who has been immersed so deeply in his learning that he can only speak gibberish and cannot be understood at all.[102] From the play's opening the limited utility of a grammar school education is made clear.

Moreover, the play discloses the potential ill-effects of learning. Siren, who attempts to lure scholars away from the schoolroom, warns:

> By study soone, fresh youth doth breake,
> The faire grow foule, the strong growe weake:
> Leave leave this musing bookish trade:
> Injoy your selves before youth fade.
> Time must be gone.
> Old age creepes on. (54–55)

Like Shakespeare's *Love's Labour's Lost* and Marston's *What You Will*, the play highlights the potential detriment of study through this metaphor of the loss of youth. Siren insists that learning destroys youth through this metaphorical shift from youth to old age, and, like *The Elder Brother*, hints at the alternative pleasures that produce manhood as she urges the boys to pursue 'choysest pleasure' before 'Gray haires will grow' (35). Many of the play's boys evade this threatened destruction of beauty, age and social utility by pursuing an alternative education. Captaine Complement and his page, Implement, tempt boys from the grammar school to learn an 'Alphabet of my Titles' (18) and the language of compliment as 'scholars' of their 'schoole', which is according to Complement 'swel[ling] with the stuffings of the Grammar brood' (20–21). These boys write down Complement's 'wise saying' in their table books and tear 'out the leaves of all their books to light tobacco pipes' so that they can 'turne fine gentlemen' (21–22). This alternative education entails an unruly imitation of the methods of the schoolroom as well as the direct destruction of the materials used. The transformation of schoolbooks to tobacco undercuts the value of reading highlighted by Philoponus by suggesting that this is the only value of the boys' schoolbooks. This sense of what is valuable is, of course, class-inflected as a number of the boys reject scholarly learning to instead learn Complement's affected, courtly behaviours. This alternative school is derided throughout the play, particularly when a cockering mother seeks to have her son, John Gingle, admitted to Complement's service. The stereotype of the interfering mother not appropriately guiding her son's education is a common one in drama of the period and is extended by the fact that Gingle's mother has previously been responsible for her son's reading.[103] Gingle's knowledge of *The Mirrour of Knighthood*, suggested by his reference to Claridana and the Knight of the Sun, is due to the fact that 'My mother hast read that booke to me' (56). This book was often associated with the recreational reading practices of the young, and Gingle's reading at the hands of his mother and his attachment to the school of Complement stand in direct contrast to the scholarly reading of Philoponus, the diligent student who is ultimately upheld as exemplary schoolboy by the end of the play.[104]

The use of schoolbooks and the additional reading of the boys who follow Complement are ridiculed in the play, an act which demonstrates the risks of keeping boys at home and puts forward the benefits of the grammar school room for young boys. Yet the play does not draw a straightforward distinction between scholars in the grammar school and those of Complement. Boys within this fictional schoolroom are also shown to deploy their learning in unconventional ways and to misuse their schoolbooks. One schoolboy, Ludio, has learned many lessons well. He demonstrates his skills as a reader when he writes notes in the margins of his books, highlights important sections and memorizes examples from his books to construct an argument. As a truant schoolboy who has only read some of his books, he marks Apollo's game of quoits in his copy of Ovid's *Metamorphoses* and takes this as a crucial example. Ludio's reading of Ovid thus teaches him that Apollo 'continues a boy' because he 'loves boyes play' (47). He writes his own note on this 'in the margine of my booke' which claims that 'sport and play besemes the gods' (48). In doing so he builds a case for the importance of play and supports his own desire to be always at play.

Apollo Shroving contextualizes Ludio's act by hinting that he is a bad reader. He is revealed to be a truant and so has missed on the full lesson. Furthermore, he misinterprets a range of lessons. The school verger, Lauriger, for instance, warns him that he needs to 'take a better lesson' (48) as he is misunderstands his reading. Yet at the same time, Ludio has learned many of his reading lessons well. In marking his book, reading selectively and using his examples to put forward a case for play, he manifests the reading skills taught to the early modern schoolboy. He insists that he has chosen to 'readest bookes only where they speake of play' (49) in order to support his argument for play. He recounts how Ovid 'describes in verse our boyes play […] Twise three stones, set in a crossed square where he wins the game/that can set his thee along in a row,/And that is sippeny morrell, I trow' (48–49). Ludio constructs a persuasive argument to the extent that Lauriger finds it difficult to contradict him and make him return to school. In this way, Ludio endorses his truancy. Furthermore, he claims that his focus on play enables a metaphorical escape from schoolroom discipline as it allows him to think of play so that 'those back blowes (which others thinke so rufull) seeme to me nothing' (50). 'He that spends his life in play', Ludio concludes, 'keepes Shrovetide (the Shrove Tuesday events) all the yeere' (50). Ludio's training as a reader and the uses to which he puts this training create an argument for perpetual play and an imagined release from authoritarian punishment: a state of carnival and misrule through which Ludio attempts to escape the normal strictures of the schoolroom.

Through the characterization of Ludio, the play demonstrates what might happen when schoolboys are trained to read in particular ways and use their learning for their own ends. He represents the boy who skilfully manipulates his grammar school training as a reader. Like the schoolboys in Brinsley's translation of *Children's Dialogues* he emerges as a schoolboy who appropriates his lessons to assert his own will and desires. As Eve Sanders points out, although the lessons of the early modern schoolroom aimed to imprint subjects by internalizing 'paradigms of exemplary masculinity' through reading, 'individual readers might choose examples that their schoolmasters would have frowned upon'.[105] Ludio's implementation of his reading for imitation facilitates his pursuit of play, in keeping with his name. His ways of reading are those taught within the schoolroom but permit the dissident pursuit of ideals not intended by the schoolroom. Moreover, through this use of his reading Ludio reimagines what it means to be a boy. He insists that Apollo is a boy because 'I have heard that he love boyes play, and therefore he still continues a boy' (47). Ludio offers an understanding of boyhood not simply as a formative stage of adult masculinity but as a distinct period with its own characteristics: a love of play. His exemplification of boyhood is in line with Henry Cuffe's characterization of this stage. In 1607, Cuffe describes boyhood as inclined 'to sportfulness, talke and learning'.[106] Ludio not only presents an argument for the importance of play to boyhood but, through his own playful talk and disruptive use of his learning, also shows how reading can be used by young boys to assert their own distinct identities as boys. The play demonstrates what might happen when schoolboys use their reading for their own ends. In Ludio's case this entails a fresh concept of boyhood and the rehearsal of the traits of boyhood that he finds in his books.

Ultimately, however, Ludio rues his decision to focus on play. The play concludes with the reprimand of the boys who have not strictly followed the ideals of the schoolroom. Ludio's punishment for his truancy and what is deemed his misreading of his texts is fixed to 'play uncessantly' (91). Although Ludio initially welcomes the promise of a 'perpetuall play-day' (91), he regrets his actions when he realizes he is doomed to a game of dice in a bottomless box—a game that he can never win or end. Ludio's celebration of boyhood play is punished by his being doomed to eternal boyhood, leaving him to wish that he had followed Philoponus' example of diligence. The play thus sets up the careful and diligent reader as the model to be followed by schoolboys. Yet, despite this moralistic conclusion, the ways in which Ludio playfully makes a case for play through the manipulation of his lessons gestures towards the alternative outcomes of schoolboy reading: the possibility of disruptive deployment of the texts read and autonomous engagement in the practices of active reading. In these texts about the schoolroom and used in the schoolroom, ranging from Brinsley's dialogues to Hawkins' play, boyhood emerges as a state distinct from the semi-literate or illiterate childhood prior to grammar school education but also distinct from the discerning literacy of manhood for which grammar school education strives. The boy is someone who has been trained in scholarly ways of reading, but who deploys his reading to undercut the structures and ideals of this institution. Ludio's engagement with his school reading, including marginalia that forge the links between the material he reads and the arguments he puts forward about play, presents a boy reader who rehearses an independent understanding of boyhood. Through his engagement with his book, Ludio reimagines and rewrites boyhood.

The performances of these books for boys in the schoolroom, whether the delivery of translated dialogues with peers or an instructor, or participation in school drama, constitute acts of reading. The various elements characterizing boyhood as wit, learning and sport coalesce in these critical moments of textual engagement in the schoolroom. These reading and performance experiences are moments in which schoolboys represent fictional versions of themselves and simultaneously use their reading to explore what it means to be a boy. Scholars have highlighted the extent to which educational performances enable young boys to try out diverse subject positions that, as Christopher Marlow highlights, are not yet familiar but which culture has constructed for them. Reading and performance might function as a way to 'shore up' and 'explore and critique' these authorized male roles their futures entailed.[107] These texts about boys and for use by boys constitute formative experiences in the ways that they advance the boys' education, providing them with the skills and knowledge to progress to adulthood. At the same time, through the performance of the roles of boys and the representation of how young boys might use their reading, these reading experiences enable boys at school to explore and critique what it might mean to be a boy.

INSCRIBING BOYHOOD

Reading in the early modern schoolroom, therefore, provides a mode through which young scholars interrogated and formed their masculine identities. While the educational programme offers an ideal model of the formation of manhood through scholarly knowledge, the physical and cultural space of learning creates an opportunity for boys to explore alternative masculine identities. Through their reading experiences in the schoolroom, they explore what it means to be a boy: an identity inflected by both gender and age as well as by learning and, most crucially, the rehearsal of this learning. The texts read by early modern schoolboys, from Latin dialogues to drama written by their schoolmasters, demonstrate the ways that boyhood might be forged through moments of independent, unruly and often disruptive uses of their reading material. The young male reader is identified specifically as a boy at moments of disruption, through reading experiences that do not conform to the development of masculine adulthood but that instead pause to reflect on how the schoolboy might resist his schoolmaster or negotiate an alternative path to traditional learning. By engaging with these schoolbooks about boys, the young participants in early modern grammar school culture potentially had an opportunity to rehearse their own boyhoods.

Whether or not early modern schoolboys 'read' or used their books in transgressive ways is, of course, difficult to determine. William Hornby's comical anecdote of the 3- or 4-year-old schoolboy who 'takes a pretty pride,/To weare the Horn-booke dangling by his side' until he discovers its utility as a weapon to hit his peers is a lively reminder that the material object of the book might have been used in any number of creative and disruptive ways.[108] Perhaps like the boys in *Apollo Shroving* schoolboys used their books to make tobacco. Or, as Lauriger humorously threatens

Ludio, 'great dicsnary[s]' (52) might have been tied at boys' heels to keep them at school. Such anecdotes aside, it is difficult, as Fred Schurink has pointed out, to prove that schoolboys encountered the vast number of books printed for them in the period at all.[109] If the boys did have access to these books, it is even more difficult to determine if and how they read them. The ideals of a humanist education in reading are well known but the gaps between pedagogical ideals and practice are difficult to determine.

Marginalia on schoolbooks are one potential source for a consideration of how historical schoolboys may have engaged with their books. Yet, like many early modern users of books, schoolboys leave their marks upon texts without necessarily demonstrating the ways in which they read the book, if indeed they read the books they marked at all.[110] Drawings and formative attempts at writing the alphabet or a name on a range of early modern books from the Bible to riddlebooks suggest that children made use of the paper in any available book to amuse themselves by drawing or developing their early writing skills.[111] However, they often 'use' school-books in interesting ways.[112] Boys and girls use the pages of a 1650 edition of Richard Hodges *The Grounds of Learning*, an instruction book for early literacy, to write their names as a mark of apparent ownership.[113] Its young female owner, Hannah Barrow, marks the blank pages extensively, writing her name but also commenting on what she had that 'Christ/mas day for diner' and practising writing the word Christmas.[114] The pages of this schoolbook, used beyond the formal schoolroom, serve as a space to practise writing but also to record the self in a diary-like manner. Barrow goes further in doing this when she addresses an imagined future reader by writing in the final blank pages 'all you that look with in this Book my name you will f[ind]'. Not only referring to this statement but also the repeated writing of her name throughout the book, Barrow consciously inscribes her self within this book, commenting on her present material experience in the form of her Christmas dinner and imagining how others might encounter her book use in the future. On occasion the blank leaves serve in less unexpected ways as a space in which the schoolboy can, very appropriately, practise what he has learned. In 1690, for instance, James Dodson practises his writing in English, then in Latin and also copies a table of numbers into the leaves of the 1585 edition of William Bullokar's *Aesopz Fablz*, a version of Aesop written in 'tru orthography' and, according to the author, particularly suited for those in their 'tender yerz'.[115] Boys reading a *c.* 1503 edition of *Sir Bevis of Southampton* in the late sixteenth and early seventeenth century similarly mark this book, which, as Nicholas Orme argues, they probably used as part of their studies. John Betts, Thomas Betts and John Gowd write their names and write short sentences in Lain, suggesting that they too take advantage of the available paper to practise their learning.[116] They also copy statements from the English text, and the woodcut illustrations, indicating the extent to which this vernacular and unusual schoolbook may have been used as the object for developing early literacy skills.[117] In addition the boys highlight various sections of the text, in keeping with the ways that they would have been taught to highlight significant examples as they read.[118] Interestingly, as Orme also points out, the boys mark parts of the narrative particularly concerned with fantasy (the descriptions of the dragon and the giant), violence (Bevis surviving on the blood and flesh of a wild boar he has killed) and sexualized bodies (the descriptions of Josian and of Bevis' relationship with her).[119] This extensive marking of parts of the story, unlikely to have been highlighted by teachers as particularly worthy of imitation, demonstrates the potential for schoolboys to apply what they have learned in terms of how to read to pursue their own literary interests. Other examples suggest that boys 'marked' their books in more unsuitable ways. In 1622 Henry Peacham recalls how his teacher beat him for drawing a picture of boys throwing stones at a pear tree in his 1606 version of William Lily's Latin grammar.[120] In a rare example of direct engagement with a schoolbook, one reader marks phrases in a 1697 edition of Charles Hoole's *Children's Talke*. While this likely schoolboy reader annotates his book to reinforce his learning by practising his alphabet, it is noteworthy, as Blaine Greteman points out, that the reader has highlighted phrases such as 'Hang the school and the master too' and 'What, shall I pray? I have more mind to curse' rather than the numerous moral teachings in this book.[121] Like the fictional Ludio, this schoolboy reader marks areas of interest, enabling the selection of reading material that was likely to have been at odds with the lessons of the schoolmaster. Through marking their texts, active schoolboy readers create an alternative script for boyhood.

The page of the schoolbook, therefore, potentially functions as another site for the production of boyhoods that disrupt the ideal notion of the diligent pupil. Manipulation of the material object of the schoolbook might offer a means of staging objections to traditional programmes of learning. In an earlier mid-fifteenth-century schoolroom drama, for instance, the disobedient schoolboy, Idleness, threatens to wash away the instruction contained in his schoolbook.[122] During a visit to a local grammar school in 1596, the Bishop of Cork discovered the 'leaf of the grammar quite torn out, which containeth in it, Elizabeth, by the grace of God Queen of England, France and Ireland, Defender of the faith' and soon realized that the same had been done in all the grammar books 'in all schools within my diocese [...] although they came new from the merchants' shops'.[123] As Pollard suggests, politically aware Irish schoolboys may have used their schoolbooks to pose their own challenge to the religious education being rolled out across Ireland under Elizabeth—although it is also possible that someone higher up the chain was modifying these texts before they came into the hands of the pupils. Although the exact identities of who annotated or modified extant schoolbooks can be difficult to determine, these examples serve as a pertinent reminder of the extent to which readers, including schoolboys, might engage with their reading material in unexpected ways.

The primary difficulty in evaluating modifications and markings to any early modern schoolbook is in determining whether or not these are signals of the engagement of a schoolboy reader. While signs such as ill-formed letters might indicate that annotations are made by someone in the earliest stages of learning to write, this does not reveal the age category of the user of the book, given that people of all ages were becoming literate in early modern Britain and given the varied standards of handwriting.[124] Unless the reader in some way marks their age, claims their status as a child (or youth, boy or girl), or leaves a name that can be directly linked to other evidence such as school records, it is difficult to identify the annotators of early modern schoolbooks. The collection of the libraries of five early modern schools in the north of England held at the University of Newcastle Library, however, contain a number of inscriptions that can be traced with more certainty to the pupils at these schools in the later seventeenth and early eighteenth centuries.[125] These samples indicate the ways in which even the simple practice of marking names on a schoolbook might function to construct boyhood. An edition of Sebastian Munster's *Dictionarium Trilingue*, printed in Basel in 1530, and held in the library of the Kepier Grammar School from the seventeenth century, contains numerous markings by schoolboys on the first and final blank leaves of the text, in English and in Latin. In some cases the boys simply mark their 'name: year'. However, J. Williams and William Shaw in 1684 elaborate on this by writing: 'When this you see: Remember mee'. It is not unusual in itself to find this statement on the leaves of books; many early moderns mark books in this way, often when giving it as a gift—they inscribe themselves upon the printed text.[126] Yet, the boys mark books from their school's collection in this way and urge future readers, like the young Hannah Barrow, to acknowledge their use of them. These markings, therefore, fix their identities as schoolboys for subsequent schoolboy readers. What is more interesting, perhaps, is that later scholars imitate this practice. In 1697 another schoolboy, John Trother, similarly records his engagement with the text, and in 1731 another four boys do the same.[127] This same practice, by the same schoolboys, can be found in a number of other texts in the collection.[128]

The repetition of this statement by these schoolboys across books and across history marks these boys as schoolboy readers. One the one hand, it fixes the status of these individuals as boys at this school in history and urges future readers to acknowledge them for this. Moreover, it forges a community of schoolboy readers, or users, both within particular years and across the period. It is this communal engagement with the schoolbook, an identification with a community of schoolboys, which allows this schoolbook to become the space in which these scholars assert a distinct culture of being boys—an alternative space for the performative act of defining themselves as boys. This identification of readers as boys in the blank leaves around these Latin texts positions this culture of boyhood outside the authorized space of the material to be learned. These readers do not define themselves as boys through the content of their curricula but in the associated spaces forge a community of boys without the intervention of the master. Like the community forged through reading aloud in the classroom, rehearsing delivery of dialogues among peers or through shared experience of participating in school drama, the material object of the book offers another space for a group of boy readers to interrogate their identities as schoolboys.

The material object of the schoolbook, therefore, becomes a space in which young scholars can inscribe their boyhood. Whether reading privately or communally in the schoolroom, or beyond it, the texts and reading practices made available by the early modern grammar school facilitate unique ways of reading, or at least using, texts to assert a distinct culture of being boys. The books produced for use in schools and the ways of reading them encouraged in the classroom might conform to humanist education's explicit aim of making boys men, but their training as independent readers opens up opportunities for the production of boyhood. Early modern grammar school boys are encouraged to read actively, to mark and select reading material to construct arguments. They are provided with opportunities to read independently and with their peers. They are taught to use their reading material, as Lynne Enterline has pointed out, to inhabit alternative identities and, as Christopher Marlow emphasizes, to test and interrogate the subject positions that culture has created for them. Ultimately, this wide-ranging and effective education in reading produces autonomous boys who are equipped to draw on their reading experiences in a range of ways. Within the ludic cultures of the schoolroom, this often results in the playful but disruptive assertion of non-traditional masculine identities; the projection of a youthful boyhood that challenges the authority of the schoolmaster. Ways of reading which encourage boys to read actively and independently encourage boys to behave as boys. This is perhaps one of the many unintended effects of grammar school. The methods of producing manhood in the community of the schoolroom forge a place for the shared experience of disruptive boyhood. In one sense, this behaviour is contained within the space of the schoolroom: it functions as part of the ludic culture of the schoolroom and as a stage of the life cycle that will ultimately be left behind. As young scholars in the process of subject formation, the testing of boundaries and rehearsal of a range of roles of subject positions is perhaps part of their formation as adult men. The playful production of boyhood via school-room reading is perhaps just another element of a developing masculinity. Nonetheless the assertion of this distinct identity through reading signals the importance of reading experiences to a gender and aged status in early modern culture. Moreover, the fate of Ludio, doomed to a 'perpetuall' boyhood, and the inscriptions of the community of schoolboys on the books of Kepier Grammar School who use their reading experience to shape their own identities as boys, demonstrates how some of these early modern schoolboys are discursively fixed in history as disruptive boys.

NOTES

1. Ben Jonson, *The Staple of News*, in *The Cambridge Edition of the Works of Ben Jonson*, ed. David Bevington, Martin Butler and Ian Donaldson (Cambridge: Cambridge University Press, 2012), Third Intermean, 37–38.
2. Margaret Spufford, *Small Books and Pleasant Histories* (Cambridge: Cambridge University Press, 1985), 72.
3. On grammar school books, see T. Baldwin, *William Shakspere's Small Latine and Lesse Greeke* (Urbana: University of Illinois Press, 1944), vol.

1, 272–531; Rebecca Bushnell, *A Culture of Teaching* (Ithaca: Cornell University Press, 1996), 132–139; Ronald S. Crane, 'The Reading of an Elizabethan Youth', *Modern Philology* 11.2 (1913): 269–271; Helen Jewell, *Education in Early Modern England* (London: Macmillan, 1998), 99–102; Rosemary O'Day, *Education and Society 1500–1800* (London: Longman, 1982), 62–76; Amanda Piesse, 'Reading English Renaissance Children and the Early Modern Stage', in *Studies in Children's Literature, 1500–2000*, ed. Celia Keenan and Mary Shine Thompson (Dublin: Four Courts Press, 2004), 19–30; John Sargeaunt, *Annals of Westminster School* (London: Methuen, 1898), 39.

4. For example, Anthony Grafton, 'The Humanist as Reader', in *A History of Reading in the West*, ed. Guglielmo Cavallo and Roger Chartier (Cambridge: Polity Press, 1999), 179–212; Alan Stewart, *Close Readers: Humanism and Sodomy in Early Modern England* (Princeton: Princeton University Press, 1997); Kevin Sharpe, *Reading Revolutions: The Politics of Reading in Early Modern England* (New Haven: Yale University Press, 2000).

5. Nicholas Orme, *Medieval Children* (New Haven: Yale University Press, 2001), 298–302; Fred Schurink, 'An Elizabethan Grammar School Exercise Book', *Bodleian Library Record* 18 (2003): 174–196.

6. Thomas Newbery, *A Booke in Englysh Metre* (London, 1563), A3v. See Chap. 3 for discussion of the books that were marketed at early modern youth.

7. Jonson, 36.

8. *OED*, 1.

9. See Edward Forset, *Pedantius Comoedia* (London, 1631); Charles Hoole, *Orbis Sensualium Pictus* (London, 1659), 198; William Hornby, *Hornbyes Hornbook* (London, 1622); William Lily, *A Short Introduction of Grammer* (Cambridge, 1621).

10. *A Pleasant Conceited Comedie, Wherein is Shewed How a Man May Chuse a Good Wife from a Bad* (London, 1602), C3r.

11. Amanda Piesse, 'Character Building: Shakespeare's Children in Context', in *Shakespeare and Childhood*, ed. Kate Chedgzoy, Susanne Greenhalgh and Robert Shaughnessy (Cambridge: Cambridge University Press, 2007), 76.

12. William Shakespeare, *The Merry Wives of Windsor*, in *The Norton Shakespeare*, ed. Stephen Greenblatt et al. (New York: W. W. Norton & Co., 2008), 4.1.11–12; John Marston, *What You Will*, ed. M. R. Woodhead (Nottingham: Nottingham Drama Texts, 1980), 2.2; Edward Sharpham, *Cupid's Whirligig* (London, 1607), I3v. On Lily's text as standard in grammar schools, see Ian Green, *Humanism and Protestantism in Early Modern English Education* (Aldershot: Ashgate, 2009), 127–154.

13. See the depiction of Prince Edward as schoolboy in Samuel Rowley, *When You See Me, You Know Me* (London, 1605), F4v.

14. Deanne Williams argues for the importance of considering the intersections between the discourses of childhood, education and theatre, proposing that these 'three major discourses "grew up" together in the early modern period, each coming to understand itself through interaction with the others'. See 'Introduction', in *Childhood, Education and the Stage in Early Modern England*, ed. Deanne Williams and Richard Preiss (Cambridge: Cambridge University Press, 2017), 3.

15. Richard Halpern, *The Poetics of Primitive Accumulation: English Renaissance Culture and the Genealogy of Capital* (Ithaca: Cornell University Press, 1991), 27; Walter Ong, 'Latin Language Study as a Renaissance Puberty Rite', *Studies in Philology* 61.2 (1959): 103–124; Diane Purkiss, *Literature, Gender and Politics During the English Civil War* (Cambridge: Cambridge University Press, 2005), 1–15.

16. Heidi Brayman Hackel, *Reading Material in Early Modern England* (Cambridge: Cambridge University Press, 2005); Bianca Calabresi, '"you sow, Ile read": Letters and Literacies in Early Modern Samplers', in *Reading Women: Literacy, Authorship, and Culture in the Atlantic World, 1500–1800*, ed. Heidi Brayman Hackel and Catherine Kelly (Philadelphia: University of Pennsylvania Press, 2008), 79–104; Margaret Ferguson, *Dido's Daughters: Literacy, Gender and Empire in Early Modern England and France* (Chicago: University of Chicago Press, 2003); Juliet Fleming, 'Dictionary English and the Female Tongue', in *Enclosure Acts: Sexuality, Property and Culture in Early Modern England*, ed. Richard Burt and John Michael Archer (Ithaca: Cornell University Press, 1994), 290–325; Kathryn Moncrief and Kathryn McPherson, '"Shall I teach you to know?" Intersections of Pedagogy, Performance and Gender', in *Performing Pedagogy in Early Modern England: Gender, Instruction and Performance*, ed. Kathryn Moncrief and Kathryn McPherson (Aldershot: Ashgate, 2013), 1–20; Eve Sanders, *Gender and Literacy on Stage in Early Modern England* (Cambridge: Cambridge University Press, 1998); Wendy Wall, 'Literacy and the Domestic Arts', *Huntington Library Quarterly* 73.3 (2010): 383–412.

17. On the ways of reading taught in the early modern grammar school, see Ann Blair, 'Reading Strategies for Coping with Information Overload ca. 1550–1700', *Journal of the History of Ideas* 64.1 (2003): 11–28; Lynn Enterline, 'Rhetoric, Discipline, and the Theatricality of Everyday Life in Elizabethan Grammar Schools', in *Performance to Print in Shakespeare's England*, ed. Peter Holland and Stephen Orgel (Basingstoke: Palgrave Macmillan, 2006), 173–190; Anthony Grafton and Lisa Jardine, *From Humanism to the Humanities: Education and the Liberal Arts in Fifteenth*

and Sixteenth-Century Europe (London: Duckworth, 1986); Peter Mack, *Elizabethan Rhetoric: Theory and Practice* (Cambridge: Cambridge University Press, 2002), 11–12; Ann Moss, *Renaissance Truth and the Latin Language Turn* (Oxford: Oxford University Press, 2003).

18. Michael Roper and John Tosh, 'Introduction: Historians and the Politics of Masculinity', in *Manful Assertions: Masculinities in Britain Since 1850*, ed. Michael Roper and John Tosh (London: Routledge, 1991), 18. On masculinity as developmental and a state that must be performed, see Gina Bloom, *Voice in Motion: Staging Gender, Shaping Sound in Early Modern England* (Philadelphia: University of Pennsylvania Press, 2007); Will Fisher, *Materializing Gender in Early Modern Literature and Culture* (Cambridge: Cambridge University Press, 2006); Alexandra Shepard, *Meanings of Manhood in Early Modern England* (Oxford: Oxford University Press, 2003).

19. On the gendering of the early modern processes of moving out of the first stage of childhood, often perceived as ending *c.* age 7, see Janet Adelman, *Suffocating Mothers: Fantasies of Maternal Origin in Shakespeare's Plays* (London: Routledge, 1992), 7; Edel Lamb, *Performing Childhood in the Early Modern Theatre* (Basingstoke: Palgrave Macmillan, 2009), 29–31; Stephen Orgel, *Impersonations: The Performance of Gender in Shakespeare's England* (Cambridge: Cambridge University Press, 1996), 15.

20. Judith Kegan Gardiner, 'Theorizing Age with Gender: Bly's Boys, Feminism, and Maturity Masculinity', *Masculinity Studies and Feminist Theory: New Directions*, ed. Judith Kegan Gardiner (New York: Columbia University Press, 2002), 113.

21. John Reading, *The Old Man's Staffe* (London, 1621), 1; Henry Cuffe, *The Differences of the Ages of Man's Life* (London, 1607), 118. See also Shepard, 21–59, on the role of age in defining early modern manhood.

22. Cuffe, 118. For a useful overview of early modern understanding of the stages of the life cycle see Paul Griffiths, *Youth and Authority: Formative Experiences in England, 1560–1640* (Oxford: Clarendon Press, 1996), 1–16.

23. Cuffe, 118.

24. Jewell, 93.

25. William Shakespeare, *As You Like It*, in *The Norton Shakespeare*, 2.7.144–146.

26. Katie Knowles, *Shakespeare's Boys: A Cultural History* (Basingstoke: Palgrave Macmillan, 2014), 104.

27. William Shakespeare, *Love's Labour's Lost*, in *The Norton Shakespeare*, 3.1.37–39 and 3.1.33. Further references are given in the text.

28. Scholars have usefully highlighted that the early modern grammar school was not an exclusively male institution. See Jewell, 11–12; Sanders, 204.

However, in many instances the sixteenth- and seventeenth-century grammar school room consisted of boys and their male teachers. Chapter 5 will consider examples of schools for girls in the period.

29. See Bushnell; Grafton and Jardine, *From Humanism*; Lynn Enterline, *Shakespeare's Schoolroom: Rhetoric, Discipline, Emotion* (Philadelphia: University of Pennsylvania Press, 2012).

30. Enterline, *Shakespeare's Schoolroom*, 7–8, 16.

31. As Michel de Certeau suggests, it is in the difference between the production of the image (in this case of the schoolboy reader) and the secondary production of that image in the process of utilization (of these books by schoolboys) that the schoolboy reader emerges. See *The Practice of Everyday Life*, trans. Steven Randall (Berkeley: University of California Press, 1988), xiii.

32. See also Carol Chillington Rutter, *Shakespeare and Child's Play* (London: Routledge, 2007), 34–95; Marjorie Curry Woods, 'Performing Dido', in *Public Declamations: Essays on Medieval Rhetoric, Education and Letters in Honour of Martin Camargo*, ed. Georgiana Donavin and Denise Stodola (Brepols: Turnhout, 2015), 253–265, on how training in rhetoric allowed boys to inhabit a range of subject positions.

33. Knowles, 1–12, 63–70.

34. Halpern, 37.

35. See David Shaw, 'The Book Trade Comes of Age: The Sixteenth Century', in *A Companion to the History of the Book*, ed. Simon Eliot and Jonathan Rose (Oxford: Wiley Blackwell, 2009), 220–231.

36. On the curricula of early modern grammar schools, particularly the recommendation of books for different forms (suggesting a progressive and varied engagement of schoolboys with their books as they moved through classes within the school), see John Brinsley, *Ludus Literarius* (London, 1612), 121; Charles Hoole, *A New Discovery of the Old Art of Teaching Schoole* (London, 1660), n.p.; Mack, 34–45; O'Day, 70–71. While there was variation across schools throughout the period, some standard authors from the mid-sixteenth century through the seventeenth century were, as Amanda Piesse points out, Ovid, Cicero, Virgil, Terence, Sallust, Prudentius, Suetonius and Castalion. See Piesse, 'Reading English Renaissance Children', 19–30.

37. Mack, 12.

38. Charles Hoole, for example, recommended that every grammar school should have its own library of specific reference works for each class and recommended 250 desirable books. See Hoole, *A New Discovery*, n.p.; O'Day, 70–71. On occasion books were chained to desks to prevent them being removed from school. See Andrew Cambers, *Godly Reading: Print,*

Manuscript and Puritanism in England, 1580–1720 (Cambridge: Cambridge University Press, 2011), 152–153.

39. Baldwin, vol. I, 494–553.
40. See O'Day, 70–71.
41. Susan Flavin, *Consumption and Culture in Sixteenth-Century Ireland* (Woodbridge: Boydell, 2014), 88; Mary Pollard, *Dublin's Trade in Books, 1550–1800* (Oxford: Clarendon Press, 1989), 34.
42. O'Day, 70.
43. William Dugard, headmaster of Merchant Taylors' School, printed his own and other school books and manuals from within the school in the 1640s. See W. R. Meyer, 'Dugard, William (1606–1662)', in *Oxford Dictionary of National Biography* (Oxford: Oxford University Press, 2004); online edn, ed. David Cannadine, 2009, http://www.oxforddnb.com/view/article/8182, accessed 11 Aug. 2017.
44. W. R. Meyer, 'Hoole, Charles (1610–1667)', in *Oxford Dictionary of National Biography*, http://www.oxforddnb.com/view/article/13701, accessed 27 Jan. 2016; John Morgan, 'Brinsley, John (*bap.* 1566, *d.* in or after 1624)', in *Oxford Dictionary of National Biography*, http://www.oxforddnb.com/view/article/3440, accessed 27 Jan. 2016. Mack, 12, notes that Brinsley's ideas are in line with those of humanist educators since the sixteenth century and therefore, although he writes in the seventeenth century, his work sheds light on common teaching methods across the early modern period.
45. John Brinsley, *Cato Translated Grammatically* (London, 1612); John Brinsley, *Corderius Dialogues* (London, 1614); John Brinsley, *Esop's Fables* (London, 1617); John Brinsley, *The First Book of Tullies Offices* (London, 1616); John Brinsley, *Ovid's Metamorphosis* (London, 1618); John Brinsley. *The Posing of Parts* (London, 1612); John Brinsley, *Sententiae Pueriles* (London, 1612); John Brinsley, *Virgil's Eclogues* (London, 1620); Charles Hoole, *Aesop's Fables* (London, 1657); Charles Hoole, *Catonis Disticha de Moribus* (London, 1659); Charles Hoole, *The Latine Grammar Fitted for the Use of Schools* (London, 1651); Charles Hoole, *A Little Vocabulary English and Latin for the Use of Little Children* (London, 1657); Charles Hoole, *Maturinus Corderius's School-Colloquies* (London, 1732); Charles Hoole, *Sentences for Children* (London, 1658); Charles Hoole, *Six Comedies of Terentius* (London, 1663).
46. H. S. Bennett, *English Books and their Readers: 1475 to 1557* (Cambridge: Cambridge University Press, 1970), 170.
47. Hoole, 'The Usher's Duty', in *A New Discovery*, 9.
48. John Brinsley, *A Consolation for our Grammar Schools* (London, 1622), 52–56; Hoole, 'The Epistle', in *A New Discovery*, A8r.

49. John Brinsley, *Pueriles Confabulatiunculae: or, Children's Dialogues, Little Conferences, or Talkings Together, or Little Speeches Together, or Dialogues Fit for Children* (London, 1617); Charles Hoole, *Children's Talke, English & Latine, Divided into Several Clauses: Wherein the Propriety of both Languages is kept, That Children by the Help of their Mother Tongue May More Easily Learn to Discourse in Good Latine Amongst Themselves* (London, 1659). Further references to Brinsley and Hoole's translations of *Pueriles Confabulatiunculae* are given in the text as *Children's Dialogues* and *Children's Talke* respectively.

50. William Kempe, *The Education of Children* (London, 1588), F4. Charles Hoole makes a similar claim, stating 'Colloquies are most suitable to children (who like nothing serious long)' (*Children's Talke*, n.p.). On the use of dialogues in Renaissance education, see Gillian Avery, 'The Voice of the Child, Both Godly and Unregenerate, in Early Modern England', in *Infant Tongues: The Voice of the Child in Literature*, ed. Elizabeth Goodenough, Mark Heberle and Naomi Sokoloff (Detroit: Wayne State University Press, 1994), 16–27; Peter Burke, 'The Renaissance Dialogue', *Renaissance Studies* 3 (1989): 1–12.

51. See Raymond Gillespie, *Reading Ireland: Print, Reading and Social Change in Early Modern Ireland* (Manchester: Manchester University Press, 2005), 165; Green, 177–180; David McKitterick, *A History of Cambridge University Press*, vol. I: *Printing and the Book Trade in Cambridge, 1534–1698* (Cambridge: Cambridge University Press, 1987), 228.

52. Joseph Webbe, *Children's Talke: Claused and Drawne into Lessons* (London, 1627).

53. Stewart, 92–121.

54. On play in the early modern schoolroom, see O'Day, 53–54. Brinsley highlights the importance of play in his *Ludus Literarius* and *Consolation*, claiming, that 'play' is the way to 'make the least to love the Schoole and Learning' (*Consolation*, 27). On the final page of his *Children's Talke*, Hoole cites Erasmus, stating: 'I matter not how I play the Boy, so it be for their profit./And I cannot tell whether any thing be better learn't then that which is learn't by play' (96).

55. See Richard Mulcaster, *Positions Wherein Those Primitive Circumstances Be Examined Which Are Necessary For the Training Up of Children* (London, 1581).

56. Foster Watson, *Tudor School-Boy Life: The Dialogues of Juan Luis Vives* (London: Frank Cass & Co., 1970), 7–8.

57. On the grammar school and social status, see Halpern, 25.

58. See discussion of *The Book of Merry Riddles* in Chap. 3, 86–87.

59. Anthony Fletcher, *Growing up in England: The Experience of Childhood 1600–1914* (New Haven: Yale University Press, 2008), 22; Michael Witmore, *Pretty Creatures: Children and Fiction in the English Renaissance* (Ithaca: Cornell University Press. 2007), 39–41.

60. Halpern, 25.

61. Mack, 135–145.

62. Brinsley, *Esop's Fables*, A2v.

63. Purkiss, 16.

64. See Lisa Jardine and Anthony Grafton, '"Studied for Action": How Gabriel Harvey Read His Livy', *Past & Present* 129 (1990): 30–78; Mack, 11–12.

65. Hoole, 'Epistle', n.p.; Hoole, 'The Usher's Duty, 50.

66. Hoole, 'The Usher's Duty', 5. Hoole continues to stress the importance of reading in English, suggesting that even when proficient in Latin the pupil should read '*Tully, Pliny, Seneca* or *Lipsus* for Epistles. *Justin, Salust, Lucius Florus*, or *Caesar* for History. *Virgil, Ovid, Lucan*, or *Horace* for Poetry' in English and Latin (122).

67. Hoole, 'The Usher's Duty', 50–51.

68. Hoole, 'The Usher's Duty', 51.

69. Brinsley, *Consolation*, 56.

70. Green, 178.

71. On the irrelevance of Latin literacy for lower classes, see Halpern, 36.

72. James Cleland, *The Institution of a Young Noble Man* (Oxford, 1607), 76. See Sanders, 58, on reading aloud as a method of developing a 'masculine' voice.

73. Lamb, 99; Ursula Potter, 'Performing Arts in the Tudor Classroom', in *Tudor Drama Before Shakespeare, 1485–1590*, ed. Lloyd Kermode, Jason Scott-Warren and Martine Van Elk (Basingstoke: Palgrave Macmillan, 2004), 143–166.

74. Hoole explicitly recommends that schoolboys perform their reading when he suggests that scholars act comedies of 'a Colloquy' 'first in private among themselves, and afterwards in the open Schoole before their fellowes' ('The Master's Method', in *A New Direction*, 142).

75. Bloom, 21–65.

76. Brinsley, *Consolation*, 61; Hoole, *A New Discovery*, 2–3.

77. Enterline, *Shakespeare's Schoolroom*, 35.

78. Hoole, 'The Master's Method', 207, 289.

79. Humanist pedagogues throughout the early modern period recommended active reading through the marking and copying of material as examples. See Bushnell, 131–134; Grafton and Jardine, *From Humanism to the Humanities*, 49; Sanders, 59–62; Sharpe, 41. Brinsley recommends that the 'very little ones' should 'make some secret markes ... with some

little dint with their naile', while older students should mark their books with ink (*Ludus Literarius*, 46–47). Hoole suggests that pupils 'cull out the most significant words, and phrases, and write them in a Pocket-book' ('The Master's Method', 139).

80. See Ian Michael, *The Teaching of English: From the Sixteenth Century to 1870* (Cambridge: Cambridge University Press, 1987), 151–152.

81. See Jennifer Richards and Fred Schurink, 'Introduction: The Textuality and Materiality of Reading in Early Modern England', *Huntington Library Quarterly* 73.3 (2010): 351–353, for a summary of critical work on the practice of reading in parts. Eugene Kintgen, *Reading in Tudor England* (Pittsburgh: University of Pittsburgh Press, 1996), suggests that reading was always for the purpose of collecting examples. Robert Bolgar, 'From Humanism to the Humanities', *Twentieth Century Studies* 9 (1973): 8–21, contends that the primary aim of the boy reader was to collect material for his own compositions and as a result texts were rarely studied in totality. Sharpe suggests that 'the commonplace method made every educated Englishman or woman into a reader who very much made his or her own meaning' (41). Mary Crane, *Framing Authority: Sayings, Self and Society in Sixteenth-Century England* (Princeton: Princeton University Press, 1993) suggests that such examples were used with little regard to their context, whereas David Scott Wilson-Okamura, *Virgil in the Renaissance* (Cambridge: Cambridge University Press, 2010), 204, disagrees, stating that although scholars were trained to excerpt quotations they were also disciplined to recognize allusions. Hoole advises his pupils to note 'where to finde them [their examples] in their Authour' when they copy phrases in their 'Pocket-book' ('The Master's Method', 139).

82. Marston, 2.2.833–836.

83. Ann Blair, 'Lectures on Ovid's *Metamorphoses:* The Class Notes of a Sixteenth-Century Paris Schoolboy', *Princeton University Library Chronicle* 50 (1989): 117–144, points out that the official curricula may not have been adopted by individual teachers and is, therefore, a problematic source of evidence on school experience. Schurink similarly highlights that it is difficult to prove that Brinsley and Hoole's methods and textbooks were used (174).

84. See Green, 179, on the extensive reprinting of Brinsley's and Hoole's schoolbooks.

85. Cited in Enterline, *Shakespeare's Schoolroom*, 49.

86. See T. H. Motter, *The School Drama in England* (London: Longman, 1929), 12–13; Michael Shapiro, *Children of the Revels: The Boy Companies of Shakespeare's Time and their Plays* (New York: Columbia University Press, 1977), 8–9; Keith Thomas, *Rule and Misrule in the Schools of Early*

Modern England (Reading: University of Reading Press, 1976). On youth groups and misrule beyond the schoolroom, see Natalie Zemon Davis, 'The Reasons of Misrule: Youth Groups and Charivaris in Sixteenth-Century France', *Past & Present* 50.1 (1971): 41–75.

87. de Certeau, 173.

88. de Certeau, xiii.

89. Marston, 2.2.882–3.

90. John Fletcher, *The Elder Brother* (London, 1637), B3r, C1r.

91. Fletcher, F1r.

92. Marston, 2.1.450–1.

93. Marston, 2.2.855–6.

94. Marston, 2.2.880–88. Halpern, 36.

95. Patricia Parker, 'Preposterous Reversals: *Love's Labour's Lost*', *Modern Language Quarterly* 54.4 (1993): 435–482.

96. H. R. Woudhuysen, 'Introduction', in *Love's Labour's Lost*, ed. H. R. Woudhuysen (London: A. & C. Black Publishers, 1998), 51.

97. Details of the play's performance are provided on the play's title page. See William Hawkins, *Apollo Shroving* (London, 1626). Further references are given in the text.

98. Sanders, 7.

99. See Jonathan Walker, 'Introduction', in *Early Modern Academic Drama*, ed. Jonathan Walker and Paul Streufert (Aldershot: Ashgate, 2008), 1–18.

100. See Shapiro, 2–5.

101. Wendy Wall, *Staging Domesticity: Household Work and English Identity in Early Modern Drama* (Cambridge: Cambridge University, 2006), 59–64.

102. See 4.4, F1r–F2r. The Latin language lesson is also reduced to the nonsensical 'Rup, tup, snup, slup, bor, hor, cor, mor – holla, holla, holla!' in Marston's *What You Will* (2.2.748–749).

103. See Ursula Potter, 'Cockering Mothers and Humanist Pedagogy in Two Tudor School Plays', in *Domestic Arrangements in Early Modern England*, ed. Kari Boyd McBride (Pittsburgh: Duquesne University Press, 2002), 244–278.

104. On *The Mirrour of Knighthood*, see Chap. 3, 79–80.

105. Sanders, 2, 62.

106. Cuffe, 121.

107. Christopher Marlow, *Performing Masculinity in English University Drama, 1598–1636* (Aldershot: Ashgate, 2013), 6. See also Steven Smith, 'The London Apprentices as Seventeenth-Century Adolescents', *Past & Present* 61 (1973): 149–61.

108. Hornby, A2r.

109. Schurink, 174–196.

110. See William Sherman, *Used Books: Marking Readers in Renaissance England* (Philadelphia: University of Pennsylvania Press, 2008), on the authors of marginalia as 'users' rather than 'readers' of books.

111. On children's marginalia, Gillian Adams, 'In the Hands of Children', *The Lion and the Unicorn* 29 (2004): 38–51; Edel Lamb, 'The Riddles of Early Modern Childhood', in *Material Worlds of Childhood in Northwestern Europe, c. 1350–1800*, ed. Philippa Maddern and Stephanie Tarbin (London: Routledge, 2017); Seth Lerer, *Children's Literature: A Reader's History from Aesop to Harry Potter* (Chicago: University of Chicago Press, 2009), 80; Sherman, 92; Keith Thomas, 'Children in Early Modern England', *Children and Their Books: A Celebration of the Work of Iona and Peter Opie*, ed. Gillian Avery and Julia Briggs (Oxford: Oxford University Press, 1989), 45–77.

112. See Jason Scott-Warren, 'Reading Graffiti in the Early Modern Book', *Huntington Library Quarterly* 73.3 (2010): 365, on such 'graffiti' as 'a useful heuristic category'.

113. See Richard Hodges, *The Grounds of Learning* (London, 1650), British Library copy, RB.23.a.37583. For more detail on the copy see Maddy Smith, 'Value in Unexpected Places: The Sole Surviving Copy of *The Grounds of Learning*, a Seventeenth-Century Schoolbook', *Untold Loves Blog*, 7 Feb. 2017, http://blogs.bl.uk/untoldlives/2017/02/value-in-unexpected-places-the-sole-surviving-copy-of-the-grounds-of-learning-a-seventeenth-century-.html

114. See Hodges, first free endpaper from front.

115. See William Bullokar, *Aesopz Fablz in tru Ortography with Grammar-notz. Her-untoo ar also joined the short sentencez of the wyz Cato translated out of Latin in-too English* (London, 1585), 3. Dodson's inscriptions are on the British Library copy, C58.c.23. He also writes: "Iames Dodson is my/name and with my/pen i write the same/and if my pen had/beene a litle better/I would mend every/Letter/1690'. Another seventeenth-century boy practises writing his name and marks ownership of his edition of *The First Five Books of Ovid's Metamorphosis* (1621, STC 18963.5, held in the Folger), writing 'Thomas Hickman is my nane [sic] and England is my nation' (6v) in a 'childish scrawl'. See James McManaway, 'The First Five Bookes of Ovid's *Metamorphosis*, 1621, Englished by Master George Sandys', *Studies in Shakespeare, Bibliography and Theatre* (1990): 81. See also Blaine Greteman, *The Poetics and Politics of Youth in Milton's England* (Cambridge: Cambridge University Press, 2013), 17, on the inscription of the alphabet on the Folger Library's copy of the 1697 edition of Charles Hoole, *Children's Talke*.

116. See Orme, 298–304.

117. See *Sir Bevys of Southampton, c.* 1503, Bodleian Douce B, subt. 234, 4–5. John Good copies 'Nowe yonge Bevys knowynge' beneath the section containing text 'Nowe yonge Bevys knowinge'.

118. See *Sir Bevys of Southampton,* 6, 8, 9, 13, 18, 19, 20, 22, 25, 39.

119. See Orme, 301–302; *Sir Bevys of Southampton,* 9, 13, 18, 39.

120. See Thomas, 'Children', 66.

121. Greteman, 17.

122. Idleness states 'geve me a litel water/That y may wesshe my book'. See Brian Lee, 'Occupation and Idleness', in *Medieval Literature for Children,* ed. Daniel Kline (London: Routledge, 2003), 275.

123. Pollard, 34.

124. Deborah Thorpe's fascinating study of doodles by fifteenth- or sixteenth-century children in a Latin medieval manuscript has recently shown that developmental psychology might offer a methodology to acquire information about the age of those drawing on early texts. This excellent case study is persuasive. However, it assumes an understanding of the abilities of children in drawing that is constant across history that would be difficult to apply to writing, given that, as I argue throughout this monograph, constructs of childhood and the processes of acquiring basic literacy vary across historical and cultural contexts. See Deborah Thorpe, 'Young Hands, Old Books: Drawing by Children in a Fourteenth-Century Manuscript, LJSMS. 361', *Cogent Arts and Humanities* (2016): 3.

125. A number of these are dated and hence can be linked to the book's location in the school library.

126. Natalie Zemon Davis, 'Beyond the Market: Books as Gifts in Sixteenth-Century France', *Transactions of the Royal Historical Society* 33 (1983): 69–88.

127. See Sebastian Munster, *Dictionarium Trilingue, In Quo Scilicet Latinis Vocabulis: In Ordinem Alphabeticum Digestis Respondent Graeca & Hebraica: Hebraicis Adiecta Sunt Magistralia & Chaldaica* (Basel, 1530), Newcastle University Library, Post Incunabula Collection, PI 492.4 MUE. The first leaf contains the writing 'Liber Scholae Keperiensis ab Hugone Hutchinson/Bibliopego Dunelmiensi de novo compactus,/ Anno Domini 1671'. It is likely that this is written by Hugh, son of Hugh Hutchinson, of Bitchburn, who married Eliza, daughter of Richard Rowe of Plawsworth, gent, and was living in 1666. See R. W. Ramsey, 'Kepier School, Houghton-Le-Sprint, and its Library', *Arcaeologia Aeliana* 3 (1907): 319. Among the signatures, demonstrating varied writing skills of the boy markers, are the names 'Thomas Dawson/1686', 'William: Shaw: 1684', 'George Canne. 1684', 'William Davison 1684' and 'Matthew: Crow his booke: Anno Domini/1684'. These markings are all

on the reverse of the final blank leaf. The dates indicate that these are written by schoolboys as the book was in the school library from at least the date of Hugh Hutchinson's annotation in 1671. It is also known that William Davison, son of Timothy Davison, gentleman, Newcastle, was a pupil at the school at this time. Following his attendance there, he was admitted to Cambridge in 1690. See Ramsey, 314. Boys writing 'When this you see: Remember mee' include Philip Douglas, Christopher Dagnia, George Baker and William Dawson in 1731.

128. The signatures of Hugh Hutchinson (1671), Christopher Dagnia (1731) and Peter Lascelles (1736) can also be found on 1537 edition of Muenster and on Valerius Maximus, *Valerius Maximus cum commento Oliverii Arzignanensis Vicentini* (Venice, 1500).

CHAPTER 5

'This Girle Hath Spirit': Rewriting Girlhood Reading

if it were not for some of the old out-of-date Grandames (who are set over the rest as their tutoresses) the young sparkish Girles would read in Shakespeere day and night, so that they would open the Booke or Tome, and the men with a Fescue in their hands should point to the Verse.[1]

against which she made so many objections, and found in many contradictions, and with all of them she still went to her father, that he sayd: this girle hath spirit averse from Calvin.[2]

These two accounts of girls as readers signal an early modern understanding of girlhood produced via reading experiences. John Johnson's satirical representation of illicit girlhood reading in *The Academy of Love* (1641) defines the students of his fantastical 'Love's University' as girls because of their use of the act of reading to sexually engage with their male counterparts in unregulated spaces beyond the watchful guidance of their mistresses.[3] In the account of Elizabeth Tanfield Cary's life, *The Lady Falkland: Her Life*, written by one of Cary's daughters in the 1640s, the young Cary is also categorized as a girl because of her transgressive reading practices.[4] It echoes Cary's father's designation of her as a 'girle' when she articulates her objections to Calvin's *Institutes* upon reading it. The girl, like the boy of Chap. 4, emerges in these accounts in moments of disruptive reading. The young female reader in these examples is defined

© The Author(s) 2018
E. Lamb, *Reading Children in Early Modern Culture*,
Early Modern Literature in History,
https://doi.org/10.1007/978-3-319-70359-6_5

as such by men, the father or male author. Via the perspective of the masculine authority figure they become girls through non-conforming reading experiences.

These mid-seventeenth-century categorizations of readers as girls are remarkable for the ways in which they define girlhood through reading, and specifically for their use of the terminology of *girl* as a reader. This monograph has argued that the child, youth and the boy are significant categories of readers in sixteenth- and seventeenth-century English-language print culture; yet the girl is not as commonly identified as a reader in early modern texts. While books addressed young female readers as maids, virgins and young women, the language of girlhood did not evolve in this context, as in many others, until the later seventeenth century.[5] Furthermore, in contrast to the 'good' child of Chap. 2 and the ideal schoolboy of Chap. 4, who are defined primarily through their engagement with their books, the ideal young woman is not defined to the same extent through active reading practices. Given high rates of female illiteracy it not surprising that literacy and reading are not the crucial defining feature of female childhood. Yet even literate girls were not always encouraged to demonstrate a commitment to books. Instead young women's interactions with their books were, according to early modern prescriptive literature, limited and controlled. Some early modern girls were celebrated for their reading abilities. Well-educated girls from higher social backgrounds such as the precocious Elizabeth Cary and Arabella Stuart were commended by their contemporaries for their exceptional education and reading practices.[6] Anne Clifford's transition from childhood to adulthood is memorably symbolized through her reading experiences in the 'Great Picture' (1646). Clifford is depicted in the left panel aged 15 surrounded by 27 books, including some religious books but predominantly literary, historical and philosophical works; on the right, the 56-year-old Clifford is accompanied by books that are primarily religious and philosophical. Her changing reading tastes are invoked to signal an increasing maturity and devotion through her life cycle.[7] Moreover, the disorderly arrangement of her books in later life implies an increasingly active engagement with her books as she ages. What and how Clifford reads is used in this portrait to represent the different stages of her life. Books and reading play a role in the production of her elite aged femininity.

Reading was not only important for elite women. As Chap. 2 demonstrated, it was increasingly seen as a crucial skill to be passed on to all girls as well as boys. It served for girls, as it did for boys, as a means of accessing knowledge, whether religious, practical or scholarly, and was for many a crucial formative and defining experience. The ways in which girls were taught to read, their access to books, and the expectations of how they engaged with that reading material meant that, as scholars such as Heidi Brayman Hackel and Eve Sanders have shown, reading experiences were gendered and produced distinct subjectivities. Building on the examination of reading and the production of an aged masculinity in Chap. 4, this chapter advances the work of feminist scholars of reading and of girlhood to ask if the reading experiences of young women produced subjectivities that were aged as well as gendered. Beginning with an examination of the gender-specific practices of teaching young children to read, it suggests that the materials, modes, aims and spaces of reading instilled gendered identities. This chapter moves between the educational spaces of early modern girls—informal instruction given in the home, the advice circulated to girls of all social backgrounds via advice books and instruction manuals, the formal school lesson within the home, and the schools for girls that developed throughout England in the seventeenth century—to consider the ways in which reading and education instilled gender traits in girls from diverse social backgrounds. The 'girl' may not have been commonly invoked as a category of reader in print culture, but this chapter will analyse the interplay of education, age, gender, sexuality and social status in the books directed at, recommended to and read by young women in these diverse instructional contexts to demonstrate the extent to which reading contributed to the production of girlhood in the early modern period. As Deanne Williams, Jennifer Higginbotham and Caroline Bicks have shown in their recent ground-breaking work, girlhood was significant conceptualizing factor for early modern women.[8] By analysing the accounts and experiences of young female readers, this chapter contends that although the language of girlhood may not have fully evolved, early modern reading cultures produced a concept of the youthful female reader that was inflected by sexual and social status as well as by age and gender. The examples of Johnson's girls and the young Elizabeth Cary gesture towards the ways in which the early modern girl as reader emerges, like the schoolboy reader, at moments of disruption, suggesting that the girl reader is characterized by autonomous reading practices. Building on Williams' reading of girlhood as marked by 'creative imagination' and Bicks' challenging of traditional narratives of girlhood as a 'space of passive presexual containment', this chapter explores how what it means to read as a girl is

creatively reclaimed in the traces of left by two early modern girls—
Elizabeth Tanfield Cary (1585–1639) and Rachel Fane (1613–1680)—of
their reading experiences.[9] This chapter thus extends *Reading Children's*
examination of the multiple childhoods produced by cultures of reading,
proposing that, although educated girls read many of the same books as
literate boys, the different purposes, ways and spaces of reading produced
alternative gendered childhoods for young female readers.

BECOMING LITERATE, BECOMING A GIRL

Girls have already been at the centre of this study. From the portrait of the
2-year-old Miss Campion holding her hornbook to exemplify the early
texts used to teach reading to boys and girls in late sixteenth- and
seventeenth-century England, to the 10-year-old Katherine Boyle urged
to read her Bible as her ABC, to the details of early encounters with books
provided by Elizabeth Isham, evidence of the experiences of young female
readers have been analysed alongside those of young male readers in the
preceding chapters.[10] Boys and girls generally learned to read using the
same basic ABC texts and religious material throughout this period. Both
sexes frequently learned to read under the instruction of their parents,
often their mothers, in the home.[11] The earliest stages of reading were
gendered experiences, and, as Elizabeth Mazzola suggests, early reading
was commonly 'anchored in an early modern women's world'.[12] In this
respect, early reading formed part of the wider social and cultural practices
that rendered early childhood feminine, through the associations with
women as the earliest carers and literacy instructors.[13] Even for children
who learned to read beyond the home, at dame or petty schools for
instance, this was also often a shared co-educational experience.[14] For
boys, the movement out of these spaces at approximately age 7, either to
the all-male schoolroom or to work accompanied by practices such as
breeching, constituted a significant developmental moment as the young
male child symbolically and materially moved away from a feminized early
childhood or 'infancy' to masculine boyhood, youth and adulthood. As
examined in Chap. 4, the advanced literacy training and the reading
experiences of the all-male schoolroom were a crucial part of this for many
early modern boys.

However, the processes of instilling distinct gendered subjectivities for
boys and girls began earlier than this transitional moment. As Eve Sanders
contends, boys and girls learned to be masculine and feminine as they

learned to read and write, and this often began in early childhood.[15] The process of becoming literate for early modern girls was a crucial part of their identity formation. In the same way that many moralists urged for boys to be removed from the effeminizing tales of childhood, they claimed that girls should learn to read and engage with appropriate stories as part of their development. In *The Lady's New-years Gift* (1688), George Savile recommends religion and the reading of 'the *Best* of *Books*' to his daughter— a way to 'cleanse our *Minds*' from the 'Legend of the *Nursery*, where Children with their *Milk* are fed with the Tales of Witches, Hobgoblins, Prophecies and Miracles'.[16] Almost a century earlier Giovanni Bruto's advice on the reading material of young girls in *The Necessarie, Fit, and Convenient Education of a Yong Gentlewoman* (1598) urges that the 'young gentlewoman', even from the 'weake age of infancie', should read or have read to her 'divers examples of virtuous gentlewomen', promoting the acquisition of gendered behaviours from the earliest stage.[17] He warns that the young gentlewoman should not read anything that might make her 'minde (very delicate of it selfe) to become more feeble and effiminate' and recommends that she be removed from the tales and stories that delight 'maids & yong girles'.[18] Ideal femininity is understood here as something to be achieved through reading. While early modern masculinity has been frequently understood as a developmental state that must be acquired through the processes of age and learning, femininity has often been overlooked in such models of gendered identity, commonly perceived instead to be the default position of the early modern child and of the individual more generally.[19] Yet, as scholars have recently shown, femininity also varied in relation to different stages of the life cycle and transition between these states was also marked by physical and cultural signifiers.[20] In his advice to his daughters, Savile offers one particular instruction in relation to ageing:

> which is, that you will let every seven years make some alteration in you towards the *Graves* side, and not be like the *Girls* of Fifty, who resolve to be always *Young*, what ever time with his Iron Teeth hath determined to the contrary; unnatural things carry a *deformity* in them near to the *Disguised*; the *Liveliness* of *Youth* in a riper Age, looketh like an *old patch* upon a *new Gown*.[21]

For Savile, the stages of the female life cycle can be divided in similar ways to that of the male life cycle, which was also commonly divided into seven-year blocks in writing on age in the period.[22] Savile suggests that biological development must be accompanied by changes in the mind and in behaviour for his daughters to become women. His image of the monstrously deformed '*Girls* of Fifty', who are 'riper' in body but young in behaviour, conceives of different states of feminine identity as dependent on behavioural signifiers. Combined with the imagery of clothing, this suggests that feminine identity is performative. From the advice of Bruto to that of Savile, ideal feminine identity is something that must be acquired as women move away from 'the weake age of infancie'.[23] The stories they encounter and how they encounter them are, in these representations, crucial to producing a desirable version of womanhood as they age. The femininity recommended by these advice books is also distinguished by social status. Bruto's young gentlewoman becomes such by reading material that strengthens her mind and distinguishes her from other women ('maids & yong girls') in terms of social status as well as age.[24] Literacy, status, gender and age converge in this advice on reading. Therefore, although childhood was generally associated with the feminine in early modern culture, attitudes towards the education of girls and their reading material shed light on an age- and literacy-inflected state of femininity specific to girlhood.

 The diverse materials for literacy acquisition also impacted on this construction of gendered, aged and social roles via early reading experiences. Early reading—and writing—materials in the domestic space included walls and samplers in addition to the traditional hornbooks and ABC books.[25] Girls may have used such alternative 'texts' in learning how to read. William Hawkins' *Apollo Shroving* (1626) hints at the samplers used by some girls as their early ABC instruction when the prologue asks Lala to read 'this one-leau'd booke./Tell the stitches in this sampler of blacke and white'.[26] Lala's stumbling attempt to sound out the letters comically juxtaposes her limited literacy with that of the schoolboys presented in the play that follows but also, as Bianca Calabresi points out, aligns the sampler and the page as gendered materials for early reading experiences.[27] It highlights the potentially different experiences of acquiring literacy for early modern boys and girls. Even the basic learning of the ABC and sounding out of words might function to shape the gendered subjectivities of young children.

As Hawkins' representation hints, the differences between boys' and girls' educational reading experiences increased as they progressed to more advanced levels of reading. Lala's exclamation at the opening of a play performed by early modern grammar schoolboys demonstrates her exclusion from this context when she fails to even sound out the play's title, claiming 'On my maidenhead this is Latine. We shall bee choaked with a dogrell Latine Play'.[28] The Latin learning provided in the male grammar school was one way of distinguishing between the sexes and, as the previous chapter argued, of instilling masculine traits. The schoolmas-ter's promise to his future wife in the final scene of Anthony Munday's *Fedele and Fortunio* (1585) offers an insight into this widespread distinc-tion between the education of male and female children, or what he terms 'boys' and 'wenches', in early modern England when he claims he will set up a great grammar school to 'teach boys the Latin tongue, to write and read,/And thou, little wenches, their needle and thread'.[29] The school-master's differentiated programme of learning at this more advanced age emphasizes scholarly education for boys and practical instruction for the 'wenches', and suggests the production of a class-specific form of girl-hood, with this term for young girls implying they are from lower social backgrounds.[30] Munday's dichotomy is simplistic. The numerous exam-ples of well-educated women in reading, writing and languages, including Latin, suggest that although it may have been a common expectation that boys would progress to scholarly education while girls pursued training in practical domestic skills, it was not definitive and differed significantly for young women of higher social status. Renowned educated early modern women from Jane Lumley to Lucy Hutchinson received intense scholarly educations in classical languages, each facilitated by their father, who pro- ✳ vided access to his library in the case of the former and who encouraged education in the latter.[31] In many instances, it seems, that advanced educa-tion was marked by a transferral of women's involvement in literacy instruction to fathers and male tutors.[32] However, this was not always the case and many girls received ongoing instruction from female tutors and family members.[33] Vives' advice on the education of women, directed primarily at royal and elite children, and which recommended an educa-tion comparable to that of the aristocratic boy, was taken forward by many. He recommended that 'when shee is of age able to learn', which others, he notes, reckon to be at age 7, the girl should 'both learne her booke, and beside that to handle wooll and flax'.[34] Female education is both scholarly and practical. The reading list that Vives offers similarly balances a desire to develop the mind but also prepare the young woman for her future roles, as he insists 'let those books be taken in hande, that may teach good manners' and read 'the Gospels, and the Acts, and the epistles of the Apostles, & the olde Testament, Saint Jerome, S. Ciprian, Augustine,

Ambrose, Hilary, Gregory, Plato, Cicero, Seneca & such other' as such books 'shall profit the life, and marvellously delight the minde'.[35] Like the humanist education offered to many early modern boys, the advanced education open to some girls trained their mind, their behaviours and also included practical preparation for their future roles. It is in the specifics of preparing for this potential future role that the books and reading practices recommended to girls differed from those recommended to boys. For girls, this role was seen to be primarily domestic. Through reading about exemplary virtuous women alongside learning to handle 'wooll and flax', Vives proposes an education that even for his royal and aristocratic audience transforms girls into wives.

The advanced education of boys and girls, and particularly male-led reading experiences in topics such as Latin and the classics, the alternative subjects, spaces and materials of learning that evolved from humanist modes of instruction, and the different recommended ends of this reading, therefore, continued 'to gender children through pedagogy'.[36] This is evident in the extant curricula of the early girls' schools. One of the earliest public grammar schools specifically for girls, the Ladies' Hall at Deptford, seems to have offered girls comparable training to the boys' grammar schools of the time in memorization and in oratory as well as in dance and needlework. The girls' appropriation of Ovid's *Metamorphosis* in their 1617 performance of a masque, *Cupid's Banishment*, suggests a wide-ranging curriculum at this school.[37] Evidence for a number of schools or 'academies' in the following decades, and their curricula of teaching needlework, writing, music and dancing, indicates the extent to which these were established as common subjects for young women at school. Mid-seventeenth-century girls' schools continued to provide training in these areas but also offered an extended curriculum of grammar, languages, rhetoric and arithmetic—comparable to boys' grammar schools in the period but with the addition of retaining the sex-specific instruction in domestic skills.[38] By the later seventeenth century, following calls for a 'universal' education, an increasing number of schools for girls developed, including Bathusa Makin's school for girls in Tottenham High Cross *c.* 1673, which offered an education in religion, work of all sorts, dancing, music, singing, writing and keeping accounts, Latin and French, and if desired Greek, Hebrew, Italian or Spanish, or limning, preserving, pastry and cookery, or astronomy, geography, arithmetic and history to girls from the age of 8 or 9.[39] This curriculum suggests an ongoing emphasis on educating girls in skills that would enhance their virtue and equip them with the practical skills and accomplishments expected in their future roles as wives. These dual aims, it seems, informed the reading experiences of young girls in their education, at home or at school.

There is limited evidence about how these subjects were taught and what books, if any, were used in instilling these advanced literacies and practical skills. There was no comparable printed textual culture for girls as there was for the early modern schoolboy. The all-male grammar school, as Chap. 4 points out, resulted in the rapid flourishing of a range of texts specifically for the youthful male pupil and offered instruction in and the material for the formation of masculine childhoods and adulthoods. Female education was not formalized, standardized or delivered so widely as to make the production of such books a profitable exercise. While many instructional manuals claim to teach women French or practical skills such as needlework, these are not specific to young women or girls.[40] Yet one extant example of a textbook for a girls' school sheds light on the subtle gendering of the books used by girls as part of their schooling and the potential of schoolroom reading lessons to impact on their girlhoods. In 1653, Charles Mauger, a French teacher in Mrs Margaret Kilvert's school in London in the mid-seventeenth century, produced what Dorothy Gardiner has called a unique 'schoolgirls' anthology'.[41] This textbook, *The True Advancement of the French Tongue*, combines rules of grammar, pronunciation and advice on how to avoid anglicisms followed by sample phrases and dialogues. Dedicated 'To The most Worthy, most Vertuous, and most Religious Gentlewoman, Mrs. *Margaret Kilvert*', but also containing dedicatory verses to more than 40 of the female pupils her school, Mauger produces a text that celebrates the school and the accomplishments of his pupils.[42] This text may have been based on the material used in teaching at this school and potentially may have acted as textbook for similar schools. Yet it is not limited to this readership. It is directed at 'the Learner (whome I suppose to be no Schollar)' (1). In this respect and in terms of content, Mauger's language lesson is comparable with earlier books of French instruction, such as Claude Holliband's much-reproduced book, adapted for women by Pierre Erondelle in 1605 as *The French Garden*. As Juliet Fleming points out, such instructional language books proclaim women as the primary readership but in fact offered an eroticized account of female body parts and dialogues aimed at male readers.[43] Mauger's text, however, attends specifically to its potential schoolgirl readers. It includes dialogues in which female learners are the main subjects, including a dialogue between 'two Gentlewomen that learne French'

(239–241), one between 'a Gentlewoman and her French Master (177–182) and one between a 'Gentleman and his daughter, that is newly come from School' (211–215). This collection of dialogues bears similarities to those produced for grammar school boys learning Latin in providing material for language learning that focuses on the experiences of the pupils.[44] However, instead of providing a set series of questions and responses, Mauger's dialogues lend themselves to improvised adaptation to suit the particular needs of his young female pupils by offering a variety of responses to each question. For instance, responses to the question of how the girls are at their lesson include commentaries on proficiency ('I find you have very well improved yourself' [212] and 'I am perfect in my Lesson' [239]) and lack of skill ('You have misspent your time' [213] and 'I can't say a word of mine' [239]). The young female readers potentially had a choice in how they used this reading material to represent their experiences, either in written translation exercises or even in quasi-performative exercises in the schoolroom. In French schoolrooms in this period, dialogues and proverbs were on occasion provided to girls for performance in the schoolroom, and it is possible that English girls' schools used similar performative techniques to their French counterparts as well as to English boys' grammar schools.[45] In this case, a book for French language instruction such as Mauger's may have functioned in similar ways: as a script for the performance of a distinct and communal school girlhood in the early schoolrooms of girls. The examples offered for use in the schoolroom, such as tale-telling ('Ile tel my Mrs what you say' and 'You are alwaies speaking English' [240]), potentially form the basis for the articulation of a distinct girlhood forged through the shared experience of the lesson in which these young women produced their gendered and aged identities through their advanced literacy levels.

The prospect that a textbook such as Mauger's may have been used in the schoolroom to facilitate the education of girls and to forge their identities as schoolgirls through independent selection of phrases and performance of these dialogues in the classroom hints at the potential production of schoolgirl identity via similar methods to school boyhood. It discloses the opportunity for this unique example of a book produced specifically for schoolgirls to be read the way comparable books were read by schoolboys to forge gendered communities of children. However, it seems that a more common practice was for girls to read the texts recommended to schoolboys. Like Lumley and Hutchinson reading classical texts on a par with their male counterparts, Rachel Fane, who will be discussed in more detail later in this chapter, read, among other things, Cato—in an edition directed to schoolboys—and Seneca and Isocrates via double translation exercises similar to those used in boys' grammar schools.[46] Yet while such texts were used to teach Latin to schoolboys, Fane used Cato to practise her hand and Seneca and Isocrates to learn French and potentially also letter-writing techniques.[47] A later seventeenth-century manuscript school exercise book belonging to Sarah Cole further discloses how girls used the same schoolbooks but for different ends. Cole, 'scholler to Elizabeth Beane', demonstrates her knowledge of Edward Cocker's *The Tutor to Writing and Arithmetick* (1664), a book that was printed for the education of young men.[48] Cole's exercise book includes drawings from this book, suggesting that she either copied directly from it or from appropriate selections made available by her writing mistress. Given that boys' teachers often produced their own manuscript textbooks for use in their schools in the period, it seems plausible that the teachers of girls may have followed similar practices. But what is most striking about Cole's engagement with Cocker's text is the way in which she combines the copied examples with a range of mathematical and linguistic problems and with lists of definitions and moral distiches. Like grammar school boys in the period this schooled girl appears to be reading selectively. In doing so, either she—or her teacher—selects material appropriate to her distinct gendered role. The mathematical examples and the word problems focus in many instances, as Sarah Powell and Paul Dingman highlight, on house-hold operations, suggesting the pervasive focus of formal education for girls towards preparation for their practical roles as wives and mothers.[49] In one sense then, this schoolgirl reader reads in similar ways to early modern schoolboys: selecting and copying appropriate examples. Yet the nature of the material selected not only advances the girls' skills as readers and writers, but is also balanced with preparation in the practical skills necessary to prepare them as housewives and the accomplishments perceived to be suited to wives. It foregrounds her future roles.

The education, informal and formal, of young girls in the period, there-fore, had similar aims to that of boys: to form their adult identities. The anticipated adult roles of wife and mother are perceived as something that must be achieved, and reading and schooling play a crucial part in this. Although some exceptional female educators in period proposed a wide-ranging education, the emphasis in schooling girls, whether in the home or the schoolroom, was on the practical training to result from reading experiences. Girls' reading was, as Kate Flint points out, seen primarily as preparation for their role within marriage.[50] The aim of girls' literacy and reading, according to prescriptive advice and educational programmes, was the production of good wives. The school reading practices recommended to boys similarly had a practical aim, as humanist schools attempted to produce civil men, prepared for professions and matters of the state.[51] However, the gendered processes of learning, the ways and the ends of reading in boys' and girls' educational experiences not only produced distinct adult identities but also shaped their childhood reading experiences. Formal female education bears similarities with the reading experiences of boys through the choice of reading material but discloses distinctions in the ways that girls engaged with or 'read' these texts. The ways and experiences of reading are what produce the distinct gendered and aged identities of these readers.

READING AS A GIRL

The examples of a schoolbook printed with specific reference to its use in a girls' school and the manuscript evidence of schoolgirls' experience of reading a book printed with the young male scholar in mind gesture towards the diverse ways in which a range of books might have been used to facilitate the education of early modern girls. These examples of young female readers engaging with books within formal contexts of learning, that is, reading their books as school exercises, are characterized by the potential that girls, like their male counterparts, were being trained as selective and active readers. In other words, these examples shed light on the ways in which early modern girls in the context of schooling, whether in the formal classroom of a school or under the guidance of a tutor in another space, chose examples from their reading material to perform or write selections most suited to their own experiences, either as schoolgirls or as future participants in the management of a household. This context of reading as schoolgirls, in lessons with guidance from teachers and with clear intended outcomes of their educational reading, impacts upon this reading experience. The 'where' of reading, as Robert Darnton emphasizes is important, and in these examples the space of the lesson shapes the experiences.[52]

However, for many literate girls in the period, reading did not take place in this formal setting of the school lesson and the methods of reading and the purposes of reading varied widely for girls in different social contexts. While some parents and guardians encouraged advanced schooling and extensive reading, others attempted to limit this. When Sir Ralph Verney writes to his godchild, Anne Denton, in 1652, he is disapproving of her education, particularly in classical languages, confessing that he did not expect her to be 'guilty of so much learning'. For him, reading the 'bible (with the common prayer) and a good plain catechism in your mother tongue' and French literacy is more 'suitable' for her 'sex'. The emphasis on French as a suitable language for girls was also reflected in the curricula of many of the early girls' schools, but for Verney it is primarily a way to access books offering domestic instruction and virtuous role models, 'for that language', he writes, 'affords many admirable books fit for you as romances, plays, poetry, stories of illustrious (not learned) women, receipts for preserving, making creams and all sorts of cookeries, ordering your gardens and in brief all manner of good housewifery'.[53] Thomas Powell goes further in his advice book that in bringing up daughters 'in stead of reading Sir *Philip Sidney's Arcadia*, let them read the ground of good huswifery'. Powell shares the belief that young women's reading should prepare them for their anticipated future as a wife, and he fears that reading of Sidney's work will instead produce a 'female Poetresse'.[54] This partially results from the class-inflected nature of this reading advice, located in a book that offers career advice to aspiring gentlemen. Yet, as Kate Flint points out, the key recommendations from Vives' sixteenth-century advice to royalty and aristocrats to seventeenth-century advice written with a growing middle-class audience in mind, was essentially the same: girls should not choose their own reading material and it should be chosen with care.[55] The specific texts recommended to girls may have varied depending on their social status, but girls' reading should be carefully monitored and controlled across all classes.

Another dimension of the advice on how women should read also cuts across social and educational as well as age divisions: that of locating and mirroring models of virtuous females in their reading material. Advice to young female readers in the 1670s that romances are 'worthy of their Observation' as they provide examples of 'generosity, gallantry and virtue', echoes Verney's recommendation of 'stories of illustrious (not learned) women' to his goddaughter.[56] Both draw on the earlier dictum of European conduct book writers, such as Vives, that women should read books containing exemplary women. In addition to the practical ends of reading, which varied depending on social context, the common advice offered to young girls as readers was to read for virtuous examples. This recommendation illuminates a significant difference in the humanist-influenced

English rationale for making boys and girls literate. In his extensive treatise on education, *Positions on the Training Up of Children* (1581), Richard Mulcaster focuses primarily on the education of 'boyes' but dedicates one chapter to 'young *maidens*' or 'girles', acknowledging that their education is both customary and a duty.[57] While he advocates reading as necessary for the training of boys' minds for access to religion, law and knowledge, for girls he suggests a much more limited rationale for learning to read. For maidens, reading is 'needefull for religion, to read that which they must know, and ought to performe', and any learning beyond the rudimentary is an 'accessory by the waye'.[58] Mulcaster admits that they may additionally receive 'direction to live by' by 'reading of some comfortable and wise discourses ... in forme of historie', but only if they 'have skill and time to reade, without hindering their housewifery'.[59] According to Mulcaster, reading for girls is primarily for religious and moral instruction and this is achieved by reflecting on the examples contained within their reading material. Women of all ages and ranks are encouraged to find virtuous models in their books and look on them as mirrors.

This is evident in the number of books produced for women, of all ages, that represent themselves as a 'mirror' or, in the case of one book specifically for girls in the mid-seventeenth century, as a 'pattern'. John Batchiler's *The Virgin's Pattern* (1661) presents 'the Exemplary Life, and lamented Death of Mrs. Susanna Perwich' 'for the use and benefit of others'.[60] It is dedicated primarily to the 'all the young *Ladies* and *Gentlewomen*, of the several *Schools* in and about the City of *London*' but '*particularly* to those of Mrs Perwich her School at Hackney'.[61] Emphasizing that their schoolmistress, who died age 25, was a 'lively example' to them in life, the dedication highlights its aim 'to set a rare Pattern and Example' in this account of her life and virtues, which is then given in both prose and poetry.[62] The book opens with an image of Perwich, accompanied by a verse to the reader, beginning 'Here's all that's left'. This address to the reader urges a literal looking upon this exemplary 'accomplished Virgin' in the book. It establishes her as a mirror image to aspire to and frames the book as the pattern for readers to follow, as the verse concludes 'what the Effigies want, the Booke will tell/On Inward splendors, looke and view them well'.[63] An earlier 'mirror' book, Thomas Salter's *The Mirrhor of Modestie* (1579) addresses three categories of women: 'Mothers, Matrones, and Maidens'.[64] Salter presents his book as a mirror for mothers and 'auncient Matrones' 'to looke in, to decke their young daughters and maidens myndes by'.[65] He presents the reading of young women as passive reflection and as mediated by their older guides, who introduce them to the appropriate examples presented in books such as this. Mothers and matrons are given responsibility for controlling the young girls' reading experiences, as Salter goes on to instruct that instead of 'bookes, ballades, Songes, sonettes and Dittles of daliance', which he claims are given to daughters by unwise fathers, the 'wise Matrone, shall reade or cause ther Maidens to reade, the examples and lives of godly and virtuous Ladies … out of the holy Scripture, and other histories both auncient and of late dayes'.[66] Such examples, Salter claims, will 'not onely delight them' but will 'pricke and incite their hartes to follow virtue'.[67] Salter thus proposes that young girls should look upon, or listen to, the examples put on in books and that these examples will form their behaviours. The girl in this recommended reading practice is subject to the guidance of parents and instructors and to the shaping influence of this passive reading experience.

Bruto's *The Necessarie, Fit and Convenient Education of a Yong Gentlewoman* (1598) offers similar advice to the 'wise matron' caring for very young gentlewomen, before offering more detailed advice on what and how the young female reader should read when she progresses to more independent reading experiences. As with Salter's reading programme, the emphasis is on reflecting on the examples of 'famous and renowned women wherewith shee may increase the notable virtues' and 'examples of all virtues, religion, holiness and loyalty'.[68] Such modes of reading are recommended to early modern women of all ages, with moralists and educators from Vives in the early sixteenth century through to Brathwait and Jacques Du Bosc in the seventeenth century recommending books to women, young and old, featuring exemplary women and morally appropriate stories.[69] A process of immediate reflection on the examples contained within books is foregrounded as an ideal reading practice for women across the life cycle. Yet Salter's and Bruto's texts emphasize the importance of such reading for young women. Salter highlights that there is 'nothyng more meete, especially for young Maidens then a Mirrhor, therein to see and beholde how to order their dooyng'.[70] Bruto claims that these 'singular examples' are 'worthy by her to be holden in memory' and are of particular 'profit to that age' during which the 'mindes of children […] are tender and delicate'.[71] Reading and memorizing good examples are recommended to all women, but are of particular significance for the young female reader. What and how the girl reads is represented in these tracts on the education and conduct of young women, especially young gentlewomen, as part of a wider process of achieving what these texts perceive to be an idealized virtuous womanhood.

The mode of reading recommended to young girls, therefore, is to read as a virtuous woman. While boys are trained to read actively and to engage with their reading in order to develop their emerging masculinities, female readers reflecting on virtuous examples are, to a certain extent, deemed to acquire the ideal traits of virtuous womanhood immediately through the process of mirroring their reading exempla. Like their male counterparts, female readers are expected to perform what they have learned through their reading through imitation of the exemplary models but this is, Sanders suggests, a passive reflection of their reading experiences rather than an active engagement with the narratives they encounter.[72] The ideal girl reader, therefore, according to educational, advice and moral tracts primarily authored by men, though also echoed by the female authors of conduct and advice books for young women, should engage with their books as mirrors seeking to reflect the good examples found within their reading material. It is unsurprising that young women were guided strictly in choosing their reading material, and were regularly warned against reading texts that might offer less positive role models. Many moralists vehemently urged against giving young girls access to song books, ballads and romances, claiming that 'lascivious stories' might lead to inappropriate behaviour.[73] If girls were trained to mirror exemplary characters in their books, the alternative was that they might mirror less desirable traits if exposed to these genres. The young susceptible female reader was thus urged to view the content of her books as models for behaviour and was accordingly urged by prescriptive literature of the period to read books containing virtuous women and, through passive imitation of these models, form her feminine identity.

However, this is only one narrative of girlhood reading shaped by prescriptive moral literature of the time. Many female readers were active readers, including Renaissance girls.[74] This was more commonly the case for girls who received a humanist-influenced education that, in spite of emphasizing the distinctions in gendered education, trained them to read in active and creative ways by encouraging limited reflection on their reading, note-taking and translation as part of their learning. However, a seventeenth-century text addressed to 'all the Female Sex, in all *Relations*, *Companies*, *Conditions*, and *states* of *Life*, even from *Child-hood* down to *Old-age*; and from the Lady at the *Court*, to the Cook-maid in the

Country' imagines a parity in terms of female reading across society.[75] *The Gentlewoman's Companion* (1673), ascribed to the author Hannah Wolley, recommends instruction in 'Letters' and 'Reading' to all and puts forward a reading list for girls 'from age of six to Sixteen' from all backgrounds.[76] This includes books for moral instruction, knowledge and recreation ranging from books of piety and divinity, namely 'Bishop Usher's Body of Divinity, Mr Swinnock's Christian-calling, Mr. Firmin's Real Christian', and including those specifically for children. 'Mr. James Janeway's book, Intituled, Acquaintance with God betimes; and his Token for Children when they are young' to romances including 'Cassandra, Clelia, Grand Cyrus, Cleopatra, Parthenessa, not omitting Sir Philip Sydney's Arcadia'.[77] This list is an extended version of that provided in Robert Codrington's earlier publication directed at young gentlewomen, _The Second Part of Youth's Behaviour, or Decency in Conversation Amongst Women_ (1664), but adapts it to direct it explicitly to 'Young Ladies, Gentle-women and all Maidens whatever' and sets this advice alongside the instructions for preserving, cooking and managing a household, which were commonly included in Wolley's manuals of cookery, medicine and household affairs.[78] This advice and reading material is represented in this book as suited to young women from all social backgrounds as a means of bettering themselves. By reading this text and practising what it teaches, the dedication to 'all Young Ladies, Gentlewomen, and all Maidens whatever' suggests, a girl from any social background can move through life and, if she desires, up through social hierarchies.[79] This utopian text equates reading with social mobility. Making young women literate, it implies, can equip them with the knowledge for any role and the manners required for a range of situations. By extension, girls' reading has the potential to erase class distinctions: an idea promoted by this female-authored text for women. It signals the potential of literacy to create autonomous girls through the deployment of reading material.

It is in moments of autonomous reading that young female readers are described as *girls* in the two examples at the opening of this chapter. The young, well-educated Elizabeth Cary is defined as a 'girle' by her father *because* of her active reading practices. Although Cary's father was the one to encourage her to read Calvin, her response to her reading material is one that he does not anticipate. 'Girl' here operates as a disruptive category; a designation of Cary's rejection of passive reflection and agreement with the model put before her by her father in the form a religious book. Although Cary's reading of material that would shape her transgressive religious beliefs as an adult differs significantly from the imagined female students termed 'girls' because of their illicit reading of amorous literature in John Johnson's account, in both cases the reader is defined as a girl when they use their reading experience to transgress the expectations of parents, moralists, educators and the authors of conduct manuals and 'mirrors' for women. To read as girl in these representations is to read in unconventional ways that challenge ideal gendered behaviours. In other words, readers become girls when their reading practices go beyond the patriarchal ideals of feminine identity.[80]

However, there are significant differences between these two categorizations of early modern readers as girls. Johnson's misogynist account uses the terminology of girlhood to suggest an illicit sexuality as the female students read beyond the established guidance of their mistresses spatially (in their closets) with alternative tutors encouraging them to read and reflect precisely the type of material that moralists were warning young girls against. Johnson's implication in calling them 'girles' is thus in keeping with many uses of the emerging language of feminine identity in the period, in which 'girl' frequently signalled wilful, independent and illicit behaviour, and was used in stark contrast to the alternative virtuous state of feminine youth, 'maid'.[81] In contrast, Cary's daughter-biographer appropriates the term to indicate her mother's emerging autonomy and strong religious beliefs. Cary, as a girl in this representation, is conveyed as unruly and disruptive, but this resistant girl is depicted positively in this text. In this deployment of the term, a daughter filters the voice of a father potentially troubled by his daughter's unconventional reading of religious material. This representation of a child's reading of Calvin forms part of the careful reimagining of the young Cary as reader that serves a particular function in this generically complex text. Scholars have generally agreed that the biography is a deliberate construction of a mother's religious beliefs and conversion, and as such is closer in form to conversion narrative or even hagiography, than a factual account of a life.[82] Indeed, the representation of Cary's childhood encounter with Calvin's *Institutes* forges a narrative of reading as central to conversion. Early commitment to reading and its potential power not only to shape but also transform religious belief signals a childhood dedication to acts that would impact on the adult Cary. Cary is represented as an active, enthusiastic learner and reader from her earliest years. She learns to read 'very soone' in life and 'loved it much' (105). According to the *Life* she is so successful that around the age of 4 or 5 she learns French, Spanish, Italian and Latin, and is proficient enough to be able to translate Seneca's *Epistles* from Latin to English (105–106).[83] Having dismissed her teacher after an initial five weeks, this self-taught programme, presumably in the home, is influenced by humanist models of teaching via translation, given that Seneca's *Epistles* were a common school exercise for boys and girls of the period. These educational acts of reading soon give way to what the *Life* portrays as an exceptional dedication to reading. Before she turns 12, the *Life* claims, Cary spends 'her whole time in reading, to which she gave herself so much that she frequently red all night' (108) and as a result her mother prevents the servants from letting her have candles. Unhindered by this, Cary's reading leads to further disruptive practices as the servants of Burford Priory recognize an opportunity for 'profitt' (108) and sell candles to her. It is soon after this, at the age of 12, that Cary's father, 'who loved to have her read', gives her the copy of Calvin and 'bids her read it' (108). Cary's disruptive reading of Calvin is represented in the *Life* as the climax of exceptional girlhood reading and as the origins of her independent engagement with religious beliefs.

These accounts of Cary's childhood reading are shaped by the representational strategies at play in this daughter's retrospective depiction of her mother. The tensions between the young Elizabeth Cary and her own mother's limitation of her reading, and the subtle resistance to the authority of her father via her reading, are mediated through the fraught familial relationships which, as has been well-documented, increased with Cary's support for her husband's move to Ireland and her later religious conversion.[84] Reading practices are further utilized to signal conversion throughout adulthood as the *Life* notes that Cary continued to 'read much' and 'when she was about twenty yeare old, through reading, she grew into much doubt of her religion', first by reading 'a Protestant booke much esteemed' (110) and then by finding more persuasive the works of St Augustine and other Catholic writers so that 'her distrust of her religion increased by reading them' (111). From the perspective of her parents, Cary is transgressive in her reading practices, reading actively and independently as a child and young adult in ways that instil what they perceived to be deviant religious beliefs. Yet, from the perspective of her Catholic daughter writing this biography at Our Lady of Consolation Convent in Cambrai, reading leads to enlightenment. Subjective comments on these acts of reading, such as 'this will not seeme strange to those that knew her well' (108), elevate the youthful Cary's reading practices to admirable characteristics in the *Life*. To read as a girl in the eyes of the father is to read disruptively; to read as a girl in the words of a father reimagined here and articulated from the perspective of Cary's daughter is a positive transformative experience. This representation of Elizabeth Cary's childhood reading experiences may or may not shed factual light on what the author read as a girl, but it illuminates imagined girlhood reading practices. Moreover, it suggests a creative autonomy available to young girls in their reading and writing that reclaims what it might mean to read as a girl. Cary's act of girlhood reading and her daughter's writing of this act of reading, are the origins of creative and independent self-fashioning.

REWRITING GIRLHOOD

Recent studies of early modern girlhood have achieved Deanne Williams' aim to 'recuperat[e]' girlhood as a separate and significant category and as a distinctive early modern identity.[85] In her important study, *Shakespeare and the Performance of Girlhood,* Williams foregrounds the 'transformative creative imagination' and persuasively argues for the 'limitless possibilities of girlhood' in the period.[86] In her work on girlhood performance and the 'incited minds' of early modern girls, Caroline Bicks also highlights the 'considerable cognitive gifts' of many early modern girls.[87] Assessing the extent to which scholarship has been influenced by early modern humoral theory, which perceived adolescent virgin girls as cognitively disadvantaged and prone to diseases of the mind, Bicks offers an alternative reading of girls on the cusp of adulthood who, no longer solely defined in relation to fathers and not yet defined by husbands, are able to 'absorb, process, store and invent' in ways that, Bicks argues, are 'unique to this particular stage of female development'.[88] The *Life's* depiction of the powerful spiritual potential of young girls' independent reading gestures towards such possibilities through critical acts of re-reading and through early modern girlhood acts of reading. The young Elizabeth Cary in one sense appropriates reading traditions to assert and construct her own transformative girlhood, and this is implied in her daughter's reconstruction of childhood reading over forty years later. However, this process had already begun in Cary's own representation of her reading practices. Around 1597 the 11- or 12-year-old Elizabeth Cary read and translated from French Abraham Ortelius' atlas, *Epitome du Théâtre du Monde.*[89] It is likely, as Danielle Clarke has suggested, that this act of reading, translating and writing—which survives in the form of a carefully prepared manuscript dedicated to

Cary's uncle, Henry Lee, and titled *The Mirror of the Worlde*—formed part of Cary's education, which, the *Life* suggests, included learning French and translation exercises.[90] Little is known about this education beyond the *Life*'s account of her temporary tutelage and subsequent independent language learning. Yet in addition to her father's mentoring of her reading and learning signalled by the *Life*, it is possible that Cary had a number of tutors throughout her childhood, including John Davies and Michael Drayton.[91] Cary's translation sheds light on her extensive lessons, which most likely took place in her home, Burford Priory. While the *Life* suggests an education in religious matters, languages and translation, in line with other well-educated girls of the period, this translation suggests that Cary also had some understanding of geography and cartography, subjects that were becoming important in the education of boys but were less likely to be prioritized in female education.[92] Lesley Peterson has suggested in her important edition of Cary's *Mirror* that the mathematical, geometrical and geographical errors in the translation are evidence that Cary lacked a formal education in these subjects. This act of reading potentially takes her beyond the formal lesson, suggesting an individual choice of reading material, perhaps influenced by her desire to impress her dedicatee, or driven by her own childhood interest in the world beyond her home and schoolroom.

Whether this act of reading occurred within the context of a tutor-guided lesson or beyond, it is an independent act of reading. As many have argued, the act of translation is more than reproduction. For early modern women, in particular, it was a mode in which readers and writers might find one of the 'multiple positions' opened by this genre's balancing of 'submission to and mastery of the text'.[93] Through translation Cary appropriates her reading to explore her own experiences and concerns.[94] This is exemplified by her deviations from her source text. While some differences might be minor errors or gaps in linguistic knowledge, others are particularly striking, especially given, as Peterson points out, that the young Cary is for the most part a careful translator.[95] For instance, while the *Life* draws attention to the young reader's disagreements with Calvin, the *Mirror* deploys Calvinist discourse when Cary refers to the 'election' (35) of God in the Holy Land. Cary's engagement with her book further becomes a means of exploring competing religious discourses when she offers an extended celebration of Italy in her translation, possibly indicating, Peterson suggests, Italy's religious and cultural authority in the mind of the young Cary.[96] Reading and rewriting this atlas of the world is a mode of exploring competing religious authorities and gestures towards Cary's ongoing interrogation of her own religious beliefs at this young age. As Peterson persuasively argues, this translation is evidence that the young Cary 'read her source text with thoughtful and often critical comprehension', creating a 'mirror of her own pre-adolescent world' with 'reflections of her childhood experiences, character and concerns'.[97] Potential 'errors' in translation, therefore, might be read as autonomous and even disruptive reading practices. Cary's translation constitutes an act of girlhood reading. Her training as a humanist reader combined with her status as a girl on the cusp of adulthood, with its imaginative and creative potential, place her in a unique position to engage creatively with her reading.

The production of the manuscript translation implies that Cary was conscious of this fact. In the dedication to her uncle, she frames her work as reflective of her youthful perspective. Representing the exercise as the 'fruites and endevours of my younge and tender yeares', she draws on the common imagery of underdeveloped youth to claim that the work is her 'viewe of the whole worlde' before 'riper yeares shall afforde me better fruites with greater judgement' (119).[98] Yet in this conventional expression of authorial humility, she establishes the work as her childhood view of the world as she clarifies that this is not a straightforward reproduction of Ortelius' text but a negotiation of her own interests and beliefs via reading and translation. By calling her version *The Mirror of the Worlde*, rather than more directly translating the title of her source version, Cary evokes the exemplary texts for women and puns on the mode of reading recommended to female readers, namely that they use books as mirrors. In contrast to offering this book as a mirror of exemplary behaviours, Cary puts forward her own distinct gendered and aged version of the world. Through the title and preface of this translation, Cary demonstrates how childhood reading might be appropriated to reflect her girlhood perspective.

The writing of early modern girls offers a potential site for young, gendered readers to engage with their reading material autonomously and creatively. As Kate Narveson highlights, humanist reading involved writing via the educational processes of copying and compiling examples. 'Methods of reading', Narveson suggests, 'spurred forays into writing'.[99] As this monograph has suggested, it is in the use of the reading material that children as readers have the opportunity to produce their own concepts of their states as children. Cary's early translation indicates the potential of written engagement with a text to reclaim girlhood and offer a distinct sense of her place in the world in relation to both her patron and her own priorities as a girl. This expression of girlhood is, of course, made possible by education. Not only has Cary has acquired the skills to read, write and appropriate what she finds in her reading material, but the pedagogical practice of translations makes this material response to her reading appropriate. Yet, as with the schoolboys of Chap. 4, it is in the moments in which the young reader departs from conventional reading practices to explore their own childhood perspective that categories of the child as reader are forged through this experience. This is exemplified by one brief engagement by Cary with her source material. In her account of 'Ditmars', Cary omits a sentence on the noteworthy stature of its inhabitants but retains the next sentence, translating it as 'There are no publique whores for to have a maide that haith lost her honor of her race or kindred is reputed for a very greate shame' (165). Peterson questions why Cary may have chosen to omit one fact and retain the latter, wondering what 'a sheltered girl would have thought on reading that this situation was considered unusual or less interesting' (165). The sexual status of the maid was perhaps of particular relevance to the girlhood of the young translator. Maidenly propriety is central to the books and reading practices recommended to girls approaching the age of marriage. The mirrors and patterns put before girls by moralists and educators instil the ideal of chastity and modest behaviour. Early modern writers and printers, as Hilda Smith has suggested, primarily divided their female readership into the categories of maid, wife and widow and, as Jennifer Higginbotham highlights, often young girls were defined by their sexual status rather than their age.[100] As a result, as Kate Chedgzoy points out, 'for early modern girls, the transition from childhood to adulthood was profoundly implicated with sexuality and the social institutions that regulate it'.[101] For girls in their early teenage years, particularly from the age of 12, the legal age for the marriage of girls, to the age of 14, which was perceived to be the time at which girls achieved sexual maturity, sexual behaviour and the appropriate management of this burgeoning sexuality, either through maintaining maidenly modesty or marriage, was a defining feature of this stage of the life cycle.[102] Cary's possibly insignificant decision to retain this comment on maidenly behaviour might also be read as a reflection on the issues relevant to her own girlhood.

The school exercise of another early modern girl highlights the crucial moral lesson for girls in the period. Dedicated to 'Mris Grace', it lists the desirable attributes of a young woman of 'tender yeares', including wisdom, humility and the four things 'comly for a virgin': 'modestie/silence/

shamesfastnes/chastitie'. Further stating that 'a mayden's blush/Is an excellent colour and a virtuous wit maketh a virgin honourable', this exercise combines a series of commonplaces about virtuous femininity in praise of this mistress and deploys the terminology of maidenhood and virginity to highlight chastity and modesty as idealized virtues of female youth.[103] The identity of this writer is unknown, but it is possible that it was one of the siblings of Lady Rachel Fane, addressing their older sister Grace, as this notebook is contained in a collection of 15 such books, 12 of which were compiled by the young Rachel Fane in the 1620s and early 1630s.[104] As early as age 10, Fane completed diverse school exercises in her notebooks, including translations, alphabets, the copying of passages to practise her writing, sermon notes and original literary writing, including poetry and drama. Fane has gained prominence in early modern childhood studies as the child author of the masques written in these notebooks in the 1620s for performance by her siblings and other children in attendance at the Mildmay-Fane household at Apethorpe.[105] Held at the Centre for Kentish Studies alongside Fane's other manuscripts, which include additional sermon notes and medicinal and culinary recipes, this collection points to her extensive reading of religious material and romance fiction, a detailed knowledge of theatrical works and practices, including Shakespeare, an education in Latin, Spanish and French, and skill in affairs of housewifery from an early age. It signals Fane's comprehensive instruction in domestic virtues, courtly behaviour and leisure activities as well as scholarly subjects. While Fane did not have access to external schooling like her brothers, it seems that she and her sisters received a formal education at Apethorpe. It is likely that this supplemented the instruction passed on to her by her grandmother, Lady Grace Mildmay, who wrote advice for her children and grandchildren in the form of her autobiography and with whom the Fane family lived from 1617 when Fane was aged 4.[106]

This combined instruction is evident in the content of Fane's notebooks. Her scholarly exercises include word lists in Latin and English and in Latin, Spanish and English (1625), compiled when Fane was aged 12; translations of French texts, including extracts from *Amadis de Gaule* in 1626, from Seneca's *Epistles* in 1629 and from Isocrates' *Epistles*; and copying of Cato's *Sentences* in secretary hand.[107] These sentences demonstrate the extent to which the content of the source material was important to the pedagogical exercise. Cato was recommended widely to young children throughout the early modern period.[108] In his distinctive phonetic rendering of select sentences, William Bullokar outlines the particular benefit of these sentences in his verse to his 'chyld', highlighting both their moral content and their brevity.[109] Such claims were reiterated in later editions aimed at schoolboys and beyond. John Penkethman's 1623 edition, *A Handful of Honesty. Or, Cato in English Verse*, for instance, claims that these are 'lessons for all sorts of persons', useful as 'copies for writing schollers' as well as 'for the furnishing of their hearts and behaviours'.[110] The moral exempla serve as a means for Fane to acquire diverse hands and they simultaneously contribute to her moral instruction. Other notebooks in the collection contain reflections on psalms, sermon notes, a reflection on Samuel Ward's *Balme from Gilead to Recover Consience* (1617) and copying the religious poetry of DuBartas to practise her secretary hand.[111] Fane's practices of reading and writing as a child, thus, bring together religious, linguistic and practical instruction. Fane reads her material actively: using sermons and psalms as the inspiration for spiritual reflection; copying extracts for content as well as style; translating creatively, like Elizabeth Cary; and, ultimately, using the tropes and images acquired through her reading and learning to write her own poems and entertainments. As Kate Chedgzoy points out, 'While education for girls was intended to form them as virtuous wives and housekeepers, Rachel Fane's career as a writer demonstrates that once acquired, the uses to which literacy may be put cannot be so easily contained and controlled.'[112] This collected evidence of Fane's reading and schooling thus demonstrates that while this girl's engagement with reading matter contributed to her religious, moral and domestic education as a young women, it was also a source of creative exploration.

Like Cary, Fane used her reading material as the starting point to explore her state as a girl through translation and original literary writing. Scholars have demonstrated the diverse ways in which she developed literary motifs, such as the liminal and erotic figure of Cupid or the characters of Shakespeare, in her dramatic writing to explore her own youthful state.[113] As well as illustrating Fane's detailed knowledge of Shakespeare's work, Williams points to the similarities between Fane's masque and Edmund Spenser's *The Shepheardes Calendar*, Philip Sidney's *Lady of May* and Mary Wroth's *The Countess of Montgomeries' Urania*.[114] Fane's dramatic writing thus gestures towards her extensive reading and her tendency to draw on this in her writing. These deployments of her reading are also manifest in the poetry and translations written by the young Fane.[115] On one level, Fane's translations seem appear to be straightforward pedagogical exercises and indicate parity with the training offered to schoolboys in ways of reading. Fane uses the method of double translation in which the student translates from the other language into English and then works from their English back into the original language, comparing this with the original, a pedagogical mode of translation recommended by Roger Ascham in the sixteenth century and used frequently into the seventeenth century.[116] For example, U269 F 38/1/10, a translation of the French 'Seneca concerning poverty', is divided into two columns with the English in the left-hand column. The layout suggests that Fane worked from a French original, and this is further supported by the fact that she often gives more than one possible translation in English.[117] Yet Fane did not complete the process of double translation. The right-hand column is largely blank, suggesting that producing an English text, possibly for her further reading, was the intent of this reading exercise. This demonstrates a level of independence in the act of translation and the potential for creative interpretation. Yet, for the most part this particular act of reading shapes Fane as an educated youth, rather than in specifically gendered terms.

However, even this use of the modes of reading commonly used by schoolboys is appropriated in gendered ways. Fane's translations of Seneca and Isocrates, in keeping with the curricula of formal girls' schools, prioritize the learning of French rather than Latin. Moreover, her reading of Seneca and Isocrates provides further instruction pertinent to her sex and her stage in the life cycle as she selects advice on what makes a good wife, modesty and virtue. In 1626, at the age of 13, Fane also translates three extracts of the romance text, *Amadis de Gaule*. As with her other translations, Fane works from a French text, namely *Le Neufvieme Livre d'Amadis de Gaule*, providing English and French on opposite pages of her notebook.[118] This is a striking choice of reading material. *Amadis de Gaule* was a widely read text throughout early modern Europe. Editions of the treasury in French and English emphasized the instructional dimensions of this book, and French editions, in particular, highlighted its role in training the young aristocracy in eloquence, virtue and generosity as well as letter writing and speech. This romance narrative thus gained a reputation as an instructional text for youth in behaviour as well as language.[119] Paynell, in his English translation, advocates it particularly to male readers so that they may learn to be 'noble orators, wise and prudent counsellors, excellent rhetoricians, expert captains, amorous companions, fervent and honest lovers, secrete messengers, obedient servants, elegant enditers of lovely Epistles, sweete pronouncers and true ortographers, of the French tong', and includes a table to direct the reader to exemplary letters depending on their needs.[120] Fane, it seems, read *Amadis* to practise letter writing in this way. Her selection of extracts, letters from book 9, chapters 6 and 65—'The answer of the Emperis Abbra to the Queene Zahara' and 'A Letter of prince Anaxertes to the infant Oriane'—implies that this translation may also be exemplary of epistle writing.[121] Yet Fane also translates the narrative section of chapter 70 which follows directly on from Anaxartes' letter to Oriane. Her reading of this text seems to extend beyond any formal school exercise.

Furthermore, the choice of *Amadis de Gaule* as pedagogical reading for a girl was potentially a problematic one. Attitudes to *Amadis* were constantly changing throughout early modern Europe, and it was deemed by many to be unsuitable for young female readers. Multiple editions of the treasury and recommendations of the book as a lesson for men countered Vives' proclamation of *Amadis* as one example of a book with 'no other purpose, but to corrupt the manners of young folkes', yet moral tracts continued to invoke *Amadis* as exemplary of the dangers of romance reading by women, deemed to be a distraction and idle waste of time to lesson in love.[122] Reading *Amadis* as a girl might be deemed in Fane's case, to use Nandini Das' expression, 'a youthful foray into the world of fiction', which was perceived to be a particularly dangerous act for young girls.[123] The comic representation of *Amadis* in the hands of a youthful female reader in Wye Salonstall's *Pictures Drawn forth into Characters* (1631) demonstrates the particular threat associated with this text to girls of a specific age. In his depiction of 'A maide' as 'a fruite that growes ripe at fifteene, and if she bee not then gathered, falls of her selfe', Salonstall draws upon the terminology of aged femininity.[124] *Amadis de Gaule* marks this specific moment of girlhood identity when at this age she takes up romance reading: 'she reades now loves historyes as *Amadis de Gaule* and the *Arcadia*, & in them courts the shaddow of love till she know the substance'.[125] This maid, on the cusp of no longer being maidenly, evinces increasing sexual desires and satisfies them through her wanton dreams and through this reading experience, a repeated reading of the 'shaddow' of love. Like the sparkish girl readers of Johnston's text, reading of romance fiction becomes a substitute for sexual activity and paves the way for illicit sexual behaviour. While Fane's reading is certainly not represented either in her own notebooks or elsewhere in these terms, Chedgzoy proposes that her reading of romance fiction offers an early exploration 'of romance tropes as a way of negotiating the expectations of heterosexual courtship' which Fane deployed in her creative writing of masques.[126] Rachel Fane's reading material *c.* age 13 is at once a safely monitored educational activity and a potential starting point to explore her emerging adolescent identity. Reading, for this aristocratic girl, informs her sense of what it means to be a girl negotiating the transition to early modern womanhood.

Fane's reading and writing does not only anticipate futurity, it also explores and characterizes her girlhood. As Deanne Williams suggests, Fane 'transforms her own reading, knowledge and experience into ... dramatic work that reflects and affirms her own world'.[127] Two poems included in her school manuscripts also illuminate the ways in which this youth used her reading and writing to explore her own distinct experience of being a girl. Her occasional poems—one written as a new year's gift to her mother and the other to mark the death of her younger sister, Francke (*c.* 1630)—put her learning into practice but also serve to articulate her own distinct position within this elite, literary family. Creative writing, imitating the models which had been read by young students, was a common pedagogical technique in the early modern grammar school, and in the elite household education it served a further function of demonstrating learning to their elders.[128] The tutees of Henry Stanford, for example, regularly wrote occasional poems in the late sixteenth and early seventeenth centuries to advance their learning through imitation of poetic models and to display their skills in the form of poetic gifts to their family. Their poems evidence extensive reading and also indicate the ways in which they used their reading as the basis for poetic expression.[129] The young George Berkley, for example, uses both classical imagery and references his reading of contemporary poems in his poetry, as he moves from references to Atlas and Hercules in a poem to his mother written he was age 11 in 1612 to an allusion to George Chapman's *An Epicede or Funerall Song* (1612) in a poem to his sister in the same year.[130] Fane's 'New Yeer's Gifte to my Lady' displays her learning and reading to her mother through this poetic gift, as, in addition to dutifully praising her mother and wishing her long life, she compares herself to Apollo, Minerva, Orpheus and Juno.[131] Her verse on her sister's death 'Upon the Death of my Sister Francke', is also an act of literary production, memorialization and a means of practising the literary tropes and images she has encountered in her reading. Her poem is replete with imagery from the schoolroom as she imagines the need for a 'new arithmiticke' in order to 'number' her sister's 'vertus' and deploys Ovidian imagery.[132] Through an extended reflection on time and the nature of life, she also suggests familiarity with early modern authors in her refiguring of the well-known Shakespearean question,

'To be or not to be?', with the statement 'To be's as not to be'.[133] Fane does not reproduce Hamlet's meditation, but uses her reading as a stimulus to craft her own response to loss. Finding her 'princly part', she negotiates her grief through her equation of birth and death as she suggests her sister now begins her life in death. Ultimately, however, she uses this opportunity to reflect on her own status. Both poems dwell on her position as author. 'New Yeer's Gift' draws comparisons with models of wisdom and poetry to convey her lesser status, as she claims her poem is 'poore shift' and 'rude lin'd' and that poetic talent is 'wanting', suggesting, like Cary, that she has not yet fully developed as a poet. Fane draws on this conventional expression of modesty again, referring to her 'unpractist hand' and concluding with an acknowledgement of her own 'unskillfull hand' that produced 'this thing', the poem.[134] The poem's reflection on the passage of time becomes a medium to encapsulate her own youthful and inexperienced state as author. This expression of inexperience highlights her youthful identity, but it simultaneously demonstrates her creative abilities to draw on the wide-ranging material of her education to explore loss, family and her own creative identity. Her notebooks and literary output written during her youth shed light on what she may have read, but moreover they disclose the diverse ways in which her training as a reader equipped her to produce literary expressions of her own emotional, familial and aged state.

READING, GENDER, AGE

Reading experiences shaped gendered identities. Scholarship on the materials, spaces, methods and ends of reading has persuasively shown that through reading and using books, early modern men and women acquired masculine and feminine traits. Reading was a gendered act and produced gendered subjectivities. These subjectivities, however, were also inflected by aged categories. Reading was a formative experience ultimately producing adult masculinities and femininities; but it also gendered the childhoods of the young boys and girls acquiring literacy, whether basic reading skills or advanced skills in reading multiple languages. As these two chapters have demonstrated, it is primarily in the ways of reading taught to early modern schoolboys and girls—who as humanist readers were taught to read actively, to select sections to express their emotions, behaviours and to inform their future roles—that young readers learned to deploy their reading material to assert their states as distinct types of readers: children. Reading as a girl or as a boy is made possible by the methods taught to these children but emerges in transgressive moments when early modern children use their reading in ways that disrupt the expectations of the older readers who taught them.

Therefore, in spite of the prescriptive attitudes on what and how early modern girls should read, girls such as Elizabeth Cary and Rachel Fane found, within the school lessons provided in their households, opportunities to read creatively, often in disruptive ways that aligned them with the derogatory categorization of what it meant to be a girl but also in creative and autonomous ways that provided the starting point for youthful meditations on the world around them and their place within it as they approached the age and rituals that would formally mark a transition from childhood to their anticipated future adult roles. For these early modern girls, it is clear that, as scholars on both authors have shown, their childhood lessons and early reading experiences informed their literary outputs. Their early educational reading experiences formed the basis for literary production that evidences their exceptional creative cognitive processes, which, Bicks argues, are not contrary to the early modern state of being a girl but are facilitated by their distinct biological state combined with their social context. The context of education enables the inventive negotiation of girlhood through written responses to their reading. For Cary, this had an ongoing influence on her future state as an adult author, as she explores as a child themes of religion, gender and sexual propriety that also preoccupy her adult writing.[135] Fane, in contrast, wrote when she was a child. Her written contribution to early modern literary cultures is inseparable from her childhood. Her writing of poetry and drama for her family extended her educational translations, meditations and copying exercises. Her engagement with literary culture in diverse ways shaped her as daughter, sister and girl. Her reading and writing were a means of navigating her girlhood identity within an elite, literary household.

Although these activities did not extend into her married adulthood, Fane's association with cultures of childhood and of childhood of reading were long-standing. Fane maintains her identity as a 'girl' into her adulthood, as Deanne Williams points out, with her first husband calling her 'my Girle', 'my good girl' and 'my sweet girl' in a series of affectionate letters.[136] This serves as yet a further reminder of the extent to which girlhood was, and is, a cultural category that might be performed at any age. Like Savile's critique of those who continue to be '*Girls* of 50', it suggests a playful refusal to leave the world of childhood behind. Reading in certain ways and deploying reading experiences are means of performing girlhood, but other behaviours can also contribute to the construction of this state. While Fane did not continue her childhood practice of creative writing throughout her life, this one-time girl reader made a substantial contribution to future generations of child readers. As mistress of her own household she paid for the upbringing of several children and in 1677 she donated money to Emmanuel College, Cambridge, for the purchase of 75 books, ensuring ongoing access to literacy for children of diverse social backgrounds through the material gift of books.[137] For just as this girl was the recipient of her grandmother's and mother's literacy and books and producer of her own texts, so as an adult Rachel Fane contributed to the reading cultures of other early modern boys and girls through this gift.

NOTES

1. John Johnson, *The Academy of Love* (London, 1641), 99.
2. Lucy Cary, *Lady Falkland: Her Life*, in *Lady Falkland: Life and Letters*, ed. Heather Wolfe (London: Continuum, 2004), 108. Further references are given in the text.
3. For an extended discussion of Johnson's representation of these readers as girls see Edel Lamb, '"Shall we playe the good girles": Playing Girls, Performing Girlhood on Early Modern Stages', *Renaissance Drama* 44.1 (2016): 73–100.
4. The *Life* was written during the years 1643–1649 by 'one of her daughters'. Wolfe has argued that Lucy Cary is the main author, working in collaboration with her siblings, Mary and Patrick.
5. On the evolution of the language of girlhood, see Jennifer Higginbotham, 'Fair Maids and Golden Girls: The Vocabulary of Female Youth in Early Modern English', *Modern Philology* 110 (2011): 171–96. On the tendency to divide the stages of the female life cycle according to sexual categories, see Hilda Smith, *All Men and Both Sexes: Gender, Politics and the False Universal in England, 1640–1832* (Philadelphia: Pennsylvania State Press, 2010), 4.
6. John Harrington recalls the young Arabella Stuart (*c.* 1587/8) reading Ariosto's *Orlando Furioso* and her ability to 'read French out of Italian, and English out of both, much better than I could' (John Harrington, *A Tract on the Succession to the Crown 1602* [London: Nicholas & Sons, 1880], 45).
7. For full list of the books in the painting, see Heidi Brayman Hackel, *Reading Material in Early Modern England* (Cambridge: Cambridge University Press, 2005), 225–227; Kevin Sharpe, *Reading Revolutions: The Politics of Reading in Early Modern England* (New Haven: Yale University Press, 2000), 297–298.

8. Caroline Bicks, 'Incited Minds: Rethinking Early Modern Girls', *Shakespeare Studies* 44 (2016): 180–202; Caroline Bicks, 'Instructional Performances: Ophelia and the Staging of History', in *Performing Pedagogy in Early Modern England*, ed. Kathryn Moncrief and Kathryn McPherson (Aldershot: Ashgate, 2011), 205–216; Jennifer Higginbotham, *The Girlhood of Shakespeare's Sisters: Gender, Transgression, Adolescence* (Edinburgh: Edinburgh University Press, 2013); Deanne Williams, *Shakespeare and the Performance of Girlhood* (Basingstoke: Palgrave Macmillan, 2014).

9. Williams, 51; Bicks, 'Instructional Performances', 205.

10. Although many of the examples have been boys and young men, this is a consequence of the nature of the extant evidence. On the challenges of accessing female reading experiences, Brayman Hackel, 196; Margaret Ferguson, *Dido's Daughters: Literacy, Gender and Empire in Early Modern England and France* (Chicago: University of Chicago Press, 2003), 3–12.

11. See Chap. 2, 34–43. On mothers as early teachers of early literacy, see Kenneth Charlton, '"Not publike onely but also private and domesticall": Mothers and Familial Education in Pre-industrial England', *History of Education* 17.1 (1988): 1–20; Elizabeth Mazzola, *Learning and Literacy in Female Hands, 1520–1698* (Aldershot: Ashgate, 2013), 25–26.

12. Mazzola, 27.

13. On the gendering of early modern childhood, see Naomi Miller and Naomi Yavneh, 'Introduction', in *Gender and Early Modern Constructions of Childhood*, ed. Naomi Miller and Naomi Yavneh (Aldershot: Ashgate, 2011), 1–16.

14. R. Houston, *Literacy in Early Modern Europe* (London: Routledge, 2014), 17.

15. Eve Sanders, *Gender and Literacy on Stage in Early Modern England* (Cambridge: Cambridge University Press, 1998), 1.

16. George Savile, *The Lady's New-Years Gift, Or Advice to a Daughter* (London, 1688), 22; 7.

17. Giovanni Bruto, *The Necessarie, Fit, and Convenient Education of a Yong Gentlewoman* (London, 1598), D6r–v.

18. Bruto, D6r, D8r.

19. See Will Fisher, *Materializing Gender in Early Modern Literature and Culture* (Cambridge: Cambridge University Press, 2006); Stephen Orgel, *Impersonations: The Performance of Gender in Shakespeare's England* (Cambridge: Cambridge University Press, 1996).

20. See Bicks, 'Instructional Performances', 207; Kate Chedgzoy, 'Playing with Cupid: Gender, Sexuality and Adolescence', in *Alternative Shakespeares 3*, ed. Diana E. Henderson (London: Routledge, 2008),

138–157; Higginbotham, *Girlhood*; Sara Mendelson and Patricia Crawford, *Women in Early Modern England* (Oxford: Clarendon Press, 1998); Kim Phillips, *Medieval Maidens: Young Women and Gender in England, 1270–1540* (Manchester: Manchester University Press, 2003).

21. Savile, 114.

22. See also Comenius' division of life cycle into comparable stages for men and women (Higginbotham, *Girlhood*, 35–37).

23. Bruto, D4r.

24. Bruto, D8r.

25. Bianca Calabresi, '"you sow, Ile read": Letters and Literacies in Early Modern Samplers', in *Reading Women: Literacy, Authorship, and Culture in the Atlantic World, 1500–1800*, ed. Heidi Brayman Hackel and Catherine Kelly (Philadelphia: University of Pennsylvania Press, 2008), 79–104; Juliet Fleming, *Graffiti and the Writing Arts of Early Modern England* (Philadelphia: University of Philadelphia Press, 2001); Margaret Spufford, 'Women Teaching Reading to Poor Children in the Sixteenth and Seventeenth Centuries', in *Opening the Nursery Door*, ed. Mary Hilton, Morag Styles and Victor Watson (London: Routledge, 1997), 47–62.

26. William Hawkins, *Apollo Shroving* (London, 1626), 5.

27. Calabresi, 84. See further discussion of this play in Chap. 4, 126–131.

28. Hawkins, 5.

29. Anthony Munday, *Fedele and Fortunio*, ed. Richard Hosley (London: Garland Publishing, 1981), 5.4.156–9.

30. See *OED*; Williams, 5.

31. See N. H. Keeble, ed., *Memoirs of the Life of Colonel Hutchinson* (London: Phoenix Press, 2000), 14; Jane Stevenson, *Women Latin Poets* (Oxford: Oxford University Press, 2005), 368–394; Marta Straznicky, *Privacy, Playreading and Women's Closet Drama, 1550–1700* (Cambridge: Cambridge University Press, 2004), 21.

32. See Michelle Dowd, *Women's Work in Early Modern English Literature and Culture* (Basingstoke: Palgrave Macmillan, 2009), 139, on how narratives of women's involvement as educators limit it in scope and duration, offering reassurance to those concerned about extent of female agency in the household.

33. For example, Sarah Coles and Rachel Fane as discussed in this chapter.

34. Juan Luis Vives, *The Instruction of a Christian Woman* (London, 1592), B4v.

35. Vives, C6r, D3v. Vives' advice was repeated in English conduct manuals for women throughout the seventeenth century. For example, Richard Brathwait recommends a similar reading list to women in *The English Gentlewoman* (London, 1631), 183.

36. Wendy Wall, *Staging Domesticity: Household Work and English Identity in Early Modern Drama* (Cambridge: Cambridge University Press, 2002), 61.

37. Robert White's masque *Cupid's Banishment* was performed by the pupils of this school at Greenwich in May 1617 and is the only record of the school. On the masque as evidence of the girls' education, see Lamb, 'Playing Girls'; Clare McManus, *Women on the Renaissance Stage* (Manchester: Manchester University Press, 2002), 164–201.

38. On the subjects taught to early modern girls and the history of girls' schools, see Caroline Bowden, 'Women in Educational Spaces', in *The Cambridge Companion to Early Modern Women's Writing*, ed. Laura Lunger Knoppers (Cambridge: Cambridge University Press, 2009), 85–96; Kenneth Charlton, 'Women and Education', in *A Companion to Early Modern Women's Writing* (Oxford: Blackwell, 2008), 3–21; Dorothy Gardiner, *English Girlhood at School* (London: Oxford University Press, 1929), 141–280; Helen Jewell, *Education in Early Modern England* (London: Macmillan, 1998), 105–106; Josephine Kamm, *Hope Deferred: Girls' Education in English History* (London: Methuen & Co., 1965), 34–82; Rosemary O'Day, *Education and Society 1500–1800: The Social Foundations of Education in Early Modern Britain* (London: Longman, 1982), 179–195; Laetitia Yeandle, 'A School for Girls in Windsor', *Medieval and Renaissance Drama in England* 17 (2005), 272–280.

39. Frances Teague, *Bathusa Makin, Woman of Learning* (London: Associated University Press, 1998), 93. See also Caroline Bicks, 'Producing Girls on the English Stage: Performance as Pedagogy in Mary Ward's Convent Schools', in *Gender and Early Modern Constructions of Childhood*, 139–153.

40. Suzanne Hull, *Chaste, Silent and Obedient: English Books for Women, 1475–1640* (Pasadena: Huntington Library Press, 1982), 65.

41. Gardiner, 215.

42. Claude Mauger, *The True Advancement of the French Tongue* (London, 1653), A2r–A6v. Further references are given in the text.

43. Juliet Fleming, 'The French Garden: An Introduction to Women's French', *English Literary History* 56.1 (1989): 19–51. On teaching French to girls in the period, see Jerome de Groot, '"Every one teacheth after thyr owne fantasie": French Language Instruction', in *Performing Pedagogy*, 33–51.

44. See Chap. 4, 113–123. For example, see 'The twelfth Dialogue, between two Gentlewomen that learne French' (239–241), which includes phrases regarding their performance at their lesson, and requests to lend and mend objects used within the schoolroom.

45. On performance in girls' schools, see Lamb 'Playing Girls', 95–96.

46. On the recommendation of Cato and Seneca to grammar schoolboys, see Chap. 4, 112–113, 144 n. 66.

47. See James Daybell, *The Material Letter in Early Modern England: Manuscript Letters and the Culture and Practices of Letter-Writing, 1512–1635* (Basingstoke: Palgrave Macmillan, 2012), 60.

48. See Emily Bowles Smith, '"Let them Compleately Learn": Manuscript Clues about Early Modern Women's Educational Practices', *A Manuscript Miscellany*, Proceedings of a Summer 2005 Institute, http://www.folger.edu/html/folger_institute/mm/EssayES.html, accessed 19 Nov. 2009; Heather Woolfe, 'Women's Handwriting', in *Cambridge Companion to Early Modern Women's Writing*, 25.

49. Sarah Powell and Paul Dingman, 'Arithmetic is the Art of Computation', *The Collation: Research and Exploration at the Folger*, September 2015, http://collation.folger.edu/2015/09/arithmetic-is-the-art-of-computation/, accessed 21 Aug. 2017.

50. Kate Flint, *The Woman Reader, 1837–1914* (Oxford: Clarendon Press, 1993), 24. See also Moncrief and McPherson, 10.

51. See Chap. 2, 33–34, on the aims of making boys literate.

52. Robert Darnton, *The Kiss of Lamourette* (New York: Norton, 1990), 167.

53. Cited in Anthony Fletcher, *Growing Up in England: The Experience of Childhood, 1600–1914* (New Haven: Yale University Press, 2010), 245.

54. Thomas Powell, *Tom of All Trades* (London, 1631), 47.

55. Flint, 22–24. On the parity of education for women across social class, see also Norma McMullen, 'The Education of English Gentlewomen 1540–1640', *History of Education* 6.2 (1977): 87–101.

56. See Hannah Wolley, *The Gentlewoman's Companion; Or, A Guide to the Female Sex* (London, 1673), 9.

57. Richard Mulcaster, *Positions Wherein Those Primitive Circumstances Be Examined Which Are Necessary For the Training Up of Children* (London, 1581), 177.

58. Mulcaster, 177, 133.

59. Mulcaster, 177.

60. John Batchiler, *The Virgin's Pattern* (London, 1661), title page.

61. Batchiler, A2r.

62. Batchiler, A2r.

63. Batchiler, opposite title page.

64. Thomas Salter, *The Mirrhor of Modestie* (London, 1579), title page.

65. Salter, A6r.

66. Salter, B3r.

67. Salter, B3r.

68. Bruto, G8r.

69. See Jacques Du Bosc, *The Compleat Woman* (London, 1639), 12–15.

70. Salter, A6r.
71. Bruto, K2v, G8r.
72. See Sanders, 67.
73. Du Bosc, 12. Du Bosc suggests that stories leave their mark on susceptible youths as although 'wee know well, they are but fictions, yet nevertheless they truly move being read' (15). See also Grace Mildmay's recollection in her *Autobiography* that her mother 'thought it ever dangerous to suffer young people to read or study books wherein was good and evil mingled together, for that by nature we ae inclined rather to learn and retain the evil than the good', in Linda Pollock, ed., *With Faith and Physic: The Life of a Tudor Gentlewoman, Lady Grace Mildmay 1552–1620* (London: Collins and Brown, 1993), 28.
74. See, for example, work on the creative ways that the teenage Jane Lumley deployed her reading in her translations, such as Deborah Uman, '"Wonderfullye astonied at the stoutenes of her minde": Translating Rhetoric and Education in Jane Lumley's *The Tragedie of Iphigeneia*', in *Performing Pedagogy*, 53–64, and work on Margaret Hoby's reading as religio-political activism, such as Julie Crawford, 'Reconsidering Early Modern Women's Reading, or, How Margaret Hoby Read her de Mornay', *Huntington Library Quarterly* 73.2 (2010): 193–223.
75. Wolley, title page.
76. Wolley, A3r.
77. Wolley, 9.
78. See Robert Codrington, *The Second Part of Youth's Behaviour* (London, 1664), 5–7. On Wolley's work, see John Considine, 'Wolley, Hannah (*b.* 1622?, *d.* in or after 1674)', in *Oxford Dictionary of National Biography*, ed. David Cannadine (Oxford: Oxford University Press, 2004), http://www.oxforddnb.com/view/article/29957, accessed 21 Aug. 2017; Dowd, 43.
79. Wolley, A3r.
80. See Lamb, 'Playing Girls', for further discussion of this representation of the girl reader.
81. See Higginbotham, 9; Williams, 4–6.
82. See Mary Beth Long, '*The Life* as Vita: Reading *The Lady Falkland Her Life* as Hagiography', *English Literary Renaissance* 38.2 (2008), 304–330; Heather Woolfe, 'Introduction', in *The Literary Career and Legacy of Elizabeth Cary, 1613–1680* (Basingstoke: Palgrave Macmillan, 2006), 1–4; Marion Wynne-Davies, *Women Writers and Familial Discourse in the English Renaissance: Relative Values* (Basingstoke: Palgrave Macmillan), 116–117.
83. Cary also learns Hebrew and Transylvanian as a child (*Life*, 106). Her exceptional mastery of languages from a young age is also noted by one

of her tutors, Michael Drayton. See Stephanie Hodgson-Wright, 'Cary, Elizabeth, Viscountess Falkland (1585–1639)', in *Oxford Dictionary of National Biography*, http://www.oxforddnb.com/view/article/4835, accessed 21 Aug. 2017.

84. On Cary's relationship with her parents, especially her mother, see Ramona Wray, 'Memory, Materiality and Maternity in the Tanfield/Cary Archive', in *A History of Early Modern Women's Writing*, ed. Patricia Phillippy (Cambridge: Cambridge University Press, 2017), 1–20.

85. Williams, 6, 51.

86. Williams, 51.

87. Bicks, 'Incited Minds', 182.

88. Bicks, 183. Bicks draws attention to significance of ages 14–15 in relation to this (180–181). On the importance of these ages to early modern girlhood see Chap. 6, 203.

89. See Lesley Peterson, ed., *The Mirror of the Worlde* (Montreal: McGill University Press, 2012), 7–22 on the dating of and source material for this translation. All references are taken from this edition and are given in the text.

90. See Danielle Clarke, 'Translation', in *Cambridge Companion to Early Modern Women's Writing*, 173. See Peterson on the presentation of manuscript as a gift for Sir Henry Lee on his admittance to the Order of the Garter in 1597 and as evidence that this translation is a 'self-conscious act of writing and literary production' (111).

91. On Cary's education, see Peterson, 50–58.

92. Peterson, 32.

93. Clarke, 169. On the authorial agency of the early modern translator, see Jaime Goodrich, *Faithful Translators: Authorship, Gender and Religion in Early Modern England* (Evanston: Northwestern University Press, 2014), 5–10; Deborah Uman, 'Translation and Community in the Work of Elizabeth Cary', in *Material Cultures of Early Modern Women's Writing*, ed. Patricia Pender and Rosalind Smith (Basingstoke: Palgrave, 2014), 76–98.

94. Jordan Carville, *Elizabeth Cary: Development of the Author*, unpublished MA dissertation (Queen's University Belfast, 2015), reads Cary's translation as a 'creative act of self-expression' in her insightful analysis of Cary's early writing. I am grateful to Carville for sharing her work with me.

95. Peterson, 25–26.

96. Peterson, 56–57, 64.

97. Peterson, 25, 4. Peterson also highlights the extended reflection on women's roles, the omission of violence and errors in translating geographical and mathematical facts as evidence of Cary's prioritization of her own concerns and 'active resistance' in her reading (27–29, 36–40).

98. See Lucy Munro, 'Infant Poets and Child Players: The Literary Performance of Childhood in Caroline England', in *The Child in British Literature*, ed. Adrienne Gavin (Basingstoke: Palgrave Macmillan, 2012), 54–68 on this conventional language in writing by children.

99. Kate Narveson, *Bible Readers and Lay Writers in Early Modern England: Gender and Self-Definition in an Emergent Writing Culture* (Aldershot: Ashgate, 2012), 12. See also Jennifer Richards and Fred Schurink, 'Introduction: The Textuality and Materiality of Reading in Early Modern England', *Huntington Library Quarterly* 73.3 (2010): 354, on the extent to which thinking about writing can help us understand reading.

100. Smith, 3–4, 53; Higginbotham, *Girlhood*, 20–27.

101. Chedgzoy, 'Playing with Cupid', 139. See also Marjorie Garber, *Coming of Age in Shakespeare* (London: Methuen, 1997), 116–173, on marriage as crucial ritual for the transition from childhood to womanhood.

102. On the significance of these ages for early modern girls, see Keith Thomas, 'Age and Authority in Early Modern England', *Proceedings of the British Academy* 62 (1976): 205–248; Ursula Potter, 'Greensickness in Romeo and Juliet: Considerations on a Sixteenth-Century Disease of Virgins', in *The Premodern Teenager: Youth in Society 1150–1650*, ed. Konrad Eisenbichler (Toronto: Centre for Renaissance and Reformation Studies, 2002), 271–291; Ursula Potter, 'Navigating the Dangers of Female Puberty in Renaissance Drama', *Studies in English Literature 1500–1900* 53.2 (2013): 421–439.

103. Centre for Kentish Studies (CKS), Sackville, U269 F 38/1/15.

104. For detailed description of the contents of this collection, see Caroline Bowden, 'The Notebooks of Rachel Fane: Education for Authorship?', in *Early Modern Women's Manuscript Writing: Selected Papers from the Trinity/Trent Colloquium*, ed. Victoria Burke and Jonathan Gibson (Aldershot: Ashgate, 2004), 157–180.

105. See Chedgzoy, 'Playing with Cupid'; Kate Chedgzoy, 'Introduction: "What, are they children?"', in *Shakespeare and Childhood*, ed. Kate Chedgzoy, Susanne Greenhalgh and Robert Shaughnessy (Cambridge: Cambridge University Press, 2007), 15–31; Higginbotham, *Girlhood*, 172–174; Munro, 54–68; Williams, 173–188.

106. Caroline Bowden, 'Fane, Lady Rachel [married names Rachel Bourchier, countess of Bath; Rachel Cranfield, countess of Middlesex] (bap. 1613, d. 1680)', in *Oxford Dictionary of National Biography*, http://www.oxforddnb.com/view/article/93575, accessed 21 Aug. 2017; Bowden, 'Notebooks'; Kate Chedgzoy, 'A Renaissance for Children?', Newcastle Upon Tyne ePrints, http://eprint.ncl.ac.uk/pub_details2.aspx?pub_id=196398, deposited 20 Nov. 2013, 6.

107. CKS U269 F 38/1/2; CKS U269 F 38/1/5; CKS U269 F 38/1/6; CKS U269 F 38/1/10; CKS U269 F 38/1/11; CKS U269 F 38/1/12;

CKS U269 F 38/1/14. I am grateful to Helen Orme at the Centre for Kentish Studies for providing copies of these documents.

108. See Chap. 4, 112–113.
109. William Bullokar, *Aesopz Fablz* (London, 1585), 3–4.
110. John Penkethman, *A Handful of Honesty* (London, 1623), n.p.
111. CKS U269 F 38/1/9; CKS U269 F 38/1/7.
112. Kate Chedgzoy, *Women's Writing in the British Atlantic World: Memory, Place and History, 1550–1700* (Cambridge: Cambridge University Press, 2007), 32.
113. See Chedgzoy, 'Playing with Cupid'; Higginbotham, 172–174; Williams, 178–187.
114. Williams, 180, 186.
115. Fane's dramatic writing has been analysed in detail for what it reveals about her familial connections and her literary knowledge, particularly her knowledge of masquing practices and of Shakespeare. Her translations and poems have received less attention. In addition to work by Chedgzoy and Williams cited above, see Alison Findlay, *Playing Spaces in Early Women's Drama* (Cambridge: Cambridge University Press, 2006), 40–43, 96–103; Marion O'Connor, 'Rachel Fane's May Masque at Apethorpe, 1627', *English Literary Renaissance* 36.1 (2006): 90–113.
116. See Joseph Loewenstein, 'Humanism and Seventeenth-Century English Literature', in *The Cambridge Companion to Renaissance Humanism*, ed. Jill Kraye (Cambridge: Cambridge University Press, 2004), 275.
117. Bowden, 'Notebooks', 168.
118. Fane works from a French version such as that published in Lyon in 1575 (British Library Reference 245 a 9). Her translation corresponds directly to Book 9, Chapters 6, 65 and 70, 72–74, 802–803 and 861–863 of this edition.
119. On the history of *Amadis de Gaule* and changing attitudes towards it, see Bowden, 'Notebooks', 170; Helen Moore, 'Introduction', *Amadis de Gaule*, ed. Helen Moore (Aldershot: Ashgate, 2004), ix–xxviii; John J. O'Connor, *Amadis de Gaule and its Influence on Elizabethan Literature* (New Brunswick: Rutgers University Press, 1970).
120. Thomas Paynell, *The Most Excellent and Pleasaunt Booke, Entitled The Treasurie of Amadis of Fraunce* (London, 1572), n.p.
121. Daybell, 60.
122. Vives, D1v. See Moore, ix–xxviii.
123. Nandini Das, *Renaissance Romance: The Transformation of English Prose Fiction, 1570–1620* (Aldershot: Ashgate, 2011), 157.
124. Wye Salonstall, *Pictures Drawn forth into Characters* (London, 1631), 17.
125. Salonstall, 19.

126. Chedgzoy, 'Introduction', 16.

127. Williams, 173.

128. See Lynn Enterline, *Shakespeare's Schoolroom: Rhetoric, Discipline, Emotion* (Philadelphia: University of Pennsylvania Press, 2012), 1–8, 22–26; Kate Chedgzoy, '"Make me a Poet, and I'll quickly be a Man": Masculinity, Pedagogy and Poetry in the English Renaissance', *Renaissance Studies* 27.5 (2013): 592–611.

129. See L. C. Black, 'Some Renaissance Children's Verse', *Review of English Studies* 24.93 (1973): 1–6; Chedgzoy, 'Make Me'; Chedgzoy, 'Renaissance'.

130. Steven May, ed., *Henry Stanford's Anthology: An Edition of Cambridge University Library MS, Dd. 5.75*, New York: Garland, 1988), items 87 and 89.

131. CKS U269 F 38/3, 6r.

132. CKS U269 F 38/3, 6v.

133. See Williams, 178–187, on Fane's knowledge of Shakespeare and the extent to which this informs her drama. Williams suggests that it is possible that Fane's awareness of the author was a result of theatrical attendance. However, it is also possible that Fane read the plays in book form, even though her grandmother, Lady Grace Mildmay, warned against 'books of idle plays and of all such fruitless and unprofitable matter which will pervert and carry the mind from all goodness and [which] is an introduction unto all evil' (Pollock, 24). See O'Connor, 93, on playbooks at Apethorpe. Other early modern girls accessed 'play books', even when parents forbade it, as the Johnson example considered in this chapter suggests. See also example of Elizabeth Isham in Chap. 6, 211. See Sasha Roberts, *Reading Shakespeare's Poems in Early Modern England* (Basingstoke: Palgrave Macmillan, 2003), 1–58, on early modern female readers of Shakespeare.

134. CKS U269 F 38/3, 7r.

135. See Carville; Peterson, 4.

136. Williams, 188.

137. Bowden, 'Notebooks', 173.

CHAPTER 6

'I Remember When I Began to Read': Remembering Childhood Reading

I had read him all over before I was twelve years old, and was thus made a Poet as immediately as a Child is made an Eunuch.[1]

The poet, dramatist and essayist Abraham Cowley memorializes his childhood reading via this striking image of transformation in his autobiographical essay 'Of Myself'. Written towards the end of his life and published posthumously in 1668, Cowley's essay positions his early textual encounters as crucial formative experiences.[2] It reflects upon the reading experiences that made him a poet, a status achieved during childhood with the publication of his *Poetical Blossoms* in 1633, a collection that contained poems written as early as 'ten yeeres age'.[3] Cowley's representation of his childhood reading is, like many of the examples considered in this study, a retrospective one. As he approaches the end of his life, he takes time to 'write of himself' (143). Childhood is recalled in order to explain his 'self'. Offering a fantastical and alluring description of the extent to which his literary career originated in the 'Stories of the Knights, and Giants, and Monsters, and brave Houses' in '*Spencer's* Works' (144), Cowley creates a quasi-magical account of artistic inspiration. He draws on multiple ideas about childhood reading to produce a narrative of the self. As this chapter demonstrates, he deploys the image of the exceptional 'good' child reader, a narrative of being a reading schoolboy and the concept of youthful immersion in tales to depict an individual formed through early reading experiences.

© The Author(s) 2018
E. Lamb, *Reading Children in Early Modern Culture*,
Early Modern Literature in History,
https://doi.org/10.1007/978-3-319-70359-6_6

Given Cowley's education at Westminster School and the indebtedness of his early poetry to classical models, it is likely that he had read Spenser by the age of 12 as he claims.[4] Yet, as many scholars have highlighted, autobiographical accounts, which involve processes of selection, rhetorical patterning and interpretation, cannot be interpreted as historical fact.[5] Cowley's representation of childhood reading experiences is arguably less interesting for what—if anything—it might reveal about the historical act of reading by a child, and is more significant for what it discloses about the ways in which writers reimagine childhood reading from the perspective of more advanced age. It reveals how childhood reading might be evoked to portray the origins of selfhood, in this case characterized by an exceptional creative talent. This chapter considers retrospective representations of childhood reading in early modern autobiographical texts to evaluate the ways in which images of the child as reader are used to write the self. Temporal distance, the desire to 'reassemble the scattered elements of [an] individual life and to regroup them in a comprehensive sketch' and the urge to memorialize a life shape such depictions of childhood and of reading.[6] This chapter examines how representations of childhood reading fulfil particular functions in early modern textual constructions of the self. It focuses on texts that recollect childhood to suggest that the autobiographical strategy of revisiting childhood reading became common in early modern spiritual narratives but was also important to diverse forms of life writing, including this essay by a professional writer.

Early modern life writing, as many have highlighted, encompassed a range of genres.[7] In the absence of established modes of autobiographical writing, early modern men and women experimented with ways of writing the self, ranging from diaries, essays and memoirs to conversion narratives, almanacs, accounts and commonplace books. This was, Julie Eckerle proposes, an 'exploratory and experimental moment' to articulate the self in writing and, as Elspeth Graham highlights 'the crucial characteristic of self-writing' was the 'exploration and exploitation of a variety of forms, rather than adherence to a recognized format for articulating the self'.[8] Early modern life writing, therefore, did not follow a prescribed format and the tendency to begin with a detailed account of childhood did not become standard until later.[9] Other than a brief acknowledgement of parentage and allusions to early education many autobiographical texts from the period do not acknowledge the author's childhood.[10] Nonetheless, while Cowley's reflection on childhood reading is remarkable, it is not unique. His description of an exceptional childhood reading experience bears similarities to Michael Drayton's representation of his childhood reading and transformation from 'goodly page' to 'Poet' in his poem 'To my most dearly-loved friend Henery Reynolds Esquire, of *Poets and Poesie*', first published in 1627.[11] More commonly, childhood reading forms an integral, albeit brief, part of spiritual accounts of the self. Early modern writers such as Grace Mildmay include descriptions of their exemplary childhoods so that their life and their text might act as model and advice for future generations. Some spiritual meditations describe youthful experiences in more detail. Influenced by Augustine's reflections on his childhood in his *Confessions*, texts by some writers, including Elizabeth Isham and Richard Norwood, appropriate the saint's account of childhood transgressions before spiritual conversion. This chapter asks what role childhood reading plays in the textual representation of early modern lives by evaluating such recollections of childhood. It proposes that there are a number of formulaic ways in which the child is retrospectively figured as reader. Covering a range of autobiographical forms, it will suggest that some patterns emerge.[12] Although the representation of the child as reader is often inflected by genre, there is no distinct trope of childhood for particular modes of writing a life in the period. Instead each representation is influenced by the context and motivation for self-reflection. For instance, in many spiritual reflections, childhood reading practices are either recalled as being indicative of the exemplary life or as a transgression that must be overcome to enable spiritual conversion. In the former, childhood reading is represented as formative of adult subjectivity; in the latter the self can only be constructed in the text through a differentiation from childhood. In narratives of professional lives, childhood reading is commemorated in distinct ways to signal exceptional talent. This chapter focuses on three retrospective representations of childhood reading that both depend upon and complicate these formulaic representations of the child as reader: Elizabeth Isham's *Booke of Remembrance*, written in her thirtieth year, *c.* 1638–1639; Elizabeth Delaval's memoirs and meditations, which she claims to have begun *c.* 1662 at the age of 14; and Cowley's 'Of Myself'. Although these writers are informed by distinct contexts, literary forms and aims, the recollection of childhood reading by these writers indicates a wider cultural recognition of how childhood relates to selfhood. They potentially draw on shared models: Isham and Delaval's memoirs, for example, are likely influenced by Augustine's *Confessions* and Calvinist-influenced texts of self-examination. Yet these examples do not indicate a chronological emergence of a standard autobiographical trope of the child as reader. Rather these exceptional cases reveal the diverse ways in which early modern writers reimagined their childhood reading to negotiate the self. Remembering childhood reading was one aspect of the experimental mode of writing a life in the seventeenth century.

In later autobiographical writing, the images of the child and childhood occupy a crucial status. As Carolyn Steedman persuasively argues, the 'child-figure' became a central 'vehicle for ideas about self and its history' in the eighteenth and nineteenth centuries, and became an apt motif following the Freudian articulation of the idea that an individual's lost past is crucial to psychic identity, or, as Steedman puts it, following the establishment of the idea that there is a 'lost child within us all'.[13] In nineteenth-century life writing in particular, Steedman points out, 'the idea of the child was used both to recall and express the past that each individual life contained' and 'the child *was* the story waiting to be told'.[14] More recent autobiographical texts interrogate the significance of childhood reading to selfhood. Francis Spufford's unusual memoir, for instance, returns to his favourite childhood books. Beginning with a self-conscious reflection on the role of childhood reading for 'self-understanding', 'autonomy' and 'transformations', Spufford proposes that reading in childhood is part of 'the primary fashioning of a self'.[15] This recollection of books read as a child functions as a narrative strategy to recount 'the origins of my life as a reader' but also to examine his life as 'a story among stories', which, Spufford admits, 'after I have been reading for a while, I can hardly tell any more which is my own'.[16] For this twentieth-century memoirist—informed by educationalists' and children's literature theorists' recognition of the ways in which children's cognitive development and emerging sense of self is shaped by their experiences of stories, narrative structures and language—childhood reading is central to the formation of identity.[17] It also serves as a literary technique for telling his life story. Early modern concepts of childhood or reading are obviously not informed by such theorizations of the child. Yet, as this monograph has shown, early modern instruction in literacy urged children, male and female, to read in order to shape their moral characters and their gendered identities, and to imitate or creatively use the examples found in books to produce their adulthoods. Early modern readers were accustomed to drawing on their reading experiences to negotiate their subjectivities. *Reading Children* has primarily argued that reading, as Ann Moss suggests, is 'a way of defining and testing the self' in early modern culture, and that young readers were shaped

by and produced their own identities as children through diverse engagements with their reading material.[18] This final chapter builds on this to
interrogate the social and literary factors that impact on early modern
writers' reflections on this early formative experience as constitutive of
selfhood and to examine how the child as reader becomes a literary trope
in this context. It contends that retrospective representations of childhood
reading illuminate the extent to which reading as a child becomes crucial
to the construction of selfhood for some early modern writers. In doing
so, it acknowledges the retrospective nature of many of the sources considered throughout this monograph to raise questions about what the
extant evidence about early modern child readers might ultimately disclose about the child and childhood in the period.

The Child Reader: An Autobiographical Trope?

Religious cultures in the sixteenth and seventeenth centuries gave rise to
diverse forms of writing about the self and about the lives of others.[19] As
Carolyn Steedman points out, English biography as a form has generally
been seen to emerge as part of a larger body of writings dealing with
spiritual journeys undertaken in individual lives, and early modern
Puritan autobiography is one of the best-known examples.[20] Alec Ryrie
notes that 'constructing and interpreting life-narratives' was 'an important part of the Protestant mindset', leading to a rise of diverse forms of
the spiritual diary in Protestant culture.[21] Such accounts were written to
'situate a life within the context of God's purpose' and, following the
Calvinist impetus to self-examination for signs of salvation, to discern
such signs in a life.[22] For many Protestant writers, identifying godly practices in their lives, including the reading of religious books, was a recurrent motif in biographical and autobiographical texts. Many writers
identify the origins of this religious reading in childhood. Lady Grace
Mildmay, for example, begins her late sixteenth-century autobiography
by stating:

> I have found by experience [and] I commend unto my children as approved,
> this to be the best course to set ourselves in from the beginning unto the
> end of our lives. That is to say: first begin with the scriptures to read them
> with all diligence and equal measure until we have gone through the whole
> book of God from the first of Genesis to the last of the Revelation and then
> begin again and so over and over without weariness.[23]

For Mildmay, reading the scriptures is a practice to be established at the beginning of life and she carefully substantiates her authority for this through the claim that this is based on 'experience'. Having highlighted the scriptures as primary reading material from childhood and throughout life, she proceeds to recommend 'the histories contained in the book of Acts and Monuments of the church' so that faith may 'be increased and strengthened', and the 'chronicles of the land' to provide knowledge of statutes and laws and, finally, 'the wise and witty sentences of the philosophers' for 'recreation'.[24] This 'book of my meditation' is written, Mildmay claims, to guide her 'daughter and her children', and this reading list is primarily directed to them.[25] Yet Mildmay goes further than recommending this reading, she demonstrates its virtue through example. This description of her life reveals her reading and 'meditations which hath been the exercise of my mind from my youth until this day'.[26] Mildmay highlights her apposite education under the guidance of a governess, who herself 'from her youth, made good use of all things that she ever did read', and her mother, who gave her books that gave her 'the first taste of Christ Jesus and his truth', namely 'The Bible, Musculus's *Common Places*, *The Imitation of Christ*, Mr. Foxe's *Book of Martyrs*'.[27] As Bedford, Davis and Kelly point out, Mildmay 'records her own life as a commendable part of [a] God-fearing lineage'.[28] Her narrative outlines her moral and spiritual practices to prove the devoutness of her own life, but also to offer this life as an example to others. In the repetition of 'from my youth' and variations on ideas of laying the 'foundation' or becoming 'better established in the whole course of my life' she impresses the importance of reading in childhood as the basis for a godly life.[29] While Mildmay's manuscript claims to inform family readers, other accounts of exemplary lives were circulated more widely. One posthumously published autobiography, *A Wise Virgins Lamp Burning [...] The Experiences of Mrs. Anne Venn* (1658), also cites childhood reading as the origin of a godly life. Venn recalls that before the age of 9 she 'began to take some delight in hearing the word, but most of all in reading to myself', and remembers that she subsequently read the work of John Dod, 'Mr Roger's evidences, and an other called the *Touchstone of true Grace*, an other called *None but Christ*, and divers others; which I did daily read on for many hours' before turning 12.[30] Venn's reading is, she claims, inspired by her childhood desire 'to read and hear all the marks of a righteous man that should go to heaven'.[31] It marks her from childhood as 'a gracious soul waiting for [God]', as the title page declares, and puts forward her life as an example for others, particularly young girls.[32]

Childhood reading experiences are also recounted in early modern spiritual autobiographies to affirm the emergence of vocations from an early age. While Mildmay recalls her early reading of herbals under the guidance of her governess, paving the way for her later medical practices, the Church of England clergyman, Ralph Josselin, describes his childhood reading in his 'summary view of my life' as the foundation of his spiritual vocation.[33] Like Mildmay, Josselin implies that early commitment to good religious practices set a pattern for life as he claims 'I confesse my childhood was taken with ministers and I heard with delight and admiracion and desire to imitate them from my youth and would be acting in corners.'[34] This enactment of his future profession from a young age is positioned alongside his 'singular affection to the historyes in the bible' from 'very yong dayes' as Josselin highlights his formative engagement with religious texts in childhood as prefiguring his future role as minister.[35] The crucial role of childhood reading in religious awakenings was not limited to Protestant texts. The Catholic Mary Ward also uses an image of childhood reading to account for her religious vocation. She describes her first desire to become a nun in her autobiographical text at the age of 15, claiming to be inspired by routines of 'prayer, some few fasts, and some austerities, and internal and external mortifications' and by delight 'in reading spiritual books'. For Ward, reading is an intense and engaging act. She claims she 'spent much time by day and sometimes by night in this employment' and, combined with her 'burning desires to be a martyr', she 'fixed' her mind 'upon that happy event; the sufferings of the martyrs appeared to me delightful for attaining so great a good and my favourite thoughts were how? And when?'[36] These intense and repetitive reading practices inspire questioning and religious commitment for Ward. This is recounted through a particular emphasis on childhood, and the crucial age of 15, and foreshadows Ward's later visions that inspire her to set up her religious community of 'English Ladies'.[37] Ward emphasizes her age and through a retrospective mode deploys the memory of childhood to vindicate subsequent decisions about religion. For Ward, inspired by the martyrs she encounters in her books, this reading works alongside prayer and fast as a bodily experience. Her reading affects both mind and body to facilitate questioning and subsequent commitment to the life she will lead as an exiled Catholic.[38] Or, at least in this literary account of her life, it facilitates the construction of her own identity as martyr-like. As with Cowley's depiction of childhood reading that makes him a poet, Ward exploits an image of childhood reading as transformative to explain a remarkable life, albeit in a very different context.

Reading is evoked in these accounts to portray exemplary lives and to justify exceptional and non-conforming life choices.[39] It is imagined as a mode through which diverse subjectivities might be formed. This depiction of childhood reading draws upon concepts of this stage of the life cycle common to early modern Protestant, Catholic and humanist ideologies, which, as this study has noted, was perceived to be a vulnerable phase during which individuals were liable to be moulded. Reading godly books, like prayer and education more generally, was perceived to be one way of shaping a self, and occupied a particular place in battling original sin, taming youthful rebellion and overcoming childhood temptations. This is reflected in stories of overcoming the dangers of youth by reading in autobiographical texts. Ann Venn remembers that when she was 'some 12 or 13 years old' the 'Divel' 'used many temptations working together with the corruptions of my own heart, in the estate of my childhood', but through the 'support' that she had from the Lord in the 'form of 'hearing and reading' she was able to resist.[40] Ralph Josselin similarly gestures towards the susceptibility of the 'estate' of 'childhood' as he acknowledges that he was preserved by the 'goodnes of God' from 'poysonous infections' and, 'though full [of] spirit, and of a nimble head and and strong memory, preserved from many untowardnesses that young [boys] fall into'.[41] Josselin admits his liability to be influenced by some reading experiences in less desirable ways. His 'continuall' reading of 'historyes' led to imaginative feats, including times when he 'would project the conquering of kingdoms and write historyes' of such exploits.[42] In addition, 'which was worse', his reading of other books inspired 'sens[ations] and 'strange prodigious uncleane lusts when I was yet a child'.[43] As Katharine Craik points out, impressionable boys in the period were seen to be drawn to unprofitable books that would incite 'emotional giddiness [...] but also engage the imaginations [...] in more subtle disturbing ways'.[44] These accounts of exemplary godly lives disclose such vulnerabilities of childhood. Reading can both distract from and enable a godly life. What makes the individuals who are tempted and exposed to books containing 'evil' such exemplary Christians is the way in which they overcome the temptations. Josselin highlights that 'god kept mee from all outward uncleanesse'.[45] He recalls childhood reading as evidence of a close relationship with God from early life, and the imaginative temptations of some reading experiences serve as signs that he was protected and marked for a godly life from childhood. The temptations of his early reading are a foil to his subsequent godliness.

In rewriting individual childhoods, these autobiographical texts produce 'fictions' or 'figures'.[46] They produce the figure of the child reader. However, this is not a singular entity. Not all early modern spiritual memoirs articulate an easy triumph over the potential ill effects of reading in childhood. Many writers instead construct a childhood characterized by what they retrospectively determine to be sinful reading. In his *Account of his Conversion and Ministry*, Vavasor Powell states that in spite of being 'trained up in learning from my Childhood [...] I was as most Youths are, not only ignorant of the knowledge of God ... but was also very active and forward in the persuit of the pleasures and vanities of this wicked world'.[47] This errant childhood is reflected in his reading interests, as he admits 'I had no esteem for the holy Scriptures, nor cared at all to look into them, but either Hystorical or Poeticall Books, Romances and the like were all my delight'.[48] A conversion happens later for Powell when by 'a choice providence I cam to find a book written by Doctor *Sibbes*, called the bruised Reed, and by reading that I found there was incouragement for weake ones'.[49] Richard Baxter, in *Reliquiae Baxterianae* (1696), also attributes a moment of spiritual awakening to reading when, through the reading of *Bunny's Resolution* 'when I was about fifteen years of age it pleased God to awaken my soul'.[50] Prior to this, in spite of his father's influence in 'set[ting] me to read the historical part of the Scripture, which suiting my nature greatly delighted me', Baxter represents his childhood as a series of sins, which include being 'bewitched with a love of romances, fables and old tales, which corrupted my affections and lost my time'.[51] Richard Norwood also cites 'delight' in romances, namely 'vayne and corrupt books as *Palmerin de Olivia*, *The Seaven Champions*, and other like' as a youthful act, which alongside 'acting a part in a play, the reading of playbooks ... alienated my heart from the Word of God' when he was aged 14 and 15, following his earlier 'childhood and tender years' of 'blessings and favours'.[52] These writers reflect on childhood and youth as corrupt stages of life and what they read figures prominently as a signifier of this corruption. Within the writing of a life, this functions to highlight a period of ignorance, described by these writers as their 'natural estate', which precedes a moment of awakening or conversion.[53] Their tales of childhood reading, commonly incorporating generic collections of material such as romances, therefore, do not necessarily reflect their historical reading but signal what they call a 'vanity of the mind' and ignorance. It represents a phase in the evolution of religious understanding through the course of a life: the transition from childish reading to the spiritual understanding which these individuals seek. Childhood is defined in these narratives by the reading of recreational or morally dubious books, as writers draw on the prevalent associations between childhood and reading for pleasure.[54] The end of childhood in these representations is marked by knowledge-able encounters with religious books.

Narrated from the perspective of the writer in adulthood, these retro-spective accounts of childhood reading also work formally to suggest a new, enlightened perspective. Childhood, commonly referred to in these texts as a time of sin, foolishness and 'childish' things, is distinguished from adulthood in terms of reading practices and this new knowledge. The recognition of the transgressions of childhood is only possible from the altered perspective. Alice Thornton reflects on a moment of under-standing achieved through reading when she was aged 12 in 1638. Reading of the 12-year-old Christ disputing with his elders 'in the Gospel of St Luke', she 'fell into a serious and deepe meditation of the thoughts of Christ's majestie, divinity and wisdom, who was able to confound the learned doctors and confute their wisome who was aged'.[55] In identifying herself with Christ, 'He being so young Himself', she proceeds to con-sider 'my owne folly and childish ignorance'.[56] Thornton's reading as child, focused on a child subject, enables her transition to understanding, and from this perspective she immediately views her childhood differently. The act of remembering facilitates consciousness of this—as Richard Norwood muses 'the remembrance of those times' is 'sweet and savoury unto the present'—but it also recasts childhood.[57] From the moment that these writers are able to understand themselves, childhood becomes a past experience and is constructed in their writing as an alternative state of being. In his autobiography, Robert Blair recalls that when reading Augustine's *Confessions* at the age of 23, what impressed him most was how in his old age he discovered his childish sins.[58] Many of these texts use a similar model. In addition to drawing on the informed perspective offered by older age, the narrative of childhood immersion in sin, particu-larly Augustine's account of stealing fruit as a boy, which echoed through-out later seventeenth-century spiritual memoirs, demonstrates the extent to which these autobiographical texts deploy formulaic conventions rather than recount the material experiences of historical individuals.[59] More advanced age, or at least a retrospective stance, enables the writer to view life from a position of self-awareness or a presumed level of self-knowledge. The retrospective form of these narratives imagines childhood from the perspective of informed adulthood. The remembered child reader is fashioned to permit the narration of a specific story from a distinct perspective. The child reader in this context is a fictional construct through which autobiographical writers chart the development of spiritual understanding.

LEAVING CHILDHOOD

These images of childhood also disclose something about the writers' subjectivities. The discourses of childhood reading form part of the writer's self-examination. Rewriting childhood reading using shared motifs is one way of negotiating the self. The child as reader may be a discursive construct in these texts, produced via the appropriation of wider cultural concepts of childhood and reading, but it functions nonetheless as a means of exploring childhood as constitutive component of individual identity, albeit one that must be left behind. This is evident in the writing of Lady Elizabeth Delaval. Delaval's untitled memoirs combine meditations, prayers, transcribed letters, a poem and linking prose sections; a series of 'scater'd papers' written 'from the time of entering into my 14th yeare' and which Delaval decides to 'colect [...] alltogether' during Lent when she is '4 month's past twenty', as a form of 'Repentance' through 'Fresh and lively representations' of sins in order to 'incline our heart's aright'.[60] Despite this ostensible spiritual motivation, Delaval's text is not, as Margaret Ezell points out, a straightforward devotional exercise and is written instead in response to moments of secular personal crisis. Delaval, Ezell proposes, 'creates in her religious meditations a chronicle of her secular life which is not bound either by the demands of conventional piety or literary genre'.[61] Beginning with a meditation 'writ in my fourteenth yeare' (28), c. 1662, that reflects on early educational and reading experiences, including her engagement with tales and books in 'childish age' (45), the text offers a detailed reflection on childhood reading experiences from the perspective of a teenage girl. Delaval imagines her writing self as situated beyond childhood, using the past tense to look back on this stage of her life. Yet, her writing betrays an ongoing struggle to move beyond the formative experiences of childhood. The representation of the various life stages covered in her text—her childhood and her youth and courtship until the age of 22—are complicated by what Julie Eckerle calls the 'layered' perspectives in the narrative. Although the sections are initially written 'from Age of forteen years old To that of Twenty' (26), with later sections written during her early twenties, some sections seem to have been added later.[62] The result, Eckerle suggests, is the presentation of 'a layered version of her former selves, in which each interpretive layer re-explains these past selves from the current moment in time'. This autobiographical text reflects on childhood from the perspective of the young teenager on the cusp of childhood and adulthood and then 'overlaid by an older, more disillusioned woman's perspective'.[63]

Age is crucial to Delaval's self-representation, not only because of this layered writing of the self at and from different temporal moments. Ezell notes that one of the most striking characteristics of the volume is the care with which she documents age.[64] Delaval provides headings for each entry, many of which highlight the age she was when it was written. In the linking narrative sections she repeatedly recalls the age at which certain events happened, identifying as early in her life as when she was a 'lettle past 8 yeare old' (29).[65] Delaval also self-consciously highlights age in presenting her emotional development. At the end of 'the prayers and meditations writ from my 14th yeare to my 20th', she reflects:

> Thus far the the [sic] thoughts which I had in the springtime of my life are set downe. Now folow's what I writ in the summer of it, which pass'd away more full of cares, and with less of innocence in it, then the former. (165)

The seasonal imagery reveals her awareness of conventional depictions of the life cycle and of the associations of these stages with states of being as she charts a movement out of the relatively innocent springtime of childhood and youth to her disappointments in love.[66] In a meditation written in her nineteenth year, she reflects on how she expected to have developed as she moved through the life cycle, writing:

> Tis true for a good while I have thought my great youth wou'd make my counsel be dispised, and now that I am grow into riper year's, alas, I grow lasy, and being weary of a troublesome world I seek ease for my self in a retirement [...] The fondnesse I have of my own peace may justly be call'd lasynesse in my nature, which at my age cannot be excused, being much less pardonable in me then in those who have long toyled in the midst of cares. (136)

Delaval demonstrates a sensitive awareness of what types of behaviour are acceptable at different ages, again drawing on motifs of ageing in the language of ripening. The recurrence of imagery of ageing hints at the ways in which her narrative is structured according to conventions. To a certain extent, Delaval seems to make her experiences fit cultural understanding of the stages of the life cycle. In addition, in this knowing reflection on the movement from 'youth' to 'riper year's' during which she becomes 'lasy', which at this 'age cannot be excused', Delaval conflates aged identities. She reflects back on her life but simultaneously lapses to reposition herself in that moment ('at my age'). The shifting tenses and language of age forges this multi-layered self.

Within this production of selfhood inflected by the perspectives of multiple aged experiences, the period around age 14 is highlighted as crucial stage. The age of 14 was a culturally significant one for many early modern children. Childhood was often perceived to end around this age, with the years between 12 and 14 more generally perceived as a crucial transitional stage for girls, as the years during which their biological transition out of childhood was marked by the symptoms of reaching sexual maturity. In the literature of the period, these years of life were frequently evoked to signify this transition out of childhood, often marked by courtship, sexual desire or marriage.[67] As the examples in this chapter have shown, it is also often highlighted in autobiographical accounts of child reading, with Venn and Thornton specifying the ages of 12 and 13 with crucial reading experiences, and Ward and Baxter associating their transformative reading experience with their 15th year. Delaval draws attention to 14 as a crucial transitional moment. It is the age at which she achieves some economic independence (an allowance from her aunt); her governess leaves and her formal education ends; she is allowed to choose her own 'young people to waight upon' (35) her; and she leaves her aunt's house, the domestic space of her childhood, to become a maid of the privy chamber to Catherine of Braganza.[68] It is also the age at which she begins to write her meditations. Furthermore, it is from the perspective of this age that she is able as a writer to reflect back on her childhood. Her first meditation, written in 'my fourteenth yeare', gives a reflective account of her earliest years by setting out to tell how 'most unhappy have I been in the beginning of my life by misplaceing of my heart' (29). Although in close proximity to this earlier state, Delaval adopts the authorial stance of maturity to distance herself from childhood and to reflect on the errors of her ways. For her, her 14th year marks the end of the earliest stage of life and gives her the vantage point to reimagine childhood retrospectively.

In doing so, Delaval depicts childhood as a period of 'folly' (45). An immersion in tales and stories, as a listener and a reader, is at the centre of this. In the first meditation she reflects back on her first 'personal crisis': the influence of her aunt's servant, Mistriss Carter since she was 'a very lettle child' (29). Recounting how Carter 'fill'd my thought's with foleish fable's' (30) and began to 'delude me with tale's of fary's' (30), Delaval claims that she 'firmely believed' these tales to the extent that she was 'longing for the appearance of my first fary' (31), took such 'great pleasure' (31) in them, and 'listen'd to all her fable's with as much attention as if her word's had been oracle's, and beleived my selfe blest in the friend I had chose' (32). While the description hints at the intensity of her engagement with these stories, this is filtered through a perspective beyond childhood. Carter's influence over her is figured from the vantage point of 14 as leading to the delusion and distraction of the child from appropriate company, learning and reading.[69] Delaval claims that Carter would take her away 'When I had a tasque set me, ether as to the reading so many chaptier's in the French Bible and so many in the English one, or that I was to learn some part of the holy scripture by heart' (29) and admits that 'So eagerly bent was I upon these thing's that I thought it altogether needlesse to pray or to read the holy scriptures' (31). The tales told by Carter are set in direct opposition to language and religious education in this recollection and represented as detrimentally impacting upon her reading in these areas. From her more mature stance, Delaval co-opts the rhetoric of the prescriptive conduct literature of the period to illustrate the dangerous ill effects of a servant's oral tales on the impressionable child.[70] She constructs her childhood experience in terms of the widespread fear that children might be corrupted by fantastical stories as they are unable to distinguish between imagined tales and reality.[71] Her language of doting, delusion and folly goes so far as to suggest an infection of the mind as a result of these stories.[72] This judgemental treatment of Carter illuminates Delaval's increased self-knowledge as she ages. However, it is not clear if Delaval is simply replicating wider fears of the effect of such tales on children or if she gently mocks them through this imaginative recreation of her childhood reading.[73]

Carter's influence, Delaval claims, also impacted on her when she had her 'own choyce' (31) of how to spend the day. Presenting herself as an avid reader, choosing this solitary activity above 'playing with my girles' (31) and 'play felow's' (32), she states that 'spent a great deal' of her own time 'in reading' (31) but bemoans that Carter:

had so fill'd my head with foly's, that … what I red was alltogether romances. I was but some few month's past ten year's old before I had read severall great volum's of them: all Cassander, the Grand Cyrus, Cleopatra and Astrea. (32)

This indulgence at the age of 10 in French romances charting the paths of young heroines in matters of love is constructed in Delaval's writing as a distraction from what she should have been doing in childhood.[74] She bemoans:

> Thus vainely pass'd the blossome time of my life, which shou'd have been spent in laying a good foundation of what is to be learnt in such book's as teach's us heavenly wisdom. (32)

Reading romance distracts her from reading spiritual books, but it also acts as dangerous formative experience. Delaval recognizes that childhood reading is the way in which the 'foundation' of the self might be acquired. Using imagery of natural development (blossoming), she recognizes childhood as an important stage in the formation of an individual. She draws on horticultural imagery to explain that Carter's influence is so dangerous because 'at that time of my life she cou'd have Turn'd me which way she pleas'd, as easely as she might have bow'd a tender Twig' (33).[75] Delaval's account of her childhood admits that she was guilty of folly as result of Carter's influence, but her language simultaneously shifts responsibility away from herself. Moreover, she does not judge these earliest errors too harshly. Her use of the imagery of childhood and of childhood reading implies that they are acts of childhood, a period in which the individual is perceived to be vulnerable and liable to such influence. In doing so, she constructs her narrative as part of her Lenten repentance but also suggests that these follies should be excused.

Moreover, Delaval implies that, as the bad judgements of vulnerable childhood, these errors might be left behind. Structurally her narrative achieves this. She ends her first meditation with an account of how she moves beyond Carter's influence. The release from her childhood companion is figured in spiritual terminology of deliverance and awakening as she recalls that she was 'deliver'd out of the misery I had thrown my selfe into before I was quite eleven year's old' (33) and that a new companion 'open'd' her eyes and 'planely made me see' (34). Appropriating the conventions of spiritual autobiographies, she suggests a moment of realization and understanding, and then, within the final paragraph of the meditation, jumps from being 'resque'd at eleven year's old' (35) to her move to court and to financial and educational independence at age 14. In terms of narrative structure, the movement beyond the influence of Carter, fairy tales and romance reading works along with a quick account of these other markers of transition to signal the end of childhood. While the folly of childhood might have been 'dangerous' (32), the structure of this text suggests that it is contained. Delaval begins her second meditation, also written in her fourteenth year, with a joyful exclamation: 'how bless'd am I in the freedeome that I now injoy' (35). Although explicitly expressing her appreciation for material ease, the juxtaposition of the two meditations suggest a celebration of escape from Carter's influence and, by extension, the release from childhood.

The text continues to depict this departure from childhood in terms of reading. For Delaval, as for many early modern writers, age is not simply determined by chronology or biology but by other factors including what and how she reads. In a meditation written in her 15th year, she reflects:

> When we are past our childish age and can attend to what we do without a perpetuall wandering fancy tis folly to spend our time any longer in reading ill chosen boock's, such as romances are, which serve onely to please our fancy not to guide our judgement, and to make our minutes passe away (tis said by some) less tediously than they wou'd do, were we otherwise imploy'd; but I have found by experience that they do rob us insenceibly of many— many houer's […] given us to worke out our salvation in. (45)

Like Mildmay, Delaval offers collective advice based on 'experience', gesturing back to her own account of reading romances as a child from her new perspective, 'past childish age'. Her statement on reading romances again emphasizes the 'folly' of her earlier reading practices, but goes further to suggest that what may have been excusable in 'childish age' is no longer acceptable. Like Powell and Baxter, Delaval suggests that she must move beyond a certain type of book.[76] By associating an indulgence in a certain types of books—in this case romances—with a stage of life, these writers create a narrative in which they can admit to reading what might be seen as 'ill chosen boock's' but by relegating this to childhood they suggest not only that they were not fully responsible but also that this is something that they can leave behind.[77] For Delaval, it is crucial to move beyond this childish state. She represents it as a vulnerable period, and further hints at the dangerous possibility of what happens to those who do not successfully negotiate the transition out of childhood in her representation of Carter acting as 'if she had been a girle her self' (29). The 14-year-old Delaval, on the cusp of childhood and a more mature state, writes in order to 'examine my own heart' (37), to consider 'how unprofitably my youth has hitherto been spent' (38) and ultimately to move beyond 'childish age'. This is a significant image in what has been read as an early modern coming-of-age narrative.

RETURNING TO CHILDHOOD

If the structure of Delaval's narrative suggests coming of age via the departure from childhood, this is belied by many features of her memoir. The form of autobiographical writing in itself involves an act of return; returning in writing to reimagine the experience of being a child. When Richard Norwood recalls his childhood reading experiences he reinserts himself into the state of being a child and positions 'we children' against a group of elders, 'they', who, he reflects, 'were willing that we children should be so persuaded of them, that we might follow our books the better and be kept in from play'.[78] Norwood discursively inhabits the space of childhood again, but this experience is altered as his older stance enables him to simultaneously interpret the intentions of the elders. This is an inevitable component of the recollection of childhood in autobiographical writing, and contributes to the 'layering' of the self in Delaval's memoirs. Despite the containment of the account of her earliest years to the first meditation and the reflective tone that marks her distance from the state of being a child, Delaval repeatedly returns to childhood. Her narrative evidences an ongoing negotiation of the impact of her childhood, particularly her childhood reading, on her future experiences. The return to childhood in her writing is affected further by her precarious age at the time of writing. Delaval may represent herself as having past 'childish age', but her writing reveals that as a 14- and 15-year-old youth she continues to navigate this transition. She remembers her earlier sins on a number of occasions throughout her teenage years. Her rhetoric works hard to associate them with a past time—using the past tense and referring, for example, to 'how unprofitably my youth has hitherto been spent' (38) or 'in my childhood' (61)—but they continue to inform her experience and her consciousness. This occurs primarily through a consideration of reading. Delaval recalls in her fourteenth year:

> How many year's of my life are now past in which I have aply'd mself to study the vaine things of this world, to be a judge of what is generally estimed good breeding, to understand the wit of a romance or a poem but not to learn wisdom and such understanding as guides us to know what the will of the Lord is. (43)

She uses this recollection of previous years to motivate a new dedication to godly reading practices, but continues to bemoan:

> Too much of mine [time] has been flung away, but now that I may walke circumspectly redeeming my time […] I will make the word of God more then ever my study; not neglect reading but be more careful what I read that I may blot out those idea's of vanity my memory is stuffed withal, and store it with what is whorthy to be treasur'd up there. (45)

The image of a memory 'stuffed', presumably with the vanities of her earlier romance reading, gestures towards the ongoing formative impact of her childhood reading on her more mature youth. It is not just what she reads, but how she reads that is at stake, and although by the following year she has committed to the reading of 'good books' in her closet, she admits that, though she 'had red some leaves in them' she had not 'remarked and retained any one good sentence' (54). Her reading practices may have changed post-childhood, at least in this representation of herself, but her childhood reading has proven to be a foundation that cannot be easily overcome. In her 16th year Delaval continues to recall one of the key 'offences of my youngest day's', neglecting her 'duty in reading thy holy word and praying' and instead finding 'nothing so pleasant as the wasting of my houer's in foleish devertisement's and in reading unprofitable romances' (62). The reading that she carefully relegates to 'childish age', both in the structure and language of her memoirs, continues to dominate the account of her youth.

These 'unprofitable romances' form the subject of her repentance as she moves beyond childhood through her teenage years; they also inform the subsequent story of her life more fundamentally. The genre of romance shapes the life memorialized in this text. As Margaret Ezell and Julie Eckerle note, Delaval's autobiographical account relies more on the conventions of romance than religious meditation.[79] Delaval acknowledges the impact of reading romance on her perspective and her relationships. She admits that in her childhood her doting on Carter was influenced by such reading, claiming that 'When ever I red any description of a whorthy good friend I presently aply'd it to her in my thought's, and as I grew up my love to her still more and more increas'd' (29). Her reading directly affects her behaviour in childhood, leading her to mistakenly dote on the villain-character of this first meditation. It continues to impact upon her expectations and her behaviour during the courtship of her later youth.

Her admission that she finds it 'a Devertion to hear' her suitor 'talke like one of the Lovers I have Red in Romances' (155) demonstrates the ongoing effect of the material of her childhood on her view of the world. On the one hand, this might function to further reinforce the dangers of romance reading, particularly during the vulnerable years of childhood. Yet Delaval's use of romance motifs to tell the story of her life also signals the ways in which the stories, narrative structures and language encountered in childhood continue to influence her negotiation of her emerging selfhood.[80] Delaval's memoirs not only return to childhood to re-present her earlier experiences as a child reader; her formative experiences as a child reader also crucially inform this construction of her life in writing as, to use Spufford's words, a 'story among stories'.[81]

Therefore, while returning to childhood is an inevitable component of much autobiographical writing, it is also a means of negotiating of the self in early modern life writing. Another example of the genre returns to youth in more detail. Begun *c.* 1638 when Elizabeth Isham was 30 years old, *My Booke of Rememberance* offers an account of Isham's life from her earliest childhood to her present.[82] Claimed as one of the earliest texts in English that is 'recognizably autobiography in the modern sense', and as 'one of the earliest female-authored prose narratives about the self', it has also been acclaimed for its attention to age and for the detailed account that Isham gives of her childhood, her family relationships, her physical and mental wellbeing and her devotional practices during this time, and particularly of her childhood reading.[83] Anne Cotterill notes that Isham's *Booke* is distinctive 'in her detailed description of being introduced to and experiencing books and writing' and in demonstrating the 'importance to her life of books'.[84] This prose account of Isham's life is complemented by what has been described as a retrospective 'diary' record: a sheet divided into squares for entries against each year of her life, starting at age 4 and ending at 40.[85] The *Diary* sheds further light on childhood reading from the perspective of adulthood, as it identifies for each year of her life a series of activities and emotions, including what Isham remembers reading. Filled with details of the range of texts that she read, the diverse ways that she engaged with them and, often, her responses to them, these autobiographical texts undoubtedly demonstrate the significance of books to her life and disclose the importance of reading as a child for this early modern writer.

Like many early modern children, Isham was given, encouraged to read and read religious matter. Such material dominates her recollection of her early encounters with books. She recalls the Bible that her father bought for her as her 'chiefest treasure' (4r). She remembers her mother giving her a psalm book (5r), a prayerbook (8r) and religious proofs (10v), and letting her keep some of her prayerbooks (16v). She read religious books aloud to her mother to comfort her during illness (17r) and read psalms with her grandmother (16v), who also passes on prayerbooks to her (16v). She recalls hearing her grandmother's maid read the Bible aloud (14r) and remembers when John Dod guided her and her siblings in the practice of reading one Old Testament and one New Testament chapter each day (12r). In line with godly reading practices of the time, Isham reads, memorizes and takes notes from all these spiritual books, and she goes even further when, at the age of 8, 'having fancied a primer' she takes it and 'put[s] it in a place where it cold not be found' (4r) and a few years later makes a miniature prayer book when she finds a page has fallen from a book (14r). Like many writers of spiritual memoirs, she presents reading as an important mode of devotion, and demonstrates her commitment to this practice from an early age. Yet, while the list of 'good' books that Isham read is in many ways conventional, her childhood reading experiences are also remarkable for their variety: a fact which she highlights. In her *Booke* she claims that she avoided 'tieing myself always to one Praire Booke for I found that viriaty quickened my Spirites [...] also for I found that in one booke which I thought I most needed—and sometime that in another booke which I most desired' (16v). The young Isham's devotional reading was determined to a certain extent by individual choice. Isham further indicates the extent to which she directed her own reading, remarking that 'it may be some think this devotion was not so fit for me. because I was a child' (16v). Recognizing that some religious material was seen to be more appropriate to her state of being a 'child' than others, she illustrates the extent to which she pursued her own interests in her reading. In remembering her childhood, Isham asserts her choice of reading.

While Isham presents herself as a committed reader of spiritual material, she presents a reading trajectory that demonstrates that this was not always easy. She recalls that when very young she 'was naturally a child apt to my worke but my Sister, was redier at her Booke' (5v); although she later notes that in her teenage years her mother asks her, rather than her sister, to read to her during periods of illness (17r). As a child she struggles to learn her catechism without proofs, claiming that she 'liked well to redd' 'Mr Pagitt's' catechism, but she struggled with her father's desire that she learn it without proofs (10v). These challenging moments of reading and learning are not presented as the errancy of youth in the way that other autobiographical writers deploy this trope. Rather, Isham presents them as part of her developing skills and identity as a reader. Her narrative is not one of an exceptional or enlightened reader; Isham presents a child exposed to a range of material, motivated to read by the spiritual example set by family readers as well as her growing 'delight' in books. As Anne Cotterill notes, she frequently speaks of 'delight' in reading: finding pleasure in hearing others read, in her individual reading and turning to her books for comfort in times of illness and grief.[86] Isham also engages with diverse forms. Noting her difficulty in learning her catechism, she admits that 'at these times I delighted so much in ballets [ballads] that I could say many by hart' (10v). She desires 'play Books' (26r) and, although her father will not lend his copies to his young daughter, by her seventeenth year she is reading 'play Bookes' that 'our nurse sent' (1625). In her late teens, Isham reads Chaucer (1626) and Ovid (20v), and in her twenties she reads Foxe's *Book of Martyrs* in the mornings, even though her 'friends' think it makes her 'mallancoly', and Philip Sidney and Edmund Spenser in the evenings (26r).[87] Isham's recollection of her experiences as a child reader is remarkable, therefore, not only for the detail provided, but also for the way in which she presents such wide range of reading experiences as part of her developing identity as a reader.

Isham's *Booke* is in many respects an account of her development as a reader or, as Julie Eckerle suggests, a literacy narrative. As Eckerle persuasively argues, it is the 'tale of the construction of a literate self' that 'also participates in the construction of her own literate self'.[88] Isham's reading material has an obvious influence on the construction of her textual self. The form that she chooses to write her life responds directly to her religious reading. The *Booke* is influenced by the increasing trend in the seventeenth century to self-examine through reading and writing, a practice recommended by many of the authors that Isham has read.[89] She presents her book as part of her process of spiritual examination as she ultimately offers it as representative of her self as 'thine own gift' to God (38r). This mode of self-examination and direct address to God is influenced by Augustine's *Confessions*, which, according to her diary, she read in 1632 and with which she links her writing when she claims she was 'imboldened by the sight of S[aint] Au[g]usti[ne's] con[fessions] ... to examine my life' (33v), calls her book 'my confessions' (1639) and imitates the Augustinian trope of stealing fruit in her youth, echoing Augustine's language in blaming her 'lickerishness' (appetite) (10r).[90] Like Delaval, Isham uses the motifs acquired through reading to shape her life in writing. However, she goes further by directly citing from her reading material to describe events of her life. Anne Cotterill has noted that Isham 'has fitted into her fabric hundreds of fragments from her reading, tested for fitness within herself'.[91] This primarily takes the form of pslams and reflections on scripture. However, on occasion Isham selects textual extracts to substitute for gaps in her memory. Noting that her birth and earliest childhood are 'that time which now I cannot call to mind' (2v), she describes her earliest days using text from the 1631 edition of Augustine's *Confessions* as well as citing from Johann Gerhard's *Meditationes*, which she references in the margins, and from a range of biblical passages.[92] The life presented in this book is composed of what she has read. Reading not only enables examination of self, it also constitutes her selfhood and—in this example—her earliest childhood.

Following this borrowed account of her birth and infancy, Isham proceeds to recollect her early years, including the birth of her siblings and their childhood illnesses, her early instruction in reading under the guidance of her mother, and her sins, including 'my natureall Stubbernes of a Childe' (3r). She recalls her life in more detail when she reaches 'the eight yeare of my age' and comes to 'a fuller knowledge' of God (3v). This knowledge correlates with increased memory of her prayers and devotional reading. However, what is most striking about Isham's reconstruction of her childhood is not simply that she recalls with detail the books she used and how she used them in her religious practice, but the ways in which books function as a trigger for these memories. Isham remembers her childhood via her encounters with books and with reading experiences. The books of her childhood work as a mnemonic device for Isham in reconstructing her life. In the *Diary* she recalls for many years of her life what she read at that time and she carries this practice of associating books with particular events or stages in her life by remembering them again in her *Booke*. Recounting her vulnerable state in her 14th year (a crucial age in her writing as for Delaval), she provides detail on her ill health, thought to be greensickness by her father, grief by her mother and wind by Isham herself, and she notes in the margin 'in this time I read some part of the second booke of Marters' (17v). Isham aligns her reading of the stories of martyrs with her own experience of a bodily regime which included exercises prescribed by her father and control of her diet, to cure her 'infirmities' (17v). The recollection of the intense physical and emotional experiences of youth work in tandem with her memories of reading.

This is also evident in the ways in which Isham reflects on reading to convey familial bonds. When she begins to 'call to mind the evill enclinations of my Childhood' (4v), this is interrupted by a memory of her grandmother reading to her mother during a period of illness. Isham claims to '[remember] well those good bookes of my Granmothers reading to my mother being weake in her Chamber, wherin they rejoyced together before thee' (4v). The memory of this reading experience, one which Isham witnesses, focuses her thoughts to give thanks for the 'unity and love betwext my father mother and grandmother' (4v). In recounting her grandmother's illness when she was in the '8 or 9 yeare of my life' (5r), Isham again relates the events of her life via memories of books. She recalls how 'comming dayly to see her lighted upon her Bookes (which lay in her window) wherein she much delighted and I gathered spirituall flowers out of the garden of her sweetnes wherein one booke I found of the nessissity of Repentance' (5r). This recollection of active spiritual reading gives way to further memories, as it causes 'to come into my mind som other things which afore those times I did (afore my Grammothers sicknes) my mother gave every one of us a Psalme booke, in which I much delighted because of the verce' (5r). One remembered act of reading invokes another memory of delight in books.

Isham's recollection of her childhood reading both shapes the construction of her self, and serves as a mode of memorializing the family members who provided the young Isham with her books and instilled good reading practices in her. Isham tells of many occasions of individual reading, including the time that she spent in her closet (10r), but she equally associates books and reading with others: from reading alongside her siblings in the early years of learning, to her sister sharing her religious exaltation following reading (28r), to Isham bringing comfort to her mother by reading to her during illness (17r), to her cousin reading aloud to her (20v), through to her later life when Isham teaches her nieces to read (1639). Yet the *Booke* does not simply record these shared reading experiences, it depicts the emotional intensity and effect of these bonds on her as child, and suggests an ongoing impact on Isham's life as she reflects upon them. For instance, Isham inserts herself within family practices of reading when she tells of her grandmother's regular reading of her great-grandfather Isham's copy of *Christian Prayers and Meditations*. When her grandmother shows the 8- or 9-year-old Isham his markings on the book, this is her stimulus to recall 'what a kind father inlaw he was to her' (16v). In her recollection of this multi-generational intimacy provoked through shared encounters with a book, Isham goes further in her *Booke* by shifting to the future, to comment that 'since I have bine very glad to meete with these places and somthing else of his owne writing yea it doth much rejoyce mee to aplie theses places for my owne use and to tred in the selfe same stepes towards heaven wherein my forefathers have walked' (16v). The descriptions of reading this book serve to reflect on the emotional bonds between three generations. As with Grace Mildmay, Isham's auto-biographical writing situates her within a family tradition of good reading and prayer. Also like Mildmay, she describes this as a practice that might potentially be passed on to future generations as she claims in a marginal note on the early pages that, although the *Booke* is primarily 'for my owne benefit', it may also 'doe my Brother or his children any pleasure I think to leave it them' (2r). Yet Isham uses this recollection of past and ongoing reading experiences as a more sustained stimulus to memory. While this depiction of an enthusiastic reader seems on one level to conventionally deploy images of spiritual reading to present her as a committed Christian from a good family in line with spiritual autobiographies of the time, her *Booke* utilizes images of childhood reading in more complex ways. She muses further on the particular prayers in her great-grandfather's and grandmother's book, noting that the devotions she liked 'of the hapines of everlasting life. and Med-itations of death' might be thought by some 'not so fit for me. because I was a child and they in yeeres' (16v). Claiming that she 'remember[s]' that this was not 'amisse but profitable to me at any time', she moves again from past to present. Recalling the effect of reading as a child, she muses on the continued impact upon her beliefs and moves to pray in the present moment of her writing, confirming her trust in and praise for God (16v). The act of remembering her reading stimulates spiri-tual reflection in the act of writing. The return to her childhood enables her religious practice and the construction of her identity in the present.

In her autobiographical writing, then, Isham returns to her childhood with emotional intensity through recollecting the feelings provoked by earlier reading experiences, and by using this as a stimulus to remember the familial bonds of her childhood and to reflect in the present. On the concluding page of her *Booke*, Isham muses on this aspect of remember-ing. She writes:

> I have observed that many in age have delighted to talke of things done in there Youth. the rememberance hereof I have found so profitable that me thinkes my Youth is renued. (38r)

Isham locates her written act of remembering among others 'in age' who 'have delighted to talke of things done in there Youth', highlighting the extent to which this activity informs her current status of 'age'. Further reflecting that as 'a childe' she 'delighted to heare old stories' from her grandfather, her grandmother and her aunt, who would recall their youths to 'tell us many good things of them, how they walked before thee my God' (38r), she represents this aged identity as informed by generational and familial practices. For Isham, the creation of 'stories' of youth is a 'profitable' and renewing act. Writing her childhood returns her to the status of a youth. This act of retelling simultaneously characterizes her 'age' and renews her youth. For Isham, the telling of her life is not just an act of memory, it works to project a return to the state of youth. This is perhaps motivated by a desire to recover some of the material energy of youth, but is also an articulation of desire for renewal in Christ. Gesturing towards alignment of early and final stages of life, it draws on the conventional image of older age as second childishness.[93] Yet for Isham, writing about childhood reading conjures up not only the individual experience of being a child or youth, but also a return. As Anne Cotterill argues, Isham's writing is in part a 'search for physical and mental well-being' as she begins writing a year after her sister's death from consumption and she acknowledges that she writes to keep a 'busy head inventing' and to resist succumbing to excessive sorrow.[94] Throughout her *Booke*, Isham highlights the role of reading in her life as a form of healing, claiming books have 'fit places to salves my owne sore' (24r). The act of remembering her reading in writing also seeks healing. The narrative of familial bonds and emotional relationships with her grandmother, mother and sister via books and shared reading experiences work to recover those now lost relationships. This deliberate return to childhood reading, therefore, seeks increased self-knowledge and spiritual understanding, but it is also a process of recovery of what has been lost. Remembering childhood reading is a way of overcoming grief; of forgetting.

MEMORIALIZING CHILDHOOD

Delaval and Isham, therefore, deploy memories of childhood reading in diverse ways. It is, of course, impossible to recover their intentions in writing their childhood and youth or to determine the historical veracity of these remembered experiences of childhood reading. Nonetheless, their texts signal the utility of the image of the child as reader in early modern self-writing. In depicting themselves as child readers, they memorialize their childhoods. Yet these childhoods—fixed in the writing of one early modern youth and a woman in her thirties reflecting back on her life—have been, like many early modern childhoods, lost until recently. Delaval's manuscript volume was overlooked until the twentieth-century, and Isham's *Booke* was only identified in the early twenty-first century.[95] These texts memorialize their authors' childhoods, yet it is only with discovery of the material and a renewed scholarly interest in early modern childhoods that they are being read for what they disclose about the experiences, and particularly the reading experiences, of early modern women and children.

In contrast, Abraham Cowley was memorialized as a child reader and author during his lifetime as well as posthumously in the cultivation of the image of an exceptional child by himself and by others. Like Delaval and Isham, he is conscious in his autobiographical essay that his representation of his early years is shaped by the restrictions of memory. Claiming to begin 'As far as my Memory can return back into my past Life' with a recollection of when he was 'a very young Boy at School' and instead of 'running about on Holy-daies and playing with my fellows; I was wont to […] walk into the fields, either alone with a Book, or with some one Companion' (143), Cowley employs an image of the child's relationship with books as an alternative to play, which had become by the mid-seventeenth century a conventional representation of the 'good child', to signal his exceptional childhood.[96] He may not directly piece together his childhood using textual fragments like Isham, but like Delaval he draws on recognizable tropes of the child. Cowley signals a youthful precocity that is marked by his refusal to 'learn without Book' at grammar school because instead he 'made a shift to do the usual [grammar] exercise out of my own reading' (143). Through this move to signal his unusual and autonomous reading practices, Cowley manipulates an image of a schoolboy reader to demonstrate early signs of his exceptional engagement with literary cultures. This is evidenced further by his demonstration of how he is 'acquainted with the Poets' from an early age, particularly Horace, and culminates in the wonderful depiction of his first encounter before the age of 12 with 'Chimes of Verse, as have never since left ringing there' and 'the tinckling of the Rhyme and Dance of the Numbers' on reading of '*Spencer's* Works' which, as cited above, 'made me a Poet as immediately as a Child is made an Eunuch' (144). At the end of his life, Cowley generates a fantastical image of childhood reading that creates the poet. He indicates the formative impact of reading as a child on the adult he would become, highlighting that 'I was then of the same mind as I am now' (143). He suggests the birth of his professional and intellectual identity through reading. Deploying well-established images of children as liable to shaping, he suggests that 'perhaps it was the immature and immoderate love of them which stampt first, or rather engraved these Characters in me: They were like Letters cut into the Bark of a Young Tree, which with the Tree still grow proportionably' (144).[97] It is specifically Cowley's state as child—his excessive and uncontrolled feeling and his malleable state—that make him receptive to the examples with which he engages. Unlike Delaval who represents this as a corruptive experience, Cowley reclaims an image of child reader overwhelmed by fantastical tales to fashion his emerging identity as a poet, inspired by and even on par with great poets.

Cowley, then, recalls his childhood to depict the development of his creative identity through early reading experiences. Earlier in the seventeenth century, Michael Drayton draws on early reading experiences in a similar way. In his poem 'To my most dearely-loved friend, Henery Reynolds Esquire, of Poets and Poesie' (1627), he claims to have been 'inclin'd to noble Poesie' from 'my cradle'.[98] The poem's speaker reflects back on childhood in this poem, presenting an imager of his earlier self as 'a proper goodly page,/Much like a Pigmy, scares ten yeares of age' who, upon asking his tutor to 'Make me a Poet [...] if you can,/And you shall see, Ile quickly be a man', received a reading list of poets from Virgil to Shakespeare and Beaumont.[99] Like Cowley's self-representation, Drayton's poem suggests that the stirrings of poetic talent in infancy are nurtured through the reading of poets in childhood.[100] Poetic virtuosity is formed through early engagement with literary models, and in specifically identifying English models both Drayton and Cowley insert themselves into English literary tradition.[101] However, while Drayton equates becoming a poet with becoming a man and the gradual development of creative talent through extensive reading, Cowley's depiction of being 'made a poet' suggests a more immediate change when he claims that he 'was made a Poet as immediately as a child is made a Eunuch'. Rather than extended reading, Cowley gives precedence to his encounter with Spenser. This reading experience is a transformative one. It makes him a poet, but does not project him into manhood. Instead the image of the child being made a eunuch, suggests not only an immediate alteration but also being fixed in the condition of youth. At the end of his life, Cowley epitomizes himself as child poet and memorializes this status.

Cowley's distinct representation of a childhood creative identity returns to his literary productivity as a child. Unlike Drayton's adult vocation as a poet, Cowley's career began early and informs a significant portion of the textual representations of him as poet. His first collection of poetry was published in 1633 when he was only 25, but contains poems that were written when he was between 10 and 12.[102] In his address to the reader, Cowley emphasizes that this work is the product of his childhood, hoping that 'a pardon may easily bee gotten for the errors of ten yeeres age' and highlighting his 'childish muse'.[103] He returns to this discourse of juvenile and inferior work as the product of childish years in his later autobiographical essay, when he selects some schoolboy verses but omits others, claiming the 'Beginning of it is Boyish, but of this part which I here set down [...] I should hardly now be much ashamed' (143). Cowley represents his early work as inferior because of his childishness.[104] Yet at the same time, by highlighting his abilities from such an early age, he implies that this is extraordinary. He identifies 'how this love [of poetry] came to be produced in me so early' (144) as the crucial question. However, his response that he 'happened to fall upon' his Mother's copy of Spenser's *Works* does not simply answer this question by proposing reading as the answer. Instead this mystical encounter with a book that lay in 'my Mothers Parlour' by mysterious 'accident' (144) suggests an extraordinary encounter with a book that effectively produces a child prodigy.

This allusion to the remarkable talent of this early modern child-author extends beyond Cowley's self-representation. His peers praise him in these terms. His 'deare Friend and Schoole-fellow', Ben Masters, suggests that Cowley is unique, asking in his poem 'on his flourishing and hopefull Blossomes', 'Could ever former Age brag of a Youth/So forward at these yeeres?'[105] In the posthumous collection of Cowley's works, Thomas Sprat notes that, spending his youth in Westminster School, Cowley 'increas'd the noble Genius peculiar to that place'.[106] During and after his lifetime, Cowley is renowned for remarkable abilities. This discourse of precocious children is common in the relatively infrequent representations of other child authors of the period. As Lucy Munro demonstrates, literary constructions of the child writer depend upon certain 'conventions of childhood'. This regularly involves, as Munro demonstrates, a discourse of 'childish incapacity'.[107] Yet, a conventional image of the exceptional child often works alongside this.[108] In the depiction of another child writer, the poet and playwright Thomas Randolph, his brother Richard West also suggests a special aptitude since infancy. He praises this poet's ability to 'lis[p] wit worthy th'Presse, as if he/Had us'd his Cradle as a Library' and represents Randolph, as Cowley depicts himself, as committed to books from an early age, claiming he chose 'Books' as his 'Toyes', 'when other Boyes/(His elders) playd with Nuts'. Stating that in order to tell Randolph's 'History', he 'must needs write miracles', West hints at extraordinary talent.[109] He constructs Randolph as another precocious child, a miraculous entity. Margaret Cavendish retrospectively represents her childhood writing in dual terms. Referring to her juvenilia as 'Baby-Books' written in 'my Baby-years' in her *Sociable Letters,* she hints at their inferior quality, yet she claims in her dedication to her biography of her husband that '*it pleased God to command his Servant Nature to indue me with a Poetical and Philosophical Genius, even from my Birth; for I did write some Books in that kind, before I was twelve years of Age*'.[110] The language of extraordinary abilities creates textual constructions of gifted children, memorialized in these depictions of their lives and talents.

Cowley's return to his childhood and his emphasis on a particular childhood reading experience that 'made' him 'a Poet' in his reflection 'Of Myself' towards the end of his life both deploys images of childhood as a formative stage and emphasizes his extraordinary childhood reading experience that shaped him as a child. It is his status as a creative and remarkable child that is ultimately memorialized in this essay. Even as he progresses to recount events of his later life, he returns to his childhood perspective of his self and the world around him, 'renewing', he claims, 'my old School-boys Wish in a Copy or Verses':

> Well then; I now do plainly see
> This busie World I shall ne're agree. (145)

Again emphasizing his own nature as something exceptional, at odds with the world around him, Cowley suggests that this experience characterizes his life. By casting this insight as one that that has persisted since his schoolboy days, he suggests an advanced knowledge of a self not yet fully formed that was confirmed rather than altered by his life experience. His deployment of the image of child as reader, therefore, functions not only to create a myth around his ongoing vocation as writer, but also suggests something remarkable in his cognitive abilities as a child. The child reader is not just a trope in this writing of a life; it is central to this characterization of this exceptional child.

The Impossibility of Childhood?

As this monograph has suggested, early modern children were urged to read and to use their reading, and they did so in ways that demonstrated the apt learning desired by teachers and parents but also the creative deployment of what they read. The retrospective representations of childhood reading in the autobiographical writings of Delaval, Isham and Cowley constitute further examples of individuals who were shaped by their early reading experiences. In writing their lives, they return to their childhood reading to produce diverse textual constructions of the self. Through this sustained engagement with their reading material, they demonstrate the formative impact of early reading experiences in early modern culture but also signal the potential autonomy early modern children had as readers. These once child readers and, in Delaval's and Cowley's cases, once child writers, draw on existing ideas about childhood to innovatively reimagine the literary figure of the child as reader. From the perspective of older age, this serves to examine their developing subjectivities. Yet, ultimately through the act of reimagining childhood, they are memorialized as remarkable child readers in these textual constructions of their lives.

This child reader is, of course, an imagined construct. As Carolyn Steedman argues, memory cannot resurrect children, 'it is memory itself that shapes them'. What and how children read is represented in these autobiographical accounts via a perspective beyond childhood. The act of remembering childhood, Steedman highlights, involves the 'rework[ing of] past time to give current events meaning, and that reworking provides an understanding that the child at that time can't possess'.[111] In this sense, childhood and the child are in Jacqueline Rose's controversial terms 'impossible'; always imagined, or reimagined, through the perspectives and fantasies of adults.[112] Many of the examples of the books and reading practices of early modern children considered in *Reading Children* have been retrospective reimaginings. Alongside fictional representations of child readers in plays, poetry, prefaces and the title pages of books claiming to address the needs of the elusive child reader, many of the children of this book have been written by adults: adults reflecting back on their own childhoods; authors addressing potential young readers; printers reaching out to a youthful market; teachers, parents and advisers offering their perspective on the child reader. The early modern child reader examined here is the product of multiple perspectives on what it means to read as a child in the period. This study has attended to alternative representations of early modern reading children through a consideration of marginalia and translations by young readers, yet it has interpreted these records too as discursive representations. Childhood is, as Anna Davin argues, 'multiple and elusive'; it is contingent and varies 'with time and place'.[113] It is precisely the multiple and contingent constructs of children as readers in early modern culture that *Reading Children* has sought to explore. It is in the intersections between representations of childhood and the representations of the experiences of children that we might locate the early modern child reader. It is by positioning the reading experiences of children alongside understandings of childhood in the books produced for them and in accounts of how they should participate in early modern textual cultures that children's participation in cultures of reading and the impact of this on what it means to be a child in the period might be disclosed.

It is perhaps, therefore, in this chapter's consideration of recollections of childhood reading in autobiographical writing that it becomes most clear how the child as reader is constructed through lived, material experiences of reading and the textual reimagining of these experiences. The child reader is evoked in these texts to serve particular ends: to signal an exemplary life; to emphasize a moment of conversion; to prove poetic aptitude; to examine the self. Childhood reading is imagined both as constitutive of adult subjectivity and as a phase to be left behind for adult concerns. Yet across all of these examples, the child and childhood reading are crucial to the writing and understanding of early modern identity. The concept of what it means to read as a child is a literary trope that might be appropriated to signal elements of development. However, as the examples considered throughout this study suggest, to read as a child also involves reading a range of materials in unexpected and exciting ways, demonstrating remarkable autonomy in selecting material and in putting recommended (as well as illicit) reading material to unexpected use. The reading that Delaval ostensibly dismisses as the stuff of an errant and vulnerable childhood, for instance, influences her writing and her understanding of her self. In her narrative of a heroine-protagonist who is informed by her childhood reading of romance, Delaval herself emerges as an author shaped by the books she has read from an early age. For literate men and women of the period, childhood reading is a crucial component of selfhood. More significantly perhaps, this reading produces childhoods, historical and fictional. It impacts on the experiences of literate early modern boys and girls. It is most discernible when it impacts on their writing, whether this takes the form of schoolboy annotations on a textbook, the translation exercises and poetry of Rachel Fane, the multi-layered narration of a life by the ageing Delaval or is evident throughout life as in the case of Abraham Cowley. Yet it undoubtedly also impacted on what it meant to be a child for those who could read but not write to convey their experiences. Early modern childhood is not an impossible fiction. Childhood—at least some version of it—is produced through the mutually informing discourses of what was understood by reading as a child and the experience of being a child reader in early modern textual cultures.

NOTES

1. Abraham Cowley, 'Of Myself', *The Works of Mr. Abraham Cowley* (London, 1668), 144. Further references are given in the text.
2. Alexander Lindsay, 'Cowley, Abraham (1618–1667)', in *Oxford Dictionary of National Biography*, ed. David Cannadine (Oxford: Oxford University Press, 2004), http://www.oxforddnb.com/view/article/6499, accessed 21 Aug. 2017.
3. Abraham Cowley, 'To the Reader', *Poetical Blossoms* (London, 1636), A4r.
4. Cowley highlights his indebtedness to his reading of Homer as a model for his poetry written during childhood ('Of Myself', 144).
5. See Ilana Ben-Amos, *Adolescence and Youth in Early Modern England* (New Haven: Yale University Press, 1994),185; Julie Eckerle, *Romancing the Self in Early Modern Englishwomen's Life-Writing* (Aldershot: Ashgate, 2013), 9–18; Andrew Murphy, *Shakespeare for the People: Working Class Readers, 1800–1900* (Cambridge: Cambridge University Press, 2008), 10; Margaret Spufford, 'First Steps in Literacy: The Reading and Writing Experiences of the Humblest Seventeenth-Century Spiritual Autobiographers', *Social History* 4.3 (1979): 407; Elspeth Graham et al., 'Introduction', *Her Own Life: Autobiographical Writings by Seventeenth-Century Women* (London: Routledge, 2003), 17; Ramona Wray, 'Recovering the Reading of Renaissance Englishwomen: Deployments of Autobiography', *Critical Survey* 12.2 (2000): 33–34.
6. Georges Gusdorf, 'Conditions and Limits of Autobiography', in *Autobiography: Essays Theoretical and Critical*, ed. James Olney (Princeton: Princeton University Press, 1980), 35. On the effect of temporal distance and memory on the conception of the self recorded in autobiography, see Kathleen Lynch, *Protestant Autobiography in the Seventeenth-Century Anglophone World* (Oxford: Oxford University

Press, 2012), 13–14; Evelyn Tribble and Nicholas Keene, *Cognitive Ecologies and the History of Remembering: Religion, Education and Memory in Early Modern England* (Basingstoke: Palgrave Macmillan, 2011), 8.

7. On definitions and forms, see Linda Anderson, *Autobiography* (London: Routledge, 2001), 1–17; Graham et al., 21; Sharon Seelig, *Autobiography and Gender in Early Modern Literature* (Cambridge: Cambridge University Press, 2006), 7; Adam Smyth, *Autobiography in Early Modern England* (Cambridge: Cambridge University Press, 2010), 1–14; Ramona Wray, 'Autobiography', in *The Cambridge Companion to Early Modern Women's Writing*, ed. Laura Lunger Knoppers (Cambridge: Cambridge University Press, 2009), 194–207.

8. Eckerle, 12; Elspeth Graham, 'Women's Writing and the Self', in *Women and Literature in Britain, 1500–1700*, ed. Helen Wilcox (Cambridge: Cambridge University Press, 1996), 213.

9. Graham et al., 21. Childhood became the common starting point for life writing in the nineteenth century. See John Burnett, *Destiny Obscure: Autobiographies of Childhood, Education and Family from the 1820s to the 1920s* (London: Allen Lane, 1982), xi; Carolyn Steedman, *Strange Dislocations: Childhood and the Idea of Human Interiority, 1780–1930* (Cambridge: Harvard University Press, 1995), 4–11.

10. Some examples of autobiographical texts beginning with an account of parentage and early education include: Margaret Cavendish, 'A True Relation of My Birth, Breeding and Life', in *Nature's Pictures* (London, 1656); Lucy Hutchinson writing in the late 1660s, see *Memoirs of the Life of Colonel Hutchinson*, ed. N. H. Keeble (London: Phoenix Press, 2000), 3–17; Lady Anne Halkett writing in the 1670s, see John Loftis, ed., *The Memoirs of Anne Lady Halkett and Ann, Lady Fanshawe* (Oxford: Clarendon Press, 1979), 9–87. Some writers offer more detailed accounts of childhood. Thomas Wythorne, for example, writes an account of his life *c.* 1576 as 'the chyld's lyfe, togyther with A young man's lyfe, and entring into the old man's lyfe'. See James Osborn, ed., *The Autobiography of Thomas Whythorne* (Oxford: Clarendon Press, 1961). Elizabeth Isham, discussed later in this chapter, starts with a detailed account of her childhood.

11. Michael Drayton, 'To my most dearely-loved friend Henery Reynolds Esquire, of *Poets and Poesie*', in *The Battaile of Agincourt* (London, 1627), 204–208.

12. As Stephen Colclough points out, 'Each author had different reasons for wishing to foreground the importance of reading in his or her intellectual or emotional development, but they often used established tropes or motifs to write about this experience.' See 'Readers: Books and

Biography', in *A Companion to the History of the Book*, ed. Simon Eliot and Jonathan Rose (Oxford: Blackwell, 2009), 60.

13. Steedman, 5.
14. Steedman, 11.
15. Francis Spufford, *The Child That Books Built* (London: Faber, 2003), 9.
16. Spufford, 210–211.
17. Spufford acknowledges such work (213). See also Arthur Applebee, *The Child's Concept of Story* (Chicago: University of Chicago Press, 1978); Bruno Bettelheim, *The Uses of Enchantment* (New York: Knopf, 1976).
18. Ann Moss, 'Literary Imitation in the Sixteenth Century: Writers and Readers, Latin and French', in *The Cambridge History of Literary Criticism*, vol. 3: *The Renaissance*, ed. Glyn Norton (Cambridge: Cambridge University Press, 1999), 109.
19. See Henk Dragstra et al., 'Introduction', in *Betraying Ourselves: Forms of Self-Representation in Early Modern English Texts*, ed. Henk Dragstra, Shelia Ottway and Helen Wilcox (Basingstoke: Palgrave Macmillan, 2000), 1–13.
20. Carolyn Steedman, *Past Tenses: Essays on Writing, Autobiography and History* (London: Rivers Oram Press, 1992), 167.
21. Alec Ryrie, *Being Protestant in Reformation Britain* (Oxford: Oxford University Press, 2013), 429, 499.
22. Steedman, *Past Tenses*, 167; Lynch, 6–7.
23. Linda Pollock (ed.), *With Faith and Physic: The Life of a Tudor Gentlewoman, Lady Grace Mildmay 1552–1620* (London: Collins and Brown, 1993), 23.
24. Pollock, 23–24.
25. Pollock, 24.
26. Pollock, 24.
27. Pollock, 23, 28.
28. Ronald Bedford, Lloyd Davis and Philippa Kelly, *Early Modern English Lives: Autobiography and Self-Representation, 1500–1660* (Aldershot: Ashgate, 2007), 168–169.
29. Pollock, 25, 28.
30. Anne Venn, *A Wise Virgins Lamp Burning* (London, 1658), 2, 4.
31. Venn, 4.
32. Venn, title page.
33. Pollock, 26.
34. Alan McFarlane, ed., *The Diary of Ralph Josselin, 1616–1683* (Oxford: Oxford University Press, 1991), 1. See John Walter, 'Josselin, Ralph (1617–1683)', in *Oxford Dictionary of National Biography*, ed. David Cannadine (Oxford: Oxford University Press, 2004), http://www.oxforddnb.com/view/article/37618, accessed 21 Aug. 2017.

35. McFarlane, 1–2.
36. M. Emmanuel Orchard, ed., *Till God Will: Mary Ward Through Her Writings* (London: Darton, Longman and Todd, 1985), 9–10. See also Susan O'Brien, 'Ward, Mary (1585–1645)', *Oxford Dictionary of National Biography*, http://www.oxforddnb.com/view/article/28699, accessed 29 June 2017.
37. On Mary Ward and her schools for 'English Ladies', see Caroline Bicks, 'Reading the Jesuitess in *A Game at Chess*', *Studies in English Literature* 49.2 (2009): 463–484; Caroline Bicks, 'Producing Girls on the English Stage: Performance as Pedagogy in Mary Ward's Convent Schools', in *Gender and Early Modern Constructions of Childhood*, ed. Naomi Miller and Naomi Yavneh (Aldershot: Ashgate, 2011), 139–153.
38. See Caroline Bicks, 'Incited Minds: Rethinking Early Modern Girls', *Shakespeare Studies* 44 (2016): 180–202.
39. See also discussion of John Rastrick in Chap. 2, 46 and Elizabeth Cary in Chap. 5, 167–170.
40. Venn, 5, 4.
41. McFarlane, 1.
42. McFarlane, 2.
43. McFarlane, 2.
44. Katharine Craik, *Reading Sensations in Early Modern England* (Basingstoke: Palgrave Macmillan, 2007), 115.
45. McFarlane, 2.
46. See Anderson, 13–14.
47. Edward Bagshaw, *The Life and Death of Mr. Vavasour Powell* (London, 1671), 1–2.
48. Bagshaw, 2.
49. Bagshaw, 3.
50. N. H. Keeble, ed., *The Autobiography of Richard Baxter* (New York: Rowman and Littlefield, 1974), 7.
51. Keeble, *Autobiography*, 5.
52. Richard Norwood, *Confessions*, in *Grace Abounding, With Other Spiritual Autobiographies*, ed. John Stachniewski (Oxford: Oxford University Press, 1998), 130, 125.
53. See also Robert Prudom, *Truth Unavail'd by Scripture-Light* (London, 1699), 150–170, who claims that he was converted at age 14 upon reading John Foxe's *Book of Martyrs*, having had a degenerate childhood during which he sang profane ballads. On the motif of books as enabling conversion in early modern narratives, see Lynch, 11.
54. See Chap. 3, 74–81.
55. Charles Jackson, ed., *The Autobiography of Mrs. Alice Thornton* (London: Surtees Society, 1875), 12.

56. Jackson, 12.
57. Norwood, 125.
58. Ben-Amos, 185.
59. On the influence of Augustine on autobiographical writing after the publication of his works in England in 1631, see Lynch, 1, 31–72; Ryrie, 301, 433.
60. Douglas Greene, ed., *The Meditations of Lady Elizabeth Delaval* (Gateshead: Northumberland Press, 1978), 26. Further references are given in the text.
61. Margaret Ezell, 'Elizabeth Delaval's Spiritual Heroine: Thoughts on Redefining Manuscript Texts by Early Women Writers', in *English Manuscript Studies, 1100–1700*, ed. Peter Beal and Jeremy Griffiths (Toronto: University of Toronto Press, 1992), 218. This text has been described as spiritual autobiography, memoir, diary, commonplace book, romance, literary narrative and coming-of-age narrative. See Jennifer Kolpacoff Deane et al., 'Women's Kinship Networks: A Meditation on Creative Genealogies and Historical Labor', in *Mapping Gendered Routes and Spaces in the Early Modern World*, ed. Merry Wiesner Hanks (London: Routledge, 2016), 238; Eckerle, 138–148; Ezell, 216–237; Sarah Read, *Menstruation and the Female Body* (Basingstoke: Palgrave Macmillan, 2013), 9.
62. Eckerle, 139. On dating of the manuscript, see Greene, 17–19; Ezell, 221–223.
63. Eckerle, 139.
64. Ezell, 225–226.
65. See also 'as soon as I was 10' (30); 'not a month past 14' (35); 'writ in the later end of my 17th yeare' (82).
66. On early modern configurations of the life cycle in terms of the seasons, see Silvana Seidel Menchi, 'The Girl and the Hourglass: Periodization of Women's Lives in Western Preindustrial Societies', in *Time, Space and Women's Lives in Early Modern Europe*, ed. Anne Jacobson Schutte, Thomas Kuehn and Silvana Seidel Menchi (Kirksville: Truman State University Press, 2001), 45–46.
67. Early modern tracts often aligned the end of childhood with the age of marriage or the age of sexual maturity. See Anon., *The Office of Christian Parents* (London, 1616), L1r; Lucy Munro, *Children of the Queen's Revels: A Jacobean Theatre Repertory* (Cambridge: Cambridge University Press, 2005), 40; Keith Thomas, 'Age and Authority in Early Modern England', *Proceedings of the British Academy* 62 (1976): 225–226. On the years between 12 and 14 as a crucial transitional stage for girls, as the years during which their biological transition out of childhood was marked by the symptoms of greensickness, see Kim Phillips, *Medieval*

Maidens: Young Women and Gender in England, 1270–1540 (Manchester: Manchester University Press, 2003), 23–60; Ursula Potter, 'Greensickness in Romeo and Juliet: Considerations on a Sixteenth-Century Disease of Virgins', in *The Premodern Teenager: Youth in Society 1150–1650*, ed. Konrad Eisenbichler (Toronto: Centre for Renaissance and Reformation Studies, 2002), 271–91; Read, 52. Ursula Potter has demonstrated how age 14 specifically is often invoked as the critical transitional age for girls in literature of the period. See 'Navigating the Dangers of Female Puberty in Renaissance Drama', *Studies in English Literature 1500–1900* 53.2 (2013), 421–439.

68. See also Margaret Ezell, 'Delaval, Lady Elizabeth (1648?–1717)', in *Oxford Dictionary of National Biography*, http://www.oxforddnb.com/view/article/68215, accessed 21 August 2017.

69. Delaval claims to be 'deluded' (30, 32) by Carter's tales and to have 'neglected' her learning (30).

70. See Chap. 3, 80–81.

71. For example, Jacques Du Bosc, *The Compleat Woman* (London, 1639), 12–15.

72. See 'doted' (29); 'deluded' (30, 32), 'foleish' (30); 'foleishly' (32).

73. See Eckerle, 139, on the complex tone of Delaval's text, which deploys elements of the romance genre but also condemns it.

74. These romances are Gaultier de Coste's *Cassandra, A Romance* and Hymen's *Praeludia*, Magdeleine de Scuderi's *Artamenes, or the Grand Cyrus* and Honoré d'Urfé's *Astrae, A Romance*.

75. On the common use of horticultural imagery to refer to the shaping of childhood, see Anna French, *Children of Wrath: Possession, Prophecy and the Young in Early Modern England* (London: Routledge, 2016), 34. For example, children are represented as fields that need tending in *The Office of Christian Parents* (Cambridge, 1616), 17, and as trees that need support in *The Court of Good Counsell* (London, 1607), Dv.

76. The reading of romances and the recognition of the dangers of this is not always equated with the shift from childhood to adulthood. However, in autobiographical texts the dismissal of romance is often aligned with other significant life changes and thus reading romance is constructed as a youthful habit to be left behind. On romance reading and its associations with youth, see Chap. 3, 79.

77. Childhood is regularly constructed in autobiographical writing as a state that can be left behind. Lady Ann Fanshawe figures this in terms of play, writing that as a 'hoyting girle' she loved riding, running and skipping, but following her mother's death she 'flung away those little childnesses that had formerly possessed me' (Loftis, 110). Lucy Hutchinson admits that as a child she was interested in 'witty songs and amorous sonnetes',

but that she subsequently 'forgo[t] those extravagancies of my infancy' (Keeble, *Memoirs*, 15). See also John Bunyan's claim that 'These things, I say, when I was but a childe' in *Grace Abounding*, in *Grace Abounding, With Other Spiritual Autobiographies*, 7.

78. Ryrie, 433.

79. Eckerle, 138–148; Ezell, 'Elizabeth Delaval's', 226. On the ways in which early modern autobiographical writing deploys other forms, see Shelia Ottway, 'They Only Lived Twice: Public and Private Selfhood in the Autobiographies of Anne, Lady Halkett and Colonel John Bampfield', in *Betraying Our Selves: Forms of Self-Representation in Early Modern English Texts*, ed. Henk Dragstra, Shelia Ottway and Helen Wilcox (Basingstoke: Palgrave Macmillan, 2000), 136–147; Ramona Wray, '[Re] constructing the Past: The Diametric Lives of Mary Rich', in *Betraying Our Selves*, 148–165; Michelle Dowd and Julie Eckerle, 'Introduction', in *Genre and Women's Life Writing in Early Modern England* (London: Routledge, 2007), 4.

80. Ramona Wray usefully highlights that the deployment of the tropes of romance in early modern women's life writing is not necessarily a conscious strategy ('[Re]constructing the Past', 152).

81. Spufford, 211.

82. All references are taken from the online edition and are given in the text. See Elizabeth Isham, *My Booke of Rememberance*, ed. Elizabeth Clarke et al., *Constructing Elizabeth Isham*, University of Warwick, http://web.warwick.ac.uk/english/perdita/Isham/index_bor.htm, accessed 7 Dec. 2011.

83. Elizabeth Clarke and Erica Longfellow, 'Introduction to the Online Edition: "[E]xamine my life": Writing the Self in the Early Seventeenth Century', *Constructing Elizabeth Isham*, University of Warwick, http://www2.warwick.ac.uk/fac/arts/ren/projects/isham/texts/, accessed 1 June 2017; Julie Eckerle, 'Coming to Knowledge: Elizabeth Isham's Autobiography and the Self-Construction of an Intellectual Woman', *a/b: Auto/Biography Studies* 25.1 (2014): 97. See also Andrew Cambers, *Godly Reading: Print, Manuscript and Puritanism in England, 1580–1720* (Cambridge University Press, 2011), 65; Kolpacoff Deane et al., 235.

84. Anne Cotterill, 'Fit Words at the "pitts brinke": The Achievement of Elizabeth Isham', *Huntington Library Quarterly* 73.2 (2010): 228.

85. All references are taken from the online edition and are given in the text according to year. See Elizabeth Isham, *Diary*, ed. Elizabeth Clarke et al., *Constructing Elizabeth Isham*, University of Warwick, http://web.warwick.ac.uk/english/perdita/Isham/index_yr.htm, accessed 7 Dec. 2011. On the retrospective nature of the diary and its relationship to Isham's

Booke, see Jill Millman, 'Northamptonshire Record Office MSIL3365 – The Other Life of Elizabeth Isham', *Constructing Elizabeth Isham*, University of Warwick, http://www2.warwick.ac.uk/fac/arts/ren/projects/isham/workshop/millman, accessed 1 June 2017.

86. Cotterill, 234.
87. On the range of books mentioned in the *Booke*, see Cotterill, 245.
88. Eckerle, 'Coming', 103. Kolpacoff Deane et al., 234, also note that Isham's text is 'so focused on her intellectual curiosity that it can be read as much as a literary narrative as a spiritual autobiography'.
89. See Clarke and Longfellow.
90. On the influence of Augustine on Isham, see Alice Eardley, '"hewen stone": Constructing Elizabeth Isham's "Booke of Rememberance"', *Constructing Elizabeth Isham*, University of Warwick, http://www2.warwick.ac.uk/fac/arts/ren/projects/isham/workshop/eardley, accessed 1 June 2017; Ryrie, 433.
91. Cotterill, 245.
92. See *Booke*, 2r–3v; Cotterill, 245.
93. On old age as a second childhood, see Gregory Semenza, '"Second Childishness" and the Shakespearean Vision of Ideal Parenting', in *Gender and Early Modern Constructions of Childhood*, 223.
94. Cotterill, 226, 229–230.
95. See Ezell, 'Delaval'; Kate Aughterson, 'Isham, Elizabeth (*bap.* 1608, *d.* 1654)', in *Oxford Dictionary of National Biography*, http://www.oxforddnb.com/view/article/68093, accessed 21 August 2017.
96. See Chap. 2, 49–56.
97. For example, children are compared to 'new waxe' and 'fresh claie' as 'fittest for good impressions' in James Cleland, *The Institution of a Young Noble Man* (London, 1607), 2.
98. Drayton, 204.
99. Drayton, 204.
100. See Kate Chedgzoy, '"Make me a Poet, and I'll quickly be a Man": Masculinity, Pedagogy and Poetry in the English Renaissance', *Renaissance Studies* 27.5 (2013): 592–611.
101. On the insertion of Drayton into a literary tradition through poetry, see Andrew Hadfield, 'Michael Drayton's Brilliant Career', *Proceedings of the Royal British Academy* 125 (2003): 131.
102. See Lucy Munro, 'Infant Poets and Child Players: The Literary Performance of Childhood in Caroline England', in *The Child in British Literature*, ed. Adrienne Gavin (Basingstoke: Palgrave Macmillan, 2012), 54.
103. Cowley, *Poetical Blossomes*, A4r.
104. On the use of this rhetoric by child authors, see Munro, 'Infant', 54–68.

105. Ben Masters, in *Poetical Blossomes*, A4v.
106. Thomas Sprat, 'An Account of the Life and Writings of Mr. Abraham Cowley', in *The Works of Mr. Abraham Cowley*, A2r. On the trope of genius in the period, see Emma Rees, *Margaret Cavendish* (Manchester: Manchester University Press, 2003), 158, 191.
107. Munro, 'Infant', 56. See also Edel Lamb, *Performing Childhood in the Early Modern Theatre* (Basingstoke: Palgrave Macmillan, 2009), 120.
108. Munro gives the example of another child author, Thomas Jordan, who is praised as being 'borne not made a Poet' ('Infant', 59).
109. Richard West, 'To the Pious Memory of My Deare Brother-in-Law, M. Thomas Randolph', in *Poems*, by Thomas Randolph (London, 1642), B3r. On Randolph, see W. H. Kelliher, 'Randolph, Thomas (*bap.* 1605, *d.* 1635)', in *Oxford Dictionary of National Biography*, http://www.oxforddnb.com/view/article/23123, accessed 21 August 2017.
110. See James Fitzmaurice, ed., *Margaret Cavendish: Sociable Letters* (London: Routledge, 1997), 140; Margaret Cavendish, *The Life of the Thrice Noble, High and Puissant Prince William Cavendish* (London, 1667), n.p.
111. Steedman, *Past Tenses*, 23.
112. Jacqueline Rose, *The Case of Peter Pan: Or, The Impossibility of Children's Fiction* (Philadelphia: University of Pennsylvania Press, 1993), 1.
113. Anna Davin, 'What is a Child?', in *Childhood in Question: Children, Parents and the State*, ed. Stephen Hussey and Anthony Fletcher (Manchester: Manchester University Press, 1999), 15.

Bibliography

Primary Sources: Manuscripts

Bodleian Library, MS Douce B subt. 234, *Bevys of Southampton, c.* 1503.
British Library, Harley Manuscript 1960, Holme Family Notebook.
Centre for Kentish Studies, Sackville, U269 F 38/1-4, Rachel Fane's Manuscripts.

Primary Sources: Other

An A.B.C. for Children. London, 1570. STC 19.5.
Abbot, Robert. *Milk for Babes.* London, 1646. Wing A69aA.
Aesop Improved. London, 1673. Wing A742.
Bagshaw, Edward. *The Life and Death of Mr Vavasour Powell.* London, 1671. Wing L2003.
Batchiler, John. *The Virgin's Pattern.* London, 1661. Wing B1076.
Batt, Bartholomew. *The Christian Man's Closet.* London, 1581. STC1011091.
Baxter, Richard. *A Breviate of the Life of Margaret.* London, 1681. Wing B1194A.
———. *A Christian Directory.* London, 1673. Wing B1219.
Bayly, Lewis. *The Practise of Pietie.* London, 1613. STC 1602.
Bevington, David, Martin Butler, and Ian Donaldson, ed. *The Cambridge Edition of the Works of Ben Jonson.* Cambridge: Cambridge University Press, 2012.
The Booke O[f] Merrie Riddles. London, 1617. STC 3322.5.
Brathwait, Richard. *The English Gentlewoman.* London, 1631. STC 3565.
Breton, Nicholas. *The Court and Country.* London, 1618. STC 3641.
———. *Melancholike Humours.* London, 1600. STC 3666.

© The Author(s) 2018
E. Lamb, *Reading Children in Early Modern Culture*,
Early Modern Literature in History,
https://doi.org/10.1007/978-3-319-70359-6

Brinsley, John. *Cato Translated Gramatically.* London, 1612a. STC 4859.
———. *A Consolation for Our Grammar Schools.* London, 1622. STC 3767.
———. *Corderius Dialogues.* London, 1614. STC 5762.
———. *Esop's Eables.* London, 1617a. STC 187.5.
———. *The First Book of Tullies Offices.* London, 1616. STC 5288.
———. *Ludus Literarius.* London, 1627. STC 3770.
———. *Ovid's Metamorphosis.* London, 1618. STC 18963.
———. *The Posing of Parts.* London, 1612b. STC 3770b.5.
———. *Pueriles Confabulatiunculae: Or, Children's Dialogues.* London, 1617b. STC 3773.
———. *Sententiae Pueriles.* London, 1612c. STC 3774.
———. *Virgil's Eclogues.* London, 1620. STC 24818.
Brown, Sylvia, ed. *Women's Writing in Stuart England.* Stroud: Sutton Publishing Limited, 1999.
Bruto, Giovanni. *The Necessarie, Fit, and Convenient Education of a Yong Gentlewoman.* London, 1598. STC 3947.
Bullokar, William. *Aesopz Fablz.* London, 1585. STC 187.
Bunyan, John. *A Book for Boys and Girls.* London, 1686. Wing B5489.
———. *A Few Sighs from Hell.* London, 1658. Wing B5516.
B[urton], R[ichard]. *Youth's Divine Pastime.* London, 1691. Wing C7363.
C., E. *An A.B.C. or Holy Alphabet.* London, 1626. STC 4264.5.
Calver, Edward. *Passion and Discretion, in Youth and Age.* London, 1641. Wing C316.
Carpenter, Andrew, ed. *Verse in English from Tudor and Stuart Ireland.* Cork: Cork University Press, 2003.
Cavendish, Margaret. *The Life of the Thrice Noble, High and Puissant Prince William Cavendishe.* London, 1667. Wing N853.
———. *Nature's Pictures.* London, 1656. Wing N855.
Cawdry, Robert. *A Shorte and Fruitefull Treatise of the Profite and Necessitie of Catechising.* London, 1580. STC 4882.
Cervantes, Miguel de. *The Ingenious Hidalgo Don Quixote de la Mancha.* Trans. John Rutherford. London: Penguin, 2003.
The Child's Bible. London, 1677. Wing C3874.
Clarke, Samuel. *A Collection of the Lives of Ten Eminent Divines.* London, 1662. Wing C4506.
Cleland, James. *The Institution of a Young Noble Man.* Oxford, 1607. STC 5393.
Clement, Francis. *The Petie Schole.* London, 1587. STC 5400.
Cobhead, Thomas. *A Briefe Instruction.* London, 1579. STC 5455.
Codrington, Robert. *The Second Part of Youth's Behaviour.* London, 1664. Wing C4878.
Coles, Elisha. *Nolens Volens.* London, 1677. Wing C5080.
Coote, Edmund. *The English Schoolmaister.* London, 1596. STC 5711.

Corin, Festus. *The Childe's First Tutor.* London, 1664. Wing C6296A.

The Court of Good Counsell. London, 1607. STC 5876.

Cowley, Abraham. *Poetical Blossoms.* London, 1636. STC 5907.

———. *The Works of Mr Abraham Cowley.* London, 1668. Wing C6649.

Craig, John. *The Mother and the Child.* London, 1611. STC 5961.5.

Craven, Wesley, and Walter Hayward, ed. *The Journal of Richard Norwood.* New York: Scholar Press, 1945.

Cuffe, Henry. *The Differences of the Ages of Man's Life.* London, 1607. STC 6103.

Dekker, Thomas. *The Gul's Horne-Booke.* London, 1609. STC 6500.

Dering, Edward. *A Briefe and Necessary Instruction.* London, 1572. STC6679.2.

Dixon, Peter, ed. *The Country Wife and Other Plays.* Oxford: Oxford University Press, 1996.

Drayton, Michael. *The Battaile of Agincourt.* London, 1627. STC 7190.

Doolittle, Thomas. *The Young Man's Instructer.* London, 1673. Wing D1906.

Du Bosc, Jacques. *The Compleat Woman.* London, 1639. STC 7266.

Ferne, John. *The Blazon of Gentry.* London, 1586. STC 10824.

Fisher, James. *The Wise Virgin.* London, 1653. Wing F1004.

Fitzmaurice, James, ed. *Margaret Cavendish: Sociable Letters.* London: Garland, 1997.

Fletcher, John. *The Elder Brother.* London, 1637. STC 11066.

Forset, Edward. *Pedantius Comoedia.* London, 1631. STC 19524.

G., J. *A Play-Book for Children.* London, 1694. Wing G37.

Graile, Edmond. *Little Timothe His Lesson.* London, 1611. STC 12171.

Greenblatt, Stephen, et al., ed. *The Norton Shakespeare.* New York: W. W. Norton & Co., 2008.

Greene, Douglas, ed. *The Meditations of Lady Elizabeth Delaval.* Gateshead: Northumberland Press, 1978.

Greene, Robert. *Alcida Greene's Metamorphosis.* London, 1617. STC 12216.

———. *Menaphon.* London, 1589. STC 12272.

Guillemeau, Jacque. *Childe-Birth.* London, 1612. STC 12496.

H., E. *David's Sling Against Great Goliath.* London, 1589. STC 14011.

Harrington, John. *A Tract on the Succession to the Crown 1602.* London: Nicholas & Sons, 1880.

Hawkins, Francis. *Youth's Behaviour.* London, 1651. Wing Y209A.

Hawkins, William. *Apollo Shroving.* London, 1626. STC 12963.

Henry, Matthew. *An Account of the Life and Death of Mr Philip Henry.* London, 1699. Wing B1100B.

Hensley, Jeannine, ed. *The Works of Anne Bradstreet.* Cambridge: Belknap Press, 1967.

H[odges], R[ichard]. *The Childe's Counting-Book.* London, 1624. STC 12573.3.

Hodges, Richard. *The Grounds of Learning.* London, 1650. ESTC R505822.

Hoole, Charles. *Aesop's Fables.* London, 1657a. Wing A691.

———. *Catonis Disticha de Moribus*. London, 1659a. Wing C1505.

———. *Children's Talke*. London, 1659b. Wing H2671.

———. *The Latine Grammar*. London, 1651. Wing H2684.

———. *A Little Vocabulary English and Latin for the Use of Little Children*. London, 1657b. Wing H2695.

———. *Maturinus Corderius' School-Colloquies*. London, 1732. ESTC T13212.

———. *A New Discovery of the Old Art of Teaching Schoole*. London, 1660. Wing H2688.

———. *Orbis Sensualium Pictus*. London, 1659c. Wing C5523.

———. *The Petty-Schoole*. London, 1659d. Wing H2688A.

———. *Sentences for Children*. London, 1658. Wing C7476.

———. *Six Comedies of Terentius*. London, 1663. Wing T736.

Hornby, William. *Hornbyes Hornbook*. London, 1622. STC 13814.

An Hundred Godly Lessons. London, c. 1686–1688. Wing H3726AB.

Isham, Elizabeth. 'My Booke of Rememberance.' In *Constructing Elizabeth Isham*, ed. Elizabeth Clarke et al. University of Warwick. http://web.warwick.ac.uk/english/perdita/Isham/index_bor.htm. Accessed 7 Dec 2011.

———. 'Diary.' In *Constructing Elizabeth Isham*, ed. Elizabeth Clarke et al. University of Warwick. http://web.warwick.ac.uk/english/perdita/Isham/index_yr.htm. Accessed 7 Dec 2011.

Jackson, Charles, ed. *The Autobiography of Mrs Alice Thornton*. London: Surtees Society, 1875.

Janeway, James. *A Token for Children*. London, 1676. Wing J478.

———. *A Token for Children. The Second Part*. London, 1673. Wing J480aA.

Johnson, John. *The Academy of Love*. London, 1641. Wing J782.

Keach, Benjamin. *Instructions for Children*. London, 1710. ESTC T121252.

———. *War with the Devil*. London, 1676. Wing K104.

Keeble, N. H., ed. *The Autobiography of Richard Baxter*. New York: Rowman and Littlefield, 1974.

———., ed. *Memoirs of the Life of Colonel Hutchinson*. London: Phoenix Press, 2000.

Kempe, William. *The Education of Children in Learning*. London, 1588. STC 14926.

Kettlewell, John. *The Practical Believer*. London, 1688. Wing K380.

Kirkman, Francis. *The Counterfeit Lady Unveiled*. London, 1673a. Wing K630A.

———. *The Famous and Delectable History of Don Bellianis of Greece*. London, 1673b. Wing K632A.

———. *The Famous and Renowned History of Amadis de Gaule*. London, 1652. Wing L2731A.

———. *The History of Prince Erastus*. London, 1674. Wing H2136.

———. *The Honour of Chivalry*. London, 1664. Wing K633.

———. *The Unlucky Citizen*. London, 1673c. Wing K638.

Lenton, Francis. *The Young Gallant's Whirligig*. London, 1629. STC 15467.

Lewis, Thomas, ed. *The Letters of the Lady Brilliana Harley*. London: Camden Society, 1854.

Lily, William. *A Short Introduction of Grammer*. Cambridge, 1621. STC 15627.3.

Locke, John. *Some Thoughts Concerning Education*. London, 1693. Wing L2762A.

Loftis, John, ed. *The Memoirs of Anne Lady Halkett and Ann, Lady Fanshawe*. Oxford: Clarendon Press, 1979.

London, William. *A Catalogue of the Most Vendible Books in England*. Newcastle, 1658. Wing L2850.

Lye, Thomas. *The Child's Delight*. London, 1671. Wing L3530.

M., J. *Sports and Pastimes*. London, 1676. Wing M48.

Marston, John. *What You Will*. Edited by M. R. Woodhead. Nottingham: Nottingham Drama Texts, 1980.

Martyn, William. *Youth's Instruction*. London, 1612. STC 17530.

Mason, John. *A Little Catechism with Little Verses and Little Sayings for Little Children*. London, 1692. Wing M916B.

Mauger, Claude. *The True Advancement of the French Tongue*. London, 1653. Wing M1352.

May, Steven, ed. *Henry Stanford's Anthology: An Edition of Cambridge University Library MS, Dd. 5.75*. New York: Garland, 1988.

McFarlane, Alan, ed. *The Diary of Ralph Josselin, 1616–1683*. Oxford: Oxford University Press, 1991.

Meres, Francis. *Palladis Tamia*. London, 1598. STC 17834.

Mulcaster, Richard. *Positions Wherein Those Primitive Circumstances Be Examined, Which Are Necessarie for the Training Up of Children*. London, 1581. STC 18253.

Munday, Anthony. *Fedele and Fortunio*. Ed. Richard Hosley. London: Garland Publishing, 1981.

The Mysteries of Love and Eloquence. London, 1658.

Newbery, Thomas. *A Booke in Englysh Metre*. London, 1563.

The Office of Christian Parents. Cambridge, 1616. STC 5180.

Osborn, James, ed. *The Autobiography of Thomas Whythorne*. Oxford: Clarendon Press, 1961.

P., H. *A Looking Glass for Children*. London, 1673.

Paynell, Thomas. *The Most Excellent and Pleasaunt Booke, Entitled: The Treasurie of Amadis of Fraunce*. London, 1572.

Penkethman, John. *A Handful of Honesty*. London, 1623.

Peters, Hugh. *A Dying Fathers Last Legacy*. London, 1651.

Peterson, Lesley, ed. *The Mirror of the Worlde*. Montreal: McGill University Press, 2012.

A Pleasant Conceited Comedie, Wherein Is Shewed How a Man May Chuse a Good Wife from a Bad. London, 1602.

Pollock, Linda, ed. *With Faith and Physic: The Life of a Tudor Gentlewoman, Lady Grace Mildmay 1552–1620*. London: Collins and Brown, 1993.

Powell, Thomas. *Tom of All Trades*. London, 1631.

The Protestant Tutor. London, 1679.

Prudom, Robert. *Truth Unavail'd by Scripture-Light*. London, 1699.

Reading, John. *The Old Man's Staffe*. London, 1621.

Rowley, Samuel. *When You See Me, You Know Me*. London, 1605.

Russel, Robert. *A Little Book for Children and Youth*. London, *c.* 1693–1696.

Salonstall, Wye. *Pictures Drawn Forth into Characters*. London, 1631.

Salter, Thomas. *The Mirrhor of Modestie*. London, 1579.

Sargeaunt, John. *Annals of Westminster School*. London: Methuen, 1898.

Savile, George. *The Lady's New Year's Gift*. London, 1688. Wing H304.

Sharpham, Edward. *Cupid's Whirligig*. London, 1607. STC 22380.

Sherman, Thomas. *Youth's Tragedy*. London, 1671. Wing S3392.

———. *Youth's Comedy*, London, 1680. Wing S3391.

A Short Catechisme for Little Children. London, 1589. STC 4803.8.

Sidney, Philip. *An Apology for Poetry*. Edited by Geoffrey Shepherd and R. W. Masten. Manchester: Manchester University Press, 2002.

———. *The Countess of Pembroke's Arcadia*. Edited by Katherine Duncan-Jones. Oxford: Oxford University Press, 1994.

Sorocold, Thomas. *Supplications of Saints*. London, 1612. STC 22932.

Sowards, J. K., ed. *The Collected Works of Erasmus*. Toronto: Toronto University Press, 1985.

Sparke, Michael. *The Crums of Comfort*. London, 1628. STC 23016.5.

Stachniewski, John, ed. *Grace Abounding, with Other Spiritual Autobiographies*. Oxford: Oxford University Press, 1998.

Storey, Matthew, ed. *Two East Anglian Diaries 1641–1729*. Woodbridge: Boydell Press, 1994.

A Table of Good Nurture. London, 1625. STC 23635.

Tyler, Margaret. *The Mirrour of Princely Deedes and Knighthood* (*c.* 1578), *The Early Modern Englishwoman: A Facsimile Library of Essential Works, I.8*. Aldershot: Ashgate, 1996.

Tymms, Samuel, ed. *Wills and Inventories from the Registers of the Commissary of Bury, St Edmund's*. London: Camden Society, 1850.

Venn, Anne. *A Wise Virgin's Lamp Burning*. London, 1658. Wing V190.

Vives, Juan. *The Instruction of a Christian Woman*. London, 1592. STC 24863.

W., S. *Most Easie Instructions for Reading*. London, *c.* 1610. STC 17.

Walker, Anthony. *The Vertuous Wife*. London, 1694. Wing W311A.

Watson, Foster. *Tudor School-Boy Life: The Dialogues of Juan Luis Vives*. London: Frank Cass, 1970.

Webbe, Joseph. *Children's Talke*. London, 1627. STC 25170.5.

White, Thomas. *A Little Book for Little Children*. London, 1702.

Whitney, Geoffrey. *A Choice of Emblemes.* London, 1586. STC 25438.
Willis, Thomas. *The Key of Knowledg[e].* London, 1682. ESTC T72530.
The Wit of a Woman. London, 1604. STC 25868.
Wolfe, Heather, ed. *Lady Falkland: Life and Letters.* London: Continuum, 2004.
Wolley, Hannah. *The Gentlewoman's Companion.* London, 1673. Wing W3276A.
Woodward, Hezekiah. *A Childe's Patrimony.* London, 1640. STC 25971.
Wright, Thomas. *The Passions of the Minde.* London, 1601. STC 26039.
Youth's Treasury. London, 1688. Wing Y212.

Secondary Sources

Ackroyd, Julie. *Child Actors on the London Stage, circa 1600.* Brighton: Sussex Academic Press, 2017.
Adams, Gillian. 'In the Hands of Children.' *The Lion and the Unicorn* 29 (2004): 38–51.
Adelman, Janet. *Suffocating Mothers: Fantasies of Maternal Origin in Shakespeare's Plays.* London: Routledge, 1992.
Andersen, Jennifer, and Elizabeth Sauer, ed. *Books and Readers in Early Modern England: Material Studies.* Philadelphia: University of Pennsylvania Press, 2002.
Anderson, Linda. *Autobiography.* London: Routledge, 2001.
Ariès, Philippe. *Centuries of Childhood.* New York: Vintage, 1962.
Avery, Gillian, and Julia Briggs, ed. *Children and Their Books: A Celebration of the Work of Iona and Peter Opie.* Oxford: Clarendon Press, 1989.
Bald, R. C. 'Francis Kirkman, Bookseller and Author.' *Modern Philology* 41, no. 1 (1943): 17–32.
Baldwin, T. W. *William Shakspere's Petty School.* Chicago: University of Illinois Press, 1943.
———. *William Shakspere's Small Latine and Lesse Greeke.* Urbana: University of Illinois Press, 1944.
Barclay, Katie, Kimberley Reynolds, and Ciara Rawnsley, ed. *Death, Emotion and Childhood in Premodern Europe.* Basingstoke: Palgrave Macmillan, 2017.
Baumann, Gerd, ed. *The Written Word: Literacy in Transition.* Oxford: Clarendon, 1986.
Beal, Peter, and Jeremy Griffiths, ed. *English Manuscript Studies, 1100–1700.* Toronto: University of Toronto Press, 1992.
Bedford, Ronald, Lloyd Davis, and Philippa Kelly. *Early Modern English Lives: Autobiography and Self-Representation, 1500–1660.* Aldershot: Ashgate, 2007.
Belsey, Catherine. *Why Shakespeare?* Basingstoke: Palgrave Macmillan, 2007.
Ben-Amos, Ilana. *Adolescence and Youth in Early Modern England.* Yale: Yale University Press, 1994.

Bennett, H. S. *English Books and Their Readers: 1475 to 1557.* Cambridge: Cambridge University Press, 1970.

Bevington, David, and Peter Holbrook, ed. *The Politics of the Stuart Court Masque.* Cambridge: Cambridge University Press, 1998.

Bicks, Caroline. 'Incited Minds: Rethinking Early Modern Girls.' *Shakespeare Studies* 44 (2016): 180–202.

Bingham, Jane, and Grace Scholt. *Fifteen Centuries of Children's Literature.* London: Greenwood Press, 1980.

Black, L. C. 'Some Renaissance Children's Verse.' *The Review of English Studies* 24, no. 93 (1973): 1–16.

Blair, Ann. 'Lectures on Ovid's *Metamorphoses:* The Class Notes of a Sixteenth-Century Paris Schoolboy.' *Princeton University Library Chronicle* 50 (1989): 117–144.

Blair, Ann. 'Reading Strategies for Coping with Information Overload *ca.* 1550–1700.' *Journal of the History of Ideas* 64, no. 1 (2003): 11–28.

Bly, Mary. *Queer Virgins and Virgin Queans on the Early Modern Stage.* Oxford: Oxford University Press, 2000.

Bloom, Gina. *Voice in Motion: Staging Gender, Shaping Sound in Early Modern England.* Philadelphia: University of Pennsylvania Press, 2007.

Bolgar, Robert. 'From Humanism to the Humanities.' *Twentieth Century Studies* 9 (1973): 8–21.

Bottigheimer, Ruth. *The Bible for Children: From the Age of Gutenberg to the Present.* New Haven: Yale University Press, 1996.

———. *Bibliography of British Books for Children and Adolescents, 1470–1770.* New York: Stony Brook University Libraries, 2008.

Boyd McBride, Kari, ed. *Domestic Arrangements in Early Modern England.* Pittsburgh: Duquesne University Press, 2002.

Brayman Hackel, Heidi. *Reading Material in Early Modern England.* Cambridge: Cambridge University Press, 2005.

Brayman Hackel, Heidi, and Catherine Kelly, ed. *Reading Women: Literacy, Authorship, and Culture in the Atlantic World, 1500–1800.* Philadelphia: University of Pennsylvania Press, 2008.

Brooks, Douglas. ed. *Printing and Parenting in Early Modern England.* Aldershot: Ashgate, 2006.

Brown, Cedric. 'Recusant Community and Jesuit Mission in Parliament Days: Bodleian MS Eng. Poet. B 5.' *The Yearbook of English Studies* 33 (2003): 290–315.

Burke, Peter. 'The Renaissance Dialogue.' *Renaissance Studies* 3 (1989): 1–12.

Burke, Victoria, and Jonathan Gibson, ed. *Early Modern Women's Manuscript Writing.* Aldershot: Ashgate, 2004.

Burnett, John. *Destiny Obscure: Autobiographies of Childhood, Education and Family From the 1820s to the 1920s.* London: Allen Lane, 1982.

Burnett, Mark Thornton. *Masters and Servants in English Renaissance Drama and Culture: Authority and Obedience.* Basingstoke: Palgrave Macmillan, 1997.

Burt, Richard, and John Michael Archer, ed. *Enclosure Acts: Sexuality, Property and Culture in Early Modern England.* Ithaca: Cornell University Press, 1994.

Bushnell, Rebecca. *A Culture of Teaching: Early Modern Humanism in Theory and Practice.* Ithaca: Cornell University Press, 1996.

Cambers, Andrew. *Godly Reading: Print, Manuscript and Puritanism in England, 1580–1720.* Cambridge: Cambridge University Press, 2011.

Campana, Joseph. 'Boy Toys and Liquid Joys: Pleasure and Power in the Bower of Bliss.' *Modern Philology* 106, no. 3 (2009): 465–496.

———. 'The Child's Two Bodies: Shakespeare, Sovereignty, and the End of Succession.' *ELH* 81, no. 3 (2014): 811–839.

———. 'Shakespeare's Children.' *Literature Compass* 8, no. 1 (2011): 1–14.

Carville, Jordan. *Elizabeth Cary: Development of the Author.* Unpublished MA dissertation, Queen's University Belfast, 2015.

Cavallo, Guglielmo, and Roger Chartier, ed. *A History of Reading in the West.* Cambridge: Polity Press, 1999.

Charlton, Kenneth. *Education in Renaissance England.* London: Routledge, 2013.

———. '"Not publike only but also private and domesticall": Mothers and Familial Education in Pre-industrial England.' *History of Education* 17, no. 1 (1988): 1–20.

Chartier, Roger. *Forms and Meanings.* Philadelphia: University of Pennsylvania State Press, 1995.

———. *The Order of Books.* Cambridge: Polity Press, 1994.

Chedgzoy, Kate. 'A Renaissance for Children?' Newcastle Upon Tyne ePrints, 2013a. http://eprint.ncl.ac.uk/pub_details2.aspx?pub_id=196398. Accessed 20 Nov 2013.

———. '"Make Me a Poet, and I'll Quickly Be a Man": Masculinity, Pedagogy and Poetry in the English Renaissance.' *Renaissance Studies* 27, no. 5 (2013b): 592–611.

———. *Women's Writing in the British Atlantic World.* Cambridge: Cambridge University Press, 2007.

Chedgzoy, Kate, Susanne Greenhalgh, and Robert Shaughnessy, ed. *Shakespeare and Childhood.* Cambridge: Cambridge University Press, 2007.

Chillington Rutter, Carol. *Shakespeare and Child's Play: Performing Lost Boys on Stage and Screen.* London: Routledge, 2007.

Colclough, Stephen. *Consuming Texts: Readers and Reading Communities, 1695–1870.* Basingstoke: Palgrave Macmillan, 2007.

Copeland, David. *Benjamin Keach and the Development of Baptist Traditions in Seventeenth-Century England.* Lewiston: Edwin Mellen Press, 2001.

Cotterill, Anne. 'Fit Words at the "Pitts Brinke": The Achievement of Elizabeth Isham.' *Huntington Library Quarterly* 73, no. 2 (2010): 225–248.

Craik, Katharine. *Reading Sensations in Early Modern England.* Basingstoke: Palgrave Macmillan, 2007.

Craik, Katharine, and Tanya Pollard, ed. *Shakespearean Sensations: Experiencing Literature in Early Modern England.* Cambridge: Cambridge University Press, 2013.

Crain, Patricia. *Reading Children: Literacy, Property and the Dilemmas of Childhood in Nineteenth-Century America.* Philadelphia: University of Pennsylvania Press, 2016.

———. *The Story of A: The Alphabetization of America from The New England Primer to The Scarlet Letter.* Stanford: Stanford University Press, 2002.

Crane, Mary. *Framing Authority: Sayings, Self and Society in Sixteenth-Century England.* Princeton: Princeton University Press, 1993.

Crane, Ronald. 'The Reading of an Elizabethan Youth.' *Modern Philology* 11, no. 2 (1913): 269–271.

Crawford, Julie. 'Reconsidering Early Modern Women's Reading, or, How Margaret Hoby Read her de Mornay.' *Huntington Library Quarterly* 73, no. 2 (2010): 193–223.

Cregan, Kate, and Denise Cuthbert. *Global Childhoods: Issues and Debates.* London: Sage Publications, 2014.

Cressy, David. *Literacy and the Social Order: Reading and Writing in Tudor and Stuart England.* Cambridge: Cambridge University Press, 1980.

Cummings, Brian. *The Literary Culture of the Reformation.* Oxford: Oxford University Press, 2002.

Cunningham, Hugh. *The Invention of Childhood.* London: Random House, 2006.

Darnton, Robert. *The Kiss of Lamourette.* New York: Norton, 1990.

Darton, F. J. Harvey. *Children's Books in England: Five Centuries of Social Life.* Cambridge: Cambridge University Press, 1982.

Das, Nandini. *Renaissance Romance: The Transformation of English Prose Fiction, 1570–1620.* Aldershot: Ashgate, 2011.

Daybell, James. *The Material Letter in Early Modern England.* Basingstoke: Palgrave Macmillan, 2012.

De Certeau, Michel. *The Practice of Everyday Life.* Trans. Steven Randall. Berkeley: University of California Press, 1988.

Demers, Patricia, ed. *From Instruction to Delight: An Anthology of Children's Literature to 1850.* Oxford: Oxford University Press, 2004.

———. *Heaven Upon Earth: The Forms of Moral and Religious Children's Literature to 1850.* Knoxville: University of Tennessee Press, 1993.

Dowd, Michelle. *Women's Work in Early Modern English Literature and Culture.* Basingstoke: Palgrave Macmillan, 2009.

Dowd, Michelle, and Julie Eckerle, ed. *Genre and Women's Life Writing in Early Modern England*. London: Routledge, 2007.

Denishoff, Dennis, ed. *The Nineteenth-Century Child and Consumer Culture*. Aldershot: Ashgate, 2008.

Dragstra, Henk, Shelia Ottway, and Helen Wilcox, ed. *Betraying Our Selves: Forms of Self-Representation in Early Modern English Texts*. Basingstoke: Palgrave Macmillan, 2000.

Dunan-Page, Anne, ed. *The Cambridge Companion to John Bunyan*. Cambridge: Cambridge University Press, 2010.

Duncan-Jones, Katherine. 'Philip Sidney's Toys.' *Proceedings of the British Academy* 66 (1980): 161–178.

Eckerle, Julie. 'Coming to Knowledge: Elizabeth Isham's Autobiography and the Self-Construction of an Intellectual Woman.' *a/b: Auto/Biography Studies* 25, no. 1 (2014): 97–121.

———. *Romancing the Self in Early Modern Englishwomen's Life-Writing*. Aldershot: Ashgate, 2013.

Eisenbichler, Konrad, ed. *The Premodern Teenager: Youth in Society 1150–1650*. Toronto: Centre for Renaissance and Reformation Studies, 2002.

Eliot, Simon, and Jonathan Rose, ed. *A Companion to the History of the Book*. Oxford: Blackwell, 2009.

Enterline, Lynn. *Shakespeare's Schoolroom: Rhetoric, Discipline, Emotion*. Philadelphia: University of Pennsylvania Press, 2012.

Ferguson, Margaret. *Dido's Daughters: Literacy, Gender and Empire in Early Modern England and France*. Chicago: University of Chicago Press, 2003.

Fisher, Will. *Materializing Gender in Early Modern Literature and Culture*. Cambridge: Cambridge University Press, 2006.

Fleming, Juliet. 'The French Garden: An Introduction to Women's French.' *ELH* 56, no. 1 (1989): 19–51.

———. *Graffiti and the Writing Arts of Early Modern England*. London: Reaktion Books, 2001.

Fletcher, Anthony. *Growing Up in England: The Experience of Childhood, 1600–1914*. Yale: Yale University Press, 2008.

Findlay, Alison. *Playing Spaces in Early Women's Drama*. Cambridge: Cambridge University Press, 2006.

Flint, Kate. *The Woman Reader, 1837–1914*. Oxford: Clarendon Press, 1993.

Fox, Adam. *Oral and Literate Culture in England, 1500–1700*. Oxford: Clarendon Press, 2000.

French, Anna. *Children of Wrath: Possession, Prophecy and the Young in Early Modern England*. London: Routledge, 2016.

Garber, Marjorie. *Coming of Age in Shakespeare*. London: Methuen, 1997.

Gardiner, Dorothy. *English Girlhood at School*. London: Oxford University Press, 1929.

Gardiner, Judith Kegan, ed. *Masculinity Studies and Feminist Theory: New Directions*. New York: Columbia University Press, 2002.

Gavin, Adrienne, ed. *The Child in British Literature: Literary Constructions of Childhood Medieval to Contemporary*. Basingstoke: Palgrave Macmillan, 2012.

Gillespie, Raymond. *Reading Ireland: Print, Reading and Social Change in Early Modern Ireland*. Manchester: Manchester University Press, 2005.

Goldberg, Jonathan. *Writing Matter: From the Hands of the English Renaissance*. Stanford: Stanford University Press, 1991.

Goodenough, Elizabeth, Mark Heberle, and Naomi Sokoloff, ed. *Infant Tongues: The Voice of the Child in Literature*. Detroit: Wayne State University Press, 1994.

Goodrich, Jaime. *Faithful Translators: Authorship, Gender and Religion in Early Modern England*. Evanston: Northwestern University Press, 2014.

Grafton, Anthony, and Lisa Jardine. *From Humanism to the Humanities: Education and the Liberal Arts in Fifteenth and Sixteenth-Century Europe*. London: Duckworth, 1986.

Graham, Elspeth, Hilary Hinds, Elaine Hobby, and Helen Wilcox, ed. *Her Own Life: Autobiographical Writings by Seventeenth-Century Women*. London: Routledge, 2003.

Green, Ian. *The Christian's ABC: Catechisms and Catechizing in England c. 1530–1740*. Oxford: Clarendon Press, 1996.

———. '"For Children in Yeeres and Children in Understanding": The Emergence of the English Catechism under Elizabeth and the Early Stuarts.' *The Journal of Ecclesiastical History* 37, no. 3 (1986): 397–425.

———. *Humanism and Protestantism in Early Modern English Education*. Aldershot: Ashgate, 2009.

———. *Print and Protestantism in Early Modern England*. Oxford: Oxford University Press, 2000.

Grenby, Matthew. 'Chapbooks, Children and Children's Literature.' *The Library* 8 (2007): 277–303.

———. *The Child Reader, 1700–1840*. Cambridge: Cambridge University Press, 2011.

Grenby, Matthew, and Andrea Immel, ed. *The Cambridge Companion to Children's Literature*. Cambridge: Cambridge University Press, 2009.

Greteman, Blaine. *The Poetics and Politics of Youth in Milton's England*. Cambridge: Cambridge University Press, 2013.

Griffiths, Paul. *Youth and Authority: Formative Experiences in England, 1560–1640*. Oxford: Clarendon Press, 1996.

Hackett, Helen. *Women and Romance Fiction in the English Renaissance*. Cambridge: Cambridge University Press, 2000.

Halasz, Alexandra. *The Marketplace of Print: Pamphlets and the Public Sphere in Early Modern England*. Cambridge: Cambridge University Press, 1997.

Halpern, Richard. *The Poetics of Primitive Accumulation: English Renaissance Culture and the Genealogy of Capital.* Ithaca: Cornell University Press, 1991.

Hayes, Kevin. *A Colonial Woman's Bookshelf.* Knoxville: The University of Tennessee Press, 1996.

Heller, Jennifer. *The Mother's Legacy in Early Modern England.* Aldershot: Ashgate, 2011.

Henderson, Diana, ed. *Alternative Shakespeares 3.* London: Routledge, 2008.

Higginbotham, Jennifer. 'Fair Maids and Golden Girls: The Vocabulary of Female Youth in Early Modern English.' *Modern Philology* 110 (2011): 171–196.

———. *The Girlhood of Shakespeare's Sisters: Gender, Transgression, Adolescence.* Edinburgh: Edinburgh University Press, 2013.

Hilton, Mary, Morag Styles, and Victor Watson, ed. *Opening the Nursery Door: Reading, Writing and Childhood 1600–1900.* London: Routledge, 1997.

Holland, Peter, and Stephen Orgel, ed. *Performance to Print in Shakespeare's England.* Basingstoke: Palgrave Macmillan, 2006.

Houston, R. *Literacy in Early Modern Europe.* London: Longman, 2002.

Hull, Suzanne. *Chaste, Silent and Obedient: English Books for Women, 1475–1640.* Pasadena: Huntington Library Press, 1982.

Hussey, Stephen, and Anthony Fletcher, ed. *Childhood in Question: Children, Parents and the State.* Manchester: Manchester University Press, 1999.

Hunt, Peter. *An Introduction to Children's Literature.* Oxford: Oxford University Press, 1994.

Immel, Andrea, and Michael Witmore, ed. *Childhood and Children's Books in Early Modern Europe, 1550–1800.* London: Routledge, 2006.

Jackson, H. *Marginalia: Readers' Writing in Books.* New Haven: Yale University Press, 2001.

Jardine, Lisa, and Anthony Grafton. '"Studied for Action": How Gabriel Harvey Read His Livy.' *Past & Present* 129 (1990): 30–78.

Jewell, Helen. *Education in Early Modern England.* London: Macmillan, 1998.

Jordanova, Ludmilla. 'New Worlds for Children in the Eighteenth Century: Problems of Historical Interpretation.' *History of the Human Sciences* 3, no. 1 (1990): 69–83.

Johns, Adrian. *The Nature of the Book: Print and Knowledge in the Making.* Chicago: University of Chicago Press, 1998.

Kamm, Josephine. *Hope Deferred: Girls' Education in English History.* London: Methuen, 1965.

Keenan, Celia, and Mary Shine Thompson, ed. *Studies In Children's Literature, 1500–2000.* Dublin: Four Courts, 2004.

Kermode, Lloyd, Jason Scott-Warren, and Martine Van Elk, ed. *Tudor Drama Before Shakespeare, 1485–1590.* Basingstoke: Palgrave Macmillan, 2004.

King, Margaret. 'Concepts of Childhood: What We Know and Where We Might Go.' *Renaissance Quarterly* 60 (2007): 371–407.

Kintgen, Eugene. *Reading in Tudor England*. Pittsburgh: University of Pittsburgh Press, 1996.

Kline, Daniel, ed. *Medieval Literature for Children*. London: Routledge, 2003.

Knowles, Katie. *Shakespeare's Boys: A Cultural History*. Basingstoke: Palgrave Macmillan, 2014.

Kraye, Jill, ed. *The Cambridge Companion to Renaissance Humanism*. Cambridge: Cambridge University Press, 2004.

Krontiris, Tina. 'Breaking Barriers of Genre and Gender: Margaret Tyler's Translation of *The Mirrour of Knighthood*.' *English Literary Renaissance* 18 (1988): 19–39.

Lamb, Edel. 'The Literature of Early Modern Childhoods.' *Literature Compass* 7, no. 6 (2010): 412–423.

———. *Performing Childhood in the Early Modern Theatre*. Basingstoke: Palgrave Macmillan, 2009.

———. '"Shall we playe the good girls": Playing Girls, Performing Girlhood on Early Modern Stages.' *Renaissance Drama* 44, no. 1 (2016): 73–100.

Lamb, Mary Ellen. 'Apologizing for Pleasure in Sidney's "Apology for Poetry": The Nurse of Abuse Meets the Tudor Grammar School.' *Criticism* 36, no. 4 (1994): 499–520.

Lerer, Seth. *Children's Literature: A Reader's History, from Aesop to Harry Potter*. Chicago: University of Chicago Press, 2008.

———. '"Thy Life to Mend, This Book Attend": Reading and Healing in the Arc of Children's Literature.' *New Literary History* 37, no. 3 (2006): 631–642.

Lesnik-Oberstein, Karin, ed. *Children in Culture: Approaches to Childhood*. Basingstoke: Palgrave Macmillan, 1998.

———. *Children's Literature: Criticism and the Fictional Child*. Oxford: Clarendon Press, 1994.

Lindley, David. *Shakespeare and Music*. London: Arden, 2006.

Loveman, Kate. *Samuel Pepys and His Books: Reading, Newsgathering, and Sociability, 1660–1703*. Oxford: Oxford University Press, 2015.

Lowenstein, David, and Janel Mueller, ed. *The Cambridge History of Early Modern English Literature*. Cambridge: Cambridge University Press, 2002.

Lucas, Caroline. *Writing for Women: The Example of Woman as Reader in Elizabethan Romance*. Milton Keynes: Open University Press, 1989.

Luke, Carmen. *Pedagogy, Printing and Protestantism: The Discourse on Childhood*. New York: State University of New York Press, 1989.

Lynch, Kathleen. *Protestant Autobiography in the Seventeenth-Century Anglophone World*. Oxford: Oxford University Press, 2012.

Lunger Knoppers, Laura, ed. *The Cambridge Companion to Early Modern Women's Writing*. Cambridge: Cambridge University Press, 2009.

Mack, Peter. *Elizabethan Rhetoric*. Cambridge: Cambridge University Press, 2002.

Maddern, Philippa, and Stephanie Tarbin, ed. *Material Worlds of Childhood in Northwestern Europe, c. 1350–1800*. London: Routledge, 2017. Forthcoming.

Marlow, Christopher. *Performing Masculinity in English University Drama, 1598–1636*. Aldershot: Ashgate, 2013.

Matz, Robert. *Defending Literature in Early Modern England: Renaissance Literary Theory in Social Context*. Cambridge: Cambridge University Press, 2000.

Mayer, Robert. 'Nathaniel Crouch, Bookseller and Historian: Popular Historiography and Cultural Power in Late Seventeenth-Century England.' *Eighteenth-Century Studies* 27, no. 3 (1994): 391–419.

Mazzola, Elizabeth. *Learning and Literacy in Female Hands, 1520–1698*. Aldershot: Ashgate, 2013.

McCarthy, Jeanne. *The Children's Troupes and the Transformation of English Theatre 1509–1608*. London: Routledge, 2016.

McKitterick, David. *A History of Cambridge University Press: Volume I: Printing and the Book Trade in Cambridge, 1534–1698*. Cambridge: Cambridge University Press, 1987.

McManaway, James. 'The First Five Bookes of Ovid's *Metamorphosis*, 1621, Englished by Master George Sandys.' *Studies in Shakespeare, Bibliography and Theatre* (1990): 69–82.

McManus, Clare. *Women on the Renaissance Stage: Anna of Denmark and Female Masquing in the Stuart Court 1590–1619*. Manchester: Manchester University Press, 2002.

McQuade, Paula. *Catechisms and Women's Writing in Seventeenth-Century England*. Cambridge: Cambridge University Press, 2017.

Mendelson, Sara, and Patricia Crawford. *Women in Early Modern England*. Oxford: Clarendon Press, 1998.

Michael, Ian. *The Teaching of English: From the Sixteenth Century to 1870*. Cambridge: Cambridge University Press, 1987.

Michals, Teresa. *Books for Children, Books for Adults: Age and the Novel from Defoe to James*. Cambridge: Cambridge University Press, 2014.

Miller, Naomi, and Naomi Yavneh, ed. *Gender and Early Modern Constructions of Childhood*. Aldershot: Ashgate, 2011.

Moncrief, Kathryn, and Kathryn McPherson, ed. *Performing Pedagogy in Early Modern England: Gender, Instruction and Performance*. Aldershot: Ashgate, 2013.

Moss, Ann. *Renaissance Truth and the Latin Language Turn*. Oxford: Oxford University Press, 2003.

Motter, T. H. *The School Drama in England*. London: Longman, 1929.

Müller, Anja. *Framing Childhood in Eighteenth-Century English Periodicals and Prints, 1689–1789*. Aldershot: Ashgate, 2009.

Munro, Lucy. *Children of the Queen's Revels: A Jacobean Theatre Repertory.* Cambridge: Cambridge University Press, 2005.

Murphy, Andrew. *Shakespeare for the People: Working Class Readers, 1800–1900.* Cambridge: Cambridge University Press, 2008.

Narveson, Kate. *Bible Readers and Lay Writers in Early Modern England: Gender and Self-Definition in an Emergent Writing Culture.* Aldershot: Ashgate, 2012.

Newcomb, Lori. *Reading Popular Romance in Early Modern England.* New York: Columbia University Press, 2002.

Newton, Hannah. *The Sick Child in Early Modern England, 1580–1720.* Oxford: Oxford University Press, 2012.

O'Connor, John. *Amadis de Gaule and Its Influence on Elizabethan Literature.* New Brunswick: Rutgers University Press, 1970.

O'Connor, Marion. 'Rachel Fane's May Masque at Apethorpe, 1627.' *English Literary Renaissance* 36, no. 1 (2006): 90–113.

O'Day, Rosemary. *Education and Society, 1500–1800: The Social Foundations of Education in Early Modern Britain.* London: Longman, 1982.

Olney, James. *Autobiography: Essays Theoretical and Critical.* Princeton: Princeton University Press, 1980.

Ong, Walter. 'Latin Language Study as a Renaissance Puberty Rite.' *Studies in Philology* 61, no. 2 (1959): 103–124.

Orgel, Stephen. *Impersonations: The Performance of Gender in Shakespeare's England.* Cambridge: Cambridge University Press, 1996.

Orme, Nicholas. 'Children and Literature in Medieval England.' *Medium Aevum* 68, no. 2 (1999): 218–246.

———. *Medieval Children.* New Haven: Yale University Press, 2001.

Pacheco, Anita, ed. *A Companion to Early Modern Women's Writing.* Oxford: Blackwell, 2002.

Parker, Patricia. 'Preposterous Reversals: *Love's Labour's Lost.*' *Modern Language Quarterly* 54, no. 4 (1993): 435–482.

Partee, Morris. *Childhood in Shakespeare's Plays.* New York: Peter Lang, 2006.

Paster, Gail Kern. *Humoring the Body: Emotions and the Shakespearean Stage.* Chicago: Chicago University Press, 2004.

Pender, Patricia, and Rosalind Smith, ed. *Material Cultures of Early Modern Women's Writing.* Basingstoke: Palgrave, 2014.

Phillippy, Patricia, ed. *A History of Early Modern Women's Writing.* Cambridge: Cambridge University Press, 2017.

Phillips, Joshua. *English Fictions of Communal Identity, 1485–1603.* Aldershot: Ashgate, 2010.

Phillips, Kim. *Medieval Maidens: Young Women and Gender in England, 1270–1540.* Manchester: Manchester University Press, 2003.

Pollard, Mary. *Dublin's Trade in Books, 1550–1800.* Oxford: Clarendon Press, 1989.

Porck, M. H., and H. J. Porck. 'Eight Guidelines on Book Preservation from 1527: How One Should Preserve All Books to Last Eternally.' *Journal of Paper Conservation* 13, no. 2 (2012): 17–25.

Postman, Neil. *The Disappearance of Childhood*. New York: Vintage, 1984.

Potter, Ursula. 'Navigating the Dangers of Female Puberty in Renaissance Drama.' *Studies in English Literature 1500–1900* 53, no. 2 (2013): 421–439.

Purkiss, Diane. *Literature, Gender and Politics During the English Civil War*. Cambridge: Cambridge University Press, 2005.

Ramsey, R. 'Kepier School, Houghton-Le-Sprint, and Its Library.' *Arcaeologia Aeliana* 3 (1907): 306–334.

Read, Sarah. *Menstruation and the Female Body*. Basingstoke: Palgrave Macmillan, 2013.

Rees, Emma. *Margaret Cavendish*. Manchester: Manchester University Press, 2003.

Relle, Eleanor. 'Some New Marginalia and Poems of Gabriel Harvey.' *The Review of English Studies* 23, no. 92 (1972): 401–416.

Richards, Jennifer, and Fred Schurink. 'Introduction: The Textuality and Materiality of Reading in Early Modern England.' *Huntington Library Quarterly* 73, no. 3 (2010): 345–361.

Roberts, Sasha. *Reading Shakespeare's Poems in Early Modern England*. Basingstoke: Palgrave Macmillan, 2003.

Roper, Michael, and John Tosh, ed. *Manful Assertions: Masculinities in Britain Since 1850*. London: Routledge, 1991.

Rose, Jacqueline. *The Case of Peter Pan: Or, the Impossibility of Children's Fiction*. Philadelphia: University of Pennsylvania Press, 1993.

Ryrie, Alec. *Being Protestant in Reformation Britain*. Oxford: Oxford University Press, 2013.

Salzman, Paul. *English Prose Fiction, 1558–1700: A Critical History*. Oxford: Oxford University Press, 1985.

Sanders, Eve. *Gender and Literacy on Stage in Early Modern England*. Cambridge: Cambridge University Press, 1998.

Saunders, Corinne, ed. *A Companion to Romance: From Classical to Contemporary*. Oxford: Blackwell, 2004.

Schurink, Fred. 'An Elizabethan Grammar School Exercise Book.' *Bodleian Library Record* 18 (2003): 174–196.

Schutte, Anne, Thomas Kuehn, and Silvana Seidel Menchi, ed. *Time, Space and Women's Lives in Early Modern Europe*. Kirksville: Truman State University Press, 2001.

Scott-Warren, Jason. 'Reading Graffiti in the Early Modern Book.' *Huntington Library Quarterly* 73, no. 3 (2010): 363–381.

Seelig, Sharon. *Autobiography and Gender in Early Modern Literature*. Cambridge: Cambridge University Press, 2006.

Shapiro, Michael. *Children of the Revels: The Boy Companies of Shakespeare's Time and Their Plays.* New York: Columbia University Press, 1977.

Sharpe, Kevin. *Reading Revolutions: The Politics of Reading in Early Modern England.* Yale: Yale University Press, 2000.

Shepard, Alexandra. *Meanings of Manhood in Early Modern England.* Oxford: Oxford University Press, 2003.

Sherman, William. *John Dee: The Politics of Reading and Writing in the English Renaissance.* Amherst: University of Massachusetts Press, 1995.

———. *Used Books: Marking Readers in Renaissance England.* Philadelphia: University of Pennsylvania Press, 2007.

Sloane, William. *Children's Books in England and America in the Seventeenth Century.* New York: Columbia University Press, 1955.

Smith, Helen. '"More swete unto the eare / than holsome for ye mynde": Embodying Early Modern Women's Reading.' *Huntington Library Quarterly* 73, no. 3 (2010a), 413–432.

Smith, Hilda. *All Men and Both Sexes: Gender, Politics and the False Universal in England, 1640–1832.* Philadelphia: Penn State Press, 2010b.

Smith, Steven. 'The London Apprentices as Seventeenth-Century Adolescents.' *Past and Present* 61 (1973): 149–161.

Smyth, Adam. *Autobiography in Early Modern England.* Cambridge: Cambridge University Press, 2010.

———. *'Profit and Delight': Printed Miscellanies in England, 1640–1682.* Detroit: Wayne State University Press, 2004.

Snook, Edith. *Women, Reading and the Cultural Politics of Early Modern England.* Aldershot: Ashgate, 2005.

Sommerville, C. John. *The Discovery of Childhood in Puritan England.* Athens: University of Georgia Press, 1992.

Spufford, Francis. *The Child That Books Built.* London: Faber, 2003.

Spufford, Margaret. 'First Steps in Literacy: The Reading and Writing Experiences of the Humblest Seventeenth-Century Spiritual Autobiographers.' *Social History* 4, no. 3 (1979): 407–435.

———. *Small Books and Pleasant Histories: Popular Fiction and its Readership in Seventeenth-Century England.* London: Methuen, 1981.

St John, Judith. 'I Have Been Dying to Tell You: Early Advice Books for Children.' *The Lion and the Unicorn* 29, no. 1 (2005): 52–64.

Steedman, Carolyn. *Past Tenses: Essays on Writing, Autobiography and History.* London: River Oram Press, 1992.

———. *Strange Dislocations: Childhood and the Idea of Human Interiority, 1780–1930.* Cambridge: Harvard University Press, 1995.

Stephens, Isaac. *Under the Shadow of the Patriarch: Elizabeth Isham and her World in Seventeenth-Century Northamptonshire.* Unpublished PhD dissertation, University of California Riverside, 2008.

Stevenson, Jane. *Women Latin Poets: Language, Gender and Authority, from Antiquity to the Eighteenth Century.* Oxford: Oxford University Press, 2005.

Stewart, Alan. *Close Readers: Humanism and Sodomy in Early Modern England.* Princeton: Princeton University Press, 1997.

Stone, Lawrence. 'The Education Revolution in England, 1560–1640.' *Past and Present* 28, no. 1 (1964): 41–80.

———, ed. *Schooling and Society: Studies in the History of Education.* Baltimore: John Hopkins University Press, 1976.

Straznicky, Marta. *Privacy, Playreading, and Women's Closet Drama, 1550–1700.* Cambridge: Cambridge University Press, 2004.

Thomas, Keith. 'Age and Authority in Early Modern England.' *Proceedings of the British Academy* 62 (1976a): 205–248.

———. *Rule and Misrule in the Schools of Early Modern England.* Reading: University of Reading Press, 1976b.

Thompson, Craig. *Schools in Tudor England.* Washington: Folger Library, 1958.

Thorpe, Deborah. 'Young Hands, Old Books: Drawings by Children in a Fourteenth-Century Manuscript, LJSMS. 361.' *Cogent Arts and Humanities* 3 (2016): 1–18.

Thwaite, Mary. *From Primer to Pleasure in Reading: An Introduction to the History of Children's Books in England from the Invention of Printing to 1914.* London: Library Association, 1972.

Traub, Valerie, M. Lindsay Kaplan, and Dympna Callaghan, ed. *Feminist Readings of Early Modern Culture.* Cambridge: Cambridge University Press, 1996.

Tribble, Evelyn. *Margins and Marginality: The Printed Page in Early Modern England.* London: University Press of Virginia, 1993.

Tribble, Evelyn, and Nicholas Keene. *Cognitive Ecologies and the History of Remembering: Religion, Education and Memory in Early Modern England.* Basingstoke: Palgrave Macmillan, 2001.

Tudor, Philippa. 'Religious Instruction for Children and Adolescents in the Early English Reformation.' *The Journal of Ecclesiastical History* 35, no. 3 (1984): 397–425.

Tuer, Andrew. *The History of the Horn-Book.* London: The Leadenhall Press, 1861.

Tupper, Frederick. 'The Holme Riddles (MS. Harl. 1960).' *Modern Language Association* 18, no. 2 (1903): 211–272.

Underwood, Lucy. *Childhood, Youth and Religious Dissent in Post-Reformation England.* Basingstoke: Palgrave Macmillan, 2014.

Vincent, David. *Literacy and Popular Culture: England 1750–1914.* Cambridge: Cambridge University Press, 1989.

———. *The Rise of Mass Literacy: Reading and Writing in Europe.* Cambridge: Polity Press, 2000.

Walker, Jonathan, and Paul Streufert, ed. *Early Modern Academic Drama.* Aldershot: Ashgate, 2008.

Wall, Wendy. 'Literacy and the Domestic Arts.' *Huntington Library Quarterly* 73, no. 3 (2010): 383–412.

———. *Staging Domesticity: Household Work and English Identity in Early Modern Drama*. Cambridge: Cambridge University, 2006.

Walsham, Alexandra. *The Uses of Script and Print, 1300–1700*. Cambridge: Cambridge University, Press, 2004.

Watt, Tessa. *Cheap Print and Popular Piety 1550–1640*. Cambridge: Cambridge University Press, 1991.

Weikle-Mills, Courtney. *Imaginary Citizens: Child Readers and the Limits of American Independence, 1640–1868*. Baltimore: John Hopkins University Press, 2012.

Wiesner Hanks, Merry. *Mapping Gendered Routes and Spaces in the Early Modern World*. London: Routledge, 2016.

Wilcox, Helen, ed. *Women and Literature in Britain, 1500–1700*. Cambridge: Cambridge University Press, 1996.

Williams, Deanne. *Shakespeare and the Performance of Girlhood*. Basingstoke: Palgrave Macmillan, 2014.

Williams, Deanne, and Richard Preiss, ed. *Childhood, Education and the Stage in Early Modern England*. Cambridge: Cambridge University Press, 2017.

Wilson-Okamura, David. *Virgil in the Renaissance*. Cambridge: Cambridge University Press, 2010.

Witmore, Michael. *Pretty Creatures: Children and Fiction in the English Renaissance*. Ithaca: Cornell University Press, 2007.

Wooden, Warren. *Children's Literature of the English Renaissance*. Lexington: University of Kentucky, 1986.

Wray, Ramona. 'Recovering the Reading of Renaissance Englishwomen: Deployments of Autobiography.' *Critical Survey* 12, no. 2 (2000): 33–48.

———. *Women Writers of the Seventeenth Century*. Tavistock: Northcote House, 2004.

Wright, Louis. 'Handbook Learning of the Renaissance Middle Class.' *Studies in Philology* 28, no. 1 (1931): 55–86.

Zemon Davis, Natalie. 'Beyond the Market: Books as Gifts in Sixteenth-Century France.' *Transactions of the Royal Historical Society* 33 (1983): 69–88.

———. 'The Reasons of Misrule: Youth Groups and Charivaris in Sixteenth-Century France.' *Past and Present* 50, no. 1 (1971): 41–75.

Index[1]

A

Abbot, Robert, 30, 39, 41
ABC for Children, 5, 33
ABC or Holy Alphabet, 37
Abc with catechism, 37, 38, 42
Ackroyd, Julie, 19
Adulthood, transition to, 3, 41, 87
Aesop Improved, 75, 91
Aesop's Fables, 72, 75, 77, 91, 112, 113
Age, 72, 75, 78–80, 84, 95, 96, 110, 155, 156, 201–205
    old, 6, 12, 40, 110, 120, 124, 125, 128, 215
Amadis de Gaule, 7, 81, 83, 174, 176–178
Apethorpe, 173–174
Apprentices, 90, 95
Archer, Issac, 31
Ariès, Philippe, 22n6
Ascham, Roger, 176

Augustine, 157, 169, 193, 200, 211, 212, 226n59
Autobiographies, 81, 191–222
    See also Diaries
Avery, Gillian, 32

B

Ballads, 48, 71, 86, 87, 90, 166
Barrow, Hannah, 94, 133, 136
Batchiler, John, 164
Batt, Bartholomew, 38
Baxter, Richard, 35, 54, 56, 72, 93, 199, 203, 206
Bayly, Lewis, 45–49, 54
Beane, Elizabeth, 161
Bedford, Ronald, 196
Berkley, George, 178
Bernard, Richard, 36
Betts, John, 93, 134
Betts, Thomas, 93, 134

[1] Note: Page numbers followed by "n" refers to notes.

Bevis of Southampton, 71, 79, 93, 133, 134
Bible, 3, 10, 29–31, 34, 35, 41, 45–47, 54, 55, 93, 94, 112, 154, 157, 163, 196, 197, 204, 210
Bicks, Caroline, 152–154, 170, 180
Blair, Robert, 200
Bloom, Gina, 121
Book of Merry Riddles, The, 86
Boy
    as reader, 3, 12, 35, 40, 43, 47, 50, 54–56, 79, 87, 92, 93, 107–137
    school, 2, 3, 34, 78–85, 90, 93, 107–137, 216
Boyhood, 11, 19, 89, 108, 110, 111, 120–137
Boyle, Katherine, 29, 30, 154
Boyle, Robert, 7
Bradstreet, Anne, 80
Brathwait, Richard, 165
Brayman Hackel, Heidi, 11, 18, 80, 153
Brechtgirdle, John, 93
Breton, Nicholas, 40
Brinsley, John, 34, 76, 112–123, 130, 131
Bruto, Giovanni, 156, 165, 166
Bull, Henry, 46
Bullokar, William, 133, 174
Bunyan, John, 43–45, 48, 58, 71, 93
Burch, Dorothy, 39
Burford Priory, 169

C
Calabresi, Bianca, 156
Calvin, John, 11, 151, 167–169, 171
Cambrai, 169
Campana, Joseph, 20, 78
Campion, Miss, 17
Campion, Thomas, 14

Carleton, Mary, 83
Carr, Robert, 4
Cary, Elizabeth, 11, 14, 17, 151–154, 167–173, 175, 178–180
Cary, Lucy, 11, 151, 168
Catechisms, 30, 33, 37–39, 41, 42, 47
Cato, 113, 114, 160, 161, 174
Cavendish, Margaret, 1, 2, 7, 14, 219
Cawdry, Robert, 38
Caxton, William, 90
C., E., 39
Centre for Kentish Studies, 173–174
Cervantes, Miguel de, 82–83
Chapman, George, 9, 178
Chartier, Roger, 9, 97
Chaucer, Geoffrey, 211
Chear, Abraham, 47
Chedgzoy, Kate, 14, 19, 20, 173, 175, 177
Childhood, 97
    construction of, 5, 20, 22n6, 220–222
    definitions of, 12, 13, 16, 17
    as formative stage, 38
    gendering of, 11, 79, 107–137, 151–181
    remembered, 17, 191–222
    studies of, 19–20
Childishness, 45, 71, 72, 80, 96
Children
    book access and ownership, 10, 11, 31, 41, 81, 89–95, 157, 209
    book annotation, 15–17, 92, 93, 112, 131–137
    books addressing, 32, 39–58, 73, 81–89, 112–118, 159
    cognitive abilities of, 6, 13–15, 39, 54, 72, 74, 76, 77, 80, 113, 117, 154, 170, 203, 204, 218, 219
    and death, 51–54

education of (*see* Education; Literacy, instruction)

as impressionable, 6, 7, 39, 198

as market, 81–89

and performance, 120, 126–132, 144n74, 158, 173

and play, 40, 41, 76, 77, 80, 81, 96, 97, 108, 109, 129, 143n54, 204

and print, 1

punishment of, 3, 115

Puritan perceptions of, 49–58, 71

and toys, 40, 43

writing by, 14, 172–179, 191–222

Children's literature scholarship, 75, 77

Cicero, 74, 112, 113, 158

Clarke, Danielle, 170

Clarke, Samuel, 17, 80

Cleland, James, 120

Clement, Francis, 40

Clifford, Anne, 45–47, 152

Cobbler of Canterbury, The, 10

Cobhead, Thomas, 38

Cocker, Edward, 92, 161

Codrington, Robert, 167

Cole, Sarah, 161

Coles, Elisha, 36

Comenius, John, 76, 113

Commonplace books, 121

Corderius, 113, 114

Corin, Festus, 42

Cork, Bishop of, 135

Cotgrave, John, 88

Cotterill, Anne, 211, 212, 215

Cowley, Abraham, 14, 47, 191–193, 197, 216–220, 222

Craig, John, 39

Craik, Katharine, 80, 198

Crashaw, Richard, 47

Cressy, David, 33

Crouch, Nathaniel, 47, 87, 90

Cuffe, Henry, 12, 110, 120, 130

Culmann, Leonard, 113

D

Darnton, Robert, 162

Darton, F. J. Harvey, 76

Das, Nandini, 177

Davies, John, 171

Davin, Anna, 221

Davis, Lloyd, 196

De Certeau, Michel, 12, 123, 141n31

Dekker, Thomas, 40

Delaval, Elizabeth, 14, 72, 193, 201–209, 211, 212, 215–217, 220–222

Demers, Patricia, 32, 36

Denton, Anne, 94, 163

Dering, Edward, 79

De Worde, Wynken, 90

Dialogues, 118–123, 159, 160

Diaries, 12, 17, 195, 209

See also Autobiographies

Dingman, Paul, 161

Doctor Faustus, 81

Dod, John, 196

Dodson, James, 133

Dolan, Frances, 21

Donne, John, 47

Doolittle, Thomas, 38

Drayton, Michael, 13, 54, 171, 217, 218

Du Bartas, Guillaume, 175

Du Bosc, Jacques, 165

Duncan-Jones, Katherine, 77–78

E

Earle, John, 1

Eckerle, Julie, 192, 201, 202, 208, 211

Education, 107–137
  in arithmetic, 74, 161, 179
  in French, 159–161, 163, 168, 175, 176
  in geography, 171
  in Latin, 36, 74, 109, 112–115, 127, 128
  in needlework, 158
  in reading (*see* Literacy instruction)
Egerton, Frances, 93
Enterline, Lynn, 19, 111
Erasmus, 76, 112
Erondelle, Pierre, 159
Ezell, Margaret, 201, 202, 208

F
Fables, 117
  See also Aesop's Fables
Fane, Rachel, 14, 17, 93, 154, 160, 161, 173–181, 222
Fathers, 31, 41, 42, 93, 153, 157, 165, 167–170, 199, 205–213
Femininity, 151–156
Ferne, John, 12
Fisher, James, 36, 56
Fleming, Juliet, 16, 159
Fletcher, John, 124
Flint, Kate, 15, 16, 161, 163
Fox, Adam, 92
Foxe, John, 46, 51, 54, 196, 211
Fryar Bacon, 81

G
Gallus, Evaldus, 118–119
Garden Of Godly Delights, The, 30
Gardiner, Dorothy, 159
Gardiner, Judith, 110
Gerhard, Johann, 212
Girlhood, 19, 151–181

Girl as reader, 6–8, 16–18, 29, 30, 43, 47, 50, 151–181, 196, 201–215
G., J., 33, 44, 86
Gouge, William, 80
Gowd, John, 93, 134
Graham, Elspeth, 192
Graile, Edmond, 39
Grandparents, 174, 210, 213–215
Grantham, Thomas, 4
Green, Ian, 38
Greene, Robert, 86
Greenhalgh, Susanne, 19
Grenby, Matthew, 15, 18
Greteman, Blaine, 15, 134
Griffiths, Paul, 73
Guillemeau, Jacques, 6

H
Hadleigh, school at, 126
Halpern, Richard, 109, 112, 117
Harley, Brilliana, 31
Harrington, John, 75
Harvey, Gabriel, 14
Hassen, Elizabeth, 94
Hatfield, Marta, 35, 36, 56
Hawkins, William, 108, 112, 126–131, 156
Heller, Jennifer, 9, 39
Henry, Philip, 47
Herbert, George, 47, 112
Heywood, Oliver, 31
Higginbotham, Jennifer, 19, 153, 173
Histories, 7, 85
Hocus Pocus Junior, 88
Hodges, Richard, 74, 94, 133
Holliband, Claude, 159
Holme siblings, 10, 91
Hoole, Charles, 33–35, 42, 77, 112–123, 134
Horace, 74, 78, 80, 113

Hornbook, 2, 3, 29, 31, 35, 36, 40, 84, 113
Hornby, William, 2–5, 97, 132
Houlbrooke, Ralph, 52
How A Man May Choose a Good Wife from a Bad, 108
Humanism
  and education, 109–121, 127, 128, 136, 166
  and reading practices, 7, 133, 144n79, 198
Hundred Godly Lessons, An, 90
Hutchins, Edward, 48
Hutchinson, John, 46
Hutchinson, Lucy, 11, 46, 157

I
Immel, Andrea, 19
Isham, Elizabeth, 10, 11, 31, 46, 93–95, 154, 193, 209–217, 220–222
Isocrates, 161, 174, 176

J
Janeway, James, 45, 51–58, 81, 95, 167
Jessey, Henry, 51
Johnson, John, 151, 153, 167–169
Jonson, Ben, 9, 108
Jonson, Nicholas, 90
Jordanova, Ludmilla, 12, 14, 19
Joscelin, Elizabeth, 39
Josselin, Ralph, 197, 198

K
Kastan, David Scott, 86
Keach, Benjamin, 33, 42, 48
Kelly, Philippa, 196
Kempe, William, 35, 114

Kepier Grammar School, 135
Kettlewell, John, 94
Kilvert, Margaret, 159
Kirkman, Francis, 73, 81–87, 89, 90, 93, 95, 96
Kline, Daniel, 76, 78
Knowles, Katie, 19, 110, 112

L
Ladies' Hall at Deptford, 158
Lamb, Mary Ellen, 89
Lee, Henry, 171
Leigh, Dorothy, 7, 30, 39, 54
Lenton, Francis, 79
Lerer, Seth, 55
Letters, 17
Lily, William, 108, 113, 134
Literacy
  instruction, 16, 31, 33–37, 41–45, 74, 154–156, 194
  levels, 21, 33, 58
Locke, John, 5, 35, 44, 49
London, William, 7
Lower, William, 94
Lucy, Lady Alice, 34
Lumley, Jane, 93, 160
Lycoris, John, 92
Lye, Thomas, 30
Lynn, Francis, 31, 92

M
Mack, Peter, 117
Makin, Bathusa, 158
Marginalia, 15–17, 92, 112, 131–137
Marston, John, 108, 121, 124, 128
Martindale, Adam, 41, 94
Martyn, William, 1
Masculinity, 77, 109–111, 120, 121
Mason, John, 41
Masters, Ben, 218

Mather, Cotton, 58
Matz, Robert, 78
Mauger, Charles, 159–161
Mazzola, Elizabeth, 154
McCarthy, Jeanne, 19
Meres, Francis, 79
Michals, Teresa, 6, 72
Mildmay, Grace, 31, 45–47, 173–181, 191–197, 206, 214
Miller, Naomi, 19
Moss, Ann, 194
Mothers, 31, 39, 79, 94, 95, 128, 129, 154, 161, 164, 165, 168, 169, 178, 196, 209–214, 218
Mothers' advice books, 39
    See also Joscelin, Elizabeth; Leigh, Dorothy
Mulcaster, Richard, 33–35, 122, 123, 164
Munday, Anthony, 157
Munro, Lucy, 19, 218
Munster, Sebastian, 135
Musculus, Wolfgang, 46, 196
Mysteries of Love and Eloquence, The, 13

N
Narveson, Kate, 172
Newbery, John, 76
Newbery, Thomas, 33, 107
Newcastle University Library, 135
Newcomb, Lori, 83, 96
Newton, Hannah, 49
North, Roger, 10
Norwood, Richard, 193
Nowell, Alexander, 37, 41

O
Occupation and Idleness, 134
Office of Christian Parents, The, 12

Ogilby, John, 91
Ong, Walter, 109
Orme, Nicholas, 93, 107, 134
Ortelius, Abraham, 170, 172
Ovid, 9, 74, 108, 113, 127, 129, 178, 211

P
Palmerin of England, 81
Parker, Patricia, 125
Paynell, Thomas, 176
Peacham, Henry, 134
Penkethman, John, 175
Pepys, Samuel, 35
Perwich, Susanna, 46, 164
Pestell, Thomas, 29–30
Peterson, Lesley, 170–173
Piesse, Amanda, 108
Pollard, Mary, 90, 135
Postman, Neill, 6
Potter, Ursula, 120
Powell, Sarah, 161
Powell, Thomas, 163
Powell, Vasavour, 72, 199, 200, 206
Prayerbooks, 36, 45–47, 155, 210
    See also Bayly, Lewis; Catechisms; Hutchins, Edward; Sorocold, Thomas; Sparke, Michael
Pregnancy, 7
Preiss, Richard, 19
Primers, 3, 37, 107
Prudom, Robert, 46
Purkiss, Diane, 118
Pynner, Francis, 93

Q
Quarles, Francis, 47

R

Randolph, Thomas, 218, 219
Rastrick, John, 10, 46
Reading
  aloud, 10, 34, 37, 120
  communities, 10, 88, 92, 112, 136, 214
  and evidence, 15–19, 135
  as formative, 6, 14, 46, 49, 155, 197
  as nourishment, 7, 30, 55
  for pleasure, 76–89, 200
  religious cultures of, 29–58, 195–201
  spaces of, 10, 12, 112, 118–137, 151, 153, 162
  ways of, 10, 11, 50–55, 88, 118–137, 145n81, 162–179
  See also Humanism
Richards, Jennifer, 5
Riddlebooks, 10, 87, 91, 92, 117
Romances, 10, 72, 78–87, 94, 116, 163, 166, 204–209, 221
Roper, Michael, 109
Rose, Jacqueline, 76, 220
Russel, Robert, 32, 45, 49–53, 57, 95
Rutter, Carol Chillington, 9, 19
Ryrie, Alec, 31, 195

S

Saint Paul's Grammar School, 122
Saint Peterborough Free School, 2
Salonstall, Wye, 177
Salter, Thomas, 164–166
Sanders, Eve, 126, 130, 131, 152–154, 166
Sansom, Oliver, 34
Savile, George, 155, 156, 180
Schurink, Fred, 5, 107
Scott-Warren, Jason, 16

Seneca, 127, 158, 161, 168, 169, 174–177
Shakespeare, William, 9, 151, 175
  As You Like It, 110
  Hamlet, 178
  Love's Labour's Lost, 110, 124–126
  Merry Wives of Windsor, The, 108
  Titus Andronicus, 10
Sharpham, Edward, 108
Shaughnessy, Robert, 19
Shaw, William, 135
Sherman, William, 16, 18, 31
Shrove Tuesday, 126
Sibbes, Richard, 72
Sibling relationships, 178, 210
  See also Holme siblings
Sidney, Philip, 13, 78, 94, 163, 175, 211
Smith, Helen, 15
Sorocold, Thomas, 48
Sparke, Michael, 46, 48
Spenser, Edmund, 9, 175, 211, 217
Sports and Pastimes, 89, 97
Spufford, Francis, 194, 209
Stanford, Henry, 178
Steedman, Carolyn, 57, 194, 195, 220, 221
Stuart, Arabella, 152
Swinnock, George, 54

T

Table of Good Nurture, A, 90
Terence, 107, 113
Themylthorpe, Nicholas, 47
Thomas, Keith, 13
Thornton, Alice, 200, 203
Tosh, John, 109
Translation, 170–176
Trother, John, 136
Tryon, Thomas, 41

Tuttoft, Jane, 7
Tyler, Margaret, 78–80, 85

V
Venn, Anne, 196, 198, 203
Verney, Ralph, 94, 163
Virgil, 72, 74, 75, 113, 127
Vives, Juan, 79, 113, 115, 116, 157, 158, 163, 165, 177

W
Walker, Elizabeth, 41, 56
Ward, Mary, 197
Ward, Samuel, 175
Weikle-Mills, Courteney, 57
West, Richard, 218, 219
Westminster Grammar School, 31, 121, 192
White, Robert, 158
White, Thomas, 30, 31, 45, 51–55, 57
Whitgift, Bishop, 34
Whittinton, Robert, 90
Whole book of psalms, 40

Williams, Deanne, 19, 139n14, 153, 170, 175, 178, 180
Williams, J., 135
Willis, Thomas, 47, 48
Withers, George, 94
Wissenden, Stephen, 90
Wit of a Woman, The, 14
Withal, John, 113
Witmore, Michael, 14, 19
Wolley, Hannah, 167
Woodward, Hezekiah, 74–77
Woudhuysen, H. R., 125, 146n96
Wray, Ramona, 17
Wright, Thomas, 14
Wroth, Mary, 175
W., S., 33
Wycherley, William, 95

Y
Yavneh, Naomi, 19
Youth
   culture, 73
   definition of, 72, 74
Youth's Treasury, 88, 97